IN THE DAYS OF OUR GRANDMOTHERS:
A READER IN ABORIGINAL WOMEN'S HISTORY
IN CANADA

From Ellen Gabriel to Tantoo Cardinal, many of the faces of Aboriginal people in the media today are women. *In the Days of Our Grandmothers* is a collection of essays detailing how Aboriginal women have found their voice in Canadian society over the past three centuries. Collected in one volume for the first time, the essays critically situate these women in the fur trade, missions, labour and the economy, the law, sexuality, and the politics of representation.

Leading scholars in their fields demonstrate important new methodologies and interpretations that advance the fields of Aboriginal history, women's history, and Canadian history. A scholarly introduction lays the groundwork for understanding how Aboriginal women's history has been researched and written, and a comprehensive bibliography leads readers in new directions.

In the Days of Our Grandmothers is essential reading for students and anyone interested in Aboriginal history in Canada.

MARY-ELLEN KELM is Canada Research Chair in Indigenous Peoples of North America at Simon Fraser University.

LORNA TOWNSEND is chair of the board of the Quesnel Museum and a graduate student in the history program at the University of Northern British Columbia.

EDITED BY MARY-ELLEN KELM AND
LORNA TOWNSEND

In the Days of Our Grandmothers

A Reader in Aboriginal Women's History in Canada

UNIVERSITY OF TORONTO PRESS
Toronto Buffalo London

© University of Toronto Press Incorporated 2006
Toronto Buffalo London
Printed in Canada

ISBN-13: 978-0-8020-4117-3 (cloth)
ISBN-13: 978-0-8020-7960-2 (paper)
ISBN-10: 0-8020-4117-5 (cloth)
ISBN-10: 0-8020-7960-1 (paper)

Printed on acid-free paper

Library and Archives Canada Cataloguing in Publication

In the days of our grandmothers : a reader in Aboriginal women's
history in Canada / edited by Mary-Ellen Kelm and Lorna Townsend.

Includes bibliographical references and index.
ISBN-13: 978-0-8020-4117-3 (bound)
ISBN-10 0-8020-4117-5 (bound)
ISBN-13: 978-0-8020-7960-2 (pbk)
ISBN-10 0-8020-7960-1 (pbk)

1. Native women – Canada – History.   2. Women – Canada – History.
I. Kelm, Mary-Ellen, 1964–   II. Townsend, Lorna

E78.C2I48 2006   305.48'897071   C2005-907518-X

University of Toronto Press acknowledges the financial assistance to
its publishing program of the Canada Council for the Arts and the
Ontario Arts Council.

University of Toronto Press acknowledges the financial support for
its publishing activities of the Government of Canada through the
Book Publishing Industry Development Program (BPIDP).

To the memory of
Bridget Moran and Mary John
who showed us all the way

Contents

Contributors

Jean Barman is Professor Emerita in the Faculty of Education at the University of British Columbia. She is the author of *The West beyond the West: A History of British Columbia* and most recently, *Sojourning Sisters: The Lives and Letters of Jessie and Annie McQueen*.

Hetty Jo Brumbach is Associate Curator of Anthropology at the University at Albany, SUNY. Most recently, she is the editor, with Robert Jarvenpa, of *Circumpolar Lives and Livelihood: A Comparative Ethnoarchaeology of Gender and Subsistence*.

Sarah Carter is a professor in the History Department at the University of Calgary. She is the author of four books, including *Capturing Women: The Manipulation of Cultural Imagery in Canada's Prairie West*.

Jo-Anne Fiske is a professor and co-coordinator of women's studies at the University of Lethbridge and Adjunct Professor in the Department of First Nations Studies at the University of Northern British Columbia. She is the author of *Cis dideen kat When the Plumes Rise: The Way of the Lake Babine Nation*.

Robert Jarvenpa is a professor of cultural anthropology at the University at Albany, SUNY. He is the author of *Northern Passage: Ethnography and Apprenticeship among the Subarctic Dene* and editor, with Hetty Jo Brumbach, of *Circumpolar Lives and Livelihood: A Comparative Ethnoarchaeology of Gender and Subsistence*.

Mary-Ellen Kelm holds the Canada Research Chair in Indigenous Peoples of North America at Simon Fraser University. She is the author of *Colonizing Bodies: Aboriginal Health and Healing in British Columbia, 1900–50*, and editor of *The Letters of Margaret Butcher: Missionary-Imperialism on the North Pacific Coast.*

Emma LaRocque is a poet and professor in the Department of Native Studies at the University of Manitoba. She is the author of *Defeathering the Indian*, and her poetry and criticism have been widely published.

John Lutz is an associate professor of history at the University of Victoria. He is the author of numerous scholarly articles and book chapters, as well as co-editor of two volumes of *The Researcher's Guide to British Columbia Directories.*

Joan Sangster is a professor in the women's studies program at Trent University and is currently director of the Frost Centre for Canadian Studies and Native Studies. She is the author of four books, including *Regulating Girls and Women: Sexuality, Family, and the Law in Ontario, 1920–1960.*

Nancy Shoemaker is a professor of history at the University of Connecticut. She has authored and edited a number of books, including *A Strange Likeness: Becoming Red and White in Eighteenth-Century North America.*

Susan Sleeper-Smith is an associate professor of history at Michigan State University. She is the author of *Indian Women and French Men: Rethinking Cultural Encounter in the Western Great Lakes* and co-editor of *New Faces of the Fur Trade: Selected Papers of the Seventh North American Fur Trade Conference, Halifax, Nova Scotia, 1995.*

Veronica Strong-Boag is a professor of women's history at the University of British Columbia. She is the author of six books, including *Finding Families, Finding Ourselves: English Canada Confronts Adoption from the 19th Century to the 1990s* and, with Carole Gerson, *Paddling Her Own Canoe: The Times and Texts of E. Pauline Johnson (Tekahionwake).*

Lorna Townsend is chair of the board of the Quesnel Museum and is a graduate student in the history program at the University of Northern British Columbia.

Sylvia Van Kirk is adjunct professor of history at the University of Toronto. She is the author of *Many Tender Ties: Women in Fur-Trade Society, 1670–1870*.

Bruce M. White has a PhD in historical anthropology from the University of Minnesota. He is the author of numerous articles on the early history of Aboriginal peoples and settlers in the Great Lakes region.

Carol Williams is a professor of women's studies at the University of Lethbridge. She is the author of *Framing the West: Race, Gender, and the Photographic Frontier in the Pacific Northwest*.

Mary C. Wright is a senior lecturer in American Indian studies and history at the University of Washington. Her work has appeared in *Frontiers: A Journal of Women Studies*, and she is the editor of *More Voices, New Stories: King County, Washington's First 150 Years*.

IN THE DAYS OF OUR GRANDMOTHERS:
A READER IN ABORIGINAL WOMEN'S HISTORY
IN CANADA

1 In the Days of Our Grandmothers: Introduction

MARY-ELLEN KELM AND LORNA TOWNSEND

'Chiefs, Matriarchs, Nobles ...' So begins the invocation to countless speeches in Nisga'a and Tsimshian feast halls. This salutation draws people to attention and welcomes them. It also stands as a symbolic reminder of the continued significance of the ancient hierarchical social structure of the Northwest Coast peoples. At the centre of this social structure are the *Sigidimanak*, the matriarchs of the Nisga'a and Tsimshian peoples. Though the *Sigidimanak* may defer to chiefs in matters of formal politics or external relations, they hold important rank because they are the ritual mothers of the matri-lineages, houses, and clans that constitute Nisga'a and Tsimshian society. These women regulate marriage and the inheritance of names and crest privileges. They also collect and distribute women's contributions to feasts, thereby directing the labour of women of lesser rank. They are, though less visible and less vocal than their male counterparts, leaders in every sense of the word.

The *Sigidimanak* seldom appear before the media. To the outside world, then, it might appear that Nisga'a women are silent, in the background.[1] Outsiders have long perceived Aboriginal women to be secondary or shadowy players in history, hard to find, hard to hear.[2] This is not, however, because Native women were not speaking. Throughout our past, Aboriginal women have expressed themselves clearly, to fur traders, to missionaries, to Native and non-Native government, and to anthropologists and historians. Indeed, a good deal of scholarship has been generated about, and increasingly by, Aboriginal women.[3] The purpose behind this scholarship, however, has changed over time. Early work tended to stress broad questions about the universality of female subjugation.[4] Later work argued for the complementarity of gender roles in pre-contact societies and asked important questions about the 'impact' of European contact on those gender roles.[5] Currently, scholars are more inclined to address the 'thirst for research,' a desire expressed by Aboriginal women who seek useable pasts, affirming research that sees beyond social pathologies to strengths and solutions.[6] Scholars both within and outside of the academy are producing 'situated knowledge' about the past that 'stresses and validates the importance of lived experiences and ... incorporates these experiences within theory.'[7] This reader honours the field of Aboriginal women's history by presenting a number of key essays in such a way as to highlight both current developments in the field and the diversity of histories to which Aboriginal women can lay claim. Just the sheer volume of work produced in this field has made selecting articles for inclusion difficult, but it has also made clear the strength of the field and, indeed, of Aboriginal women themselves. Refuting the myth of silence, this reader amplifies the persistent voice of Aboriginal women over three centuries of Canadian history.

Changing Theoretical Paradigms

Nineteenth- and early twentieth-century anthropology had little interest in women. If women were discussed at all, it was usually as anonymous participants in birthing rituals, child care, or food preparation. Typically, since male anthropologists chose male informants, the world of Aboriginal women remained a mystery to researchers, apart from what they could observe from a distance.[8] For this reason, and because they had privileged access to them,[9] early women anthropologists were drawn to Aboriginal women. Some women researchers sought a retreat from modernity and turned to First Nations as a refuge, coming to find common cause with the Aboriginal women with whom they lived and worked.[10] Still others looked to add what they learned about women to a larger body of research about the development of social, exchange, kinship, and gender relations.[11] The desire to find grand theories of social evolution generated provocative work and productive debate.[12] For example, Michelle Rosaldo used Ruth Landes' early ethnographic work on the Ojibwa to argue that the 'separate spheres' characterizing gender relations among First Nations were the source of universal male dominance. Eleanor Leacock countered that female subordination was the product of capitalism and Christianity.[13] These early feminist scholars brought the study of Aboriginal women to an international audience.

Yet many Aboriginal women found these studies unsatisfying and homogenizing.[14] They demanded that academic research be crafted to meet their present needs. They insisted that it not replicate colonialism in its research questions, its conceptual practices, its methodologies, or its modes of representation.[15] Some argued that a feminist analysis was unsuited to Native women because it failed to understand how Aboriginal women framed their experiences.[16] Scholars, too, found that universalizing tendencies of feminist theory were unhelpful in producing histories of Aboriginal women that truly respected difference.[17]

Subsequent generations continued to debate large social questions, but through the use of particular case studies, they sought nuance and sophistication rather than generalization. Few today would argue that male dominance is or was universal. Most now accept that the majority of First Nations organized their gender roles around reciprocity and complementarity, but that there was considerable variation across space and over time.[18] In the literature today, Aboriginal women are seldom labelled 'powerful' or 'powerless.'[19] Nevertheless, an interest in the role that European contact and colonization played in gender roles and the status of women persists. Beginning in the 1990s, the work of Michel Foucault increasingly informed definitions of power, emphasizing its fluidity. The impact of colonialism and the power relations of gender on women's lives is a central theme of this collection.

Since the 1990s scholars have made three key contributions to the field. First, they have been increasingly critical of the nature of existing documentary sources and how historians have used these sources. Poststructuralist critics of the colonizing archive have built on the previous generation's awareness of the flaws of the documentary record. Feminist historians of First Nations have long been critical of the ways that Aboriginal women have been portrayed in the popular media, in the records of church and state, in the correspondence of traders, and by previous ethnographers.[20] Sylvia Van Kirk raised many of these issues two decades ago in her *Many Tender Ties*, lamenting that so many of her sources were written by white men who were distanced by culture, gender, and often class from the women about whom they wrote. So historians sought ways to use the existing record despite its flaws. Bruce White, for example, places his own struggle with biased and often troubling sources at the forefront of his article included in this volume. And sometimes even when historical observers' conclusions were drawn solely from their own cultural frameworks, they recorded valuable data. Wendy Wickwire discovered that the ethnographer of

Nla'ka'pamux and Secwepmc peoples, James Teit, was a remarkable exception to the rule of anthropological androcentrism.[21] Similarly, in this collection, we see Mary Wright use Teit's work to find out a great deal about the private lives of Plateau women.[22] In addition, feminist historians and literary critics have reintroduced the writing of women travellers in order to glean what they have to say about Native women. The international literature on women's travel writing has asked the question 'what difference did gender make?' Canadian writing on this subject reveals that much depended on timing and demographics, but, in some cases, women's writing reveals the interconnections among women, instead of a stark racial divide.[23] Finally, the abundant photographic record of Aboriginal women is receiving some serious analysis, as Carol Williams's award-winning study, *Framing the West*, reveals.[24] Much can be learned, as Jennifer Brown and Elizabeth Vibert remind us, in 'reading beyond [the] words' of existing historical sources.[25]

Historians have learned much from poststructuralist critics. Concepts such as 'experience,' 'difference,' 'dominance,' and 'voice,' and even the category 'woman,' must be interrogated and situated.[26] Few historians today think of language as a simple purveyor of truth; nor do they balk at recognizing that the line between history and fiction is sometimes unclear.[27] Yet the power relations that are inherent between scholars and those they study are not easily undone. The historian's use of sources and her way of writing can sometimes 'continue to work to ... "veil" the epistemic violence that is inevitable in the Native/colonial confrontation [and can] still stage the show.'[28] Creating space for a plurality of voices within our written work, to unfetter ourselves from crippling white solipsism, to embrace what Ruth Roach Pierson calls 'epistemic humility,' is precisely the path that many of the historians whose writing is collected here have followed.[29] The claims and the criticisms of poststructuralism and postcolonialism were neither unwelcome nor unheard among historians of Aboriginal women. At the same time, the theme of the problematic nature of historical sources returns repeatedly throughout this anthology, drawing attention to the fact that reading through the colonizing intention of many of the available sources remains an inescapable feature of research on Aboriginal women.

The 1990s brought another welcome addition to the field – the sophisticated use of oral history. While oral history itself was not a new methodology, feminist historians and anthropologists expressly sought to create new sources and to capture women's voices that were otherwise silent in standard historical accounts. Such recuperation, Sherna Gluck says, is, in and of itself, a 'feminist encounter.' But the meaning of the words women speak is not something that historians today take for granted. Rather, as Joan Sangster reminds us, oral history allows us an opportunity to explore 'the construction of women's historical memory.'[30] Probably the most significant contributor to the re-visioning of Aboriginal women's history and its methods is Julie Cruikshank. Her award-winning *Life Lived like a Story* has been called 'the most original and creative example of understanding and documenting northern women's lives.'[31] She discusses how the oral-history recordings produced with three female elders were shaped by *their* desires to communicate how they came to understand their changing world. They saw Cruikshank as their way to reach a wider audience. Cruikshank argues that these women's stories should not be reduced to nuggets of evidence, but rather should be seen as 'statements of cultural identity.' Cruikshank's approach has alerted historians to the inherent and often silenced dialogues that exist within all historical sources.

Finally, historians have become increasingly attentive to gender as 'a useful category of historical analysis,' to repeat the title of Joan Scott's generative article.[32] Moving beyond a preoccupation with 'roles,' gender is being used to explicate power relations of all kinds. Most often, gender is the mechanism through which the construction of the categories 'woman' and 'man' is made explicit, but it can also be the entry through which those categories are problematized.[33] While an awareness of gender has always been implicit to women's history, current work on women, like that of Jean Barman and Sarah Carter included here, examines the historical processes through which 'woman' and 'Aboriginal' were made. John Lutz's article here opens discussion on the differential impact of colonialism and the global economy on Aboriginal men and women, masculinity and femininity.

This historiographical trend is in keeping with a profoundly influential shift within international scholarship towards seeing imperialism as a gendered phenomenon. Imperialism envisioned its subjects (both colonized and colonizing) through a lens of racialized masculinities and femininities. In this literature, scholars have demonstrated that the racial hierarchies and gendered identities crafted in the colonies were imported and applied to the genders, classes, and ethnicities at home.[34] Canadian Aboriginal history, built on these new insights and situated in a colonial context in which the colonized and the colonizer resided as neighbours, opens up new possibilities for understanding the influence of colonial discourses, and the Aboriginal people they sought to frame, in the history of Canada. We have begun to ask ourselves: how did gendered discourses associated with colonialism worldwide affect, in particular and local ways, constructions of Aboriginal femininity and masculinity? How did these constructions, in turn, impact the gendered identities and racialized self-conceptions of all Canadians and, indeed, of Canada itself?[35] Feminist historians in Canada are beginning to answer these questions (some of their thoughts are found in the articles included here), but there is much more that can be done, especially, perhaps surprisingly, on Aboriginal men.[36] Thus, by using sources creatively and critically, through an engagement with oral history, and by an increasingly acute awareness of gender, feminist scholarship has radically altered how we study Aboriginal women's pasts.

There is still much work to do, and this reader reveals that too. Students will find that some regions within Canada are much better represented in this scholarship than others. British Columbia, and the West more generally, has been a fruitful ground for new scholarship, while Aboriginal women in the Maritimes, despite their prominence in the agitation against the Indian Act in the late twentieth century, remain understudied.[37] Ruth Phillips's work on women's production for the tourist market in eastern Canada is a notable exception, but much more work needs doing.[38] Similarly, Inuit studies have followed other trajectories, while American scholars studying the Inuit of Alaska more commonly pose questions relating to women and gender.[39]

Indeed, the border troubled us as we drew together articles for this reader. On the one hand, we wanted to add something to the study of Canadian history, and yet, on the other hand, we also recognized that Aboriginal women's history often challenges our very notions of what is Canadian. We are pleased with the present collection, not just because of the substantive gaps the articles address, but because they question and augment historical methodologies and common historical conceptualizations. We believe that good women's history (and good gender history) will change the way we see society, will illuminate relations of power, will challenge our assumptions about 'how things are.' And these articles have done just that; indeed, they have caused us to wonder about Canada. For clearly, as the articles by Susan Sleeper-Smith, Mary Wright, and Bruce White make plain, the border made little sense to the First Nations whose territories crossed it, whose kinship and community connections were truly trans-boundary.[40] 'Canada' made its most profound impact on First Nations through laws and institutions that were part of a totalizing agenda, a 'liberal order framework' as Ian McKay describes it. But that has more to do with the imaginings, the aspirations, the imperatives of non-Natives than the views of Native people.[41] Even at this level, we must recognize that Canadian relations with First Nations were never as distinct from American policy or that of the other settler colonies of Britain as Canadians would like to think.[42] In this reader, then, Canada is a category that was useful to us, but may not have had much relevance to the women whose lives are recorded herein. All in all, however, there is much for students in this field to contribute: to new definitions of Canada, to new work on Aboriginal women in under-represented regions, to the examination of gender more broadly. As in our own work, we hope students will find a springboard here in the work of others in this field.

The Fur Trade

For many First Nations, fur trade and first contact were synchronic. On both the Atlantic and the Pacific coasts, Aboriginal traders greeted European explorers with furs, ready to make exchanges.[43] In other places, European goods obtained through trade were the first introduction Aboriginal people had to the newcomers who would gradually move across the land. The various trading companies introduced by the French and then the monopoly of the Hudson's Bay Company also assured that subsequent historians would have plenty of records with which to understand the fur trade. In the 1970s, a new fur-trade history flourished. Building on Harold Innis's staples theory, the fur-trade histories that emerged in the 1970s and early 1980s typically argued that the Aboriginal traders were shrewd economic strategists pursuing their own best interests.[44] Few of these new works said much about women's part in the trade. On the other hand, early work by feminist historians and anthropologists using the same archives showed that women played important roles. Sylvia Van Kirk's *Many Tender Ties* and Jennifer Brown's *Strangers in Blood* were two early analyses of women's relationship to the fur-trading world.[45] Van Kirk and Brown proved that women were far from exploited, but rather that they played pivotal parts. Subsequent work explored the nature and impact of women's expanding role in the fur-trade period.[46] Susan Sleeper-Smith's work, for example, explores how women used their fur-trade marriages and their conversion to Catholicism to solidify their place as cultural mediators and to enhance the wealth and prestige of their kin. Rather than being peripheral players in the world economy of fur, they assumed leadership roles, influenced commodity production, and became independent traders. Bruce White criticizes much of the standard historiography for ignoring gender, and women in particular, in the fur-trade. He suggests that women occupied liminal positions within Aboriginal societies, expressed through stories about women breaching the divide between animals and humans. This position allowed them to act as conduits of exchange, among First Nations and between Aboriginal people and Europeans, and so placed them in key positions within the fur-trade.

The Church

Like the fur trade, the role of the church in First Nations history has been the subject of much historiographical debate. In the 1980s, Eleanor Leacock's groundbreaking work argued that it was the Jesuits' adherence to patriarchy and their conflation of women's subordination with 'civilization' that undermined women's roles in Montagnais-Naskapi society. Subsequent scholarship debated this point, stressing gendered responses to missionaries. Carol Devens, for instance, contended that Algonkian women had much to lose by adhering to Christian belief systems, while men had much to gain. Women lost autonomy and status in the course of colonization, Devens argued, and therefore their struggles to 'retain customary ways (even if somewhat modified) can be seen as efforts to offset the disruptive influence of alien ideas, social structure, and technology and to maintain cultural integrity.'[47] The association of 'woman' with 'traditional' only redoubled missionary attempts to undermine the power of women. In more recent times, the casting of women as 'bearers of tradition' has produced mixed results. As Emma LaRocque pointedly put it, 'There is no choice, as women we must be circumspect in our recall of tradition.'[48] Aboriginal women facing the first wave of cultural assault may have faced this same dilemma.

More recent work on the history of missions and the church has demonstrated the complexity of women's responses to Christianity, the multiple readings and uses of Christian beliefs, icons, and rituals that were made by Aboriginal women over time. Nancy Shoemaker's article shows clearly how one fairly disadvantaged woman, Kateri Tekakwitha, was able to take from Catholicism symbols and rituals that gave her a sense of personal power, subverting Jesuit patriarchy. Speaking about the other half of the missionary encounter, Natalie Zemon-Davis similarly has argued that Catholicism in New France offered 'a hybrid space rather than a transplantation of European order.'[49] Others have shown that, like their male counterparts, Aboriginal women used conversion to Catholicism to gain greater access to trade goods, to increase both personal autonomy and public voice. Catholicism, some argue, was particularly easy to syncretize with indigenous beliefs, which allowed Aboriginal women to forge new paths of religious leadership that adhered both to indigenous spiritual practice and the new authority of the church.[50] The icons of Catholicism were especially useful as the Virgin Mary provided a potent symbol of women's powers to Aboriginal women in contact with Catholicism across North America. Salish women, for example, found in Mary not a martyr or a saint, but a warrior.[51]

Indigenous women also formed productive partnerships with Protestant missionaries. Carol Williams uses photography, particularly honorific portraits, to explore Aboriginal women's reasons for embracing Christianity. While missionaries used photography to illustrate their success, a careful contextual reading of their photographic record yields clues to the complex motives for conversion. On the north coast of British Columbia, where missionaries were often critical of the government's land policy, chiefly women allied themselves with missionaries for strategic reasons. Like other resources, the missionary could be managed to assist noble women in meeting the needs of their people. Alternatively, women whose experiences with the colonizers had diminished their status, found the Christian message and the promise of 'rebirth' realized as they returned to their home villages to re-enter Aboriginal society.

The Coming of Settlement

When Europeans were reliant on indigenous societies in order to survive, whether as fur-traders or as missionaries, the accommodating trend among First Nations was to adapt to what they needed and to ignore what served no purpose. However, the coming of settlement and disease shifted the demographics of intercultural relations, and, in turn, the power relations of that contact also changed. Sarah Carter explores the ways in which Aboriginal women were constrained by the establishment of colonial and state relations during the early settlement era in Western Canada. Looking at the discursive formations developed to contain the public perception of 'Aboriginal women,' the social relations that developed, and the work of the state in limiting the Native women's options, Carter explores the trajectory of patriarchal domination, which followed colonization and capitalist development onto the Canadian Prairies. Sylvia Van Kirk also uses the fascinating photographic archives to study the later lives of women who had married high-ranking fur-traders. Settled in Victoria as élites, these women were subjected to a program of colonization that was intent on erasing aboriginality and promoting acculturation to European norms. Their daughters still used marriage as a strategy of social mobility. But as Van Kirk argues, 'race could trump class,' and with the growing determination of settler society to mark the divide between 'Native' and 'white' as insurmountable, these women were gradually rejected as marriage partners for settlers' sons. Subsequent generations would eventually 'write out' their Native grandmothers from the family histories, seeking to highlight only their Hudson's Bay Company roots.

Subsistence and Paid Labour

Early feminist scholars sought to situate declining women's status within the rise of capitalism and the positioning of Aboriginal women as a reserve army of labour. This process, however, was not immediate or uniform. Women's work in the fur-trade, a mercantilist endeavour, for example, shows that Aboriginal women's labour in that phase of economic development was anything but superfluous. Indeed, Sylvia Van Kirk called it essential. The article by Jo Brumbach and Robert Jarvenpa shows that our perceptions of a rigid division of labour based on gender may, in fact, be a historical artifact. In the context of an anthropological inquiry concerning gender roles and modes of production, Jarvenpa and Brumbach broke new ground to argue that woman too could be 'the hunter.' Here they argue that Cree women were highly involved in hunting and other forms of economic activity described as 'male' by early anthropologists and that it was a change in reproductive labour that limited women's economic roles. John Lutz's article, focusing on the Lekwammen of southern Vancouver Island, uses a long-term analysis to show that integration into the global economy did not impact gender roles once but many times and in a variety of ways. Lutz attends to rank and age as well as gender in his analysis and discovers that commoners more than nobles, and that women more than men, most often benefited from the economic opportunities brought by the newcomers. Welfare colonialism was the most damaging to Lekwammen people's access to work and wealth.

Sexuality and Reproduction

Ann Laura Stoler's scholarship on sexuality and colonialism in nine-teenth-century Indonesia demonstrates the centrality of colonialism in making sexuality, in Foucault's words, a 'dense transfer point for rela-tions of power,' both in the colonies and in the metropole.[52] Several articles in this collection focus similarly on the connections between women's bodies, sexuality, colonialism, and power. Although the no-tion of the female body as a symbol of inferiority, submissiveness, and passivity can be dated back to the ancient Greek era in Western socie-ties, ethnohistorians often argue that female bodies have been more positively idealized in Aboriginal societies and cultures.[53] Many First Nations cultures, for example, have traditionally equated the female body with Mother Earth or a similar unifying metaphor for Aboriginal physical and spiritual existence. Scholars also argue that the power and social status of pre-contact Aboriginal women emanated from their biological and reproductive roles, and that such 'mythological repre-sentations of traditional women's roles' continue to serve as an 'ideo-logical basis for contemporary action.'[54] Symbols of motherhood remain powerful and provide legitimacy to women's demands for change and justice within Aboriginal communities.[55]

Mary Wright's article, 'The Woman's Lodge: Constructing Gender on the Nineteenth-Century Pacific Northwest Plateau,' is a wonderful con-tribution to this area of feminist anthropological inquiry, as it offers unique insights into the significance of the 'woman's lodge' for defining female gender identities within several early nineteenth-century Pacific Northwest First Nations groups, including the Thompson, Lillooet, and Okanagan of British Columbia. It was in these secluded female-built structures that puberty, menstrual, and birthing rituals took place, and where Aboriginal women's wisdom and skills were transmitted from one generation to the next. Wright explains how menstrual seclusion, puberty rites, and birthing rituals associated with the 'woman's lodge' went into decline around the end of the nineteenth century, largely because of the effects of colonization, including epidemics, socio-economic change, land issues, and cultural misinterpretation. Work among Athapaskan women further reveals the relevance of puberty seclusion to the building of strong, empowered gendered identities and documents a similar decline in these rituals at the beginning of the twentieth century.[56] In recent years, a resurgence of puberty and other female rituals is permitting young girls, once more, to 'become' women according to cultural customs on traditional land, and in the process is also reaffirming their rights to 'use these experiences for political, social, cosmological and legal purposes.'[57]

Colonization dramatically affected the social construction of the female body.[58] Aboriginal female bodies were double burdened by the racism and sexism of patriarchal colonialism. Theories of evolution and racial difference developed alongside prevailing misogynistic views of sexuality, and colonial forces subscribed to Victorian ideals of female subservience and passivity and to the notion of the body as a subject of scientific study.[59] In this collection, Jean Barman and Joan Sangster explore the various ways that First Nations' women's bodies and sexuality have been historically constructed, along with 'race,' through the laws and politics of colonialism. Both authors draw on the work of Foucault and such feminist writers as Anne McClintock, Catherine Hall, and Ann Laura Stoler to emphasize the significance of gender, race, sexuality, and colonialism as interrelated systems of inequality.[60]

In 'Taming Aboriginal Sexuality: Gender, Power, and Race in British Columbia, 1850-1900,' Barman examines what she calls the 'tripartite alliance' among missionaries, government officials, and Native men, demonstrating how these three male-dominated factions attempted to control Aboriginal women's sexuality in late nineteenth-century British Columbia. Barman deconstructs the language of colonialism to show how, because 'sexuality' was a forbidden topic, the tropes of 'prostitution' and 'concubinage' were used to sexualize Aboriginal women, as colonizers attempted to recreate these women in the image of domestic, chaste, European female ideals.

The Law and the State

Tracking the impact of the law and the role of the state in the lives of Aboriginal women has incorporated the ever-increasing interdisciplinary framework of contemporary historical scholarship. Over the past two decades, anthropologists, historians, lawyers, sociologists, activists, and Native and non-Native scholars alike have contributed greatly to our understanding of how Euro-Canadian laws have significantly altered Native identities. Their work also reminds us that 'tarred with their patriarchal inequalities, imperialism and colonialism drew their darkest lines along boundaries of gender.'[61] Aboriginal women's interactions with the law further codified their sexualized and subordinated status vis-à-vis the Canadian state. Joan Sangster shows how male authorities used Aboriginal women's sexuality to construct notions of 'race' and to regulate *all* women. Sangster also explores the changes that have occurred to Aboriginal ideologies regarding sexuality, showing how, over time, legal and social interventions led First Nations peoples to begin seeking assistance from the Euro-Canadian legal system to deal with what they had come to consider as 'immoral' behaviour of their men and women. Both Barman and Sangster make clear that we must contextualize the attempts to regulate Native women's sexuality within broader notions of gender, race, colonialism, and the evolving relationships between 'customary law' and the Canadian legal system. As these articles point out, it is important that 'customary law' be interpreted as a process, and 'tradition' as an ideological concept, in order to avoid abuses of power and further oppression of women.[62]

Jo-Anne Fiske discusses the relationship between colonialism and Native women's socio-political status in her 'Political Status of Native Indian Women: Contradictory Implications of Canadian State Policy.' Fiske is one of many scholars who have found their attention drawn to the Indian Act's restrictive impact on Aboriginal women.[63] Her historical overview begins with the passing of the Indian Act in 1876 and includes details of the legislative changes leading up to 1985, and the subsequent negative effects of Bill C-31. Fiske describes how, in spite of increasing autonomy, previous assimilation policies and the influences of state patriarchy have had lingering negative impacts on Native women's status within First Nations communities. As a result of the contradictory and ambiguous nature of Native women's political status, the implications for self-government in Native communities could result in either an increased status for females with greater political and social opportunities, the maintenance of the status quo, or a continued patriarchal socio-political structure. Fiske further suggests that divisive state policies could also lead to irreparable conflicts among Aboriginal women, and, in turn, result in weakened female kin links.

Writing and Representation

By focusing on literature in the final portion of our collection, we wish to emphasize further the interdisciplinary nature of Aboriginal women's scholarship and draw attention to the important contributions that First Nations women have made to the academic synthesis of critical theory, history, and literature. We begin by looking back at the place of Pauline Johnson in intercultural dialogue. For a long time, Johnson's place in Canadian history was overlooked; however, recent biographies by Veronica Strong-Boag and Carole Gerson and by Charlotte Gray have placed her once again in the public eye.[64] Like many of the women discussed in this reader, Johnson occupied the liminal space between Aboriginal and European cultures and negotiated an identity that spanned both. In so doing, she lived in ways that contradicted the stereotypes of racist culture, that undermined the dominant society's disavowal of First Nations' presence, and that demanded the construction of a Canadian nationalism that embraced First Nations. From the other end of the twentieth century comes Emma LaRocque's powerful exhortation to end the silence that has surrounded Aborignal women's history. She writes of the continuing impacts of colonialism on Aboriginal women, who are doubly burdened by racism and sexism. She expresses caution about the too ready acceptance of 'tradition,' especially when it is predicated on women's passivity. Her conclusion is a call to arms and is worth repeating here: 'If we wish to act on history rather than be acted on, we can ill afford to be silent or to stay content in the shadows of our male contemporaries ... History demands of us to assume our dignity, our equality, and our humanity. We must not move toward the future with anything less. Nor can we pursue scholarship in any other way.'

One theme in this reader should by now be clear. Research and writing are potent political forces. Whether in history or any other academic discipline, in writing for a scholarly or a popular audience, the production of knowledge is powerful. This force can be harnessed to consolidate the dominant position of Europeans, to deny First Nations access to land and resources, or to loosen their ties to each other. It can also be used to create social change and to promote justice. For many years, the knowledge that was produced about Aboriginal women served the colonizers. It reduced Aboriginal women to beasts of burden, it sexualized them, it deprived them of their status, and it fit them into categories, whether scientific or sociological, that emphasized the pathological. As we write today, over five hundred Aboriginal women are still missing from cities across Canada. We write from British Columbia's central interior, where a hitherto respected provincial court judge has recently been convicted of the violent sexual assaults of young Aboriginal women. The 'categories and terrains of exclusion' that Sarah Carter talks about continue to contribute to the epistemic and very physical forms of violence that Aboriginal women endure today.

Feminist scholars early on recognized the connection between the violence of the word and the violence of the body. Intent on reclaiming women's lives from the distortions of the historical record, feminist historians turned their attention to Aboriginal women's history. Their perspectives and their frameworks of analysis were sometimes no less silencing than those of their male counterparts. Sometimes, feminist work submerged Native women in the uniformity of feminist theory. Sometimes it romanticized Native history, turning Aboriginal women into princesses or goddesses. In the long run, however, feminist political commitment to hearing the voice of women meant that these scholars could not ignore the fact that Aboriginal women have never been silent. The political stance of feminist scholarship made a space for conversation and debate among women, both Native and non-Native. This conversation was not always comfortable for the academics; often, it was infuriating for the Aboriginal women. There have been and continue to be misunderstandings. But that is the nature of communication, and where there was once silence there is now a chorus of voices, a multiplicity of perspectives, anything but a unified stance. This reader, we believe, is testament to that.

We also wish it to be a testament to all our grandmothers, both Native and non-Native, who communicated and worked together as women to improve their communities, to work for social change, to make justice happen. We have dedicated this reader to the memory of Sai'kuz elder Mary John and the Irish-Canadian social worker Bridget Moran. Bridget and Mary worked together for nearly forty years to expose the racism of late twentieth-century Canadian society, particularly around the communities of British Columbia's central interior. Together Bridget and Mary produced the remarkable text *Stoney Creek Woman*, which added Mary John's life story to the history of British Columbia. The pair travelled across the North giving talks, and Bridget went on to work with other Carrier elders to produce two more books. Neither woman shied away from controversy, but neither sought the limelight for her own ends. Like many northern British Columbian women, we were inspired by Bridget and Mary and by the promise of cross-cultural communication they represented. We hope this reader will prompt dialogue and debate and will inspire students, as we have been, to add their voices to this important and growing field.

NOTES

1 Media coverage of the negotiation and recent signing of the Nisga'a agreement emphasized the place of Aboriginal male leadership, particularly that of Joseph Gosnell. Nor has subsequent analysis of the treaty

foregrounded the impact on women, although marriage law has been
discussed. For an overview of Canadian media coverage of the Nisga'a
agreement, see http://www.canoe.ca. For Hansard on Nisga'a treaty and
matrimonial rights, see http://www.parl.gc.ca/36/1/parlbus/chambus/
house/debates/217_1999-04-28/han217_1445-e.htm and http://www
.parl.gc.ca/36/1/parlbus/chambus/house/debates/218_1999-04-29/
han218_1430-e.htm. For subsequent discussion of the treaty, see, for
example, *BC Studies* 120 (Winter 1998–9).

2 Laura F. Klein and Lillian A. Ackerman, 'Introduction,' in *Women and
Power in Native North America* (Norman: University of Oklahoma Press,
1995), 3; Marjorie Mitchell and Anna Franklin, 'When You Don't Know the
Language, Listen to the Silence: An Historical Overview of Native Indian
Women in BC,' in *Not Just Pin Money*, ed. Barbara K. Latham and Roberta J.
Pazdro (Victoria: Camosun College, 1984), 17–34; Armand Guest Ruffo,
'Out of Silence – the Legacy of E. Pauline Johnson: An Inquiry into
Lost and Found Work of Dawendine-Bernice Loft Winslow,' in *Literary
Pluralities*, ed. Christl Verduyn (Peterborough, ON: Broadview Press,
1998), 211–23.

3 Jo-Anne Fiske, 'By, For and About? Shifting Directions in the Representa-
tion of Aboriginal Women,' *Atlantis* 25.1 (Fall/Winter 2000): 11–27. For the
growth of Aboriginal women's history in North America, see: Beatrice
Medicine, 'The Role of Women in Native American Societies: A Bibliogra-
phy,' *Indian Historian* 8 (1975): 51–3; Rayna Green, *Native American Women:
A Contextual Bibliography* (Bloomington: Indiana University Press, 1983);
Gretchen M. Bataille and Kathleen Mullen Sands, *American Indian Women:
A Guide to Research* (New York: Garland, 1991).

4 Pauline Turner Strong, 'Feminist Theory and the "Invasion of the Heart"
in North America,' *Ethnohistory* 43.4 (Fall 1996): 683–703; Kathleen
Jamieson, '"Sisters under the Skin": An Exploration of the Implications of
Feminist-Materialist Perspective Research,' *Canadian Ethnic Studies* 13.1
(1981): 131.

5 For an example of a study of the 'impact' of colonization that produces a
too simplistic portrayal, see Somer Brodribb, 'The Traditional Roles of
Native Women in Canada and the Impact of Colonization,' *Canadian
Journal of Native Studies* 4.1 (1984): 85–103. And for two studies that assess
the impact of colonialism on the same First Nations group, each coming to
its own conclusion, see Carol Cooper, 'Native Women of the North Pacific
Coast: An Historical Perspective, 1830–1900,' *Journal of Canadian Studies*
27.4 (Winter 1992–3): 44–75; and Jo-Anne Fiske, 'Colonization and the
Decline of Women's Status: The Tsimshian Case,' *Feminist Studies* 17.3 (Fall
1991): 509–35.

6 Patricia Chuchryk and Christine Miller, 'Introduction,' in *Women of the First Nations: Power, Wisdom and Strength* (Winnipeg: University of Manitoba Press, 1996), 3–10; Fiske, 'By, For and About?' 11–27; Patricia Albers and Beatrice Medicine, 'Introduction,' in *The Hidden Half: Studies of Plains Indian Women* (Lanham, MD: University Press of America, 1983), 14; Rayna Green, 'Native American Women,' *Signs: Journal of Women in Society and Culture* (1980): 248–67.

7 Luni Sunseri, 'Moving beyond the Feminism versus Nationalism Dichotomy,' *Canadian Woman Studies / Les cahiers de la femme* 20.2 (2000): 143–8.

8 Jo-Anne Fiske, 'Ask My Wife: A Feminist Interpretation of Fieldwork Where the Women Are Strong and the Men Are Tough,' *Atlantis* 11.2 (Spring 1986): 59–69.

9 Alice Beck Kehoe, 'Transcribing Insima: A Blackfoot "Old Lady,"' in *Reading beyond Words: Contexts for Native History*, ed. Jennifer S.H. Brown and Elizabeth Vibert (Peterborough, ON: Broadview Press, 1996), 381–402.

10 Margaret Jacobs, *Engendered Encounters: Feminism and Pueblo Cultures, 1879–1934* (Lincoln: University of Nebraska Press, 1999); Karen J. Blair, 'The State of Research on Pacific Northwest Women,' *Frontiers* 23.3 (2001): 49–50.

11 Ruth Landes' work has most often been criticized for being ethnocentric and for being an uncritical extension of the dominant paradigms of the day; see Ruth Landes, *The Ojibwa Woman* (New York: Norton, 1971). See also Eleanor Leacock, 'Women's Status in Egalitarian Society: Implications for Social Evolution,' *Current Anthropology* 33 (Fall 1992): 225–36; and Jamieson, '"Sisters under the Skin,"' 133. Another classic is Louise S. Spindler, *Menomini Women and Culture Change*, American Anthropological Association, Memoir 91 (February 1962). See also Robin Ridington, 'Stories of the Vision Quest among Dunne-za Women,' *Atlantis* 9.1 (Fall 1983): 68–78.

12 Karen Sachs, 'Engels Revisited: Women, the Organization of Production and Private Property,' and Sherry Ortner, 'Is Female to Male as Nature Is to Culture?' in *Women, Culture and Society*, ed. Michelle Zimbalist Rosaldo and Louise Lamphere (Stanford: Stanford University Press, 1974), 207–22 and 67–87.

13 Michelle Zimbalist Rosaldo, 'Women, Culture and Society: A Theoretical Overview,' in Rosaldo and Lamphere, eds, *Women, Culture and Society*, 16–42; Eleanor Burke Leacock, 'Matrilocality in a Simple Hunting Economy (Montagnais-Naskapi),' *Southwest Journal of Anthropology* 11(1955): 31–47.

14 Rayna Green, 'The Pocahontas Perplex: The Image of Indian Women in American Culture,' in *Native American Voices: A Reader*, ed. Susan Lobo and Steve Talbot (New York: Longman, 1998), 182–92; Rayna Green, 'Review

Essay: Native American Women,' *Signs: Journal of Women in Culture and Society* 7 (Winter 1980): 248–67; Jennifer Nez Denetdale, 'Representing Changing Woman: A Review Essay on Navajo Women,' *American Indian Culture and Research Journal* 25.3 (2001): 1–26.

15 Denetdale, 'Representing Changing Woman,' 2. See also Linda Tuhiwai Smith, *Decolonizing Methodologies: Research and Indigenous Peoples* (New York and London: Zed Books, 1999), 151.

16 Lisa J. Udel, 'Revision and Resistance: The Politics of Native Women's Motherwork,' *Frontiers* 22.2 (2001): 43–62.

17 Strong, 'Feminist Theory,' 687.

18 Nancy Shoemaker, 'Introduction,' in *Negotiators of Change: Historical Perspectives on Native American Women*, ed. Nancy Shoemaker (New York and London: Routledge, 1995), 7.

19 Klein and Ackerman, *Women and Power*, 12.

20 Katherine Weist, 'Beasts of Burden and Menial Slaves: Nineteenth Century Observations of Northern Plains Indian Women,' and Alice Kehoe, 'The Shackles of Tradition,' in Albers and Medicine, eds, *Hidden Half*, 29–53 and 53–77; Green, 'Pocahontas Perplex'; Bataille and Sands, *American Indian Women: Telling Their Lives* (Lincoln: University of Nebraska Press, 1984), 1–46; David Smits, 'The Squaw Drudge: A Prime Index of Savagism,' *Ethnohistory* 29 (1982): 281–306; Gail Guthrie Valaskakis, 'Sacajawea and Her Sisters: Images and Native Women,' *Canadian Journal of Native Education*. 21.1 (1999): 117–35; Martha Harroun Foster, 'Lost Women of the Matriarchy: Iroquois Women in the Historical Literature,' *American Indian Culture and Research Journal* 19.3 (1995): 121–40.

21 Wendy Wickwire, 'Women in Ethnography: The Research of James A. Teit,' *Ethnohistory* 40.4 (Fall 1994): 539–62.

22 Mary C. Wright, 'The Woman's Lodge: Constructing Gender on the Nineteenth-Century Pacific Northwest Plateau,' *Frontiers* 24.1 (2003): 1–18; Wickwire, 'Women in Ethnography.' For a different conclusion about Teit, see Nadine Schuurman, 'Contesting Patriarchies: Nlha7pamux and Stl'atl'imx Women and Colonialism in Nineteenth-Century British Columbia,' *Gender, Place and Culture* 5.2 (1998): 141–58.

23 See, for example, Alison Blunt, *Travel, Gender and Imperialism: Mary Kingsley and West Africa* (New York: Guilford Press, 1994); Sara Mills, *Discourses of Difference: An Analysis of Women's Travel Writing and Colonialism* (London: Routledge, 1991); Nancy Pagh, 'Imagining Native Women: Feminine Discourse and Four Women Traveling the Northwest Coast,' in *Telling Tales: Essays in Western Women's History*, ed. Catherine Cavanagh and Randi R. Warne (Vancouver: UBC Press, 2000); Carole Gerson,

'Nobler Savages: Representations of Native Women in the Writings of Susanna Moodie and Catharine Parr Traill,' *Journal of Canadian Studies* 32 (Summer 1997): 5–21. For an example of one woman's writing in which relationships between the writer and Aboriginal women are evident, see Margaret A. Ormsby, *A Pioneer Gentlewoman in British Columbia: The Recollections of Susan Allison* (Vancouver: University of British Columbia Press, 1976). For a fuller contextualization of the relations between Aboriginal and white women in British Columbia, see Adele Perry, *On the Edge of Empire: Gender, Race, and the Making of British Columbia, 1849–1871* (Toronto: University of Toronto Press, 2001).

24 Carol J. Williams, *Framing the West: Race, Gender and the Photographic Frontier in the Pacific Northwest* (Oxford: Oxford University Press, 2003); Laure Meijer Drees, 'Aboriginal Women in the Canadian West,' *Native Studies Review* 10.1 (1995): 61–3; Dorinda M. Stahl, 'Moving from Colonization to Decolonization: Reinterpreting Historical Images of Aboriginal Women,' *Native Studies Review* 12.1 (1999): 115–16.

25 Taken from the title of Brown and Vibert, eds, *Reading beyond Words*.

26 Ruth Roach Pierson, 'Experience, Difference, Dominance and Voice in the Writing of Canadian Women's History,' in *Writing Women's History: International Perspectives* (Bloomington: Indiana University Press, 1991), 79–106; Joan Wallach Scott, *Gender and the Politics of History*, rev. ed. (New York: Columbia University Press, 1999).

27 Julia Emberley, 'Aboriginal Women's Writing and the Cultural Politics of Representation,' in Miller and Chuchryk, eds, *Women of the First Nations*, 97–112. For the mainstream nature of these criticisms today, see the introduction to Cavanaugh and Warne, eds, *Telling Tales*, 5.

28 Julia Emberley, '"A Gift for Languages": Native Women and the Textual Economy of the Colonial Archive,' in *Thresholds of Difference: Feminist Critique, Native Women's Writings, Postcolonial Theory* (Toronto: University of Toronto Press, 1993), 100–26.

29 Pierson, 'Experience, Difference, Dominance and Voice.'

30 Joan Sangster, 'Telling Our Stories: Feminist Debates and the Use of Oral History,' in *Rethinking Canada: The Promise of Women's History*, 4th ed., ed. Veronica Strong-Boag, Mona Gleason, and Adele Perry (Don Mills, ON: Oxford University Press, 2002), 222.

31 Charlene Porsild, 'Coming In from the Cold: Reflections on the History of Women in Northern Canada,' *Atlantis* 25.1 (Fall/Winter 2000): 63–7.

32 Joan Wallach Scott, 'Gender: A Useful Category of Historical Analsysis,' in *Gender and the Politics of History*, ed. Joan Wallach Scott (New York: Columbia University Press, 1988), 28–52.

33 For a discussion of trends involving gender history, see vol. 1, no. 1, of the journal *Gender and History* (1989). For Canadian discussion on gender history and women's history, see Kathryn McPherson, Cecilia Morgan, and Nancy M. Forestall, 'Introduction: Conceptualizing Canada's Gendered Pasts,' in *Gendered Pasts: Historical Essays in Femininity and Masculinity in Canada*, ed. McPherson, Morgan, and Forestall (Toronto: Oxford University Press, 1999), 1–11; Gail Cuthbert Brant, 'Postmodern Patchwork: Some Recent Trends in the Writing of Women's History,' *Canadian Historical Review* 72.4 (1991): 441–70; Joan Sangster, 'Beyond Dichotomies: Re-assessing Gender History and Women's History in Canada,' *Left History* 3.1 (1995): 109–21; and the responses: Karen Dubinsky and Lynn Marks, 'Beyond Purity: A Response to Sangster,' *Left History* 3.2 (Fall 1995): 205–21, and France Iacovetta and Linda Kealey, 'Women's History, Gender History and Debating Dichotomies,' *Left History* 4.1 (Spring 1996): 221–8.

34 Ann Laura Stoler and Frederick Cooper, 'Between Metropole and Colony: Rethinking a Research Agenda,' in *Tensions of Empire: Colonial Cultures in a Bourgeois World*, ed. Frederick Cooper and Ann Laura Stoler (Berkeley: University of California Press, 1997), 4–11; Antoinette Burton, *Burdens of History: British Feminists, Indian Women and Imperial Culture, 1865–1915* (Chapel Hill: University of North Carolina Press, 1994); Ann Laura Stoler, *Carnal Knowledge and Imperial Power* (Berkeley: University of California Press, 2002); Catherine Hall, *Civilising Subjects: Colony and Metropole in the English Imagination, 1830–1867* (Chicago: University of Chicago Press, 2002)

35 Perry, *On the Edge of Empire*.

36 See Elizabeth Vibert, *Traders' Tales: Narratives of Cultural Encounters on the Columbia Plateau: 1807–1846* (Norman: University of Oklahoma Press, 1997) and Mrinalini Sinha, *Colonial Masculinity: The 'Manly Englishman' and the 'Effeminate Bengali' in the Late 19th Century* (Manchester: Manchester University Press, 1995) are just two examples from this field.

37 Janet Silman, *Enough Is Enough: Aboriginal Women Speak Out* (Toronto: Women's Press, 1987).

38 Ruth B. Phillips, 'Nuns, Ladies and the "Queen of the Huron": Appropriating the Savage in Nineteenth-Century Huron Tourist Art,' in *Unpacking Culture: Art and Commodity in Colonial and Postcolonial Worlds*, ed. Ruth B. Phillips and Christopher B. Steiner (Berkeley: University of California Press, 1999), 33–50.

39 For example, see Barbara Bodenhorn, '"I'm not the great hunter: my wife is": Inupiat and Anthropological Models of Gender,' *Etudes/Inuit/Studies* 14.1–2 (1990): 55–74; Margaret Blackman, *Sadie Brower Neakok: An Inupiaq*

Woman (Seattle and London: University of Washington Press, 1989); Sheilagh Grant, 'Inuit History in the Next Millennium: Challenges and Rewards,' in *Northern Visions: New Perspectives on the North in Canadian History*, ed. Kerry Abel and Ken S. Coates (Peterborough, ON: Broadview Press, 2001), 91–106.

40 Sarah Carter, 'Transnational Perspectives on the History of Great Plains Women: Gender, Race, Nations, and the Forty-ninth Parallel,' *American Review of Canadian Studies* 33.4 (Winter 2003): 565–96.

41 Ian McKay, 'The Liberal Order Framework: A Prospectus for a Reconnaissance of Canadian History,' *Canadian Historical Review* 81.4 (Dec. 2000): 617–46.

42 Perry, *On the Edge of Empire*, 6.

43 Bruce G. Trigger and William R. Swagerty, 'Entertaining Strangers: North America in the Sixteenth Century,' in *The Cambridge History of the Native Peoples of the Americas*, Vol. 1, *North America*, Part 1, ed. Wilcolm Washburn (Cambridge: Cambridge University Press, 1996), 327; T.J. Brasser, 'Early Indian-European Contacts,' in *The Handbook of North American Indians*, Vol. 15, *The Northeast* (Washington, DC: Smithsonian Institution, 1978), 79; Barbara S. Efrat and W.J. Langlois, eds, 'The Contact Period as Recorded by Indian Oral Tradition,' in *nu:tka: Captain Cook and the Spanish Explorers on the Coast*, ed. Efrat and Langlois, *Sound Heritage* 7.1 (1978): 54–8; Daniel Clayton, 'Captain Cook and the Spaces of Contact at "Nootka Sound,"' in Brown and Vibert, eds, *Reading beyond Words*, 95–123; Yvonne Marshall, 'Dangerous Liaisons: Maquinna, Quadra, and Vancouver in Nootka Sound, 1790–95,' in *From Maps to Metaphors: The Pacific World of George Vancouver*, ed. Robin Fisher and Hugh Johnson (Vancouver: UBC Press, 1993), 160–76; George R. Hamell, 'Strawberries, Floating Islands and Rabbit Captains: Mythical Realities and European Contact in the Northeast during the Sixteenth and Seventeenth Centuries,' *Journal of Canadian Studies* 21.4 (Winter 1986–7): 72–4; Christopher L. Miller and George R. Hamell, 'A New Perspective on Indian-White Contact: Cultural Symbols of Colonial Trade,' *Journal of American History* 73.2 (Sept. 1986): 311–28.

44 See, for example, A.J. Ray, *Indians in the Fur Trade: Their Role as Hunters, Trappers and Middlemen in the Lands Southwest of Hudson Bay, 1660–1870* (Toronto: University of Toronto Press, 1974); Arthur J. Ray, *The Canadian Fur Trade in the Industrial Age* (Toronto: University of Toronto Press, 1990); Arthur J. Ray and Donald B. Freeman, *Give Us Good Measure: An Economic Analysis of Relations between the Indians and the Hudson's Bay Company before 1763* (Toronto: University of Toronto Press, 1978); Charles A. Bishop, *The Northern Ojibwa and the Fur Trade: An Historical and Ecological Study*

(Toronto: Holt, Rinehart and Winston, 1974); Robin Fisher, *Contact and Conflict: Indian-European Relations in British Columbia, 1774–1890*, 2nd ed. (Vancouver: UBC Press, 1992); Daniel Francis and Toby Morantz, *Partners in Furs: A History of the Fur Trade in Eastern James Bay, 1600–1870* (Kingston and Montreal: McGill-Queen's University Press, 1983).

45 Sylvia Van Kirk, *Many Tender Ties: Women in Fur-Trade Society in Western Canada* (Winnipeg: Watson & Dwyer Publishing, 1980); Jennifer S.H. Brown, *Strangers in Blood: Fur Trade Company Families in Indian Country* (Vancouver: University of British Columbia Press, 1980).

46 See, as just one example, Bruce M. White, 'The Woman Who Married a Beaver: Trade Patterns and Gender Roles in the Ojibwa Fur Trade,' *Ethnohistory* 46.1 (Winter 1999): 109–47.

47 Carol Devens, *Countering Colonization: Native American Women and Great Lakes Missions 1630–1900* (Berkeley: University of California Press, 1992), 121–2.

48 Emma LaRocque, 'The Colonization of a Native Woman Scholar,' in Miller and Chuchryk, eds, *Women of the First Nations*, 14.

49 Natalie Zemon-Davis, *Women on the Margins: Three Seventeenth-Century Lives* (Cambridge, MA: Harvard University Press, 1995), 254–7.

50 Susan Sleeper-Smith, *Indian Women and French Men: Rethinking Cultural Encounter in the Western Great Lakes* (Amherst: University of Massachusetts Press, 2001).

51 Laura Peers, '"The Guardian of All": Jesuit Missionary and Salish Perceptions of the Virgin Mary,' in Brown and Vibert, eds, *Reading beyond Words*, 284–303.

52 Stoler, *Carnal Knowledge and Imperial Power*, 46, 140.

53 For an excellent overview of the history of Western sexuality, see Robert Nye, ed., *Sexuality* (New York: Oxford, 1998).

54 Jo-Anne Fiske, 'Carrier Women and the Politics of Mothering,' in Strong-Boag et al., eds, *Rethinking Canada: The Promise of Women's History*.

55 Lisa J. Udel, 'Revision and Resistance: The Politics of Native Women's Motherwork,' *Frontiers* 12.2 (2001): 43–62.

56 Julie Cruikshank, 'Becoming a Woman in Athapaskan Society: Changing Traditions on the Upper Yukon River,' *Western Canadian Journal of Anthropology* 5.2 (1975): 1–14.

57 Georgina Elizabeth Marucci, *Lake Babine Women's Rites of Passage: An Archaeological Inquiry* (M.A. thesis, University of Northern British Columbia, 2000), 122.

58 Mary-Ellen Kelm, *Colonizing Bodies: Aboriginal Health and Healing in British Columbia, 1900–50* (Vancouver: UBC Press, 1998), xvii.

59 See, for example, Wendy Mitchinson, *The Nature of Their Bodies: Women and Their Doctors in Victorian Canada* (Toronto: University of Toronto Press, 1991).
60 See for example, Stoler, *Carnal Knowledge*; Anne McClintock, *Imperial Leather: Race, Gender, and Sexuality in the Colonial Conquest* (New York: Routledge, 1995); and Hall, *Civilising Subjects.*
61 Ann McGrath and Winona Stevenson, 'Gender, Race, and Policy: Aboriginal Women and the State in Canada and Australia,' in *Labour / Le Travail* 38 (Fall 1996): 39.
62 See, for example, Jo-Anne Fiske, 'The Supreme Law and the Grand Law: Changing Significance of Customary Law for Aboriginal Women of British Columbia,' *BC Studies* 105/6 (Spring/Summer 1995): 183–99.
63 See, for example, Kathleen Jamieson, 'Sex Discrimination and the Indian Act,' in *Arduous Journey: Canadian Indians and Decolonization*, ed. Rick J. Ponting (Toronto: McClelland and Stewart, 1986), 112–36; Jamieson, *Indian Women and the Law in Canada: Citizens Minus* (Ottawa: Advisory Council on the Status of Women, 1978); L.E. Krosenbrink–Gelissen, 'Caring Is Indian Women's Business, but Who Takes Care of Them? Canadian Indian Women, the Renewed Indian Act and Its Implications for Women's Family Responsibilities, Roles and Rights,' *Law and Anthropology* 7 (1994): 107–30; Val Napoleon, 'Extinction by Number: Colonialism Made Easy,' *Canadian Journal of Law and Society* 16.1 (2001): 113–45; and Mary Ellen Turpel, 'Patriarchy and Paternalism: The Legacy of the Canadian State for First Nations Women,' *Canadian Journal of Women and the Law* 6 (1993): 174–92.
64 Veronica Strong-Boag and Carole Gerson, *Paddling Her Own Canoe: The Times and Texts of E. Pauline Johnson (Tekahionwake)* (Toronto: University of Toronto Press, 2000); Charlotte Gray, *Flint and Feather: The Life and Times of E. Pauline Johnson, Tekahionwake* (Toronto: Harper Collins, 2002).

2 Women, Kin, and Catholicism: New Perspectives on the Fur Trade

SUSAN SLEEPER-SMITH

...

This article focuses on four Native women, married to French fur traders, whose lives offer insight into the process of sociological and cultural adaptation that occurred as Indian villages of the western Great Lakes became increasingly involved in the trade. This essay suggests that Richard White's conception of the 'middle ground' is a viable way in which to describe interaction between Indians and Euro-Americans and that it should be expanded to emphasize the prominent role that Native women played as cultural mediators. The Indian women who married fur traders were 'negotiators of change.'[1] They lived in a region where the exchange process occurred primarily at wintering grounds or in villages, and, because trade had social as well as economic ramifications, intermarriage played an integral role in the trade's evolution. Traders who married these women thus had an advantage over their rivals. Marriage, either in the 'manner of the country' or performed by missionary priests, assured traders inclusion as members of indigenous communities and facilitated access to furs.[2]

A fur trader's presence enhanced the importance of the community where he lived and simultaneously enhanced his wife's authority and prestige among her people. Native women did not marry out; rather, they incorporated their French husbands into a society structured by Native custom and tradition.[3] Although access to trade goods enhanced the power and influence of these Native women, they did not simply reinvent themselves as French. Although early Jesuit records, particularly marital and baptismal registers, provide the opportunity to study such women's lives, unfortunately they also effectively mask indigenous identity. Many women were simply identified by their baptismal names or by the surname of their husbands.

The Native women who are the focus of this article can be identified in Jesuit records by both their Indian and Christian names. Because we are aware of their Native ancestry, we can consequently see how they were involved in the creation of Catholic kin networks. These women repeatedly served as godmothers to numerous children of mixed ancestry. Over time, these Catholic kin networks became increasingly more complex, as large numbers of such children and godchildren entered the fur trade. Baptism and marriage provided the means through which these diverse real and fictive kin networks could be continually expanded. Marital and baptismal records suggest that such networks, created by Catholicism, facilitated access to peltry while simultaneously allowing women to negotiate for themselves positions of prominence and power. Also, many of the traders who married into these networks became prominent fur-trade figures. Therefore, by the mid-eighteenth century, identifiable Catholic kin networks had evolved that were compatible with and often parallel to those of indigenous society.

Female members – especially of the Barthe, Bourassa, Chaboyer, Chevalier, La Framboise, and Langlade families – appear frequently in baptismal registers of the western Great Lakes. These women were godmothers to each other's children and grandchildren, and their surnames span generations. The godparenting roles modelled by mothers were emulated by daughters and granddaughters.

The contention that Catholicism had important social ramifications that enhanced female autonomy contradicts the view that Catholicism instituted a male patriarchal order, which increasingly subordinated Native women to men. This later perspective, espoused by Carol Devens's *Countering Colonization* and Karen Anderson's *Chain Her by One Foot*, views Christianity as the means through which indigenous female autonomy was subverted.[4] These conclusions do not appear uniformly applicable to all Native communities in the western Great Lakes. Instead, this article suggests that Catholicism could also serve as a pathway to social prominence.[5] The Jesuits generally recruited catechizers or instructors among Native women. These female converts were often the most visible proof of Jesuit success. It would have been foolhardy for these priests to foster female subjection to the authority of men whom the Jesuits frequently despised. Indeed, most missionary priests viewed the fur-trade husbands of these converts as licentious drunkards who undermined Christian ideals; the Jesuits even vigorously supported a seventeenth-century royal policy that banished traders from the western Great Lakes. The Jesuits also frequently dismissed the elders of Native communities, many of whom scorned Christianity.

Therefore, it would have been problematic for the Jesuits to support the establishment of a male patriarchal order that subjected their pious female converts to the authority of male fur traders and unconverted headmen.

Just as the profit-making dimensions of the fur trade were mediated by the Algonquian-French political alliance, the repressive patriarchal order was mediated by the Jesuits' reliance on Native women. During the eighteenth century, these women were also the beneficiaries of the dramatic decline in the number of Jesuit priests. Not only did missionary fervour wane, but in the last quarter of the century the Jesuits were temporarily disbanded. In the absence of priests, many female converts fashioned a type of 'frontier Catholicism' in which they assumed the role of lay practitioners.

Amid the dynamics of this changing social landscape, Indian women who married fur traders relied on the interface between two worlds to position themselves as mediators between cultural groups, to assume leadership roles in religious training, to influence commodity production, and eventually, at least in a few cases, to establish themselves as independent traders. Through it all, these women retained their Indian identity, as evidenced by their language, names, and tribal affiliations. More important, they relied on their Catholicism to maintain relative autonomy in relation to their husbands. The complicated dynamics of such behaviours are evidenced by four women, whose lives spanned the seventeenth and eighteenth centuries. Two of the women were Illini: Marie Rouensa-8cate8a[6] and Marie Madeleine Réaume L'archevêque Chevalier.[7] Each used Catholicism to resist and reshape indigenous societal constraints. Rouensa lived during the early years of the fur trade, when Catholicism was shaped by Jesuit missionaries. Réaume lived later in the eighteenth century, when priests were few in number, lay practitioners became increasingly important, and 'frontier' or 'folk' Catholicism emerged.[8] Over time, the syncretic nature of Catholicism facilitated the creation of an ever-expanding kin network that extended the parameters of women's worlds from those of their immediate family and community to fur-trade posts throughout the Great Lakes and Mississippi River valley.

These women used the fictive ties created by godparenting to create an ever-expanding kinship network, and by the end of the eighteenth century these networks had evolved as strategic alliances that enabled some Native women to successfully establish themselves as independent fur traders. This was the case for Magdelaine Marcot La Framboise and Thérèse Marcot Lasaliere Schindler, who were raised in Odawa communities and were incorporated from birth into the Catholic kin networks of fur-trade society.[9] They negotiated the hazardous world of the late eighteenth- and early nineteenth-century fur trade, when Frenchmen were displaced, first by the English and later by American traders. Both La Framboise and Schindler prospered because their centrality in indigenous kin networks gave them access to a stable supply of furs. These women retained their independence because they were at the locus of Catholic kin networks that were rooted in indigenous communities and that structured Great Lakes fur-trade society.[10]

These women, who have appeared tangentially in the fur-trade literature, have been depicted either as historical outliers or as women who did not challenge traditional spheres of male authority.[11] White uses Rouensa to exemplify the cultural inventions of an evolving middle ground, when compromise, rather than force, convinced Rouensa to marry the fur trader Michel Accault. After her marriage, Rouensa disappeared from the 'middle ground.'[12] Marriage, however, was not her gateway to invisibility. Marriage, coupled with her Catholicism, afforded access to power and prestige, which is apparent when examining the whole of Rouensa's life.[13]

Her centrality as a historical actor resulted from the economic and social adaptations that Indian communities experienced as they became increasingly involved in the western Great Lakes fur trade. Rouensa's village, located just south of Lake Michigan, became involved in the fur trade in the late 1670s, when Robert La Salle established a French presence in the Illinois Country. Her father was an important headman among the Kaskaskia, one of the seven nations of the Illiniwek Confederacy.[14] In 1790 he arranged for Rouensa to marry a fur trader who had ventured west with La Salle in 1679.

Among the Kaskaskia, women were free to reject such arranged marriages. But in the 1690s, when the Fur Trade Wars engulfed the Great Lakes, access to trade goods and alliances with the French were considered important strategies that countered Iroquois hostilities. Rouensa would have experienced tremendous community pressure to accede to her father's request and to the wishes of her village. Had she acquiesced to such pressure, her behaviour would have escaped historical attention. But Rouensa refused to marry, and she turned to the Jesuit Father Jacques Gravier for support.

Rouensa was one of Gravier's more prominent female converts among the Kaskaskia, of whom the Jesuits converted more women than men.

Their efforts reinforced the Illini matrifocal households, which linked women in communal living arrangements and encouraged female conversions.[15] A 1712 Jesuit letter described how this process occurred among the Illinois: 'We call those instructors, who in other missions are called catechists, because it is not in the Church, but in the wigwams that they instruct the catechumens and the proselytes.'[16]

Gravier's enthusiastic search for converts encouraged these young women to speak out, and he (perhaps inadvertently) provided the tools for social empowerment to them.[17] In turn, female proselytes used Christianity to challenge the traditional wisdom of the tribal elders. Many young women became known for 'mock[ing] the superstitions of their nation':[18]

> Although this nation is much given to debauchery, especially the men, The Reverend Fathers of the Jesuits, who talk their language with perfect ease manage ... to impose some check on this by instructing a number of girls in Christianity, who often profit by their teaching, and mock at the superstitions of their nation, which often greatly incenses the old men and daily exposes these Fathers to ill treatment, and even to be killed.[19]

Given this scenario, it is not surprising that the Jesuits could 'find hardly a single young man upon whom we can rely for the exercises of religion.'[20]

Christian conversion enabled Rouensa to position herself as a teacher among her people. She expanded the culturally innovative dimensions of the middle ground when she translated Gravier's Christian message into her Kaskaskia language. Because she was an effective mediator of that message, Gravier loaned Rouensa books with pictures that supplemented her Christian storytelling and privileged her among the Kaskaskia: 'Not only did she explain them at home ... speaking of nothing but the pictures or the catechism, – but she also explained the pictures on the whole of the Old Testament to the old and young men whom her father assembled in his dwelling.'[21]

Gravier further reinforced such behaviours of young female proselytes when he shared with them stories of female saints. Virtue and mystical experiences produced European celibates, and strong similarities in indigenous behaviour encouraged the Kaskaskia converts to dedicate their lives to the church. Illini women who traditionally elected to remain single usually entered the warrior society. Christian conversion created an alternative option, and, facing the threat of an undesirable marriage, Rouensa 'resolved to consecrate her virginity to God.' Catholic conversion encouraged her to resist a proposed marriage, even though it was arranged by her parents. Her professed devotion to virginity, to the love of Christ, intensified when her parents chose for her husband Michel Accault, a fifty-year-old grizzled veteran of the fur trade. Rouensa called on Gravier to defend her decision to remain a celibate Catholic woman:[22] 'She had resolved never to marry, in order that she might belong wholly to Jesus Christ. She answered her father and her mother, when they brought her to me in company with the frenchman whom they wished to have for a son-in-law, that she did not wish to marry; that she had already given all her heart to God.'[23]

Gravier supported his young convert's decision. To have abandoned her would have resulted in the inevitable loss of his female congregation. Gravier was ridiculed by the fort commandant, and Rouensa's father banned his people from attending mass. Few attended, and although Gravier proposed prayer as the solution for the impasse, Rouensa proposed a more practical solution. She consented to marry the disreputable French trader if her parents agreed to become Christian converts. They readily assented to her demands.

In this manner Rouensa used Catholicism to reshape an otherwise potentially dismal outcome.[24] A marriage 'in the manner of the country' would have given her minimal control over a husband who was 'famous in this Illinois Country for all his debaucheries.'[25] Now she could demand Christian reformation of Accault's character. As the priest's able assistant, Rouensa helped define what was expected of a Christian husband, and she relied on both her parents and her community to apply the necessary social pressures. Her parents' conversion was soon followed by the baptism of an additional two hundred people, and Gravier, obviously pleased with Rouensa's solution, counted more than three-fourths of the Kaskaskia present during catechism.[26]

Catholic marriages were sanctioned by Illini headmen, and consequently Christian strictures about the sanctity of marriage were incorporated into enforceable communal norms. Rouensa's father publicly proclaimed that 'the black gowns were the witnesses of true marriage; and that to them alone God had given orders to pray for all who wished to marry, and they would be truly married.'[27] Although marriage 'in the manner of the country' often acquired long-range stability, marriage partners like Accault, better known for their wayward ways than their faithful behaviour, were problematic husbands. Not surprisingly, after his marriage Accault publicly proclaimed himself a reformed man.

Surrounded by Christian Indians, he atoned for his sins. The sincerity of Accault's confession may be questioned, but Rouensa's matrifocal household, as well as her larger community, relied on Christian strictures about the sanctity of marriage to establish the invisible but effective links that ensured a reliable supply of well-priced trade goods.

French fur traders were eager to marry Native women with extensive kin networks, particularly socially prominent women like Rouensa. The exchange of trade goods for peltry occurred on a face-to-face basis, along a kinship continuum. Kin networks controlled access to furs, and marriage ensured Euro-American men inclusion as kin. When French traders married Illini women, they joined their wives' household. This gave women, who controlled productive resources, increased access to trade goods. Trade goods reinforced ritual gift-giving and enhanced both the power and prestige of matrifocal households and individual women.

Households, like that of Rouensa, remained rooted within indigenous society and proved highly resistant to any efforts to impose patriarchal authority. Gravier was justifiably reluctant to accord Accault authority over his wife, for she was both an effective Catholic proselytizer and a more rigorous and faithful Christian than her husband. In this instance Catholicism proved to be a socially innovative mechanism that enhanced female authority. Simultaneously, access to trade goods reinforced the continued viability of Rouensa's matrifocal household, when it came under the stress of recurrent relocations.

...

During Rouensa's life, the Kaskaskia migrated south to settle on the Mississippi's rich alluvial lands near St Louis. Rouensa was left a widow after seven years of marriage to Accault, after which she married another Frenchman, Michel Philippe. He arrived in the Illinois Country as an obscure voyageur, or canoeman, who probably earned less than a thousand livres a year.[28] For the next twenty years, the Kaskaskia baptismal records detail the evolution of their increasingly large family. Rouensa gave birth to six more children, and by her death in 1725 she had amassed an estate that was sufficient to probate and inventory. The estate was divided between her second husband and her children from both marriages.

Before her death, Rouensa dictated her will to Father Baptiste Le Boullenger, and it was written down by a notary. The will was then read to her twice, in her Illini language. Her request that the document be written in her Native tongue indicated that Rouensa's household and children were probably conversant in her language, rather than in her husband's French tongue. Each of her children, upon maturity or marriage, received 2,681 livres from an estate valued at 45,000 livres. Her property included several agricultural tracts of land. Two substantial houses, each thirty-six by twenty feet with stone fireplaces, were located within the Kaskaskia village. There were two barns filled with hay to feed the livestock; oxen, thirteen cows, three horses, thirty-one pigs, and forty-eight chickens. There were ox and horse carts and ploughs to cultivate the fields. Rouensa owned four African slaves (two couples, both married) as well as an Indian slave.[29] The female slaves probably planted and harvested the oats, wheat, and maize. The male slaves were more likely to work in the fur trade, but they were also woodcutters, for there were nine tons of wood, cut and debarked. The barns also contained wheat and oats. The wheat, valued at 3,300 livres, had been sheaved but not yet ground at the nearby mill. Nineteen to twenty arpents of maize or Indian corn remained to be harvested.[30]

The community of Kaskaskia itself underwent a complex evolution as a result of these relationships. It was a mature settlement, which historians have often erroneously identified as founded by the French. The fur traders intermarried among the indigenous people. Although numerous French names appear in marital and baptismal registers, Native women baptized by missionary priests assumed Christian names. During the first twenty years following European contact, there were few French women. As a consequence, of the twenty-one baptisms recorded by the Jesuits, only one was the child of a French woman.[31] There was a ready market in supplying fur traders as well as in shipping agricultural produce and furs north to Montreal and, in some instances, south to New Orleans. The establishment of Kaskaskia in close proximity to Cahokia created a new centre of farming activity in the American Bottoms. Rouensa's household profited from the fur trade.[32]

Over time, communities like Kaskaskia evolved as a blending of indigenous and French cultures, but for the first generation they were more Illini than French.[33] Agriculture, for instance, remained the province of women. The continuity of these matrifocal households encouraged French husbands to become traders rather than farmers. But fields mounded in Indian fashion or cultivated by the small French *en bardeau* ploughs led travellers to condemn French men as lazy, simply because Native women's agricultural work was invisible to Euro-American outsiders. These women also resisted the women's work associated

with French households. Among the probated wills and inventories of
the river community residents there were none of the traditional tools
associated with French home industry – spinning wheels, looms, or
even knitting needles.[34] In these communities it appears that indigenous gender roles gave women the management and allocation of
resources. Even in the Illinois lead mines in the Fox-Wisconsin riverway
region, women engaged in mining and seem to have influenced mining
techniques and access to the mines.[35]

The fur trade and Catholicism enhanced not only the authority of
women, but it also accorded them new avenues to social prominence.
Women became Christian instructors. They also rang the chapel bells
that summoned Catholic Indians to services in the morning and
evening.[36] One of the most important figures at the River L'Abbe Mission, the French colonial church for the Cahokia Indians on Monks
Mound, may have been the Illini woman who was buried with the
chapel bell.[37] It was Rouensa who achieved one of the highest honours,
however, for she was buried inside the Kaskaskia mission church.

...

Distinctive métis communities eventually evolved from these Catholic kin networks as mixed-ancestry women married Frenchmen or mixed-
ancestry fur traders. Métis communities existed at important fur-trade
posts, like Michilimackinac and Green Bay, but at smaller fur-trade
communities the lives of these women continued to be shaped by the
indigenous communities in which they lived. The power of habit structured their lives, just as it organized Indian society and enabled traditional economies to meet the demands of an emerging transatlantic
market economy.[38]

Catholic kin networks were indispensable to the fur trade because
they linked the larger fur-trade posts (the centres of exchange) with the
smaller fur-trade posts (the sources of supply). How that kinship system operated is apparent in the life of another Illini woman, Marie
Madeleine Réaume, the daughter of Simphorose Ouaouagoukoue and
Jean Baptiste Réaume.[39] She was born early in the eighteenth century,
shortly before Rouensa's death. Although both were Illini women and
Catholic converts, their lives differed dramatically. Unlike Rouensa,
Réaume did not have social prominence, and her conversion was of no
particular significance to any of the Jesuit fathers. Nor did she possess
sufficient wealth to leave legacies for her children. In every respect, she
was a less conspicuous historical figure, and consequently she left no
written records or will for the perusal of curious historians. But Réaume's

life was illustrative of the prominent role women played in the evolution of fur-trade communities. Her life bridged two disparate worlds and illustrated how kin networks linked indigenous and French societies. Exchange remained embedded in social relationships, kinship mediated that process, and Catholic kin networks linked the distant fur-trade outposts of an expanding fur-trade society. For Native people, however, trade remained a process of collective exchange, while for Europeans exchange was an increasingly individualistic transaction within an emerging transatlantic market economy.[40]

Réaume, like the other women discussed in this article, was married 'in the eyes of the church.' Her husband was Augustin L'archevêque, a licensed trader in the Illinois Country.[41] During the course of their sixteen-year marriage, Réaume gave birth to six children and remained relatively anonymous until her husband's death.[42] Her name then started to appear in the fort's reimbursement records. Now identified as the Widow L'archevêque, she was reimbursed by the St Joseph commandant for 'one fat pig, a heifer, an ox, four pairs of snowshoes, a bark canoe, and another fat pig.' Other invoices indicate that the widow also supplied packs with wheat, oats, and corn.[43] It is clear that Réaume's household produced both a marketable agricultural surplus as well as specific goods for the trade.[44] Her agricultural holdings paralleled those of Rouensa, although they were far less significant. Réaume had 'ten houses, good lands, orchards, gardens, cattle, furniture, [and] utensils.'[45] Such women, and the agriculturally oriented communities in which they lived, were common throughout the Great Lakes. As far north as Michilimackinac, other Indian communities served as agricultural suppliers of the trade. At Waganagisi (L'Arbe Croche or Crooked Tree) the Odawa 'raised large surpluses of corn and vegetables, produced fish, and later maple sugar, and manufactured canoes, snowshoes, and clothing essential to the Great Lakes fur trade.'[46]

These communities experienced seasonal population shifts, but they acquired an increasingly larger core of permanent residents. Réaume, for instance, lived at Fort St Joseph for almost seventy years; because of this longevity, she gradually established under the umbrella of Catholicism fictive and real kin networks that linked her household with similar fur-trade communities throughout the Great Lakes.[47]

Réaume's first attempt to expand her familial and fictive kin network to other prominent fur-trade families took place after her husband's death.[48] She had kin connections in the Illinois Country, but it was Michilimackinac that was emerging as the most important entrepôt of the eighteenth-century fur trade. In the summer of 1748, the thirty-eight-year-old widow travelled north to Michilimackinac. This was a journey of more than three hundred miles, which she made in a birch-bark canoe with her three-year-old son and her two eldest daughters, seventeen-year-old Marie Catherine and fifteen-year-old Marie Joseph Esther. Réaume relied on baptism and marriage to incorporate her family into the more prominent Catholic kin network of Michilimackinac. Members of the Bourassa and the Langlade families served as godparents to Réaume's son and as witnesses at the weddings of her daughters.[49] The ceremonies and celebrations completed, Réaume returned to St Joseph. Both daughters and their fur-trader husbands returned to St Joseph and became part of Réaume's household.[50]

After the marriage of Réaume's daughters, increasingly complex behavioural strategies enveloped this entire household and included not just the children but also Réaume herself. Three years after the 1848 trip to Michilimackinac, Réaume, then forty-one years old, gave birth to a son. The child's father was a prominent Michilimackinac trader, Louis Thérèse Chevalier, whom Réaume later married at the St Joseph mission.[51] Chevalier was thirty-nine.[52] Although Chevalier had married among the Odawa, he nevertheless married this forty-two-year-old widow and relocated to the southeastern shore of Lake Michigan.

The apparent marital strategy of Réaume was to join her prosperous agricultural household to Michilimackinac, which was the most important trading outpost in the western Great Lakes. For Chevalier marriage extended his already extensive kin network and provided him with an entrée into the prosperous St Joseph trade. Following Chevalier's marriage to Réaume, the Chevaliers garnered a substantial portion of the St Joseph trade. Chevalier's father had traded there in 1718, but he subsequently did not receive a permit for the area. His eldest sister and her husband had lived in the community for more than twenty years, but reimbursement invoices signed by the post commandant were for Louis Deschêtres's work as a blacksmith. The Chevaliers were Michilimackinac traders who were long denied entrée into the St Joseph trade. The other men in the Chevalier family had all married Native women on the western shore of Lake Michigan. In fact, Chevalier himself had married, in the manner of the country, an Odawa woman before his Christian marriage to Réaume, through whom he planned to enter the St Joseph trade.[53]

The Chevalier kin network was gradually integrated into the St Joseph community. One of Réaume's daughters married Chevalier's younger brother, Louis Pascal Chevalier.[54] Another daughter married her stepfather's Montreal trading partner, Charles Lhullic *dit* Chevalier. The groom was a recent forty-five-year-old widower; the bride, Angelique L'archevêque, was twenty-one.[55] Réaume's youngest daughter, seventeen-year-old Anne, also married a fur trader, and they initially remained part of the St Joseph community.[56]

Marriage integrated these two distant families, and in time the offspring migrated to other fur-trading communities. Mobility strengthened kinship ties not only with Michilimackinac but also to the south, creating a network that became increasingly important to the entire St Joseph River valley when the British took control of the western Great Lakes. During the 1850s Réaume's two eldest daughters, their husbands, and their children moved to Fort Pimiteoui, now Peoria, and eventually to Cahokia.[57] Réaume's fourth daughter, Marie Amable, and her husband also eventually joined their L'archevêque kin at Cahokia.

Geographically distant kin links were also greatly reinforced by the godparenting roles that siblings played to each other's children. For example, Réaume's daughters were frequent godparents to their nieces and nephews.[58] After they no longer lived in the Fort St Joseph community, they returned annually when missionary priests arrived from distant posts. Louis Chevalier's siblings also became godparents to the L'archevêque grandchildren, and Réaume's daughters were godmothers to the Chevalier grandchildren.

During the mid-eighteenth century, an important demographic shift took place when Fort St Joseph reverted to a predominantly indigenous settlement, and an increased number of Potawatomi became Catholic converts. By 1755 there was no longer a resident priest. In addition, many of the French families who had earlier lived at St Joseph had now moved to Detroit.[59] Consequently, Réaume became the community's most important lay practitioner.[60] She employed Catholicism as a socially integrative tool that incorporated increased numbers of Native people. *Panis*, or Native slaves, and Indian women were baptized at the St Joseph mission church. Réaume, for instance, was the godmother to Marie Jeanne, a thirteen-year-old slave, as well as to Thérèse, a forty-year-old Potawatomi woman.[61] One Miami couple, Pierre Mekbibkas8nga and his wife, had their 'Indian style marriage' sacramentally sanctioned by a visiting priest.[62] The incorporation of their four adult daughters through baptism revealed even more strongly the influence of the L'archevêque-Chevalier family. One daughter selected Louis

Chevalier as her godfather; two other daughters chose Réaume as their godmother.[63]

The French departure did not signal the demise of St Joseph as a fur-trade community. Instead, the number of furs harvested increased dramatically. More engagements or contracts for hiring canoemen were issued in this decade than in any previous period, and fur exports increased.[64]

By 1755, Réaume and Louis Chevalier were linked through trade and intermarriage to the Potawatomi villages of the St Joseph River valley. Their son, Louison, probably married among the Potawatomi. In this smaller fur-trade community, on the banks of the St Joseph River, Réaume and Chevalier remained part of an indigenous kin system.

Kinship facilitated fur-trade exchange and had political, as well as social and economic, dimensions. French authority over the North American interior rested on the hegemony of these kin networks. The French traders living among Native people were central to New France's highly effective communications network that linked distant western outposts. French traders relayed messages, solicited warriors, and mediated potentially disruptive disputes. Following the French and Indian War, when the British displaced the French, these kin networks frustrated the transfer of power. The garrisoning of former French forts proved an explosive event, when fur traders failed to assume their traditional role as mediators. Instead, in the uprising of 1763, they remained passive observers as the forts at Le Boeuf, Michilimackinac, Miami, Ouiatenon, Presqu'Isle, St Joseph, Sandusky, and Verango fell to Native-American forces.[65]

England lacked a sufficient presence to govern through force, and when the English ignored or attempted to displace French traders and their Native wives, this threatened to destabilize the highly complex, kin-related world of the upper Great Lakes region. Although Chevalier was described by the British as 'so connected with the Potawatomis that he can do anything with them,'[66] his influence was actually attributable to his wife. Réaume had lived at Fort St Joseph for more than fifty years and had incorporated Chevalier into her kin network.[67] Communities like St Joseph were the locus of Catholic kin networks, and women like Réaume were the demographic links in a world defined by kinship. Her behaviour followed the pattern of godparenting common in the western Great Lakes. She was the godmother to the children of her children, her slaves and their offspring, fellow Native-American converts, and even to the children of unconverted Native women. Eventually, Réaume's kinship networks extended south to St Louis, Cahokia, and Kaskaskia; north to Michilimackinac; and west to Green Bay. Both her mother and first husband were people of the Illinois Country. Her uncle Simon Réaume was considered the most important trader at Fort Ouiatenon until his death in the 1730s.[68] Her father eventually established himself as a Green Bay trader, and her younger sister, Suzanne, was raised in that community. Réaume's oldest daughter was the godmother to Suzanne's son.[69] Réaume's marriage to Chevalier was the impetus for incorporation of the Chevalier kin at Michilimackinac into the Fort St Joseph community. Chevalier's Montreal trading partner[70] and his younger brother (Louis Pascal Chevalier) both married Réaume's daughters.[71]

...

English commandants who ignored women such as Réaume and their French fur-trader husbands thwarted effective governance in the western Great Lakes. Those francophobic English commandants who advocated removal of French fur traders failed to appreciate that many mixed-ancestry offspring were now indistinguishable from the Indian people among whom they lived. In 1780, when Patrick Sinclair, the Michilimackinac commandant responsible for the St Joseph post, ordered the forcible removal of the forty-eight French people resident at St Joseph, including Réaume and Chevalier, he learned a bitter lesson about the folly of ignoring these kinship ties.[72] Shortly after their arrival, the English fur traders sent to Fort St Joseph were attacked by Réaume's Illinois kin network. This force was composed of her immediate family, her son-in-law, and thirty of his friends. Although this first raid was unsuccessful, it was followed by a larger, more effective force from Cahokia, Kaskaskia, and St Louis, with Madeleine's son, thirty-year-old Louison Chevalier, as the guide and interpreter. The Potawatomi reckoned the number to be 'one hundred white people and eighty Indians,' while other estimates placed the number at sixty-five white men and a large Native-American contingent.[73] Young Louison Chevalier ensured the attack's success because he divided the British goods among the St Joseph Potawatomi. The attack proved devastatingly effective, and the invaders were gone when the British arrived the next day.[74]

The St Joseph invasion is often described as a minor skirmish of the Revolutionary War, but such descriptions fail to appreciate the extent to which such events reflected fur-trade rather than military rivalries. This 1781 incident prevented the establishment of British traders in the

St Joseph River valley and secured the economic interests of the L'archevêque-Chevalier kin network.

Kinship facilitated the exchange process, and by the beginning of the nineteenth century, access to the best peltry in the western Great Lakes was increasingly controlled by these complex kin networks. When the American Fur Company entered the Great Lakes trade, company managers relied on this established kinship network and chose to supply two Odawa women, rather than their male competitors. They were Thérèse and Magdelaine Marcot, who were born into the St Joseph kin network. They were part of an intermediate link that joined that river valley to the Odawa community fifty miles father north, in the Grand River valley. Direct access to trade goods encouraged their emergence as independent traders.

Thérèse and Magdelaine were the children of an Odawa woman known as Thimotée and a French trader named Jean Baptiste Marcot. Marcot was a St Joseph trader whose family, along with the Chevaliers, had been forcibly removed in 1781.[75] Thimotée returned with the children to her Odawa community in the Grand River valley, while her husband relocated to present-day Wisconsin.[76] He was killed in 1783, when Thérèse and Magdelaine were young children of three and four. They were raised as Odawa, since their mother was the daughter of Chief Kewinaquot (Returning Cloud).[77] Both children were baptized at Michilimackinac, and their godparents were members of generationally prominent fur-trade families, part of the Chevalier, Barthe, and La Framboise kin networks. Thérèse and Magdelaine, despite being Catholic and the daughters of a French father, were identified as Odawa by the missionary priest.[78]

At first, the lives of both Thérèse and Magdelaine were remarkably similar to that of Marie Rouensa and Marie Madeleine Réaume L'archevêque Chevalier. Like their predecessors, Thérèse and Magdelaine were raised in indigenous society and married French fur traders. They married young, at fourteen, and their husbands paid the bride-price required by the Odawa. Magdelaine remained in the Grand River valley with her husband, Joseph La Framboise, and he traded among her people; Thérèse moved with her fur-trader husband, Pierre Lasaliere, to the St Joseph River valley.[79] After several years Lasaliere and Thérèse separated, and he moved to the west side of Lake Michigan to join the Wisconsin trade.[80] Like her mother, Thérèse returned to raise her daughter in her Odawa village in the Grand River valley. Then in 1799 she took her nine-year-old daughter to Michilimackinac to be baptized.[81]

Once again, the Michilimackinac priest identified both Thérèse and her child as Odawa, not French. After her husband's departure, Thérèse remained an attractive marital prospect because of her dual-kinship heritage. Her second husband was an Anglo fur trader, George Schindler, who started trading among the Odawa in 1800.[82]

Early in the nineteenth century, the lives of the two sisters changed dramatically. In 1804 their country marriages were consecrated by a missionary priest at Michilimackinac. Well-known Catholic fur-trade families witnessed the event, including their old friends the Chevaliers from St Joseph. Joseph La Framboise had lived with Magdelaine for ten years, and they had two children.[83] After Thérèse's marriage to Schindler, she moved to his house on the island. Now legal kin, the La Framboise and Schindler families also formed a business partnership. They planned to obtain trade goods from Claude La Framboise, Joseph's brother in Montreal, but unfortunately the business alliance never fully materialized.[84] In 1806, several years after the Michilimackinac celebration of his marriage, Joseph was killed by an irate Indian.[85] Magdelaine buried her husband and continued on her journey to the Odawa wintering ground with her infant son Joseph, two African-American slaves, Angelique and Louison, and twelve voyageurs.[86]

After her husband's death, Magdelaine, then in her twenties, emerged as an independent trader. She chose not to remarry, unlike Marie Rouensa and Marie Madeleine Réaume. Magdelaine's centrality in the Catholic kin networks of fur-trade society, her social prominence as a young Odawa woman, and her experience in the fur trade coincided with trader John Jacob Astor's eager search for an entrée into the Great Lakes trade. Kinship worked to Magdelaine's advantage and encouraged her independence. For the next fifteen years, until she retired from the trade in 1822, she travelled annually between the Grand River valley and Michilimackinac to exchange peltry for trade goods. She lived among her Odawa kin in the Grand River valley, and each year wintered with them. Magdelaine established herself as Madame La Framboise, obtained trading licences, first from the British and then, after the War of 1812, from the Americans. She hired voyageurs to accompany her, secured trade goods on credit, and returned each June to Michilimackinac to sell her furs and resupply her outfit.

Several years after Joseph La Framboise's death, a stroke left George Schindler an invalid.[87] Thérèse, like Magdelaine, became an independent fur trader, but traded at L'Arbe Croche, the Odawa community closest to Michilimackinac. Thérèse's operations rapidly expanded. She often served as Magdelaine's supply source for the Grand River valley trade, but she also supplied a large number of French fur traders, men drawn from her kin network.[88] She sold goods to traders from the Barthe, Chevalier, and La Framboise families, all members of her fictive kin network. Men from her Catholic kin network all appeared regularly on the pages of her fur-trade journals. Thérèse increasingly acquired prominence as a supplier, while her sister Magdelaine remained an active, independent trader.[89]

In 1816, when the American Fur Trade Company acquired greater control of the Great Lakes trade, it incorporated both women. By 1818 their supplies came from the American Fur Trade Company.[90] Magdelaine may have earned as much as five thousand to ten thousand pounds a year, while the average fur trader probably earned no more than a thousand pounds a year. The Grand River territory shipped about one hundred packs of furs a year to Michilimackinac. In 1800 furs were valued at twenty pounds per pack, and Magdelaine secured the majority of furs exported from the Grand River valley. She eventually retired from the fur trade and moved next door to her sister on Michilimackinac.[91]

These women negotiated for themselves positions of prominence in an era when the fur trade proved to be a precarious male venture. Many independent male traders were eliminated when John Jacob Astor and the American Fur Company gained control of the Great Lakes trade. The furs Thérèse Schindler and Madame La Framboise had first sold to Ramsay Crooks, Astor's representative in the Great Lakes, established their standing credit with Astor's newly formed American Fur Company.[92]

Marie Rouensa, Marie Magdelaine Réaume L'archevêque Chevalier, Magdelaine Marcot La Framboise, and Thérèse Marcot Lasaliere Schindler were part of a world where identity was defined not by nationality but by kinship. Kin networks, like those of the St Joseph community, characterized every fur-trade community in the western Great Lakes. The fictive and familial relationships created by the umbrella of frontier Catholicism further strengthened and expanded an already complex indigenous kinship system.[93] The Catholic kin network, in which these women played so prominent a role, served a socially integrative function, which enhanced the role and importance of these women.

In 1680 and 1711, Rouensa and Réaume were born into a demographically chaotic and socially unstable world. The Fur Trade Wars pitted Iroquois against the Algonquian-speaking people. The Jesuits contributed to that social disruption when they condemned fur traders as licentious and dismissed shamans as 'jugglers.' Indian women emerged as the cultural mediators of this eighteenth-century landscape. The Jesuit presence offered Native women an opportunity to interface between two disparate worlds, and as Catholic converts these women constructed an ever-expanding world of real and fictive kin under the umbrella of Western religion. They raised children conversant with European and indigenous cultures, drew a livelihood for themselves and their households from the emerging market economy, and facilitated the evolution of the fur trade in the western Great Lakes. Fur-trade exchange was clearly much more than the simple economic transaction of a marketplace economy; instead, it was defined by kinship and friendship. The fur trade remained collective on one side and individualistic on the other, and this world of individual and collective exchange was bridged by Native women. These women's lives mirrored the complex interactions of indigenous societies and demonstrated how traditional economies met the demands of an emerging transatlantic economy.

Great Lakes people defined themselves by their relatives, while Anglo outsiders identified them as French or Native-American. During the nineteenth century, a distinctive métis society developed from the intermarriages within kin networks, especially those involving the more prominent fur-trade families, such as the Barthes, Chevaliers, Bourassas, Langlades, and La Framboises, who resided in the larger fur-trade communities like Detroit, Michilimackinac, Green Bay, and St Louis.[94]

...

Change for these women was always defined by the extensive kin networks that controlled and mediated the exchange process of the fur trade. Three of these women were daughters of fur traders, and many of their daughters married fur traders. Marriage served as a planned extension of familial kin networks, further extended through the fictive kinship of Catholic ritual. Therefore, as offspring moved to other fur-trade communities, mobility became the warp on which the fabric of the fur trade was woven.

Native women married to fur traders played a pivotal role in brokering social change. These multilingual translators fostered the spread of Christianity among Great Lakes people, just as they mediated the face-to-face exchange of goods for peltry. These women suggest alternative perspectives from which we might revise prevailing views about the fur trade and Catholicism. Native women were 'negotiators of change,' and Rouensa, Réaume, Schindler, and La Framboise were indicative of how that occurred and how women were active participants and emerged as central actors in the colonial era of the western Great Lakes.

NOTES

1 Richard White, *The Middle Ground: Indians, Empires, and Republics in the Great Lakes Region, 1650–1815* (New York, 1991); Clara Sue Kidwell, 'Indian Women as Cultural Negotiators,' *Ethnohistory* 39.2 (1992): 97–107. The term 'negotiators of change' is borrowed from Nancy Shoemaker's *Negotiators of Change: Historical Perspectives on Native American Women* (New York, 1995).
2 'Marriage "after the custom of the country" was an indigenous marriage rite which evolved to meet the needs of fur trade society ... Although denounced by the Jesuit priests as immoral, the traders had taken their Indian wives according to traditional Native marriage rites and distinct family units had developed' (Sylvia Van Kirk, *Many Tender Ties: Women in Fur-Trade Society, 1670–1870* [Norman, OK, 1983], 28). These marriages combined both Indian and European marriage customs; the unions, although not always permanent, were neither casual nor promiscuous. For a further explanation of how marriage *à la façon du pays* became institutionalized as integral to the Great Lakes fur trade, see especially Jacqueline Peterson's 'Prelude to Red River: A Social Portrait of the Great Lakes Métis,' *Ethnohistory* 25 (1978): 41–67, in which she shows how 'the force of tribal custom ... French peasant practices and the *coutume de Paris*' encouraged intermarriage. See also Jennifer S.H. Brown, *Strangers in Blood: Fur Trade Company Families in Indian Country* (Norman, OK, 1980), 62–3; Jacqueline Peterson and Jennifer S.H. Brown, eds, *The New Peoples: Being and Becoming Métis in North America* (Fort Garry, MB, 1985), especially Peterson's 'Many Roads to Red River: Métis Genesis in the Great Lakes Region, 1680–1815,' 37–73; Sylvia Van Kirk, 'The Custom of the Country: An Examination of Fur Trade Marriage Practices'; and John E. Foster, 'The Origin of the Mixed Bloods in the Canadian West,' in *Essays on Western History*, ed. Lewis H. Thomas (Edmonton, 1976), 49–68, 71–80.
3 Sylvia Van Kirk, 'Towards a Feminist Perspective in Native History,' in *Papers of the Eighteenth Algonquian Conference*, ed. José Mailhot (Ottawa, 1987), 386.
4 For a discussion of missionization among Native American women that relies on an assimilationist model, see Karen Anderson, *Chain Her by One*

Foot: The Subjugation of Women in Seventeenth-Century New France (New York, 1991); Carol Devens, *Countering Colonization: Native American Women and Great Lakes Women, 1630–1900* (Berkeley, CA, 1992); Eleanor Burke Leacock, 'Montagnais Women and the Jesuit Program for Colonization,' in *Myths of Male Dominance: Collected Articles on Women Cross-Culturally*, ed. Eleanor Leacock (New York, 1981), 43–62.

5 For the parallel circumstance of Catholic women among the Iroquois, see Nancy Shoemaker, 'Kateri Tekakwitha,' in *Negotiators of Change*, ed. Nancy Shoemaker (New York, 1995), 49–71; and Natalie Zemon Davis, 'Iroquois Women, European Women,' in *Women, 'Race,' and Writing in the Early Modern Period*, ed. Margo Hendricks and Patricia Parker (New York, 1994), 243–61.

6 The number eight appears throughout the St Joseph baptismal register and indicated the phonetic equivalent for parts of Native-American languages that were not spelled in French. The 8 was a digraph or shorthand for *ou*.

7 Before their conversion to Catholicism, the Illini were polygamous, and this has been attributed to the high ratio of women to men. Early observers reported that women outnumbered men four to one and for this reason men espoused the younger sisters of their first wives. Village dwellings consisted of substantial oblong cabins that housed from six to twelve families. Consequently, village houses brought substantial numbers of women together. These women also exercised control over productive resources, and men turned over the food of the hunt to them. Women owned all household possessions, while a man's property consisted only of his weapons and clothes. See Clarence Walworth Alvord, *The Illinois Country, 1673–1818* (Chicago, 1920), 41–6.

8 The term 'frontier Catholicism' suggests that lay Catholics were instrumental in the spread of Catholicism in the western Great Lakes. This was a result of the scarcity of priests, a situation worsened in 1762 by the secularization of the Jesuits. The role lay people played in the transmission of dogma is unclear. The term 'baptized conditionally' appears frequently in baptism registers and indicates that a child had previously received lay baptism when a priest was unavailable.

9 The Odawa were semi-sedentary and moved their villages only when the soil was no longer fertile or when enemies threatened attack. Women remained resident in the village, while hunting parties were an all-male activity. Although divorce was uncommon, when it did occur the children remained with the women. Children belonged to the women, and for this reason it appears that descent was traced through women. See James E. Fitting and Charles E. Cleland, 'Late Prehistoric Settlement Patterns in the Upper Great Lakes,' *Ethnohistory* 16 (1969): 295–6; W. Vernon Kinietz, *The Indians of the Western Great Lakes* (Ann Arbor, MI, 1990), 270–4.

10 All four women – Marie Rouensa-8cate8a, Marie Madeleine Réaume
    L'archevêque Chevalier, Magdelaine Marcot La Framboise, and Thérèse
    Marcot Lasaliere Schindler – were Catholic; hence the presence of Chris-
    tian names.
11 Carl J. Ekberg with Anton J. Pregaldin, 'Marie Rouensa-8cate8a and the
    Foundations of French Illinois,' *Illinois Historical Journal* 84 (Fall 1991): 146–
    60; John E. McDowell, 'Therese Schindler of Mackinac: Upward Mobility
    in the Great Lakes Fur Trade,' *Wisconsin Magazine of History* 61 (Winter
    1977–8): 126–7; David A. Armour, 'Magdelaine Marcot La Framboise,' *Dic-
    tionary of Canadian Biography* (Toronto, 1991), 7:582–3; McDowell, 'Madame
    La Framboise,' *Michigan History* 56 (Winter 1972): 271–86; Keith R. Widder,
    'Magdelaine La Framboise, Fur Trader and Educator,' *Historical Women of
    Michigan: A Sesquicentennial Celebration*, ed. Rosalie Riegle Troester (Lansing,
    MI, 1987), 1–13. *Dictionary of Canadian Biography* is cited hereafter as *DCB*.
12 White, *Middle Ground*, 70–5.
13 See Louise Tilly, 'Gender, Women's History, and Social History,' *Social
    Science History* 13 (1989): 339–480 (esp. 447), which suggests that women's
    history become more analytical and address issues central to the historical
    agenda.
14 The Algonquian-speaking Illinois included several groups: the Cahokia,
    Chipussea, Coircoentanon, Kaskaskia, Michigamea, Moingwena, Peoria,
    and Taponero. The French referred to the area as 'Illinois Country,' which
    included the present state of Illinois, plus eastern Missouri and eastern
    Iowa. See Emily J. Blasingham, 'The Depopulation of the Illinois Indians,'
    Ethnohistory 3 (1956): 193. The term *Iliniwik* comes from *ilini* or man; *iw* is
    ek, the plural termination and was changed by the French to *ois* (Alvord,
    Illinois Country, 31).
15 In a matrifocal household, the woman is the focus of the relationship but
    not the head of the household. Women evolved as the centre of economic
    and decision-making coalitions with their children, despite the presence of
    a husband-father. See Raymond Smith, 'The Matrifocal Family,' in *The
    Character of Kinship*, ed. Jack Goody (New York, 1973), 124–5.
16 From Father Gabriel Marest, missionary of the Society of Jesus, to Father
    Germon of the same Society, 9 November 1712, *Lettres édifantes* (Toulouse,
    1810), 6:207.
17 Raymond E. Hausner, in 'The *Berdache* and the Illinois Indian Tribe during
    the Last Half of the Seventeenth Century,' *Ethnohistory* 37 (1990): 54,
    has suggested that the status of Illinois women was limited by sororal
    polygyny and that brothers played an important role in the selection of a

husband. The conversion to Catholicism would have clearly ended the practice of polygyny as well as the marital influence exercised by men.

18 DeGannes, 'Memoir of DeGannes Concerning the Illinois Country,' in *The French Foundations, 1680–1692*, ed. Theodore Calvin Pease and Raymond C. Werner, *Collections of the Illinois State Historical Library* (Springfield, IL, 1934), 23:361.

19 Mary Borgias Palm, *The Jesuit Missions of the Illinois Country, 1673–1763* (Cleveland, 1933), 25; DeGannes, 'Memoir ... Concerning the Illinois Country,' 38–40.

20 Rebuen Gold Thwaites, ed., *The Jesuit Relations and Allied Documents, Travels and Explorations of the Jesuit Missions in New France, 1610–1791* (Cleveland, 1896–1901), 65:67; hereafter cited as *JR*.

21 *JR*, 64:229.

22 *JR*, 64:205, 195–205.

23 *JR*, 64:195.

24 Rouensa married Accault within the church. Gravier described the circumstances of the wedding and baptized their first son, Peter Accault, on 20 March 1695 at Pimiteoui. For the baptism, see 'Kaskaskia Church Records,' *Transactions of the Illinois Historical Society* [Springfield, IL] 2 (1904): 394; Marthe F. Beauregard, *La population des forts français d'Amérique* (Montreal, 1982), 2:108.

25 *JR*, 64:213.

26 *JR*, 64:233; Palm, *Jesuit Missions*, 26.

27 *JR*, 64:209.

28 Magaret Brown and Laurie C. Dean, *The Village of Chartres in Colonial Illinois, 1720–1765* (New Orleans, LA, 1977), 871; Ekberg, 'Marie Rouensa,' 156.

29 For a description of African-American slavery in the Illinois Country, see Carl J. Ekberg, 'Black Slavery in Illinois, 1720–1765,' *Western Illinois Regional Studies* 12 (1989): 5–9. For Native-American slavery in the Great Lakes, see Russell M. Magnaghi, 'Red Slavery in the Great Lakes Country during the French and British Regimes,' *Old Northwest* 12 (Summer 1996): 201–17.

30 An arpent is a French unit equal to about 0.84 acres or, when used as a linear measurement, equal to 192 English feet. See Winstanley Briggs, 'Le Pays des Illinois,' *William and Mary Quarterly* 47 (1990): 38.

31 Palm, *Jesuit Missions*, 42; Beauregard, *La population*, 2:107–81.

32 Daniel H. Usner, in *Indians, Settlers, and Slaves in a Frontier Exchange Economy* (Chapel Hill, NC, 1992), 7, indicates that the Illinois Country was

under the political administration of New Orleans but was economically more integrated with the Great Lakes.

33 Palm, *Jesuit Missions*, 42–3, 80.

34 Susan C. Boyle, 'Did She Generally Decide? Women in Ste. Genevieve, 1750–1805,' *William and Mary Quarterly* 44 (1987): 783–4.

35 Lucy Eldersveld Murphy, 'Autonomy and the Economic Roles of Indian Women of the Fox-Wisconsin River Region, 1763–1832,' in Shoemaker, ed., *Negotiators of Change*, 72–89; see esp. 81–2.

36 Gilbert J. Garraghan, 'New Light on Old Cahokia,' *Illinois Catholic Historical Review* 11 (1929): 99–146.

37 John A. Walthall and Elizabeth D. Benchley, *The River L'Abbe Mission: A French Colonial Church for the Cahokia Illini on Monks Mound*, Studies in Illinois Archaeology, no. 2 (Springfield, IL, 1987), 71–3.

38 See chapter 3, 'Structures, Habitus, Practices,' in Pierre Bourdeau, *The Logic of Practice* (Stanford, CA, 1980), 52–65.

39 Marie Madeleine Réaume's father was the trader, Jean Baptiste Réaume. The first official reference to Jean Baptiste Réaume was in 1720, when the New France governor, Vaudreuil, sent him to the re-established Fort St Joseph post with two canoes loaded with gifts for the Miami. In 1717 her father served as the post interpreter and later moved onto Green Bay. Marie Madeleine Réaume first appears in the St Joseph register when she was listed as a godmother, in March 1729, and was identified as the daughter to Simphorose Ouaouagoukoue and the post's interpreter, Sieur Jean Baptiste Réaume. See 'St. Joseph Baptismal Register,' *Mississippi Valley Historical Review* 13 (June 1926–March 1927): 212.

40 For an explanation of exchange in indigenous societies, see Marcel Mauss, *The Gift: The Form and Reason of Exchange in Archaic Societies* (New York, 1990).

41 Variant spellings for *L'archevêque* include *Larchesveque* and *Larche* (Certificate, Montreal, signed de Villiers, 18 July 1745; *ANCol*, CIIA, 117: 325). In 1741 Augustin L'archevêque contracted to hire canoemen to accompany him to the Illinois Country. For engagements or contracts hiring canoemen at St Joseph during 1722–45, see *Rapport de l'Archiviste de la Province de Québec*, 1929–30: 233–465; hereafter cited as *RAPQ*.

42 The daughters lived to maturity, but the son probably did not reach adulthood. The first daughter, Marie Catherine, was born the day after her mother and father were married. She was baptized on 13 January 1731. Her godfather was the post commandant, Nicolas Coulon de Villiers, and her godmother was Marie Catherine, of the Illinois nation. See 'St. Joseph Baptismal Register,' ed. Rev. George Paré and M.M. Quaife, *Mississippi*

Valley Historical Review 13.2 (Sept. 1926): 213. The second daughter, Marie
Esther (referred to as Marie Joseph Esther), was born sometime in 1733
and baptized one year later at Michilimackinac on 1 January 1734. See 'The
Mackinac Register,' *Collections of the State Historical Society of Wisconsin*,
19:4; hereafter cited as *WHC*. The third daughter, Marie Anne, was twenty-
one months and eight days old at the time of her baptism at St Joseph in
April of 1740. Her godfather was Nicolas Coulon de Villiers, the post
commandant, and her older sister, Marie Joseph Esther ('St. Joseph Register,' 218). The fourth daughter, Marie Amable, was baptized at St Joseph
on 27 July 1740 by the post commandant, Nicolas Coulon de Villiers, and
subsequently by Father Lamorine on 29 June 1741. The godparents were
Claude Caron and Charlotte Robert, the wife of the post interpreter ('St.
Joseph Register,' 219). The fifth daughter was Angelique (Agathe), baptized in March 1744. Her godfather was Monsieur de Lespiné de Villiers, a
cadet in the troops of the colony's marine detachment. Her godmother
was her oldest sister, Marie Catherine ('St. Joseph Register,' 221).
43 Joseph Peyser, *Fort St. Joseph Manuscripts: Chronological Inventory and
    Translations* (Niles, MI, 1978), 121, 104.
44 The seventeenth-century Jesuits attested to the lushness of the St Joseph
    River valley and to the profusion of wild grapes that grew along
    riverbanks. The dune area around southern Lake Michigan also produced
    large quantities of huckleberries, wild currants, gooseberries, and black-
    berries. Plum, crabapple, and cherry trees grew along the river bottoms.
    See James Brown, *Aboriginal Cultural Adaptations in the Midwestern Prairies*
    (New York, 1991), 60; *JR*, 55:195.
45 'Petition of Louis Chevalier,' reprinted from the Haldimand Papers,
    Canadian Archives, Ottawa, *Michigan Pioneer and Historical Society: Collec-
    tions and Researches* (hereafter *MPHC*) 13 (1889): 61.
46 James M. McClurken, 'Augustin Hamlin, Jr.: Ottawa Identity and the
    Politics of Persistence,' in *Being and Becoming Indian*, ed. James A. Clifton
    (Chicago, 1989), 85.
47 These communities had a settled agricultural appearance. There were
    agricultural fields, log cabins, framed houses, and fruit orchards. The
    usual markers of European society, houses and cabins, were also indica-
    tive of Native-American society. At Réaume's St Joseph village, a French
    carpenter had built a house for a Potawatomi headman. A jail was even
    constructed by the blacksmith Antoine Deschêtres. It was made of stone
    and measured eight feet by ten feet (Certificate, St Joseph, signed Piquoteé
    de Belestre, 13 May 1750; *ANCol*, CIIA, 96:313). The post interpreter Pierre
    Deneau *dit* Detailly submitted a certificate to receive a thousand livres for

building a house for a medal chief (Certificate, St Joseph, 30 April 1760, Archives Nationales, V7, 345:99, Ottawa, National Archives of Canada).

48 In Sainte Genevieve, Illinois Country, French widows were more active in the local economy and were more likely to file legal grievances than either single or married women. See Boyle, 'Did She Generally Decide?' 788–9.

49 Augustin L'archevêque was baptized on 7 July 1748. He probably never reached adulthood. His godfather was Augustin Langland, and his godmother was Marie Catherine Lerige Bourassa ('Mackinac Baptisms,' WHC, 19:24–5); Marie Catherine married Jean Baptiste Jutras (Joutras), and the wedding took place at St Ignace on 7 July 1748. He was a trader from Trois Rivières. Witnesses included Legardeur de St Pierre Verchere, Bourassa, Langlade, and Charles Langlade ('Mackinac Register,' WHC, 18:475). The wedding of Marie Joseph Esther and Jacques Bariso de La Marche took place at St Ignace on 2 August 1748. Some witness signatures were illegible, but both those of Langland and Bourassa remain legible ('Mackinac Register,' WHC, 18:476). The bridegroom was probably related to the Montreal merchant with whom Réaume's father had traded. In 1729 Jean Baptiste Réaume owed Charles Nolan LaMarque 4,000 livres in furs (RAPQ, 1929–30: 244–408). Joseph Esther was twice widowed, and at the age of forty-six, on 8 June 1779, she married Thomas M. Brady. He became the Indian agent at Cahokia. She had children and grandchildren living in Cahokia until well into the 1800s (Webster and Krause, Fort Saint Joseph, 115).

50 Catherine married Jean Baptiste Jutras (Joutras). Her youngest daughter, Esther, married Jacque Bariso de La Marche, who was probably related to the Montreal merchant with whom Réaume's father had traded. He was the son of a Montreal merchant, which would have guaranteed the St Joseph community an adequate and annual supply of trade goods.

51 The Chevaliers were a large French family. There were seventeen children. Jean Baptiste Chevalier and his wife, Marie Françoise Alavoine, probably moved from Montreal to Michilimackinac in 1718. Baptismal registers at Michilimackinac and St Joseph provide information about fifteen of the seventeen children born to Chevalier and Alavoine: five, possibly six, children were born at Montreal; eleven were baptized at St Ignace. The four children born in Montreal included Charlotte (1712), Marie Anne (Chabouillez) Catherine (1714), Michel Jean Baptiste, and Marie Josephe (1718). The eleven children baptized at the St Ignace Mission included Constance (1719), Louis Thérèse (1720), Marguerite Josephe (1723), Marie Magdaleine (1724), Anne Charlotte Veronique (1726), Charles (1727),

Joseph Maurice (1728), Louis Pascal (1730), Anne Thérèse Esther (1732), Angelique (1733), and Luc (1735). See John M. Gram, 'The Chevalier Family and the Demography of the Upper Great Lakes,' unpublished paper, Mackinac Island State Park Commission, Lansing, MI, 1995.

52 Their marriage coincided with the baptism of their son, Louis, who was born in October 1751 and was baptized by his uncle, Louis Pascal Chevalier. In April 1752 he was baptized by the priest, Father DuJaunay. His godfather was his oldest stepsister's husband, Joutras, and his godmother was another stepsister, Madeleine Chevalier ('St. Joseph Register,' 223).

53 Gram, 'The Chevalier Family,' 20.

54 Marie Magdalaine L'archevêque appears to have been one of Madeleine's daughters, but this cannot be confirmed by the baptismal registers. Louis Pascal was baptized at Michilimackinac on 2 July 1730. He died before 1 January 1779. Louis Pascal and his wife had four children baptized at St Joseph between 1758 and 1773. See 'St. Joseph Register,' 223, note 38; *WHC* 19:3; Webster and Krause, *Fort Saint Joseph*, 120–1.

55 The Chevaliers were partners, but they were not related. Charles Lhullic Chevalier's trading partner now became his stepfather-in-law. Charles and Angelique were married at St Joseph, where three of their children were later baptized. Chevalier died in 1773; he was about sixty-four. His death was the last entry in the St Joseph baptismal register. See Webster and Krause, *Fort Saint Joseph*, 115–17; Dunning Idle, 'The Post of the St. Joseph River during the French Regime 1679–1761' (Ph.D. diss., University of Illinois, 1946), 253–4, note 104; 'St. Joseph Register,' 230.

56 The register does not mention the marriage of Anne L'archevêque and Augustin Gibault. When she served as godmother to the daughter of her sister Marie Joseph in 1756, she was identified as Anne L'archevêque. By 1758 she was identified as Gibault's wife ('St. Joseph Register,' 228, 230).

57 Marie Amable married Jean Baptiste François Lonval. Lonval's ties were to the fur-trade community at Trois Rivières. The Lonvals settled in Cahokia, where they appear on the 1787 Cahokia census (Webster and Krause, *Fort Saint Joseph*, 117–18; 'St. Joseph Register,' 231, 233–4).

58 Both Joseph Esther's and Marie Amable's children were baptized at the Fort St Joseph Mission. Four of Esther's children were baptized there. In 1753 her sister Catherine was the godmother to her sixteen-month-old son, Louis, and to her three-year-old son, Etienne Joseph. Esther's sister Anne was the godmother to her three-year-old daughter, Marie Joseph. In 1756, Esther's sister Magdeleine was the godmother to her five-month-old daughter, Angelique ('St. Joseph Register,' 225, 225–6, 228). In 1761 Amable's

two-month-old daughter was baptized at St Joseph ('St. Joseph Register,' 233–4).

59 The prolonged absence of priests at frontier missions led lay Catholics and even non-Catholics to perform baptisms. Priests were only intermittently assigned to the St Joseph Mission, but they did serve continuously from 1750 to 1761. During other times, the post was reliant on the missionary priests assigned to the Illinois Country; generally these priests resided at either Cahokia or Kaskaskia. Growth of the frontier Catholic church was hampered in 1762, when the French government decreed secularization of the Jesuits. The Supreme Council of New Orleans put the decree into effect on 3 July 1763. Father Meurin was allowed to remain in the Illinois Country at Sainte Genevieve on the Spanish side of the river. Priests from other orders were at the St Joseph Mission in 1761, 1768, and 1773. A new missionary priest, Father Gibault, was assigned to the Illinois Country in 1773. See 'St. Joseph Register,' 204–5; George Paré, *The Catholic Church in Detroit, 1701–1888* (Detroit, 1951), 78–103. For an account of the banishment, see *JR.*

60 The term 'baptized conditionally' appears frequently in baptismal registers and indicates that a child had previously received lay baptism when a priest was unavailable. For an explanation of the term 'baptized conditionally,' see 'The Mackinac Register, 1696–1821: Register of Baptisms of the Mission of St Ignace de Michilimackinak,' *WHC*, 19: 7, note 25.

61 'St. Joseph Register,' 218, 238.

62 His godfather was Mr Marin de La Perrière's wife. Her godfather was Louis Metivier, a master carpenter, and the godmother was Marie Fafard, Metivier's wife. Five years later Marie, Pierre's wife, died ('St. Joseph Register,' 221–3).

63 On 22 April 1752 one of Pierre's daughters, 8abak8ik8e, was baptized. She was about thirty-five years old and took the name Marie as her Christian name. Louis Chevalier signed as the godfather. On 1 May 1752 three more of Pierre's children, all women, were baptized; one was twenty-six or twenty-seven, the second was twenty-five, and the third was fifteen or sixteen. The eldest, a widow and identified as Temagas8kia, took the name Marguerite. Her godmother was Marguerite of the Saki nation. Both other daughters elected Marie Madeleine Réaume Chevalier as their godmother. The middle daughter, age twenty-five, was identified as being married to Pi8assin, who was listed as still unconverted. The third daughter took the name Suzanne. See 'St. Joseph Register,' 222–3.

64 Idle, 'Post of the Saint Joseph River,' 182; *RAPQ*, 1929–30: 233–465.

65 Howard Peckham, *Pontiac and the Indian Uprising* (Detroit, 1994); Ian K.

Steele, *Warpath: Invasions of North America* (New York, 1994), 237–42; Charles E. Cleland, *Rites of Conquest: The History and Culture of Michigan's Native Americans* (Ann Arbor, MI, 1994), 134–43; White, *Middle Ground*, 269–314; Gregory Evans Dowd, 'The French King Wakes Up in Detroit: Pontiac's War in Rumor and History,' *Ethnohistory* 37 (1990): 254–78; Gregory Evans Dowd, *A Spirited Resistance: The North American Indian Struggle for Unity, 1745–1815* (Baltimore, 1992).

66 'To General Gage from Lt. Campbell, April 10, 1766,' Gage Papers #308, Ayers Manuscript Collections, Newberry Library, Chicago, Illinois; 'To General Haldiman from A.S. DePeyster, August 15, 1778,' *MPHC* 9 (1886): 368.

67 British traders who attempted to break the exclusionary St Joseph trade barrier met a dire fate. In 1773 four English traders were murdered near St Joseph by the Potawatomi. Chevalier was suspected, but the British were reluctant to remove him. See Gérard Malchelosse, 'St. Joseph River Post,' *French Canadian and Acadian Genealogical Review,* nos. 3–4 (1970): 189.

68 Joseph L. Peyser, 'The Fate of the Fox Survivors: A Dark Chapter in the History of the French in the Upper Country, 1726–1737,' *Wisconsin Magazine of History* 73 (Winter 1989–90): 110; R. David Edmunds and Joseph L. Peyser, *The Fox Wars: The Mesquakie Challenge to New France* (Norman, OK, 1993), 144.

69 'The Mackinac Register,' *WHC*, 19:25.

70 The Chevaliers were partners, but they were not related.

71 Louis Pascal was baptized at Michilimackinac on 22 July 1730. He died before 22 July 1740. Pascal and his wife had four children baptized at the mission church between 1758 and 1773. See 'St. Joseph Register,' 223; *WHC*, 8:490, 19:3.

72 Memorial of Louis Joseph Ainsse, 5 August 1780, *MPHC* 13 (1889): 58–9, 10:415. The pretense for removal was Governor General Haldimand's order that the trader whose loyalty was questionable be prevented from living among the Indians (Haldimand to DePeyster, 6 May 1799, *MPHC* 9 [1886]: 357–8). See also Keith R. Widder, 'Effects of the American Revolution on Fur Trade Society at Michilimackinac,' in *The Fur Trade Revisited: Selected Papers of the Sixth North American Fur Trade Conference, Mackinac Island, Michigan, 1991*, ed. Jennifer S.H. Brown, W.J. Eccles, and Donald Heldman (East Lansing, MI, 1994), 307.

73 'Indian Council held at Detroit 11th March, with the Pottewatimies from St. Josephs, Tere Coupe, and Coueur de Cerf,' *MPHC* 10:453–4.

74 The attack from Cahokia was led by Thomas Brady and Jean Baptiste Hamelin. Brady had married Réaume's widowed daughter, Marie Joseph,

and Hamelin kin were frequent godparents for St Joseph children. Descriptions of the attack and destruction of Fort St Joseph include Joseph Peyser, ed., *Letters from New France: The Upper Country, 1686–1783* (Chicago, 1992), 219–21; A.P. Nasatir, 'The Anglo-Spanish Frontier in the Illinois Country during the American Revolution, 1779–1783,' *Illinois State Historical Society Journal* 21 (1928): 291–358; Ralph Ballard, *Old Fort St Joseph* (Berrien Springs, MI, 1973), 46–8; Gérard Malchelosse, 'The St. Joseph River,' *French Canadian and Acadian Genealogical Review*, nos. 3–4 (1970): 204–6; Rufus Blanchard, *The Discovery and Conquest of the Northwest* (Chicago, 1880), 165–6; B.A. Hinsdale, *The Old Northwest* (New York, 1888), 173–4; Charles Moore, *Northwest under Three Flags* (New York, 1900), 257–60; John Francis McDermott, *Old Cahokia: A Narrative and Documents Illustrating the First Century of Its History* (St Louis, 1949), 31–2, 200; Clarence W. Alvord, 'The Conquest of St. Joseph Michigan, by the Spaniards in 1781,' *Michigan History* 14 (1930): 398–414.

75 Thimotée is also called Marie Neskesh by the Jesuits. Thérèse was ten and Magdelaine was six when they were baptized on 1 August 178 ('Mackinac Register,' *WHC*, 19:86).

76 'Census of the Post of St. Joseph,' *MPHC* 10:406–7.

77 In 1783, Marcot was killed by Indians at the portage between the Fox and Wisconsin Rivers. His widow returned to her Native Odawa village to raise her children among her people. Magdelaine was the youngest of seven children. See McDowell, 'Therese Schindler.'

78 Baptisms of Native-American women occurred most frequently during the summer months, and multiple baptisms took place in a day.

79 'Marguerite-Magdelaine Marcot (La Framboise),' *DCB*, 7:582; Milo M. Quaife, *Lake Michigan* (Indianapolis, 1944), 201–6.

80 *WHC*, 19:86, 117, 118; 11:164–5.

81 'Mackinac Register,' *WHC*, 19:117–18.

82 Quaife, *Lake Michigan*, 115.

83 'Mackinac Register,' *WHC*, 18:507–8.

84 George Schindler to Solomon Sibley, 9 July and 22 August 1807, and Claude La Framboise to John Kinzie, 11 June 1807, Solomon Sibley Papers, Burton Historical Section, Detroit Public Library; McDowell, 'Therese Schindler,' 131.

85 Claude La Framboise to John Kinzie, 11 June 1807, Solomon Sibley Papers, Burton Historical Collection, Detroit Public Library.

86 Elizabeth Thérèse Baird, 'Reminiscences of Early Days on Mackinac Island,' *WHC*, 14:38–9.

87 Baird, 'Reminiscences of Early Days on Mackinac Island,' *WHC*, 14:22;

Elizabeth Thérèse Baird, 'Reminiscences of Life in Territorial Wisconsin,' *WHC*, 15:213.

88 'Account Book of Mackinac Merchant,' Michigan Manuscripts, C, in Archives Division, State Historical Society of Wisconsin; *Michigan Pioneer and Historical Collections*, 37:143; McDowell, 'Therese Schindler,' 135–6.

89 Baird, 'Reminiscences of Mackinac,' *WHC*, 14:2; Baird, 'Reminiscences of Life in Territorial Wisconsin,' *WHC* 15:213; 'Account Book of a Mackinac Merchant,' Michigan Manuscripts, C, in Archives Division, State Historical Society of Wisconsin; *MPHC* 27:143; McDowell, 'Therese Schindler,' 128, 135–6.

90 Ida Amanda Johnson, *The Michigan Fur Trade* (Grand Rapids, MI, 1971), 130–1; *DCB*, 7:582.

91 Gordon Charles Davidson, *The North West Company* (Berkeley, CA, 1918), 72; McDowell, 'Madame La Framboise,' 278.

92 John Denis Haeger, *John Jacob Astor: Business and Finance in the Early Republic* (Detroit, 1991), 149–52.

93 When increased numbers of mixed-ancestry offspring migrated to larger fur-trade communities, such as Michilimackinac, Green Bay, and St Louis, they increasingly intermarried among themselves. These intermarriages resulted in the emergence of a distinctly métis community. As the number of mixed-hereditary offspring continued to increase, young women of mixed marriages appeared with increasing frequency as the spouses of French fur traders, but these favoured marital choices had kin networks rooted in indigenous society. Kinship networks ensured access to peltry and insured viability as a fur trader. Women with extensive kinship networks remained the most desirable marriage partners. It was for this reason that Marie Madeleine, at age forty, was a desirable fur-trade widow.

94 For a description of the St Louis community, see especially Tanis C. Thorne, *The Many Hands of My Relations* (Columbia, MO, 1996).

3 The Woman Who Married a Beaver: Trade Patterns and Gender Roles in the Ojibwa Fur Trade

BRUCE M. WHITE

In 1904, Kagige Pinasi (John Pinesi), an Ojibwa (Anishinaabe)–French man living at Fort William on the north shore of Lake Superior, told the anthropologist William Jones a story about a young woman who married a beaver. With blackened face she went to fast for a long time during a vision quest. She saw a person in human form who spoke to her. He asked her to come live with him. She did and eventually agreed to marry him. She was well provided with food and clothing and soon gave birth to four children.[1]

She soon noticed something very odd that led her to realize for the first time that she had married a beaver. From time to time the woman's husband or children would leave with a human being who appeared outside their house. 'And back home would they always return again. All sorts of things would they fetch – kettles and bowls, knives, tobacco, and all the things that are used when a beaver is eaten; such was what they brought. Continually they were adding to their great wealth.' They would go to where the person lived and the person would kill the beavers. Yet the beavers were never really killed. They would come back home again with the clothes and tobacco that people gave them. The beavers were very fond of the people and would visit them often. The woman herself was forbidden to go by her husband, but this is what she heard.

Eventually the woman's husband died and she returned to live with human beings. She lived a long time after that and often told the story of what happened while she lived with the beavers. She always told people that they should never speak ill of a beaver or they would never be able to kill any: 'If anyone regards a beaver with too much contempt, speaking ill of it, one simply [will] not [be able to] kill it. Just the same as the feelings of one who is disliked, so is the feeling of the beaver. And he who never speaks ill of a beaver is very much loved by it; in the same way as people often love one another, so is one held in the mind of the beaver, particularly lucky then is one at killing beavers.'

Referring to stories like this one, the philosopher Jean-François Lyotard wrote that such accounts are a succinct record of the beliefs of the societies in which they are told. 'What is transmitted through these narratives,' Lyotard wrote, 'is the set of pragmatic rules that constitutes the social bond.' He noted that such stories 'recount what could be called positive or negative apprenticeships.' They tell of the success or failure of a hero, whose adventures define a society's 'criteria of competence' and delineate a range of possible actions for members of the society.[2]

A primary purpose of such accounts is educational. Ojibwa elders told stories like this, usually in winter, to teach young people about the world while entertaining them.[3] As such, these narratives are also a useful way for outsiders to learn about the people's worldview and understand their view of their history.[4] Kagige Pinasi may have had a variety of reasons for wishing to instruct the anthropologist William Jones by telling him this story. Jones's biographer, Henry M. Rideout, spoke of the informant as 'an old chief' and an experienced trapper who made Jones examples of animal traps. He also told Jones a number of odd experiences he had had hunting and trapping with his sons. He also recounted, for Jones's transcription, more than fifty stories, which Jones praised for their artistry.

Jones wrote that the man developed a fondness for him – the anthropologist was of Fox and British-American ancestry – and tried to convince him to 'come and live here, take to myself a wife, and be one of the people.' Telling Jones this story of a kind of intermarriage may have been a form of subtle encouragement.[5]

Beyond Kagige Pinasi's own personal motives, this story is, like all Ojibwa stories, interesting on many levels. It instructs young people, especially girls, on the importance of the vision quest, the means through which an Ojibwa person obtained a relationship with powerful beings who would be helpful to her and could chart a unique course for her life. Further, it is a basic description of and commentary on the cooperative arrangements that many Ojibwa people believed existed between different kinds of beings in the world. Ojibwa people who hunted, fished, or gathered plants had to be aware of their reciprocal obligations with the natural world and give back something to the animals, fish, or plants from which they harvested. In taking small plants in the woods, or bark from the trees, people often left a gift of tobacco. After a bear was killed, they held an elaborate ceremony of thanks and gave presents to the bear. The beaver story shows that reciprocity was necessary to keep the system operating. Without gifts and respect, animals would not be so helpful to humans. They would hold themselves back and not allow themselves to be used by people. Without gifts and respect, the system would cease to function.[6]

Ojibwa people also applied the principle of reciprocity to their dealings with people, including non-Indians. In their earliest interactions with the French and the British, the Ojibwa made use of the same gifts, ceremonies, and words that they used in dealing with animals, plants, and other beings.[7] The logic of approaching Europeans in this way was solid; interaction with Europeans was important because of the valuable technology Europeans brought with them. Reciprocity was necessary to keep the system operating. Without gifts and respect, Europeans would not be so helpful to Indian people. They would withhold their technology from Indian people. Without gifts and respect, the system would cease to function.

Dealing with animals differed, of course, from dealing with Europeans. The Ojibwa quickly worked out a variety of strategies that were specific to the newcomers. For example, they gave different things. The story of the woman who married the beaver describes a reverse fur trade. In the European fur trade, Indian people gave furs in return for tools, kettles, and tobacco, but this story tells of a relationship in which people gave tools, kettles, and tobacco to beavers in return for the animals' furs.

There is yet another striking feature of the story: it delineates an intermediary role for women in the interaction between people and animals, suggesting a role for women in the interaction between the Ojibwa and Europeans. This story is not an origin tale.[8] It does not describe the beginnings of the reciprocal arrangement between people and animals. For the people in the story, the relationship was a well-established, functioning system. Yet the story explains the system and how it works through the experiences of a woman. If the story was intended to teach, in Lyotard's words, 'positive or negative apprenticeships,' there was clearly a special message in it for young women about what was possible. Women, it would appear, have power to cross boundaries, explaining one world to another, in this case through a marriage relationship. This power had implications for the workings of the fur trade.

Gender and Fur Trade Historiography

Many accounts of the fur trade imply that trade took place mainly between Native and European men, with women playing an adjunct role. Until recent years, few studies of the fur trade mentioned women specifically. Harold A. Innis, in his major economic study, *The Fur Trade in Canada*, seldom spoke of gender. Although he noted that 'the personal relationship of the trader to the Indian' was essential under 'conditions of competition,' he did not discuss the role that intermarriage played between male traders and Native women in the trade.[9] Historian Arthur J. Ray, in several major studies, explored the coming together of Native people and Europeans in the fur trade. In one book he analysed 'the set of institutions which developed as a compromise between the customs and norms of traditional Indian exchange and those of European market trade.' However, he failed to consider in his detailed work any differing impact that men and women may have had upon this composite trade.[10]

More recently, the historian Richard White has examined the accommodation between Native people and Europeans in a complex set of relationships that took place in what he called a cultural, social, and political 'middle ground' of the Great Lakes of the seventeenth and eighteenth centuries. White argued that the 'fur trade proper is merely an arbitrary selection from a fuller and quite coherent spectrum of exchange that was embedded in particular social relations.'[11] White wrote mostly of the role of diplomacy in Native-European interactions – diplomacy in which women apparently had a smaller role than men – and emphasized the role of men as speechmakers, negotiators, and warriors. Nonetheless, White referred at many points in his study to the role of women in trade. For example, in describing a speech by a Potawatomi man in Montreal, White noted that the man was representing, in part, the women in his community who 'by implication, were a major force in exchange.' Similarly, White wrote that much of the 'petty trading' of French traders in Native villages was 'probably with women.' But neither point was developed in detail.[12]

The major work on the differing roles of men and women in the fur trade has come, not surprisingly, from the research of women historians and anthropologists. Anthropologist Jennifer Brown, in her 1980 study *Strangers in Blood*, examined the dynamics of Canadian fur-trade societies established within the institutional frameworks of the North West and Hudson's Bay Companies. She showed the joint effect of Native and European cultures on the available roles for men and women and the formation of trade cultures and institutions.[13]

Feminist historian Sylvia Van Kirk, in *Many Tender Ties*, also emphasized the Canadian fur trade in her look at the role of women in fur-trade society. She stated that her study 'supports the claims of theorists in women's history that sex roles should constitute a category of historical investigation' because the experience of women 'has differed substantially from that of their male counterparts.' She suggested that 'the lives of both sexes must be examined if we are to fully understand the dynamics of social change.'[14] Van Kirk emphasized the role of Native women as 'women-in-between,' a situation 'which could be manipulated to advantage.' She stated that Native women in general may have had a vested interest in promoting cordial relations with the whites and that 'if the traders were driven from the country, the Indian women would lose the source of European goods which had revolutionized their lives.' She argued that Native women sometimes received better treatment and had more influence at the trading post than in Native villages. She suggested that they had a more sedentary life and had more help in doing their work when married to a trader. All of these facts may have led some women to choose new roles from among those available to them.[15]

Jacqueline Peterson's influential 1981 dissertation, 'The People in Between,' took another look at men and women in the fur trade. She examined Indian-white marriages and the formation of a mixed-blood people in the Great Lakes between the seventeenth and nineteenth centuries. Peterson viewed the culture of the Great Lakes fur-trade communities as a 'unique lifeway – an occupational subculture' that gave birth to a people who would later be called the Métis. In particular, Peterson explored the key role played by Native women in these communities, as social, economic, and cultural intermediaries between Europeans and Native societies.[16]

Despite these broad examinations of the role of women in the fur trade, detailed and focused studies of gender relations in the Ojibwa fur trade have yet to be done. Discussion of the role of Ojibwa men and women in the fur trade has come largely in the context of ethnographic and historical studies of Ojibwa women. In such work, the differing roles of men and women in relation to the fur trade have been interpreted in light of theories about the autonomy and power of Ojibwa women – the control of women over their own activities and the power they exerted in the society as a whole.[17]

Pioneering work was done by the anthropologist Ruth Landes in her book *The Ojibwa Woman,* a classic study based on fieldwork in northwestern Ontario in the 1930s. Although often interpreted as a contemporary description of the roles of Ojibwa women, the work was to a large extent historical. It contained stories of women's lives – told to her by her informant Maggie Wilson – dating back to the mid-nineteenth century, a period during which the fur trade continued to be a major influence on Ojibwa society.[18] In this study, Landes provided a rich view of Ojibwa women's lives, including examples of women who had significant roles as hunters, warriors, and healers. Landes, however, appeared to believe that these women were exceptions to the rule that women and their accomplishments were devalued or simply ignored in modern Ojibwa society. She noted, for example, that men's work was considered 'infinitely more interesting and honorable' than women's work and spoke of 'men's supremacy' in Ojibwa society.[19] In a brief discussion of the fur trade, Landes suggested that women had little role in trading either in the 1930s or earlier. She noted that Ojibwa men had learned to barter furs and meat 'which they had secured in hunting,' since they, 'rather than the women, possessed the material desired by the Whites.'[20]

Landes' comments on Ojibwa gender roles, if not the examples she gave, seemed to imply that a devaluation of women was ingrained in Ojibwa society and would have been present during the fur-trade era and perhaps even earlier. Anthropologist Eleanor Leacock took issue with at least one aspect of this implication in a 1978 article. Writing about the Ojibwa and other 'egalitarian band societies,' Leacock stated that nothing in the structure of such societies 'necessitated special deference to men.' Leacock took particular issue with Landes' conclusions about the Ojibwa, asserting that Landes exhibited a 'lack of a critical and historical orientation toward her material' as well as a 'downgrading of women that is built into unexamined and ethnocentric phraseology.' In keeping with a Marxist approach to the topic, Leacock suggested that the situation of women in egalitarian societies often changed when the products of labour began to be treated as commodities in trade with Europeans. Women became dependent on men only when the trade made men's products more 'commercially relevant' than their own.[21]

More recent studies have echoed such views. In her analysis of the responses of Great Lake Native women to Christian missionaries and to the fur trade, Carol Devens wrote that before contact with Europeans, Ojibwa society had a gender balance upon which the communities depended. This balance was disrupted by European missions and trade. The trade, in particular, acted as a 'catalyst for modification in social structures throughout Native bands.' Devens argued that the trade favoured 'intensive production in order to accumulate and then exchange surplus goods.' Disruption of Native gender roles occurred because 'French traders wanted the furs obtained by men rather than the small game, tools, utensils, or clothing procured or produced by women.' She suggested that 'most of the items given in exchange by the French were tools and weapons intended to facilitate trapping.' This caused 'daily and seasonal life' of Native communities to 'revolve around the trade.' Women became 'auxiliaries to the trapping process' rather than 'producers in their own right.' Devens wrote that the fur trade led to a decrease in women's 'direct contribution to the community welfare.'[22]

The basic argument advanced in slightly different ways by Landes, Leacock, and Devens is that women had little direct role in the fur trade. Leacock and Devens argued that this lack of participation and authority in making decisions about an increasingly important economic endeavour led to a devaluation of women in Ojibwa society. The basis of this change, they suggested, was that men were the primary traders because the product of women's labour was not in great demand in the trade.

In fact, this theory has yet to be thoroughly demonstrated using the records of the fur trade. A major problem with doing so is simply that the sources used to describe the trade are marred by misconceptions about the roles of women in Native societies. This point was made by Priscilla K. Buffalohead in a 1983 study of the roles available to Ojibwa women during the fur-trade era. Buffalohead noted that the common view in earlier sources on the Ojibwa was that Native men were lazy and Native women were overworked 'drudges.' Buffalohead pointed out that many eighteenth- and nineteenth-century sources on the Ojibwa viewed men's and women's roles from the point of view of European beliefs about the desirable roles for men and women. These beliefs made it difficult to accurately gauge Ojibwa peoples' own beliefs about the autonomy of women and the value placed upon them in the society. The derogatory statements by European men about Native women are sometimes wrongly seen as descriptive of Ojibwa beliefs or social structures, providing unwarranted support for a belief that the fur trade led to a devaluation of Ojibwa women.[23]

Buffalohead's work dealt with the explicit beliefs of those who reported on Ojibwa women and their role in society. Just as problematic was the frequent lack of mention of women in the narratives of European inter-action with the Ojibwa. Based on the evidence of many written sources, one might assume that the Ojibwa were a people entirely without women. Thomas Vennum Jr, in his study of the use of wild rice among the Ojibwa, provided an example of this problem. He quoted a 1804–5 journal of François Victoire Malhiot, a North West Company trader at Lac du Flambeau (Wisconsin). In a translation of the original French, Malhiot stated that on 10 September 1804, a leader named L'Outarde, or Goose, 'started yesterday with his young men to gather wild rice at [Trout Lake], where his village is.'[24]

Without other evidence, this passage might be interpreted to suggest that gathering wild rice was a band activity, led by a male leader and carried out by his 'young men,' or followers. Vennum noted, however, that such a statement 'should be taken to mean that the band went to establish its rice camps, and not that the men were the harvesters.' Vennum based his conclusions on more recent ethnographic and his-torical evidence, the preponderance of which suggests that women, rather than men, managed and did most of the wild-rice harvesting until the twentieth century. While the wild-rice harvest was under way, Vennum noted, men were more generally involved in fishing and hunt-ing geese.[25]

Using ethnographic materials in this way is a technique that has been called 'upstreaming.' The term was initially used by the anthropologist William Fenton. In an influential 1952 essay on the training of 'historical ethnologists,' Fenton argued that 'major patterns of culture tend to be stable over long periods of time,' so that it was possible to proceed 'from the known to the unknown, concentrating on recent sources first because they contain familiar things, and thence going to earlier sources.' Fenton noted, however, that it was important to show 'a preference for those sources in which the descriptions of the society ring true at both ends of the time scale.'[26]

As Fenton went on to state, ethnographic sources from the nineteenth and twentieth centuries and earlier accounts were all historical sources. They were all the product of points of view and perspectives, which must be considered in evaluating the information they contain. In argu-ing in favour of upstreaming, Fenton was reacting against those who assumed 'acculturation,' or inevitable change of Native cultures in the face of European cultural conquest. Although the concept of accultura-tion has become less accepted, a related view – which should perhaps be called 'downstreaming' – persists. This is the belief that, lacking detailed written documentation, the cultural attributes of Native people in the nineteenth and twentieth centuries cannot be assumed to have existed earlier.[27]

The assertion that seventeenth-century Native people shared cultural values, gender relations, or social organization with nineteenth-century Native people simply because they shared languages or tribal names is one that sometimes needs to be demonstrated, given the many social, economic, and political changes that took place in the Great Lakes in those two hundred years. On the other hand, to presume that there was no similarity in culture between such groups is equally problematic. In fact, many aspects of seventeenth- and eighteenth-century Ojibwa history may be totally inexplicable without the guidance from later ethnographic sources.[28] To insist too strictly on the primacy of early French or British documents is to suggest that Native people of more recent times have nothing useful to say about their own past. It can also lead to ignoring, as the earlier documents often do, the role of Native women, simply because they are not mentioned in documents written by European men, who recorded only interaction with Native men.

Ethnographic sources can and should be used to pose questions about earlier events and patterns, to investigate what is said and, often more important, what is not said in earlier historical documents. The rich works of Johann Georg Kohl, Frances Densmore, M. Inez Hilger, and Ruth Landes herself, all of which are cited in this article, describe the lives, skills, and beliefs of Ojibwa women in more detail, providing some alternative explanations that avoid the value judgments inherent in many historical sources. Perhaps more than anything, such ethnographic work suggests the need to acknowledge individual experience and motives in the interpretation of historical documents. When interacting with Europeans, Ojibwa men and women were presented with new situations, ones that involved the application and alteration of culturally received ideas. In many ways these new situations provided more rather than fewer opportunities for men and women. Evidence from the fur trade illuminated with the knowledge gained from later ethnographic work demonstrates that Ojibwa men and women had many ways to participate in the fur trade. As I argue, the nature of the possibilities available to both Ojibwa men and women calls into question the belief that the trade provided a mechanism for transforming an earlier egalitarian society into one in which men dominated women.

Gendered Patterns of Trade

Pierre Radisson and his brother-in-law Medard Chouart des Groseilliers spent the winter of 1659-60 in the region south of Lake Superior, living among a mixed group of Huron, Ottawa, Ojibwa, and later, Dakota. For a period of time they lived at an unnamed village by a lake. The cultural identity of the inhabitants is not altogether clear from the narrative, though they may have been Ojibwa speakers. Radisson stated on his arrival: 'We destinated [presented] three presents, one for the men, one for the women, and the other for the children – to the end that they should remember that journey, that we should be spoaken [sic] of a hundred years after, if other Europeans should not come in those quarters and be liberal to them, which will hardly come to passe [sic].' Each present was in fact a group of presents:

The first [for the men] was a kettle, two hattchets [tomahawks], and six knives, and a blade for a sword. The kettle was to call all nations that weare their friends to the feast which is made for the remembrance of the death; that is, they make it once in seaven years; it's a renewing of friendship ... The hattchets were to encourage the young people to strengthen themselves in all places, to preserve their wives, and show themselves men by knocking the heads of their ennemyes with said hattchets. The knives were to show that the French were great and mighty, and their confederats and friends. The sword was to signifie that we would be masters both of peace and of wars, being willing to help and relieve them and to destroy our ennemyes with our arms.

The second gift [for the women] was 2 and 20 awls, 50 needles, 2 gratters [scrapers] of castors, 2 ivory combs and 2 wooden ones, with red painte [vermilion], 6 looking-glasses of tin. The awls signifieth to take good courage that we should keepe their lives and that they with their husbands should come down to the French when time and season should permit. The needles for to make them robes of castor because the French loved them. The two gratters [scrapers] were to dress the skins; the combs [and] the paint to make themselves beautifull; the looking-glasses to admire themselves.

The third gift [for the children] was of brasse rings, of small bells, and rasades [beads] of divers colours, and given in this manner. We sent a man to make all the children come together. When they were there we throw these things over their heads. You would admire what a beat was among them, everyone striving to have the best. This was done upon this consideration, that they should be always under our protection, giving them wherewithal to make them merry and remember us when they should be men.[29]

Radisson and Groseilliers were seeking to encourage Native demand for European goods and to encourage participation in the fur trade. Their gifts communicated what they sought to accomplish, as well as their understanding of Native culture. Clearly, not all of their gifts were to the point. The gift of the tools of adornment to the women, for example, ignored the fact that many later sources suggest that Ojibwa men were as much concerned with such things as Ojibwa women.[30] Similarly, though the kettle may have been intended to symbolize the feast of the dead in which men may have been instrumental, kettles came to be used more often by women in cooking, making maple sugar, and parching wild rice.[31]

On the other hand, as indicated by the gifts of hatchets, usually called tomahawks, to the men and awls and scrapers to the women, the Frenchmen clearly understood some aspects of the gendered division of labour among the Ojibwa. On the simplest level, as recorded in a variety of later sources, men hunted, trapped, and went to war, and women gathered rice, made maple sugar, gardened, fished, processed a variety of foods, built bark houses, and wove mats. In doing these things, both men and women, as Buffalohead put it, clearly managed and directed their own activities. Even in cooperative work, there was a division of labour. For example, in the making of birchbark canoes, men shaped ribs and thwarts, while women sewed the panels of bark to the framework.[32]

The tools used to perform these tasks symbolized, for the Ojibwa, the gendered nature of the activities.[33] Frances Densmore wrote of the Ojibwa custom of burying with people who died a variety of tools that would be useful to them on the journey of death: 'A pipe and tobacco pouch, with flint, steel, and punk were buried with a man and, if he were a good hunter, his gun might be placed beside him. A woman's favourite ax or pack strap might be buried with her.'[34] Similarly, writing in 1836, the French ethnographer Joseph N. Nicollet stated that tools like this were a means of teaching children about gender. When a male child was born, men in the village would sing and dance around the family's house, firing shots. Then they would enter the house and give the child a small rifle carved out of wood, a leader saying: 'I found your rifle. It seems you did not take good care of it. We bring it back to you. Here it is. Indeed, you must hunt to survive and you must defend yourself when the enemy strikes. Keep it safely.' Similarly when a female child was born, women in the village would dance, each one with a hatchet, 'singing and dancing around the lodge and making gestures of women busy chopping wood.' Then they would give the child a little wooden hatchet, saying: 'We found your hatchet. It appears you did not take good care of it. We bring it back to you. Here it is. Indeed, you must chop wood to stay warm, and chop more wood to fortify your lodge should the enemy attack.'[35]

In many ways, this picture of the gendered nature of Ojibwa labour and the manner in which traders like Radisson and Groseilliers accommodated it accords with the views of Leacock and Devens. The gift of awls and scrapers could be seen as bearing out Devens's suggestion that French gifts were intended to encourage trapping. The only outstanding question would appear to be whether or not this encouragement actually made changes in Ojibwa gender and subsistence patterns as all labour became geared to the production of furs.[36]

The problem with this view of Ojibwa participation in the fur trade, however, is that it is simplistic, revealing nothing of the complex nature of the fur trade, a trade that provided varied opportunities for direct participation by both men and women. Gifts such as these were not representative of the entire relationship between Ojibwa and European traders, either in 1659 or for the next 250 years. From the seventeenth century on, the fur trade was important to the Ojibwa, who had a continuing, though variable, interest in obtaining European merchandise to use in their daily lives, in hunting, cooking, and religious ceremonies.[37] Trade goods offered material benefits, increased status, and much more. But from the beginning, traders accommodated Ojibwa demand by bringing a rich assortment of goods, including cloth, blankets, utensils, tools, silver jewellery, thread, and beads. In return, traders needed more from the Ojibwa than furs. They also needed a rich variety of products that only women could provide. All these factors meant that both Ojibwa men and women had a variety of roles to play and methods of exerting power and influence over the trade process.

The major role of women in the fur trade was not evident in the earliest years of French-Ojibwa interaction, when canoe-loads of people from the western Great Lakes went east to Montreal to trade their furs with the French. It may be that women were involved in these expeditions, although most accounts suggest that the participants were mainly men.[38] Later, however, when the location of trade shifted to Native villages, at the time of Radisson and Groseilliers, women became crucial to the trade.

In the context of the trading post and the village, Ojibwa men and women had distinct and often different relationships with traders. The fur trade was never simply an exchange of furs for trade goods. It included a variety of other kinds of transactions. Traders needed to get food from Native people; without it, they could not survive the winter in the western Great Lakes. They simply could not bring in or collect enough food to feed themselves, while at the same time carrying on the fur business. At the same time, as described later in more detail, traders needed a variety of Native-manufactured supplies. The multifaceted nature of this trade meant that Native people interacted with traders in many ways.

The varied interactions of Ojibwa men and women with traders were manifested in the complex set of trade patterns that made up a complete trading year. In the eighteenth century, a trading year in a Southwestern Ojibwa community would begin with the arrival in the fall of the trader with a new supply of goods. Once established in a fort or trading house, he gathered members of the community and gave and received ceremonial gifts. Goods such as clothing and utensils designed to help the Ojibwa survive the winter were then given out on credit, and customers went on their fall and winter hunts. The trader often purchased supplies of wild rice for his own survival and in some cases hired a hunter and his family to provide him with meat during the winter. Later, the trader or his men might visit Native families to collect the furs they produced. Similarly, Native people might revisit the trading post bringing in furs. In such circumstances, there could be further gifts and further credit. At the end of the trading year in the spring, before the trader's departure, certain goods were traded in direct exchanges and there might be concluding gifts and ceremonies.[39]

...

Men appear to have been the most frequent participants in trade ceremonies, as they were in other kinds of non-trade-related diplomacy. Leading men in the community gave speeches and sometimes, especially at the beginning of the trading year, presented gifts of furs or food. In return, they were given gifts of liquor, which they appear to have shared with men and women alike. It was also on such occasions that leading men were presented with chief's coats and other symbols of their role in the trade and in the community. Sometimes they were 'made chiefs,' that is, given status by the trader that they did not actually have in the community. It should be noted that the skilful leader – one who understood the need of leaders to give things away in order to increase their own status in the community – often gave away the clothing and other symbols of power given them by traders.[40] Such gifts may have gone to women as well as men. In any case, trade ceremonies also involved more general gifts to men and women in the community. Alexander Henry, the younger, a North West Company trader on the Red River in 1800, made this clear in his account of the transactions that took place on his arrival in the region of trade. On 21 August of that year, he presented several male community leaders with scarlet-laced coats, laced hats, red feathers, white linen shirts, leggings, breech cloths, and flags, as well as tobacco and alcohol. A few weeks later, in addition to unspecified goods on credit to the amount of twenty skins' worth each to a number of individuals, he also gave 'an assortment of small articles gratis, such as one Scalper, two Folders, and four Flints [apiece to the men], [and to the] Women, two awls, three needles, one seine of net Thread, one fi[r]e steel, a little Vermilion, and a half f[atho]m of Tobacco.'[41]

It is usually asserted that men were the primary traders of furs. This is hard to document, given the fact that few furs were actually traded directly. Instead, as noted, they were exchanged in credit/debt transactions. Traders seldom listed the goods they gave out on credit or even to whom credit was given, though usually traders recorded debts in the names of men.[42] It is impossible to know whether women or men chose the goods given out in this fashion. It could be argued that even if the credit was granted to the hunters or trappers who were expected to produce the furs, this does not preclude the possibility that women were involved in the choice of goods or that men discussed with their wives what the wives or children needed for the winter. Given the documented concern of Ojibwa people for their families, it is hard to picture Ojibwa men who acted like mythical 'economic men' in the theoretical sense, maximizing their own self-interest at the expense of their families.[43] This would, perhaps, have been productive for them in the short run, but would have lowered their status in the community.[44]

As for the repayment of the debts during the winter, a variety of people could be involved, including the hunter or trapper, his children, and his wives or female relations. Often the trader would be notified that a particular group of trappers had produced some furs.[45] He would then send off his men to pick them up. Subsequently, the hunter or other members of the family would be given a gift of alcohol in some form, which would, again, be shared among men and women.[46] It should also be noted that there were occasions when women traded furs directly.[47] While men were the primary hunters and trappers in Ojibwa communities, women processed the furs, a fact that would have given them greater authority in deciding what would happen to the furs, as well as the opportunity to trade them.

The occasional role of women in bartering furs was part of a larger role in bartering. Food was an important part of women's trade. They supplied wild rice and maple sugar, both of which were mainstays for the trader. As noted, the characteristic return for such items of food was liquor. However, there were exceptions to this pattern. For example, food was sometimes traded for a variety of trade goods other than liquor, especially in times of scarcity. Michel Curot, a young clerk trading along the St Croix River in 1803–4, for example, stated that because food supplies were scarce during the winter, traders were paying blankets for wild rice. In other years, this was an unusual transaction, and after paying a two and-a-half-point blanket to one woman in late February 1804, Curot felt obligated to explain: 'I resolved to give the blanket, having only a single fawn of rice for provisions.' Normally such a blanket was worth three beaverskins or more. He went on to describe the failure of his men to obtain fish to feed them.[48]

Wild rice was important not only as a trade item to be consumed by traders while living in an Ojibwa village near the Great Lakes, but also as an important way to feed brigades travelling further west. One account of large-scale trading of wild rice suggests something of women's power in the trade and in the Ojibwa community. The British trader Alexander Henry, the elder, went west of Lake Superior for the first time in 1775. When he reached Lake of the Woods, he and his men received a warm welcome:

> From this village we received ceremonious presents. The mode with the Indians is, first to collect all the provisions they can spare, and place them in a heap; after which they send for the trader, and address him in a formal speech. They tell him, that the Indians are happy in seeing him return into their country; that they have been long in expectation of his arrival; that their wives have deprived themselves of their provisions, in order to afford him a supply; that they are in great want, being destitute of every thing, and particularly of ammunition and clothing; and what they

most long for, is a taste of his rum, which they uniformly denominate milk. The present, in return, consisted in one keg of gunpowder, of sixty pounds weight; a bag of shot, and another of powder, of eighty pounds each; a few smaller articles, and a keg of rum. The last appeared to be the chief treasure, though on the former depended the greater part of their winter's subsistence.

In a short time, the men began to drink, while the women brought me a further and very valuable present, of twenty bags of rice. This I returned with goods and rum, and at the same time offered more, for an additional quantity of rice. A trade was opened, the women bartering rice, while the men were drinking. Before morning, I had purchased a hundred bags, of nearly a bushel measure each. Without a large quantity of rice, the voyage could not have been prosecuted to its completion. The canoes, as I have already observed, are not large enough to carry provisions.[49]

There was a great deal more going on in this encounter than is evident in Henry's description. In this trading encounter, men played their usual ceremonial role, describing what it was they sought from the traders. Their words, along with their 'ceremonious presents,' suggest that their aim was to establish a continuing relationship, one that would ensure them of a supply of merchandise, not just a one-time interaction. Unfortunately, Henry was only passing through. The ceremony did not initiate a full year's worth of credit, debt, trade, and gift.[50] Instead, the only Native product to be traded was wild rice, a product largely harvested by women and for trading purposes, under their control. Given the limited nature of the encounter and the need, and the pressing schedule of the trader, these women had the power to obtain not just alcohol, but, apparently, a full range of goods. This interaction differs strikingly from the picture of women made powerless by a trade that had no need for what they controlled, the picture suggested by Ruth Landes in her study done 160 years later in the very same region.[51]

Women's role in the trade was evident in relation to other resources. Canoes – the product of both men's and women's labour – were often traded by women and were a useful way to obtain a full range of trade goods. In one case, a woman at Fond du Lac traded Curot a small canoe in return for two capotes, a two-and-a-half-point blanket, and two pots of mixed rum. Together this was worth more than ten beaverskins.[52] Supplies for maintaining canoes were also produced by women. In early April 1804, Curot and his men left their Yellow River wintering post to camp out on the St Croix River. Curot's canoes were badly in need of repair, and the trader sent off one of his men with rum and cloth 'to hire the women to make gum that I absolutely need, since we cannot make use of any of our canoes without it filling immediately.' It was not until 1 May that Curot was able to purchase gum from a woman named La Petite Riviere, or Little River, in return for a three-point blanket, generally worth three or four beaverskins. Curot obtained birchbark and *wadab*, the spruce roots used for tying panels of bark, from an unidentified person – possibly from Little River – in return for some jewellery, and the next day his men were able to repair the canoes. They finally set off for Grand Portage the following day.[53] Little River, who was unusual in being identified by her own name, also tanned three deerskins in return for two pairs of wool leggings, which together were worth four beaverskins.[54]

Considering their role in trading a wide variety of food and supplies, it may be that women were more often involved in direct trade than men. Curot's journal provides some statistical evidence on this point. As suggested by the examples given here, Curot not only used his journal as a way of recording a narrative of trade activities, but also for recording specific trade transactions. While he was generally vague about the quantity of goods given on credit – usually recording only the name of the person given credit – he was more specific about direct trade. Throughout the pages of the journal, Curot recorded sixty-four separate transactions that were clearly examples of direct trade. Of these, nineteen involved men and twenty-two involved women. In addition, there were twenty-three transactions in which the gender of the person trading was not evident. Given the frequency with which Curot named the male Ojibwa with whom he traded, and the fact that most of the men had received credit from him, it is very likely that most of the anonymous trade transactions were also examples of trade with women. This suggests that the vast majority of Curot's direct trade transactions were with women.[55]

Beyond these opportunities for women to trade their own products for a wide range of goods, some women took part in the ceremonial trading roles of giving and receiving gifts and getting credit, the more typical role of men. A prime example was Netnokwa, the Ottawa mother of the adopted white captive John Tanner, who lived with her family among Ojibwa west of the Red River around 1800. On the occasion of trading with one trader, according to Tanner, Netnokwa 'took ten fine beaver skins, and presented them to the trader. In return for this accustomed present, she was in the habit of receiving every year a chief's dress and ornaments, and a ten gallon keg of spirits.'[56] Around the time described in the narrative, Charles Chaboillez, a North West Company trader, stated that on arriving in the region of the Red River, he exchanged presents with and gave credit to the 'Old Courte Oreille [Ottawa] & Two Sons.' This was clearly a reference to Netnokwa, Tanner, and Tanner's adopted brother. Later, Chaboillez stated that he gave her a present of rum and tobacco, 'to encourage her to return' with furs and other products, a suggestion of her primary role in trading.[57] How typical Netnokwa was of other women in the community in which she lived is not clear. Laura Peers pointed out that 'while Netnokwa was an exceptionally strong and charismatic woman ... her influence was presumably neither unprecedented nor unparalleled.'[58]

There were various explanations for Netnokwa's participation in trade rituals more frequently undertaken by men. For one thing, when she and her family were coming west several years before, Netnokwa's husband had died. Death or illness of a husband and other emergencies appear to have been important reasons for women to undertake activities that were normally the work of men, as it would have been for men to undertake the work of women on occasion. Ruth Landes argued that women were 'reserve material' capable of doing men's work when necessary for survival. In fact, though Landes gave many examples of women who hunted, traded, and went to war when they had to, she could only provide one example of a woman who resisted doing men's work when left alone by the death of her husband.[59]

In the case of Netnokwa, however, her transcendence of usual gender roles was evident even before her husband's death. As an older woman who had been married to a younger husband with two other wives, Netnokwa was, according to Tanner, considered to be the head of the household, even before his adopted father's death. Tanner stated that Netnokwa was seventeen years older than her husband, was an accomplished trader, and was owner of most of the family's wealth. Tanner said, perhaps exaggerating, that she was 'notwithstanding her sex, ... regarded as principal chief of the Ottawwaws,' and that 'whenever she came to Mackinac, she was saluted by a gun from the fort.' Perhaps most significant of all – in terms of Ojibwa and Ottawa culture – Netnokwa was, as described by Tanner, a person of strong spirituality, and she used her power to aid her sons in hunting.[60]

Dreams and visions were often cited as providing authorization for Ojibwa men and women to transcend the gendered division of labour. Despite the tendency of scholars to analyse gender roles based on material factors, including participation in the fur trade, power in an Ojibwa community was never purely material, and even material power was usually seen as having a non-material basis. Gwen Morris, in a remarkable recent study of women in Ojibwa society, notes that women, on the beginning of menstruation, were seen as having a unique source of power, made clear by its perceived danger to men.[61] Beyond that, as recounted in the story of the woman who married the beaver, girls fasted at puberty, seeking to gain a continuing relationship with a being who could help them in their lives. Having this relationship – especially when it was renewed from time to time through ceremony and further visions and dreams – helped men in important activities like hunting and war. For women, such a relationship might aid them in activities usually described as women's work.[62] Similarly, as Morris notes, such dreams and visions could help define a particular and unique course for their lives that transcended their own gender. This may have been the case with Netnokwa, whose spirituality was evident in her actions, though her own puberty visions were never recorded.[63]

Thus, despite the existence of a well-understood division of labour, described as rigid in many generalized descriptions of the Ojibwa, the more recent ethnographic evidence suggests that the Ojibwa gave cultural acceptance to those who violated the usual gender roles, and who demonstrated competence brought about by spiritual aid. Such cultural acceptance suggests that for many Ojibwa, creative, dynamic women forging a unique course were seen as having a beneficial effect on their communities. This is also evident in a major aspect of the role of women in the fur trade, their role as the wives of traders. As I show, this unique role – one that Ojibwa men could not fill – had a major social and economic impact on the trade.

Fur Trade Marriages

Claude-Charles Le Roy, *dit* Bacqueville de La Potherie, stated that in the late seventeenth century the Dakota, residing in what is now north-central Minnesota, made an alliance with the Ojibwa, then living mainly at the eastern end of Lake Superior, based on a desire for European trade goods. Because they 'could obtain French merchandise only through the agency of the Sauteurs,' they made 'a treaty of peace with the latter by which they were mutually bound to give their daughters in marriage on both sides. That was a strong bond for the maintenance of entire harmony.'[64] The agreement appears to have been encouraged by the French diplomat Daniel Greysolon, Sieur du Lhut, who, in mid-September 1679, convened a meeting of representatives from various 'nations of the north,' including Dakota, Assiniboine, and probably Ojibwa, at Fond du Lac, the present site of Duluth. He later wrote: 'I was able to gain their esteem and friendship. In order to make sure that the peace was more durable among them, I found that the best way to cement it was by bringing about reciprocal marriages. I was not able to do this without a great deal of expense. During the following winter, I brought them together again in the woods where I was, so that they could hunt together, feast, and by this means, create a closer friendship.'[65]

Among the Ojibwa, marriage was defined by the decision of two parties, sometimes through the intercession of parents or other relations, to sleep, live, and carry on their day-to-day lives together. Although the event was not marked by the ceremonies with which Europeans were familiar, it could involve ceremonial exchanges of gifts.[66] From the point of view of the Native community, marriages between traders and Native women could help achieve the important aim of ensuring a steady supply of merchandise. Ties of affection could increase the likelihood that a trader would return to the community in future years and that he might be more generous with gifts and in the rates exacted for direct exchange.

Historian Jacqueline Peterson wrote that 'tribal people, throughout the fur trading era, saw intermarriage as a means of entangling strangers in a series of kinship obligations. Relatives by marriage were expected not only to deal fairly, but to provide protection, hospitality, and sustenance in time of famine.' Peterson stated that 'in addition to assuming positions of economic and political leverage, traders' wives used to advantage their symbolic status as links between two societies by serving as spies, interpreters, guides, or diplomatic emissaries ...'[67]

For fur traders, their wives or the wives of their employees could prove to be useful socially and economically. The evidence suggests that leading traders often married the daughters of Ojibwa leaders, although it is sometimes hard to say which came first.[68] In marrying a leader's daughter, a trader gained a powerful ally among his Indian customers. Since the authority of a leader was in part the result of extended kin ties, the trader may have formed ties with a large number of people. The leader's influence over kin and non-kin alike depended also on his persuasive oratory.[69] Thus, through marriage, the trader gained an alliance with a man of demonstrated ability to influence his fellows. The father-in-law could become, in a sense, an economic agent for the trader, useful in persuading the people to be friends and clients.

Simon Chaurette, a head trader for the North West, XY, and American Fur Companies, mostly at Lac du Flambeau, between 1795 and the early 1820s, was married to the daughter of Keeshkemun (Sharpened Stone or La Pierre à Affiler), an important leader who was a member of the Crane clan. According to François Victoire Malhiot, a rival trader in the region in 1804–5, Keeshkemun was allied in trade terms with Chaurette, although this alliance did not lessen the trader's obligation to give gifts and fulfil other Native expectations of him. As for Keeshkemun's daughter, little has been written about her. Mostly she is identified in trade documents by the name of her husband or father. However, American Fur Company documents show that a woman named Keenistinoquay (or Cree Woman), identified as Chaurette's wife, was so important to the company's operation at Lac du Flambeau that she was employed as a trader there during 1819–21, receiving an average of more than $200 per year, around half of her husband's yearly salary.[70]

Another trader who benefited from a connection to a prominent Native family was Charles Oakes Ermatinger, who, from a base at Sault Ste Marie, shipped goods to trading posts south and west of Lake Superior from 1800 to the mid-1820s. Ermatinger married Charlotte, the daughter of Kadowaubeda, or Broken Tooth, a member of the Loon clan and a civil leader described by Henry R. Schoolcraft, an Indian agent and a noted writer on Ojibwa culture, as 'patriarch' of the region around Sandy Lake and the upper Mississippi, the area of Ermatinger's trade. After her husband's retirement in the 1820s, Charlotte went to live with him and her children in Montreal, where she spent the rest of her life.[71]

Important traders like Chaurette and Ermatinger were not the only members of their companies married to Native women. It is apparent from accounts of stable trading posts south of Lake Superior in Wisconsin and Minnesota that some fur company outfits were linked to the Indian community from top to bottom of the trade hierarchy, meaning that fur companies had access to an extensive kinship network.[72] Because traders were unsystematic in recording genealogical information on themselves and their employees, it is not always possible to pin down the parameters of these networks. However, the unofficial and supposedly non-economic network that existed around each trading post was probably as important to companies as was the network of suppliers and shippers through which they obtained their supplies of trade goods. As Jennifer Brown suggested in her study of Hudson's Bay Company and North West Company social life, women associated with the trading post could provide a more certain food supply.[73] When the North West Company wintering partner John Sayer was stationed on the St Croix River, his Ojibwa wife went to the sugar bush in 1803 and 1804 to process maple sugar for their food supply.[74] When food was scarce at the trading post, traders were sometimes fed by their wives' families. On 17 March 1804, George Nelson wrote: 'Brunet with my permission goes with his family to his father in law's lodge, as we have nothing here to eat. I give him a little ammunition & a few silverworks to trade provisions – for we have now nothing else to trade. We subsiste [sic] upon indian Charity.'[75]

Beyond providing food, Native women and the trade kinship networks served as a source of information for traders as much as for Indian people. In 1804, Michel Curot learned that one Ojibwa family did not want to give their furs to the opposition North West trader because the man was out of rum. Curot said he had heard it from the wife of his man Savoyard, who had in turn heard it from the wife of the North West trader's clerk.[76]

...

The implication of some accounts of marriages arranged by traders and the parents of Native women is that women were passive objects like the furs, food, and merchandise exchanged in the fur trade ... It is open to question whether this was the case with most such marriages. To be effective in achieving the purposes Native communities might envision for such marriages, women could not be passive. They had to exert influence and be active communicators of information. Further, there is evidence that marriages were not simply arranged by male and female elders in communities. Rather they were embraced by many women themselves as a way of achieving useful purposes for themselves and for the communities in which they lived.

Marriages between traders and Native women were based on a variety of factors, not just material motives. Jacqueline Peterson, in her study of Great Lakes Métis society, suggested that marriages with fur traders took exceptional women, people with unusual ambitions, influenced by dreams and visions – like the women who became hunters, traders, healers, and warriors in Ruth Landes' account of Ojibwa women. One example Peterson gave was Oshahgushkodanaqua, a woman from the western end of Lake Superior who married the Sault Ste Marie trader John Johnston in the 1790s.[77] Oshahgushkodanaqua was the granddaughter of Mamongeseda (Big Foot or Big Feet), a La Pointe leader noted for his prowess in war and diplomacy. One of Mamongeseda's daughters – one source suggests her name was Obemaunoqua – was the wife of John Sayer, who was in charge of the entire Lake Superior area for the General Company of Lake Superior and the South in the 1780s and the North West Company from 1794 to 1805. One of Mamongeseda's sons, Waubojeeg (White Fisher), also based at La Pointe, was as renowned in war and diplomacy as his father. Waubojeeg was the father of Oshahgushkodanaqua.[78]

Oshahgushkodanaqua's marriage was preceded by a dream during the vision quest she undertook at puberty. She told the story many years later, after her husband's death, to a visiting British writer named Anna Jameson. The story of the dream has some interesting parallels to the story of the woman who married the beaver.

According to Jameson, Oshahgushkodanaqua fasted 'according to the universal Indian custom, for a guardian spirit.' She went to a high hill and built a lodge of cedar boughs, painted herself black, and then began to fast:

> She dreamed continually of a white man, who approached her with a cup in his hand, saying, 'Poor thing! why are you punishing yourself? why do you fast? here is food for you!' He was always accompanied by a dog, which looked up in her face as though he knew her. Also she dreamed of being on a high hill, which was surrounded by water, and from which she beheld many canoes full of Indians, coming to her and paying her homage; after this, she felt as if she were carried up into the heavens, and as she looked down upon the earth, she perceived it was on fire, and said to herself, 'All my relations will be burned!' but a voice answered and said, 'No, they will not be destroyed, they will be saved'; and she knew it was a spirit, because the voice was not human. She fasted for ten days, during which time her grandmother brought her at intervals some water. When satisfied that she had obtained a guardian spirit in the white stranger who haunted her dreams, she returned to her father's lodge.[79]

Some time after this dream, John Johnston appeared at her parents' home at Chequamegon to trade for furs. He asked the woman's father, Waubojeeg, for her hand in marriage. Her father at first was scornful of Johnston because he did not believe the trader was seeking a long-term relationship. He told Johnston to return to Montreal in the spring and if he still wished to marry her, he could come back to Lake Superior and marry her, 'according to the law of the white man *till death.*' Johnston returned to Lake Superior and the marriage was arranged.

The young woman, however, was not keen on the idea and took some persuasion to stay with her husband. Given the possibilities for dissolving marriage among the Ojibwa, this fear may have been due in part to Johnston's insistence on marriage until death. Once she consented, however, the couple remained married for thirty-six years.[80] All evidence suggests that she served an important and influential role in relations between her people and her husband, who was an important trader in the Lake Superior region from the 1790s to the 1820s. According to Jameson, Oshahgushkodanaqua throughout her life carried on a variety of subsistence activities characteristic of Ojibwa women – activities that would have been advantageous for her husband's business. She sugared every year and fished. In addition, Jameson noted, in words that could have appeared in one of Ruth Landes' accounts of remarkable women, that 'in her youth she hunted, and was accounted the surest eye and fleetest foot among the women of her tribe.'[81]

Later in her life, Oshahgushkodanaqua also taught Ojibwa and Ojibwa culture to her children and to visitors to the region, including her son-in-law, Henry R. Schoolcraft. Her career transcended the fur trade, lasting into an era when Ojibwa people had need for intermediaries who would help them in dealings with the U.S. government. All in all, Oshahgushkodanaqua actively made use of the situation in which she found herself.[82]

It should be said that Oshahgushkodanaqua's interpretation of the vision quest experience may have evolved over the years. It may have been coloured by the death of her husband. It may have been shaped by her Christian conversion, as suggested by some of the imagery and wording in the story. On the other hand, her experience bears the clear imprint of Ojibwa culture. The vision quest, though an apparently solitary endeavour pursued by young people, was shaped in part by the Ojibwa educational process, including the telling of stories, some of which, in Oshahgushkodanaqua's case, may have resembled the story of the woman who married the beaver. The process of seeking a vision was also usually supervised by adults, who encouraged certain desirable results.[83]

It may be that in this way, Oshahgushkodanaqua's experience was shaped by community needs. Her story contains the suggestion that a marriage with an outsider could be of benefit to the woman's relations, that there was some social purpose in undertaking the marriage with such a person who could provide something useful to the community. She felt some fear about the risks involved to herself and her community, but in the long run, the marriage was a good one. In her life, she achieved a great deal.

All of these elements were found, too, of course, in the story of the woman who married the beaver, a story which tells a great deal about how the Ojibwa community did honour to women who followed unique destinies. The nature of the message communicated by the story can be seen by comparing it to another of Kagige Pinasi's stories, a humorous tale about a young man named Clothed-in-Fur, a trickster-like figure, who marries, in turn, a wolf, a raven, a porcupine, a Canada Jay, a beaver, and finally a bear. Most of the marriages are unsuccessful, due to drawbacks Clothed-in-Fur finds in the various wives: the wolf could not carry heavy loads, and the raven was a bad cook and a poor housekeeper, for example. But in the course of the story, Clothed-in-Fur learns valuable lessons on how to treat with respect the bones of animals he kills so that the animals will come back to life. There was another version of this same story, collected by Schoolcraft. In this version, the young man marries a nighthawk, a marten, a beaver, and a bear. The story ends with the man's bear-wife giving herself up to a hunter to be killed. The man spoke to the hunter and gave him important instructions about the proper way to treat bears: 'You must ... never cut the flesh in taking off the skin, nor hang up the feet with the flesh when drying it. But you must take the head and feet, and decorate them handsomely, and place tobacco on the head, for these animals are very fond of this article, and on the *fourth* day they come to life again.'[84]

Both of these versions have a humorous tone, as the hapless hero discovers the identity and drawbacks of each marriage partner and her faults. The serious portion of the story is in its instructions about the treatment of animals, comparable in some ways to the injunctions given in the story of the woman who married the beaver. In telling the latter story, however, Kagige Pinasi had something more in mind than entertaining and instructing about the proper treatment of animals. There was an important message about women. In particular, this is revealed in a description of the woman's discovery by the trappers who found her in the beaver lodge many years after her marriage. Hearing her voice calling to them, they broke open the beaver lodge, and one of them reached in his hand and touched her, 'whereupon he found by the feel of her that she was a human being; all over did he try feeling her –

on her head; and her ears, having on numerous ear-rings, he felt. And when he had forced a wide opening, out came the woman; very white was her head. And beautiful was the whole mystic cloth that she had for a skirt; worked all over with beads was her cloak; and her moccasins too were very pretty; and her ear-rings she also had on; she was very handsomely arrayed.'[85]

This key description captures something of the awe with which the woman was viewed, in the story and by the storyteller. Her white hair, beaded clothing, and earrings were all symbols of power, spiritual and material, and the honour she would have in an Ojibwa community. Unlike the man who married the beaver, the birds, the bear, and the other animals, the woman who married a beaver is an object of respect and reverence.[86]

This story, together with the other accounts given here, can serve as a guide to interpreting experiences and events, suggesting other ways of looking at them and providing Ojibwa alternatives to scholarly scenarios. Far from being beasts of burden, subsidiary to interactions with outsiders, Ojibwa women were central to the process, honoured for the role they played. The way in which these and other women used their relationships with outsiders for their own benefit, the benefit of the communities, or of their husbands – and in the process influenced the patterns of interaction with outsiders – must be evaluated based on all the available details, on a case-by-case basis. It would be wrong to see in any of the women described here a single set of motives or a single path for Ojibwa women.[87] Nonetheless, it is only by considering all the available Ojibwa models of women's roles as warriors, shamans, wives, suppliers of food, traders, intermediaries, brokers, and teachers, that one can hope to understand the role of Ojibwa women in the fur trade.

Conclusion

The fur trade is sometimes seen simply as an exchange that took place between men of European and Native cultures. However, an examination of the trade among the Ojibwa of Lake Superior shows that women and men both participated in the trade. They also had different opportunities, different expectations, and different roles to play. As acknowledged by traders in their gift-giving and trade, men and women sought a different assortment of trade goods. Women also played an important role in providing the resources that were their responsibility in Native life: wild rice, maple sugar, and a variety of vital supplies necessary for the function of trade. While most women did not usually participate in trade ceremonies or receive credit from traders, they were able to trade the products of their labour for goods they needed. Finally, women also could serve as a vital link between their communities and European traders by marrying traders. Such marriages could ensure a steady supply of merchandise for a community by providing an incentive for traders to return to the communities from which their wives came and, possibly, by increasing their generosity toward their wives' relations. Although such marriages were encouraged and often arranged by men, women were not mere objects to be exchanged. The value of such marriages to a Native community could only be achieved if women exercised influence on the trader and served to increase the flow of information and merchandise in both directions.

The challenge of examining the differing roles of Ojibwa men and women in the fur trade means using both early documents and later ethnographies in an ongoing creative process. This process may not always provide a satisfying narrative of exactly what occurred in the past, but it does reveal a catalogue of possible roles for men and women, roles that they may have assumed at various times in the past.

The multiple nature of the fur trade and of Ojibwa women's roles in relation to that trade suggests that the theories of Landes, Leacock, and Devens need revision. The fur trade provided more than a few opportunities for Ojibwa women. While the fur trade was important to Native communities, both men and women had distinct and powerful roles to play in relation to a trade that was never simply one of furs for merchandise. Women had many opportunities to trade food, supplies, and, on occasion, furs to obtain what they needed and wanted from traders.

This does not deny the possibility that there may have been particular situations in which women had fewer opportunities to trade the products of their work for the things that they needed. With the improvement of transportation methods and the growth of white population centres in the Great Lakes, traders may have been able to bring better supplies of food, allowing them to trade for furs more exclusively. It should be noted, however, that while later fur traders may have had less use for Ojibwa women's food and supplies, there was a contemporaneous growing market for maple sugar, wild rice, and berries among lumbermen, settlers, and city people, which may well have provided greater opportunities for women than before. This was certainly the case along the Minnesota frontier in the late nineteenth century.[88]

The extent to which Ojibwa women's power and status in their own communities may have changed since contact with Europeans remains to be demonstrated. A major problem with describing the course of changes in Ojibwa society in the last four hundred years is the difficulty of reconstructing Ojibwa gender relations in the era prior to European contact using only documents that result from that contact. Analysis of the changes in Ojibwa society in the era of the fur trade also requires care, especially if it is based on documents that interpret Ojibwa gender from a European point of view of how men and women should live their lives. Scholars must take into account some of the Ojibwa beliefs about women's spiritual power and the accounts of individual women's lives and dreams discussed here. Though the Ojibwa did have a distinct division of labour, one that may have changed at various times in response to interaction with Europeans, women could make a distinct course for themselves through their spiritual power.

One way or another, however, care should be taken in attributing the condition of Ojibwa society and culture in the late twentieth century to the effects of the fur trade. To do so is to ignore the effects of treaties, a declining land base, limitation of opportunities to use natural resources, pervasive mass media, urbanization, and poverty, all of which have occurred in the years since the decline of the fur trade.

Further work is needed on the gendered patterns of the fur trade among the Ojibwa. It is important to take a fresh look at all primary sources to consider the gender dimensions of every transaction involving traders and Native people, reading between the lines when necessary. Whether or not such an examination will suggest alterations in existing theories about gender and about other aspects of the impact of the fur trade on the Ojibwa, it will provide a richer view of the fur trade itself.

NOTES

1 William Jones, *Ojibwa Texts*, ed. Truman Michelson, Publications of the American Ethnological Society, vol. 7, part 2 (New York, 1919), 215–57. For further information on Kagige Pinasi (Forever-Bird) or John Pinesi, see Jones, *Ojibwa Texts*, vol. 7, part 1 (Leiden, 1917), xvii; and Henry M. Rideout, *William Jones: Indian, Cowboy, American Scholar, and Anthropologist in the Field* (New York, 1912), 98, 110–11. The story of the woman who married a beaver is reprinted in Thomas W. Overholt and J. Baird Callicott, *Clothed-in-Fur and Other Tales: An Introduction to the Ojibwa World View* (Washington, DC, 1982), 74–5.

2 Jean-François Lyotard wrote of what he called 'popular stories.' See Lyotard, *The Postmodern Condition: A Report on Knowledge* (Minneapolis, 1984), 20, 21

3 Overholt and Callicott, *Clothed-in-Fur,* 26

4 Overholt and Callicott use the stories to help explain Ojibwa worldview in ibid., 24–9.

5 Rideout, *William Jones,* 98, 109–11. Notes entitled 'Penessi goes hunting' are found in the William Jones Papers, American Philosophical Society, Philadelphia.

6 For a discussion of these beliefs and their bearing on the fur trade, see Bruce M. White, '"Give Us a Little Milk": The Social and Cultural Meaning of Gift Giving in the Lake Superior Fur Trade,' in *Rendezvous: Selected Papers of the Fourth North American Fur Trade Conference, 1981,* ed. Thomas C. Buckley (St Paul, MN, 1984), 187–8.

7 Bruce M. White, 'Encounters with Spirits: Ojibwa and Dakota Theories about the French and Their Merchandise,' *Ethnohistory* 41 (Summer 1994): 376–81; B. White, '"Give Us a Little Milk,"' 189–92; Richard White, *The Middle Ground: Indians, Empires, and Republics in the Great Lakes Region, 1650–1815* (Cambridge, 1991), 95, 112–14.

8 On Native American origin tales, see Stith Thompson, *The Folktale* (1946; reprint, Berkeley and Los Angeles, 1977), 303.

9 Harold A. Innis, *The Fur Trade in Canada: An Introduction to Canadian Economic History* (1930; rev. ed., Toronto, 1956), 40.

10 Arthur J. Ray and Donald B. Freeman, *'Give Us Good Measure': An Economic Analysis of Relations Between the Indians and the Hudson's Bay Company* (Toronto, 1978), xv. See also Arthur J. Ray, *The Indians in the Fur Trade: Their Role as Hunters, Trappers, and Middlemen in the Lands Southwest of Hudson Bay, 1660–1870* (Toronto, 1974), which also lacks a detailed discussion of the role of gender.

11 R. White, *Middle Ground,* 94, 105

12 Ibid., 74, 130. R. White's primary discussion of women in the book concerns sexual and marriage relations between Frenchmen and Indian women, 60–75.

13 Jennifer Brown, *Strangers in Blood: Fur Trade Company Families in Indian Country* (Vancouver, 1980).

14 Sylvia Van Kirk, *Many Tender Ties: Women in Fur-Trade Society, 1670–1870* (1980; first American ed., Norman, OK, 1983), 5.

15 Ibid., 75–7, 80. See also Sylvia Van Kirk, 'Toward a Feminist Perspective in Native History,' in *Papers of the Eighteenth Algonquian Conference,* ed. William Cowan (Ottawa, 1987): 377–89.

16 Jacqueline Peterson, 'The People in Between: Indian-White Marriage and the Genesis of a Métis Society and Culture in the Great Lakes Region, 1660–1830' (Ph.D. diss., University of Illinois at Chicago, 1981), 2. An important chapter of Peterson's dissertation, for the point of view of trade patterns, was published as 'Women Dreaming: The Religiopsychology of Indian-White Marriages and the Rise of a Métis Culture,' in *Western Women: Their Land, Their Lives,* ed. Lillian Schillel, Vicki L. Ruiz, and Janice Monk (Albuquerque, 1988), 49–68.

17 For a discussion of the varying themes covered in the study of gender among Native-American groups, see Patricia Albers, 'From Illusion to Illumination: Anthropological Studies of American Indian Women,' in *Gender and Anthropology: Critical Reviews for Research and Teaching,* ed. Sandra Morgen (Washington, DC, 1989): 132–48.

18 The stories in Ruth Landes' book refer to Ojibwa people going to war against the Sioux or Dakota, suggesting this was a part of people's lives at the time, though Landes acknowledged that war between the two groups had not existed in at least fifty years. See Landes, *The Ojibwa Woman* (1938; reprint, New York, 1971), 4, 17, 132, 133, 141, 143, 162, 163, 171. Maggie Wilson (see vii) was of Cree descent but spoke Ojibwa, had married an Ojibwa man, and had lived all her life among the Ojibwa.

19 Ibid., 131, 137. On the range of roles available to women, see 135–71.

20 Ibid., 134. Landes noted, however, that 'today when rice and berries and maple sugar are commanding some white attention, the women also are learning to function as dealers.'

21 Eleanor Leacock, 'Women's Status in Egalitarian Society: Implications for Social Evolution,' *Current Anthropology* 19 (June 1978): 249–52, 254, 255. Another useful critique of Landes' work appears in Sally Cole, 'Women's Stories and Boasian Texts: The Ojibwa Ethnography of Ruth Landes and Maggie Wilson,' *Anthropologica* 37 (1995): 3–25, especially, 13, 17, 31. Harold Hickerson, who largely ignored gender in his influential work on the Ojibwa, appears to have agreed with the theory that the fur trade devalued women's roles. In one of his last published works, a study of 'fur trade colonialism,' he argued that among the Huron, the fur trade inevitably led to a decline in women's roles and importance. He suggested that men naturally assumed the major role in dealing with traders. See Hickerson, 'Fur Trade Colonialism and the North American Indians,' *Journal of Ethnic Studies* 1 (Summer 1973): 15–44.

22 Carol Devens, *Countering Colonization: Native American Women and Great Lakes Missions, 1630–1900* (Berkeley, CA, 1992), 13, 14, 15–16, 17, 18.

23 Priscilla K. Buffalohead, 'Farmers, Warriors, Traders: A Fresh Look

at Ojibway Women,' *Minnesota History* 48 (Summer 1983): 237. One
nineteenth-century example is Peter Grant, 'The Sauteux Indians around
1904,' in *Les Bourgeois de la Compagnie du Nord Ouest*, ed. Louis F.R. Masson
(1890; reprint, New York, 1960), 2:321. Grant stated that Ojibwa women,
'for all their work and devotion, are regarded by the men little better than
slaves to their will, or mere beasts of burden for their conveniency.'

24 Thomas Vennum Jr, *Wild Rice and the Ojibway People* (St Paul, MN, 1988),
108, 109. The translation is from R.G. Thwaites, ed., 'A Wisconsin Fur-
Trader's Journal, 1804–5,' *Collections of the State Historical Society of Wisconsin* 19 (1910): 197.

25 Vennum, *Wild Rice*, 108, 109. It should be noted, in addition, that François
Victoire Malhiot in his original journal used the term 'gens' to refer to
L'Outarde's followers, a word that could be translated as 'people' or even
'band.' Even this translation, however, may imply a more important role
for men in ricing than is warranted. See Malhiot journal, 15 (10 September
1804), McGill University Libraries, Rare Books and Special Collections.

26 William Fenton, 'The Training of Historical Ethnologists in America,'
American Anthropologist 54.3 (1952): 33, 335.

27 Ibid., 333. R. White, at the beginning of *The Middle Ground*, wrote that 'the
technique of using ethnologies of present-day or nineteenth-century
Indian groups to interpret Indian societies of the past' had a 'bias toward
continuity' that he tried to avoid (R. White, *The Middle Ground*, xiv).
Scepticism toward contintuity in the analysis of Native-American history
is sometimes allied with the application of globalizing theories, as in Carol
I. Mason, 'Indians, Maple Sugaring, and the Spread of Market Economies,'
in *The Woodland Tradition in Western Great Lakes: Papers Presented to Elden
Johnson* (Minneapolis, 1990), 37–43.

28 Even scholars who argue for radical change in Native-American cultures
due to contact with Europeans often make use of later ethnographic works
as evidence for their understanding of Aboriginal culture. See, for example, Calvin Martin, *Keepers of the Game: Indian-Animal Relationships and
the Fur Trade* (Berkeley, CA, 1978), 72, a work that relies heavily on the
twentieth-century ethnography of A. Irving Hallowell.

29 Quotations, with modernized orthography and pragraph breaks added,
are from Pierre Radisson, *Voyages of Pierre Esprit Radisson* (Boston, 1885),
199–200. Grace Lee Nute convincingly dates these events to 1659–60. See
Nute, *Caesars of the Wilderness: Médard Chouart, Sieur des Groseilliers and
Pierre Esprit Radisson, 1618–1710* (1943; reprint, St Paul, MN, 1978), 58, 62.
The term *destinated* is a borrowing by Radisson of the French verb *destiner*,
meaning 'to intend something for someone or for some use,' though in

this context, 'present' may be a better translation. Such borrowings from the French were typical of Radisson's narrative.

30 On Ojibwa facial adornment in the nineteenth century, see Johan Georg Kohl, *Kitchi-Gami: Life among the Lake Superior Ojibwa* (1860; reprint, St Paul, MN, 1985), 18.

31 Among Eastern groups, kettles clearly had an important symbolism in the feast of the dead, which may explain Radisson's reference here. See Laurier Turgeon, 'The Tale of the Kettle: Odyssey of an Intercultural Object,' *Ethnohistory* 44 (Winter 1997): 11. Harold Hickerson gives an analysis of the Algon-quian feast of the dead, with occasional reference to the roles of men and women, in Hickerson, 'The Feast of the Dead among the Seventeenth-Century Algonkians of the Upper Great Lakes,' *American Anthropologist* 62 (1960): 90. The use of kettles in various activities among the Ojibwa is described in Vennum, *Wild Rice*, 118–19; and Alexander Henry, the elder, *Travels and Adventures in Canada and the Indian Territories* (1809; reprint, New York, 1976), 149.

32 Buffalohead, 'Farmers, Warriors, Traders,' 238. Landes (*Ojibwa Woman*, 125) noted that there was a similar division of labour in the manufacture of cradleboards.

33 Ivan Illich, in an illuminating definition, wrote in *Gender* (New York and Toronto, 1982), 99, that 'gender not only tells who is who, but it also defines who is when, where and with which tools and words; it divides space, time and technique.' The gendered nature of material culture is of special interest to some archaeologists. For a discussion that focuses in particular on Dakota women's uses of awls and other tools of Native and European manufacture, see Janet D. Spector, *What This Awl Means: Feminist Archaeology at a Wahpeton Dakota Village* (St Paul, MN, 1993), including 30–9. See also Spector, 'Male/Female Task Differentiation among the Hidatsa: Toward the Development of an Archeological Approach to the Study of Gender,' in *The Hidden Half: Studies of Plains Indian Women*, ed. Patricia Albers and Beatrice Medicine (Lanham, MD, and London, 1983), 77–99.

34 Frances Densmore, *Chippewa Customs* (1929; reprint, St Paul, MN, 1979), 74.

35 Joseph N. Nicollet, *The Journals of Joseph N. Nicollett: A Scientist on the Mississippi Headwaters*, ed. Martha Coleman Bray (St Paul, MN, 1970), 181–2.

36 It should be noted, however, that each item on the list would clearly be useful for other activities aside from preparing furs for trade. In fact, preparation of furs for use as clothing probably involved more scraping than preparing furs for trade, especially once traders no longer put a

premium on beaver pelts that had been worn as beaver robes. See M. Inez Hilger, *Chippewa Child Life* (1951; reprint, St Paul, MN, 1992), 129–33; Densmore, *Chippewa Customs*, 31, 163–5; James L. Clayton, 'The American Fur Company: The Final Years' (Ph.D. diss., Cornell University, 1964), 96, 101, 108, 109; Ray, '*Give Us Good Measure*,' 159.

37 The argument here is in favour of a desire for and an interest in European merchandise, not necessarily a complete dependence upon it. For a longer discussion of the multiple nature of this interest in merchandise, see B. White, 'Encounters with Spirits,' 376–81. For one trader's account of Ojibwa interest in merchandise, see Henry, *Travels and Adventures*, 196. For a discussion of 'dependency' in relation to Great Lakes Indian groups, see R. White, *Middle Ground*, 482–6.

38 For accounts of expeditions to Montreal, see Nicholas Perrot's account in *Indian Tribes of the Upper Mississippi Valley and Region of the Great Lakes*, ed. Emma H. Blair (Cleveland, 1911): I:175, 210–20. In an earlier period, around 1609, Algonquin men and women from the upper Ottawa River, perhaps related to Great Lakes Algonquin peoples, did travel together to trade with the French at Montreal. See Bruce G. Trigger, *The Children of Aetaentsic: A History of the Huron People to 1660* (1976; reprint, Montreal, 1987), 249. See also a nineteenth-century account of a seventeenth-century Ojibwa husband and wife travelling east to discover the French, cited in B. White, 'Encounters with Spirits,' 373.

39 Bruce M. White, 'A Skilled Game of Exchange: Ojibway Fur Trade Protocol,' *Minnesota History* 50 (1987): 229–40.

40 On the generosity of Ojibwa leaders, see Kohl, *Kitchi-Gami*, 66.

41 *The Journal of Alexander Henry the Younger, 1799–1814*, ed. Barry M. Gough (Toronto, 1988), I:26, 53. These entries correspond to 48, III, in the original journal transcript in National Archives of Canada, Ottawa.

42 Traders mentioned credit books or ledgers in their narrative journals, but none have been found for this period. Even credit books, however, do not make clear the role of the hunter's family in choosing the goods received on credit. For an analysis of a credit book from a later period, one kept using pictograph symbols, see George Fulford, 'The Pictographic Account Book of an Ojibwa Fur Trader,' *Papers of the Twenty-third Algonquin Conference* (Ottawa, 1992), 190–217.

43 Illich, *Gender*, 9–11; Lionel Robbins, *An Essay on the Nature and Significance of Economic Science* (1931; reprint, London, 1952), 94–9.

44 On Ojibwa attitudes toward generosity, see Kohl, *Kitchi-Gami*, 66.

45 For examples of women notifying the trader of available furs and other items, see Michel Curot's journal, 8 (22 September 1803) and 19 (13 No-

vember 1803) (original in Masson Collection, National Archives of Canada). A garbled translation of this narrative was published as 'A Wisconsin Fur-Trader's Journal, 1803–4,' *Collections of the State Historical Society of Wisconsin* 20 (1911): 396–471.

46 Curot journal, 10 (13 October 1803), (14 October 1803), 13 (24 October 1803).

47 Some examples of direct trade of furs by womeni n Curot's journal include 23 (2 December 1803) and 32 (9 February 1804).

48 Ibid., 3 (17 and 18 August 1803), 6 (12 September 1803), 9 (4 and 5 October 1803), 23 (2 December 1803), 28 (17 December 1803), 29 (23 December 1803), 32 (9 February 1804), 33 (20 February 1804), 41 (18 March 1804), 47 (15 and 16 April 1804).

49 Henry, *Travels and Adventures*, 243–4.

50 There are many examples in trade literature of food gifts to initiate the trading year. See B. White, '"Give Us a Little Milk,"' 187–93.

51 As quoted earlier, Landes did acknowledge that women learned how to trade when their food was in demand outside their communities (Landes, *Ojibwa Woman*, 134).

52 Curot Journal, 3 (17 August 1803). The estimate of the value of these goods is based on values found in accounts kept by Malhiot (originals in Rare Books and Special Collections, McGill University Libraries).

53 Curot did some trading and collecting furs during the period when he was camped on the St Croix River. See Curot journal, 46 (7 April 1804), 47 (15 April 1804), and 50 (8–10 May 1804). See also 5 (5 September, 1803), in which it is noted that David can go nowhere because of a lack of gum for his canoe. On *wadab*, see John D. Nichols and Earl Nyholm, *A Concise Dictionary of Minnesota Ojibwe* (Minneapolis, 1995), 113; Densmore, *Chippewa Customs*, 150.

54 Curot Journal, 47 (15 April 1804).

55 Figures on trade transactions were compiled from the Curot journal by the author.

56 John Tanner, *A Narrative of the Captivity and Adventures of John Tanner* (1830; reprint, New York, 1975), 64, 69, 70, 75, 78, 101–2.

57 Harold Hickerson, ed., 'Journal of Charles Jean Baptiste Chaboillez,' *Ethnohistory* 6 (1959): 275, 299, 374.

58 Laura Peers, *The Ojibwa of Western Canada* (St Paul, MN, 1994), 56–7. For other examples of powerful Ottawa women involved in trading, see David Lavendar, *The Fist in the Wilderness* (1964; reprint, Albuquerque, 1979), 264–5.

59 Landes, *Ojibwa Woman*, 162–3, 169, 173, 176, 177. Men also may have occasionally performed duties assigned to women, in the absence of their wives. See Tanner, *Narrative*, 56.

60 Tanner, *Narrative*, 36, 37, 39, 40. Tanner demonstrates Netnokwa's ability as a trader in the transaction through which she obtained him from his original captors. On her dreams used to help her sons hunting, see 52, 72.

61 Gwen Morris, 'Gifted Woman Light around You: Ojibwa Women and Their Stories' (Ph.D. diss., University of Minnesota, 1992), 50–8.

62 Landes, *Ojibwa Woman*, 20; Kohl, *Kitchi-Gami*, 126–8.

63 Such visions or dreams were not usually discussed casually. See Kohl, *Kitchi-Gami*, 203.

64 Blair, ed., *Indian Tribes*, I:277. On Ojibwa-Dakota intermarriage in the region of the St Croix River, see William Warren, *History of the Ojibway People* (1885; reprint, St Paul, MN, 1984), 164.

65 Author's translation from Pierre Margry, *Découvertes et etablissements des français dans l'ouest et dans le sud de l'Amerique septentrionale* (1879–88; reprint ed., New York, 1974), 7, 32.

66 For descriptions of marriage customs, see Densmore, *Chippewa Customs*, 72–3; Hilger, *Chippewa Child Life,* 158–60; and Grant, 'The Sauteux Indians,' 320.

67 Peterson, 'The People in Between,' 71, 88

68 It is sometimes unclear whether the extensive influence of the Ojibwa leader made the trader successful, or whether traders backed with large capital helped increase the renown of Ojibwa leaders. This is an area that needs further research.

69 For a discussion or oratory and other leadership qualities, see James G.E. Smith, *Leadership among the Southwestern Ojibwa* (Ottawa, 1973), 17.

70 Malhiot journal, 6 (5 August 1804) and 27 (4 February 1805); George Nelson journal, 16 (7, 8, and 14 November 1803), original in Metropolitan Toronto Public Library; Warren, *History of the Ojibway People*, 48, 192, 318, 325, 372–7; Bruce M. White, *The Fur Trade in Minnesota: An Introductory Guide to Manuscript Sources* (St Paul, MN, 1977), 38, 45, 375. Even more distant Indian-trader kinship was still useful. According to Warren, 302, trader Michel Cadot, at Lac du Flambeau in the 1870s, derived benefits from the intercession of his wife's uncle. Warren does not give the name of this man, but it may be Keeshkemun.

71 B. White, *Fur Trade in Minnesota,* 41; Lawrence Taliaferro journal, 8 (9 October 1837): 92, Minnesota Historical Scoeity; Thomas L. McKenney et al., *The Indian Tribes of North America* (Edinburgh, 1934), 2:316–19; Kohl, *Kitchi-Gami*, 147–8; Henry R. Schoolcraft, *Personal Memoirs of a Residence of Thirty Years with the Indian Tribes on the American Frontiers* (Philadelphia, 1851), 293. Information on Charlotte, sometimes listed as Charlotte Kattawabide, after her father, is found in Montreal Protestant church

registers, compiled in MG 19, A2, series 4, National Archives of Canada, Ottawa. Charlotte died on 9 July 1850 at the age of seventy-five. See also the Ermatinger family history in MG 25, G38, National Archives of Canada.

72 For examples, see Malhiot journal, 32 (12 April 1805), 33 (26 April 1805), 34 (18 May 1805); Curot journal, 2 (14 August 1804), 16 (4 November 1804), 17 (6 November 1804); Nelson journal, 25 (13 March 1804).

73 Brown, *Strangers in Blood*, 81.

74 On Sayer's wife making sugar, see Curot journal, 39 (8 March 1804); John Sayer's journal, erroneously printed as that of Thomas Connor in Charles M. Gates, ed., *Five Fur Traders of the Northwest* (1933; reprint, St Paul, MN, 1965), 270 (1 March 1805); Nelson journal, 25. See also Douglas A. Birk, ed., *John Sayer's Journal, 1804–5* (Minneapolis, 1989), 49.

75 Nelson journal, 25.

76 Curot journal, 51 (15 May 1804).

77 The Ojibwa name Oshahgushkodanaqua, spelled in various ways, was translated by the woman's son-in-law, Henry R. Schoolcraft, as 'Woman of the Green Valley.' See Schoolcraft, *Personal Memoirs of a Residence of Thirty Years*, 431, 662, 676. It may be that the name is a garbled misspelling of some combination of the Ojibwe words for green (*ozhawaawashko-*, the lexical prefix for green or blue, occurring on verbs and on some nouns and participles), prairie or plain (*mashkode*), and woman (*ikwe*). See Nichols and Nyholm, *Concise Dictionary*, xii, 64, 78, 111.

78 Charles H. Chapman, 'The Historic Johnston Family of the 'Soo,' *Michigan Pioneer and Historical Collections* 32 (1903): 305–43. On 341, in letter six of a series of autobiographical letters written by John Johnston, there is reference to Mamongeseda's daughter as being a 'Mrs. Jayer.' However, an examination of the original letter (filed with the first letter of the series, 14 January 1828) in the Henry R. Schoolcraft Papers, Library of Congress, Washington, DC, suggests that the name should really be read as Sayer. On John Sayer, see Douglas A. Birk, 'John Sayer and the Fond du Lac Trade: The North West Company in Minnesota and Wisconsin,' in Buckley, ed., *Rendezvous*, 51–61. For the name of Sayer's wife, see Thomas L. McKenney, *Sketches of a Tour to the Lakes* (1827; reprint, Minneapolis, 1959), 485.

79 Anna Jameson, *Winter Studies and Summer Rambles in Canada* (London, 1838), 3:211–14.

80 Ibid., 217.

81 Ibid.

82 Chapman, 'The Historic Johnston Family,' 308, 313; Philip Mason, ed., *The Literary Voyager or Muzzeniegun* (Lansing, MI, 1963), xxv, xxxiii.

83 On the cultural nature of dreams experienced during vision quests, see
    Paul Radin, 'Some Aspects of Puberty Fasting among the Ojibwa,' *Museum
    Bulletin* 2: 69–78, and 'Ojibwa and Ottawa Puberty Dreams,' *Essays in
    Anthropology Presented to Alfred Kroeber* (Berkeley, CA, 1936), 233–64;
    Landes, *Ojibwa Woman*, 9–10.
84 Jones, *Ojibwa Texts*, vol. 7, part 2, 207–41; Henry R. Schoolcraft, *Schoolcraft's
    Indian Legends* (1956; reprint, Westport, CT, 1974), 87–91.
85 Jones, *Ojibwa Texts*, vol. 7, part 2, 256.
86 The word used by Kigage Pinasi for 'mystic cloth' was *manidowagin*,
    sometimes translated as 'spirit skin,' a term sometimes used to refer to the
    woollen cloth brought initially by French traders. Similarly, his word for
    beads was *manidominasa* or 'spirit seeds.' See Jones, *Ojibwa Texts*, vol. 7,
    part 2, 256. Both terms reflect the early wonder of the Ojibwa at European
    technology. For a discussion of these words and the beliefs behind them,
    see B. White, 'Encounters with Spirits,' 397, fn. 11, 398, fn. 12. Landes's
    informant described a woman with storng ability as a 'sucking doctor' in
    similar fashion. 'She dressed in red, green, blue, yellow, black, and wore
    beads of all colors and different kind of ribbons in her hair, and a feather
    sticking on her head and earrings, and beaded moccasins, and her face
    was painted' (Landes, *Ojibwa Woman*, 158).
87 As Ruth Landes noted in writing of women who tested the flexible bound-
    aries of Ojibwa gender roles: 'It cannot be assumed that one woman's
    motivations are similar to those of other women' (Landes, *Ojibwa Woman*,
    148). Landes also noted, 'The important factor is that a girl grows up
    seeing these unconventional possibilities about her, and sees them easily
    accepted' (140).
88 Maude Kegg, growing up around 1900, near Mille Lacs Lake, Minnesota,
    stated: 'That's the way they made their living, selling berries and buying
    lard, flour, sugar, whatever they needed.' See Kegg, *Portage Lake: Memories
    of an Ojibwa Childhood* (Edmonton, 1991), 47. Early examples of Indian
    people selling game, wild rice, and maple sugar in early Minnesota
    communities are described in Marjorie Kreidberg, *Food for the Frontier:
    Minnesota Cooking from 1850 to 1900* (St Paul, MN, 1975), 15–16, 18, 199.

4 Kateri Tekakwitha's Tortuous Path to Sainthood

NANCY SHOEMAKER

Kateri Tekakwitha died at Kahnawake in 1680 in the odour of sanctity (a sweet odour filled the room). Pilgrims from all over New France journeyed to her tomb to ask her to intercede with God on their behalf. In 1683, Tekakwitha's divine intervention saved several Jesuits from certain death when a windstorm caused the mission church at Kahnawake to collapse around them.[1] Ten years later, André Merlot's 'inflammation of the eyes' healed after he made a novena to Tekakwitha, rubbing his eyes with a solution of water, earth from Tekakwitha's grave, and ashes from her clothing.[2] Columbière, canon of the Cathedral of Quebec, testified in 1696 that his appeal to Tekakwitha relieved him of 'a slow fever, against which all remedies had been tried in vain, and of a diarrhea, which even ipecacuana could not cure.'[3] The Roman Catholic Church acknowledged Tekakwitha's holiness by declaring her venerable in 1943. In 1980, Tekakwitha was beatified. Perhaps soon, Tekakwitha will pass the next and final step of canonization and be recognized as a saint. She is the only Native American to rise so far in the saintly canon of the Catholic Church.[4]

Kateri Tekakwitha appears in most historical accounts of missionization in New France except, oddly enough, those that deal explicitly with women and missionization.[5] The now classic research of Eleanor Leacock and two recent books on women and missionization, one written by Karen Anderson and the other by Carol Devens, do not mention Tekakwitha.[6] More surprising is that the historical literature on Native women and religion in New France ignores the Iroquois, even though there is a voluminous literature debating the power of Iroquois women before and after European contact.[7] Leacock and Devens confined their studies to the Montagnais (an Algonquian-speaking tribe), while

Anderson's research focused on the Montagnais and Huron, who were culturally and linguistically related to the Iroquois but often at war with them.

Tekakwitha's experience does contradict the usual argument that missionaries forced Native people to adopt patriarchy along with Christianity and that missionization helped to devalue women's role in Native societies. The usual narrative of missionization's impact on Native women in New France describes how epidemic disease and progressively deeper involvement in the fur trade created an economic imbalance and a crisis of faith within Native communities; the Jesuits' persistent vilifying of Native customs, especially marriage customs, eventually led missionized Indians to abandon the old ways and accept the basic tenets of Christianity and Western culture.

The choicest pieces of evidence used to support the argument that Native people in New France ultimately conformed to missionary preachings and Western patriarchy come from a 1640 Jesuit account of the Montagnais mission at Sillery, which was recovering from a severe smallpox epidemic. One particular incident figures prominently in the arguments of Leacock, Anderson, and Devens. Several Montagnais women complained to the Jesuits that the men had brought them to a council to reprimand them:

> 'It is you women,' they [the men] said to us [the women], 'who are the cause of all our misfortunes, – it is you who keep the demons among us. You do not urge to be baptized; you must not be satisfied to ask this favor only once from the Fathers, you must importune them. You are lazy about going to prayers; when you pass before the cross, you never salute it; you wish to be independent. Now know that you will obey your husbands.'[8]

Leacock and Anderson gave this as evidence of missionized Indian men dominating women. Devens used this example to show that Native women resisted Christianity, partly because of its patriarchal implications. However, Devens's argument is weakened by her own discussion of how some Native women eagerly embraced Christianity.

These arguments presume a linear, assimilationist model of change and seem to come from a Western narrative tradition that depicts people as one thing, and after a crisis of some sort, they become another thing. However, it seems more likely that historical change is constantly in motion, perhaps moving in many different directions at once. Crisis may not lead automatically to permanent change but instead may simply be the moment in time when competing interests clash in a visible and tangible way. Smallpox made 1640 an especially stressful year in this Montagnais village, and men and women may have become embattled as they sought to reassert some control over their lives. Montagnais men were probably not successfully dominating women, but they may have been trying to and may have tried using the symbols of Christianity to do so. Some women may have in similar moments called upon the symbols of Christianity to assert their own identity and authority within the Native community

This narrative of a decline into patriarchy appeals to those of us with historical hindsight; however, even though we may view Christianity as part of a patriarchal, Western tradition that assisted in the conquest of America, Native people may have interpreted it differently. First, Roman Catholicism, especially in the way the Jesuit missionaries presented it, paralleled Iroquois religious beliefs, allowing certain aspects of Christianity to be easily incorporated. Second, Roman Catholicism, perhaps more than any other Christian religion, employs feminine imagery, such as the Virgin Mary and women saints, which could be co-opted by women as symbols of power. And third, while scholars of missionization in New France have emphasized Jesuit efforts to enforce monogamous, life-long marriages on Native converts as crucial to women's disempowerment, they have ignored the Jesuits' even more profound admiration of women who refused to marry, a novel idea when introduced to the Iroquois and one that some women may have appreciated as an alternative to their prescribed role within Iroquois society The Jesuits preached patriarchy but also brought to the Iroquois a toolkit of symbols, stories, and rituals that portrayed women as powerful or that gave women access to power. Just as Native people transformed Europeans' material toolkit of guns, blankets, and glass beads to suit their own needs, Iroquois women and men may have sometimes adopted, sometimes rejected, but continually worked to transform the spiritual and symbolic toolkit of Christianity to meet the needs of the moment.

The Jesuit compulsion to missionize in the Americas was partly the product of a religious revival that swept through élite circles in France in the early 1600s.[9] Jesuits first arrived at the French colonial settlement of Quebec in 1625. After briefly losing the colony to an alliance of English colonists and the disaffected French Protestants known as Huguenots, France re-established Quebec in 1632, and within the year the Jesuits arrived again, this time to set up permanent missions. At first, the Jesuits concentrated their missions among the Hurons, Montagnais, and Algonquins. They made several attempts to missionize the Iroquois but did not survive long in any of the Iroquois villages. However, some Iroquois, many of them Huron or Algonquin war captives who had been adopted into Iroquois families, left their villages to form Christian communities. One of the largest and must successful of these 'praying towns' was Kahnawake.

Kahnawake (or Caughnawaga) originated at La Prairie de la Madeleine near Montreal in the late 1660s. La Prairie consisted of three distinct, but interacting, communities: the Jesuit mission of St Francis Xavier, a village of French colonists, and a growing Native village of Algonquins, Hurons, and Iroquois. The first Native settlers at La Prairie were Catherine Gandeacteua, an Erie woman, and her Huron husband, Francois Xavier Tonsahoten. Both of them had previously learned about Christianity at Jesuit missions, but had then been taken captive and adopted into the Oneida tribe, one of the five Iroquois nations. By the early 1670s, Gandeacteua, Tonsahoten, and other members of their family had left their Oneida village and permanently settled near Montreal. For a variety of reasons, the Native village and the mission moved a few miles up the St Lawrence River to Sault St Louis in 1677. Although the French usually called this Indian settlement 'the Sault,' the Native inhabitants named their village Kahnawake, meaning 'at the sault' or falls in Mohawk, a reflection of the growing number of Mohawks who had joined the community. As the easternmost of the Iroquois tribes, the Mohawks were the first to feel most intensely the disruptive consequences of European contact, and many Mohawks came to see Kahnawake, with its strict prohibitions against alcohol, as a haven from the alcohol-induced violence plaguing Iroquois villages in the late 1600s.[10]

According to Tekakwitha's two hagiographers, the Jesuits Pierre Cholenec and Claude Chauchetière, Tekakwitha was one of the many Mohawks who sought refuge at Kahnawake.[11] She was born in 1656 at Gandaouague (now Auriesville, New York) near present-day Albany. Her mother was an Algonquin who had been missionized by the Jesuits at Trois-Rivières, and her father was Mohawk and a 'heathen.' When Tekakwitha was about four years old, a smallpox epidemic killed her immediate family and left Tekakwitha disfigured and with weak eyes that could not bear bright light. She was raised by her aunts and by an uncle who was considered one of the most powerful men in the village as well as a vehement opponent of Christianity.

As a young girl, Tekakwitha did what all Iroquois girls did. (However, she was also 'gentle, patient, chaste, innocent, and behaved like a well bred French child.')[12] She helped gather firewood, worked in the cornfields, and became skilled at various decorative crafts. And although she later 'looked back upon it as a great sin' requiring 'a severe penance,' she arrayed herself in typical Iroquois finery and engaged in other vanities.[13] When Tekakwitha reached marriageable age, her relatives began pressuring her to marry. At one point, they even arranged a marriage, but when the intended bridegroom came into the longhouse and seated himself next to Tekakwitha, by which custom the arranged marriage was revealed to her, she 'left the lodge and hid in the fields.'[14]

Tekakwitha first encountered the Jesuits as a young girl when Fathers Frémin, Bruyas, and Pierron stayed in her uncle's lodge while arranging to establish missions among the five Iroquois nations. It was not until several years later, however, that Tekakwitha received her first instruction in Christianity. Jacques de Lamberville, then Jesuit missionary to the Mohawk, visited Tekakwitha's lodge and found her eager to hear more, or at least she was one of the few Iroquois he could get to listen. (Her eye problems and other ailments often kept her confined to the longhouse while other women went to work in the cornfields.) He baptized her in 1676 and gave her the Christian name of Catherine.[15] Harassed by the non-Christian majority, Tekakwitha fled to Kahnawake about a year and a half later, arriving shortly after the village had relocated from La Prairie to Sault St Louis.

While at Kahnawake, Tekakwitha's enthusiasm for Christianity became more intense. She moved in with her adopted sister and faithfully learned Christian prayers and the lives of the saints from Anastasia, 'one of the most fervent Christians in the place' and the matrilineal head of the family in that longhouse.[16] Her first year there, she went on the winter hunt, as was the custom for residents of Kahnawake, but could not bear being deprived of Mass, the Eucharist, and daily prayer. She built her own shrine, a cross, in the woods and prayed to it, but would have preferred to be back in the village. The next winter, she refused to go on the hunt, which meant that she also chose to go without meat for the entire winter.

Once again, Tekakwitha's relatives, including Anastasia, pressured her to marry. They even solicited Cholonec's assistance in convincing Tekakwitha of the importance of marriage. At first Cholonec took the side of the relatives, for he knew that in Iroquois society women were dependent on men for clothing (provided through the hunt and later through the fur trade), and that, without a husband to contribute meat and hides to the longhouse, Tekakwitha was not helping herself or her longhouse family. But Tekakwitha insisted that she could 'have no other spouse but Jesus Christ.' Finally persuaded that she was 'inspired by the Holy Spirit,' Cholenec changed sides in the family dispute and began to defend Tekakwitha's decision to remain unmarried.[17]

Meanwhile, Tekakwitha had formed a close friendship with another young woman, Marie Therese. They dedicated themselves to each other, to Christianity, and to leading lives modelled after that of the nuns in Quebec and Montreal. Cholenec ascribed their knowledge of the nuns to Tekakwitha, and said that she had for herself seen how the hospital nuns in Montreal lived and had learned of their vows of chastity and penitential practices.[18] However, Chauchetière credited a third young woman, Marie Skarichions, with suggesting to Tekakwitha and Marie Therese that they model themselves after the nuns.[19] Skarichions was from Lorette, a community similar to Kahnawake but located near Quebec, and she had once been cared for there by the Sisters de la Hospitalière.

These three women determined to form their own association, in which they dedicated themselves to virginity and helped each other in their self-mortifications. Tekakwitha's penances were many and varied. She walked barefoot in ice and snow, burned her feet 'with a hot brand, very much in the same way that the Indians mark their slaves [war captives],' put coals and burning cinders between her toes, whipped her friends and was whipped by them in secret meetings in the woods, fasted, mixed ashes in her food, and slept for three nights on a bed of thorns after hearing the life story of Saint Louis de Gonzague.[20] Tekakwitha's self-mortification eventually took their toll and she became ill, so ill that Cholenec, making an exception for her, had to bring all his ritual equipment to her in her lodge to perform the last rites. She died at age twenty-four on 17 April 1680.

This narrative of Tekakwitha's life needs to be interpreted from two different perspectives. First, there is the issue of Tekakwitha as a Jesuit construction. Why did they think she might be a saint? How did their own culture shape the narrative of Tekakwitha's life story? Second, what was she really doing? Was she forsaking traditional Iroquois beliefs to become Christian or did her actions make sense within an Iroquois cultural framework?

Undeniably, Tekakwitha was to some extent a Jesuit construction.[21] If you were to strip this narrative of its occasional Iroquois element – the longhouse, women in the cornfields, the winter hunt – it could have taken place in fourteenth-century bourgeois Siena. Her life story follows the hackneyed plot-line typical of women's hagiographies, especially that of Saint Catherine of Siena, except that Tekakwitha did not live long enough to become an adviser to popes and kings.[22] First, there are the unrelenting relatives who try to force Tekakwitha into marriage, purportedly for her own sake but primarily for the economic advantage of the family as a whole. Then, there is her complete devotion to Christian ritual: persistent prayers, a particular emotional intensity expressed for the Holy Eucharist, and her feelings of desperation and longing when deprived of the ritual experience. And finally, like other women who by the seventeenth century had been recognized as saints or likely saints, Tekakwitha's reputation for holiness was based entirely on her dedication to virginity and her proclivity for abusing her own body. Because Tekakwitha's life story follows an established hagiographical model, it could be that Cholenec and Chauchetière fictionalized their narratives to make her life fit the model. However, it is more likely that they thought she might be a saint because her life fit the model so well.

There were other potential saints among the Indians at Kahnawake. There was, for instance, Catherine Gandeacteua, the founder of the Native village at La Prairie. The Jesuits praised her effusively, but according to the other model typical for women saints. Instead of being a self-mortifying virgin, Gandeacteua, 'like Saint Anne,' impoverished herself through her charity to others. She died before the village moved to the Sault, and so her body was buried at La Prairie. When the Native village moved, the Indians and the French colonists at La Prairie vied for who should possess her corpse.[23] The Indians probably planned to rebury Gandeacteua's body near the new village. The French at La Prairie, however, must have thought Gandeacteua had virtues worthy of a saint, for they wanted the body, 'the relics,' presumably so they could have access to her intercessory powers with God. It was the custom in Europe to pray for a saint's intercession at the tomb or to the more portable relics (the saint's bones, clothes, dirt from near the tomb, whatever had physically been the saint or been touched by the saint).[24] French colonists were probably suffering from saint-deprivation, for there were as yet no saints' tombs in New France and most of the more easily transported relics were still in Europe. In this unusual colonial struggle, the French won and Gandeacteua's body remained at La Prairie.

There were even more saintly possibilities among Tekakwitha's peers at Kahnawake. She was merely one of many to join in a penitential fervour that raged through the village in the late 1670s and early 1680s. According to Chauchetière,

> The first who began made her first attempt about Christmas in The year 1676 [the year before Tekakwitha arrived at Kahnawake], when she divested herself of her clothing, and exposed herself to The air at the foot of a large Cross that stands beside our Cemetery. She did so at a time when the snow was falling, although she was pregnant; and the snow that fell upon her back caused her so much suffering that she nearly died from it – as well as her child, whom the cold chilled in its mother's womb. It was her own idea to do this – to do penance for her sins, she said.[25]

Chauchetière then described how four of her friends, all women, followed her example but invented other, more elaborate forms of penance. Tekakwitha learned about penance from other Indians at Kahnawake and did not initiate the practice.[26]

Moreover, penitential practices seem to have reached their peak after Tekakwitha's death. Chauchetière gave the clearest account of this development in his short history of the mission at the Sault. After referring to how, in 1680, the 'mission gave to paradise a treasure which had been sent to it two years before, to wit, the blessed soul of Catherine Tegakwita, who died on the 17th of april,' Chauchetière recounted the events that transpired later that year:

> The demon [the devil], who saw the glorious success of this mission, used another kind of battery. Transfiguring himself as an angel of light, he urged on the devotion of some persons who wished to imitate Catherine, or to do severe penance for their sins. He drove them even into excess, – in order, no doubt, to render christianity hateful even at the start; or in order to impose upon the girls and women of this mission, whose discretion has never equaled that of catherine, whom they tried to imitate. There were Savage women who threw themselves under the ice, in the midst of winter. One had her daughter dipped into it, who was only six years old, – for the purpose, she said, of teaching her penance in good season. The mother stood there on account of her past sins; she kept her innocent daughter there on account of her sins to come, which this child would perhaps commit when grown up. Savages, both men and women, covered themselves with blood by disciplinary stripes with iron, with rods, with

thorns, with nettles; they fasted rigorously, passing the entire day without eating, – and what the savages eat during half the year is not sufficient to keep a man alive. These fasting women toiled strenuously all day – in summer, working in the fields; in winter, cutting wood. These austerities were almost continual. They mingled ashes in their portion of Sagamité; they put glowing coals between their toes, where the fire burned a hole in the flesh; they went bare-legged to make a long procession in the snows; they all disfigured themselves by cutting off their hair, in order not to be sought in marriage ... But the Holy Ghost soon intervened in this matter, enlightening all these persons, and regulated their conduct without diminishing their fervor.'[27]

For the Jesuits, who knew that one saint was rare and ten or twenty completely implausible, the only way to explain this was to distinguish Tekakwitha's self-mortifications as inspired by God and everyone else's as inspired by the devil.

Despite their attempts to isolate Tekakwitha as especially holy, the Jesuit accounts show that the entire village of Kahnawake, both men and women, but especially the women, were taking Christianity to an extreme. The Jesuits frequently mentioned having to intervene to 'regulate' penitential practices, and as Chauchetière admitted, 'The Savage women sometimes propound to us doubts in spiritual matters, as difficult as those that might be advanced by the most cultured persons in France.'[28] The Christian Indians at Kahnawake were inventive and self-motivated, exhibiting an independence and intensity which frightened the Jesuits because they risked being unable to control it. But still, from the Jesuits' perspective, Tekakwitha and the other Indians at Kahnawake were behaving in ways that were comprehensible as Christian.

However, the historical literature on missionization in New France has shown how Christian Indians created a syncretic religion, a new religion that melded traditional Native beliefs and Christian rituals.[29] The Jesuits assisted the syncretic process in their accommodationist approach to Native cultures. Similarities between Christianity and Iroquois religious beliefs, which the Jesuits rarely admitted to, also made syncretism possible.

The Jesuits' previous missionizing experiences and their scholarly emphasis led them to develop a somewhat sly missionary philosophy. They learned the Native language and worldview in order to package Christianity in a conceptual framework that was familiar to the people they were attempting to missionize. In China, the Jesuits had first tried to ease into Chinese society by looking and acting like Buddhist monks. They then switched to the more comfortable role of scholar, and began to dress and act like the Chinese literati.[30] In New France, the Jesuits retained their usual style of dress, which is why the Indians called them 'Black Robes,' but slid into the only social category that approximated what they were: shamans. And even though the Jesuits saw themselves as superior to the Native 'conjurors,' they did act just like shamans. They performed wondrous miracles by foretelling eclipses.[31] They interpreted 'visions,' while railing against Native shamans who interpreted 'dreams.'[32] To cure people, they had their own set of mysterious and powerful rituals, such as bleeding, songs and prayers, and strange ritual implements.[33] Since they feared backsliders and usually only baptized adults who were on the verge of death, they were often perceived as either incompetent shamans or shamans who used their powers for evil purposes.[34] But, in any case, the Indians were able to view them as people who had access to special powers.

These special powers were most observable in the new rituals which the Jesuits introduced to the Indians. Tangible manifestations of Christianity proved to be more important than theology in assisting the missionizing effort. Visual images and stories about people, either Bible stories or saints' lives, were the most efficacious missionary tools. Chauchetière was especially proud of his collection of religious paintings and drawings, some of which he drew himself or copied from other works. His depiction of 'the pains of hell' was 'very effective among the savages.' The mission church at Kahnawake also had on display 'paintings of the four ends of man, along with the moral paintings of M. le Nobletz,' and eventually, after Tekakwitha's death, a series of paintings by Chauchetière depicting events in her life.[35]

Although the Jesuits may have shied away from attempting to explain the abstract principles of Christianity, which could not easily be translated into Native languages anyhow, there were conceptual similarities between Iroquois religious beliefs and seventeenth-century Catholicism which also furthered missionization. Christian origin stories, from Adam and Eve to the birth of Jesus Christ, are similar to the Iroquois origin story, which even has an Immaculate Conception.[36] The Holy Family – the somewhat distant and unimportant Joseph, the powerful and virtuous Virgin Mary, her mother, St Anne, and the son, Jesus Christ – was structurally more like the matrilineal Iroquois family than the patriarchal nuclear family of Western culture.[37] And the rosary, a string of beads with spiritual significance, resembled Iroquois wampum, belts and necklaces made of shell beads, which had spiritual and political meaning.[38] Indeed, many of the actions of Christianized Indians, which the Jesuits proudly recorded and took credit for, conformed to the cultural norms of traditional Iroquois society. Gandeacteua's Christian virtues – her generosity, especially in giving food and clothing to the poor, and her complete disavowal of all her personal possessions when she heard, mistakenly, that her husband had died – were more than virtues among the Iroquois; they were established customs.[39]

In emphasizing the syncretism of Christianity at Kahnawake, however, I do not want to belittle the significance of becoming Christian as people at the time perceived it. Christian Indians did see themselves as different, and non-Christian Indians ascribed a distinct identity to Christian Indians, even if they lived within the same village and spoke the same language. Also, even though the Indians at Kahnawake maintained many of their traditional beliefs and customs, they agreed to conform to some Jesuit demands, such as their prohibition of divorce.[40] For an Iroquois in the seventeenth century, becoming Christian and choosing to live near the Jesuits would have been a difficult decision, for the Iroquois rightly associated Christian missions with the French, who were, except for brief interludes, their enemies. The tensions arising from such a decision reached their peak in the early 1680s, when the Iroquois at Kahnawake reluctantly joined the French in a war against the main body of Iroquois to their south.[41]

Also, despite the conceptual similarities between Iroquois beliefs and Christianity, those who converted to Christianity do seem to have been already marginal within their communities. As Daniel Richter has observed, many of the residents at Kahnawake were former war captives who had been adopted into Iroquois families.[42] This might also explain the prominence of women in the mission accounts of Kahnawake. Since female war captives were more likely than men to be adopted permanently into the tribe, many Iroquois women had a dual ethnic identity. Tekakwitha's marginality came from two directions: her mother and her disfigurement from smallpox. The Mohawks in Tekakwitha's original village thought of her as an Algonquin, suggesting that her mother, although presumably formally adopted as Iroquois, still strongly identified as Algonquin or was strongly identified by others as Algonquin.[43] According to her hagiographers, Tekakwitha was also self-conscious about her weak eyes and her smallpox scars. Unlike other Iroquois women, she always tried to keep her face covered with her blanket.

Supposedly, some of her fellow villagers ridiculed her and said, after she died, 'that God had taken her because men did not want her.'[44]

The marginality of Tekakwitha and adopted Iroquois women might explain why they, and not others, chose Christianity, but it does not explain what they saw in Christianity. In Tekakwitha's case, there seem to have been three conceptual similarities between Iroquois beliefs and seventeenth-century Catholicism which make her actions comprehensible from both the Iroquois and Jesuit cultural perspectives. First, the Iroquois Requickening ceremony and the Christian ceremony of' baptism, though conducted through different kinds of rituals, achieved the same end of renewal through imitation. Second, the Iroquois and the Jesuits employed voluntary societies as an additional level of social organization beyond the family and the political council. Voluntary societies served as an avenue by which individual women and men could acquire prestige, authority, and kin-like bonds within the larger community. And third, Iroquois and Jesuit beliefs about the body, the soul, and power were similar enough to allow for a syncretic adoption of self-denial and self-mortification as spiritually and physically empowering acts.

Undeniably, the Jesuits favoured men in their daily administration of the mission. If given the choice, the Jesuits would have preferred to have more male converts, especially men of influence, than female converts. The Jesuits also granted men more authority and prestige by giving them roles as assistants in church services and by making them 'dogiques' (Native catechists). However, women turned Christianity to their advantage and incorporated the ritual of baptism, Christian societies, virginity, and penance as means to establishing a firmer place for themselves in a changing Iroquois society.

First, the Christian ritual of baptism resembled an Iroquois Requickening ceremony. In both ceremonies, someone assumed the name and the metaphorical identity of an important person who had died. In both ceremonies, water played a purifying role. The Jesuits sprinkled holy water to mark the baptismal moment, whereas the Iroquois drank 'water of pity' to signify the transition to a new identity. Among the Iroquois, names of important people were passed on within clans. Individuals from later generations assumed these names and were expected to live up to them by imitating the person who had died and by fulfilling the obligations that went along with the name. For instance, when the Jesuit Lafitau arrived as a missionary at Kahnawake in 1712, the Iroquois requickened him in the place of Father Bruyas.[45]

Although men and women could be renamed and 'requickened,' the ceremony was also held as part of the Condolence ceremony, the raising up of a new chief, and therefore was in its most prestigious manifestation held as a ceremony for men.[46]

The Jesuits introduced the Iroquois to new images of women in their stories of the Virgin Mary and women saints, and then provided the ritual, baptism, which encouraged imitation of these seemingly powerful women. When Tekakwitha was baptized, 'the spirit of Saint Katherine of Sienna and of other saints of this name, was revived in her.'[47] She was at the same time requickened as Saint Catherine of Siena, a woman whom the Jesuits featured prominently in their stories and devotions. Tekakwitha probably was deliberately modelling herself after her namesake. She would have heard the story of Saint Catherine's life many times – the fasting and penitential practices, her refusal to marry and her marriage to Jesus Christ in a vision, and her later role as an adviser to male political leaders. Tekakwitha and the other women at Kahnawake may have sensed the underlying patriarchy of the Jesuit mission, but also heard the Jesuits talk of powerful women, like Saint Catherine of Siena, and were urged to imitate them.

Second, the women at Kahnawake used the model of the Christian society to enhance their collective role as the women of the village. One such Christian association was the Confraternity of the Holy Family, an organization of men and women which the Jesuits established at Kahnawake to bind the most devoted Christians together.[48] Women appear to have been among the most active participants in this organization. Perhaps the Jesuits' use of the 'holy family' as the model for this society's devotions inspired its members to assume a matrilineal organization for determining members' relationships, mutual obligations, and decision-making powers.

The Jesuits viewed the Confraternity of the Holy Family as a successful operation, but expressed some doubts about the indigenous Christian organizations sprouting at Kahnawake. For example, Tekakwitha and her two friends attempted to form a nunnery. They planned to leave the village and set up a separate community of Christian women on Heron Island, until Father Frémin talked them out of it.[49] Chauchetière described another women's organization in connection with the penitential practices adopted at Kahnawake:

The use of these [instruments of penance] Daily becomes more general. And, as The men have found that the women use them, they will not Let themselves be outdone, and ask us to permit them to use these every Day; but we will not allow it. The women, to the number of 8 or 10, Began The practice; and The wife of the dogique – that is to say, of him who Leads the Singing and says The prayers – is among the number. She it is who, in her husband's absence, also causes The prayers to be said aloud, and Leads The Singing, and in this capacity she assembles the devout women of whom we have spoken, who call themselves sisters. They tell One another their faults, and deliberate together upon what must be done for The relief of the poor in the Village – whose number is so great that there are almost as many poor as there are Savages. The sort of monastery that they maintain here has its rules. They have promised God never to put on their gala-dress ... They assist One another in the fields; They meet together to incite one another to virtue; and one of them has been received as a nun in The hospital of monreal.[50]

Chauchetière's account suggests that women deliberately formed these societies as an alternative to the gender-mixed Confraternity of the Holy Family and that the men at Kahnawake viewed women's societies as a challenge to their own authority and status.

However, 'confraternities' were fundamental, well-established components of Iroquois village life. Iroquois women used similar 'confraternities' to organize their work and acknowledge women's achievements.[51] The Iroquois also had healing societies, like the False-Faces, which possessed a specialized knowledge and their own healing rituals.[52] The women at Kahnawake added to this familiar kind of social institution the newly introduced, Christian example of the nunnery, of which several existed in New France. In Quebec in 1639, the Ursulines arrived to start a mission school for Indian girls and the Sisters de la Hospitalière opened a hospital. Later, Montreal also had some hospital sisters.[53] Although the Catholic Church restricted the authority of women's religious orders by making them ultimately subject to a male director, the women at Kahnawake were more likely to be aware of how these women, because of their unusual lifestyle and their healing activities, appeared to be powerful and respected members of French colonial society. As their husbands became the Jesuits' 'dogiques,' women may have refashioned their work-oriented organization after the Christian model to reassert a traditional balance of power, which the Jesuits were disrupting by appointing men to positions of power and high status. The women's dedication to penance, and the envy among the men which this inspired, further suggests that both men and women at Kahnawake came to view penance as an empowering ritual.

Iroquois and Jesuit philosophies about the relationship between the body, the soul, and power illuminate why Tekakwitha and the other residents of Kahnawake accepted the Christian ideals of virginity and penance. In Catholic and Iroquois religious traditions there was an ambivalence about the connection between the body and the soul. Both belief systems characterized the soul as a separate entity from the body, but elaborate funerary rites and the homage paid to soulless corpses show that they were reluctant to disavow all connections between the soul and the body. In Catholic theology, the soul left the body upon death and, in the case of saints and other holy people, resided in heaven. The Iroquois believed the soul left the body at death and lived an afterlife that would be like life on earth, but better.[54] The Iroquois also believed that the soul left living bodies while they were asleep. Dreamers made trips to this other world and brought back important messages needing interpretation. Shamans' skills included diagnosing these dreams so that they could be acted upon for the good of the individual and the community.[55] Although Iroquois dream interpretation was from the Jesuit point of view one of the most despicable and pagan aspects of Iroquois culture, in the Catholic tradition, holy people also bridged these two worlds. In their lifetime, they might have visions which connected them to the Virgin Mary or Jesus Christ, and after their death, they became the intercessors for others.

Saints functioned like guardian spirits, which in Iroquois culture were not people who had died but instead were animals or some other being that was part of the natural world.[56] In Iroquois tradition, a token (which might be a feather, a pebble, or a piece of oddly shaped wood) was the physical key to the spiritual world, just as Catholics prayed to the saint's physical remains, to a relic, or at the tomb to reach guardian angels and saints.[57] Since the Iroquois believed everything in nature had a soul, unlike Christians who believed only people did, their range of possible guardian spirits was broader. However, the idea of appealing to a guardian spirit for miraculous cures, success in hunting and warfare, for love and happiness, or for special powers was part of both religions. Among the Iroquois, everyone and everything had some power, or 'orenda,' but some had more than others.[58] This power could be called upon by appeals to guardian spirits, and could be used for either good or bad. The Jesuits believed that only a few were graced with divine power. And even though they had earthly authority as administrators of Christianity, it was a rare Jesuit who was also graced with divine authority, as a martyr or as someone who exhibited such extreme devotion to Christian ideals that they had to be a saint.

Within the Christian tradition, it was difficult for women to acquire authority on earth, but mystical experiences and Christian virtue carried to extremes produced saints. Self-mortification, virginity, and especially fasting appear in most hagiographies but especially dominate in the stories of women saints' lives. Refuting other scholars' claims that bodily abuse was an expression of women's hatred of their bodies, Rudolph Bell in *Holy Anorexia* and Caroline Walker Bynum in *Holy Feast and Holy Famine* argued that women seeking a sense of identity and self-assertion tried to control their world through the only means available, by controlling their own bodies and by controlling the symbols of women's domestic authority, such as food distribution. By fasting, making a vow of chastity, and engaging in penitential self-abuse, Catherine of Siena and other women saints revealed that they were among the select few graced with divine authority. As in the case of Catherine of Siena, a woman saint's divine authority could bring her some earthly authority as well, authority over her own life as well as over the lives of others. Saint Catherine of Siena's marriage to Jesus Christ in a vision partly explained why she could not marry on earth and also gave her the authority to tell kings and popes what to do.

In Iroquois society, one could similarly acquire power by controlling one's own body through fasting and sexual abstinence. Although life-long celibacy struck the Iroquois as odd, virginity and sexual abstinence were conceived of as sources of power.[59] Virgins had certain ceremonial rules, and Iroquois legends told of there having once been a society of virgins.[60] The Iroquois viewed sexual abstinence as an avenue to physical and spiritual strength and as essential to men's preparations for war and the hunt. Fasting and tests of physical endurance also could be used as a means to acquire power. The Iroquois coming-of-age ritual for young men and women was a vision quest.[61] They went into the woods by themselves, fasted, and hoped to receive a vision or token from a guardian spirit. Those with especially powerful visions might become shamans (professional healers and visionaries).[62] Since some Indian residents at Kahnawake accused Tekakwitha of being a 'sorceress,' apparently the same acts that inspired the Jesuits to think of her as holy also gave her access to 'orenda.'[63]

Bell and Bynum revealed how virginity and fasting had a special meaning for women saints in medieval Europe. In contrast, among the Iroquois, virginity and fasting seem to have been equally available to men and women as sources of individual empowerment. Still, Bell's and Bynum's analyses of the relationship between food and control can shed light on why the Iroquois had a more democratic understanding of who could acquire 'orenda' and how. Although Iroquois women controlled the distribution of food, both men and women made important, complementary contributions to food production. Women grew corn, and men hunted meat. Moreover, both men and women equally shared in their fear of starvation during winter. Iroquois rituals – many of which involved fasting, feasting, or cannibalism – all show an obsession with food, which may have been a cultural expression of their daily anxieties about an uncertain supply of food in the future.

Virginity and fasting resonated with Iroquois traditions. Penance was an entirely new ritual, but one that paralleled Iroquois ritual torture of war captives. The Iroquois adopted all war captives into the place of deceased clan members, and clans then chose whether the adoptee would live or die in the spirit of their namesake. Those consigned to die in the place of a mourned relative were put through a lengthy and painful series of tortures, after which parts of their body might be eaten. If the captive had died an especially brave death, he (usually it was a he) was more likely to be eaten because his body parts were seen as possessing that strength and courage. Through ritual torture, war captives became the repositories for violent emotions; by directing anxiety, stress, and grief for dead relatives outward, the Iroquois kept peace among themselves.[64]

Although the Jesuits condemned Iroquois torture, they recognized awkward similarities between Iroquois cannibalism and the Eucharist. The Eucharist is a metaphoric ritual in which participants eat the body of Christ and drink his blood, a reference to the theological notion that Christ sacrificed himself so that others might live. Fearing that the Iroquois might think they condoned cannibalism, the Jesuits translated the Eucharist to mean a feast and did not tell the Iroquois about its sacrificial connotations.[65] If it had not been so uncomfortably reminiscent of Iroquois ritual cannibalism, the Eucharist might have been a useful missionizing tool, with which the Jesuits could have offered the Iroquois a ritual to replace the torture of war captives.

However, David Blanchard has argued that the Indians at Kahnawake replaced the ritual torture of war captives with ritual self-torture. They called their penitential practices 'hotouongannandi,' which Chauchetière translated to mean 'public penance.'[66] According to Blanchard, a better translation of the term would be 'They are making magic,' suggesting that the Iroquois saw penitential practices as a ritual source of power. Blanchard emphasizes the importance of this ritual in helping the Iroquois, as in their dreams, to leave the world on earth and visit 'the sky world.'[67] It is also important to emphasize, however, that they used visits to 'the sky world' to control and improve life on earth.

The Indians at Kahnawake probably saw penance as a powerful healing and prophylactic ritual. Since the penitential practices at Kahnawake began at about the same time as a 1678 smallpox epidemic, which ebbed quickly and caused little damage, penitents at Kahnawake may even have viewed penance as an especially effective ritual to counter new diseases like smallpox.[68] The rise of penitential practices in Europe, evident in such movements as the Flagellants, which emerged after the Bubonic Plague, suggests that Christians in fourteenth-century Europe also thought that self-induced abuse of the body was a means to control the uncontrollable.[69] Also, the Iroquois at Kahnawake may have viewed penance as a prophylactic ritual to prevent torture and death at the hands of one's enemies. The Jesuits deliberately drew analogies between Christian hell and the torture of war captives practised by northeastern Indians, and promised that Christian devotion would save one from an eternity in hell.[70]

In conclusion, the Iroquois who adopted Christianity did so for reasons that made sense within an Iroquois cultural framework. Certain Christian rituals fit easily into traditional Iroquois beliefs, while the new ritual practices, like penance, offered a special power lacking in traditional Iroquois rituals. Whereas the Jesuits emphasized the importance of Christian ritual in determining one's place in the afterlife, Tekakwitha and other Christian Iroquois had new and pressing needs for empowering rituals to control the increasingly uncertain, earthly present. Smallpox, increased warfare, alcohol, and the economic and political assaults on traditional gender roles did create a growing sense of crisis in Iroquois communities. To deal with that crisis and control their changing world, many Iroquois women and men turned to Christianity. However, they did not become Christian in the way the Jesuits intended; instead, they transformed Christianity into an Iroquois religion.

During one particular moment of crisis at Kahnawake in the 1670s and 1680s, Iroquois women and men struggled to reshape the Jesuits' preachings into something meaningful for them. Part of the struggle had to do with the patriarchal structure of Christianity. The Jesuits supported male authority in the village by promoting men as administers of Christianity and Church activities. Women responded by using Christian symbols to assert their authority and identity within the community. Through a syncretic transformation of the ritual of baptism, the Christian society, virginity, and self-mortification, Tekakwitha appeared holy and Christian to the Jesuits while pursuing status and a firmer sense of her own identity within Iroquois society. The Jesuits tried to implement patriarchy at their missions, but they also brought the symbols, imagery, and rituals women needed to subvert patriarchy.

NOTES

The author thanks Deborah Sommer and Louis Dupont for their help with this article.

1 Claude Chauchetière in 'Annual Narrative of the Mission of the Sault, from Its Foundation until the Year 1686,' in *The Jesuit Relations and Allied Documents: Travels and Explorations of the Jesuit Missionaries in New France, 1610–1791 (JR)*, ed. Reuben Gold Thwaites (New York: Pageant, 1959), 63:229. Pierre Cholenec more elaborately tells how Tekakwitha appeared to Chauchetière in a vision and prophesied the destruction of the church in 'The Life of Katharine Tegakoüita, First Iroquois Virgin' (1696), Document X, in *The Positio of the Historical Section of the Sacred Congregation of Rites on the Introduction of the Cause for Beatification and Canonization and on the Virtues of the Servant of God Katharine Tekakwitha, the Lily of the Mohawks*, ed. Robert E. Holland (New York: Fordham University Press, 1940), 312.

2 Peter Rémy to Father Cholenec, 12 March 1696, Document IX, in *The Positio*, 227.

3 Columbière is quoted in 'Letter from Father Cholenec, Missionary of the Society of Jesus, to Father Augustin Le Blanc of the Same Society, Procurator of Missions in Canada,' in *The Early Jesuit Missions in North America: Compiled and Translated from the Letters of the French Jesuits, with Notes*, ed. William Ingraham Kip (Albany: Joel Munscll, 1873), 115.

4 'Lily of the Mohawks,' *Newsweek* 12 (1 August 1938), 27–8; 'The Long Road to Sainthood,' *Time* 116 (7 July 1980), 42–3. At about the time of Tekakwitha's beatification, the Catholic Church undertook a major reform of the saint-making process and reduced the number of miracles required for beatification and canonization. Under the old rules, Tekakwitha needed two

documented miracles to be beatified or declared 'blessed.' Under the new rules, she only needed one. However, even though Tekakwitha is credited with many miracles, not one was able to meet the documentation standards required by the Catholic Church. Pope John Paul II waived this requirement for her, perhaps to give American Indians a saint of their own. To be canonized, and thereby declared a 'saint,' she would need two miracles according to the new rules, but since the documentation standards have already been waived for her, it is not clear whether there are any remaining obstacles to her canonization. See Kenneth L. Woodward, *Making Saints: How the Catholic Church Determines Who Becomes a Saint, Who Doesn't, and Why* (New York: Simon and Schuster, 1990), 99, 117–88, 208, 217.

5 James Axtell, *The Invasion Within: The Contest of Cultures in Colonial North America* (New York: Oxford University Press, 1985), 23–127; Cornelius J. Jaenen, *Friend and Foe: Aspects of French-Amerindian Cultural Contact in the Sixteenth and Seventeenth Centuries* (New York: Columbia University Press, 1976); Daniel K. Richter, *The Ordeal of the Longhouse: The Peoples of the Iroquois League in the Era of European Colonization* (Chapel Hill: University of North Carolina Press, 1992), 105–32.

6 Eleanor Burke Leacock, 'Montagnais Women and the Jesuit Program for Colonization,' in *Myths of Male Dominance: Collected Articles on Women Cross-Culturally*, ed. Eleanor Burke Leacock (New York: Monthly Review Press, 1981), 43–62; Karen Anderson, *Chain Her by One Foot: The Subjugation of Women in Seventeenth-Century New France* (New York: Routledge, 1991); Carol Devens, *Countering Colonization: Native American Women and Great Lakes Missions, 1630– 1900* (Berkeley: University of California Press, 1992), 7–30. An exception is Natalie Zemon Davis's article 'Iroquois Women, European Women,' which argues that Christianity may have given Indian women in New France access to a public voice denied them in traditional Iroquois oratory. This article is in *Women, 'Race,' and Writing in the Early Modern Period*, ed. Margo Hendricks and Patricia Parker (New York: Routledge, 1994), 243–58, 350–61.

7 W.G. Spittal, *Iroquois Women: An Anthology* (Ohsweken, ON: Iroqrafts, 1990).

8 *JR*, 18 (1640): 105–7; Leacock, 'Montagnais Women,' 52; Anderson, *Chain Her by One Foot*, 219; Devens, *Countering Colonization*, 7.

9 W.J. Eccles, *France in America* (New York: Harper and Row, 1972); Cornelius J. Jaenen, *The Role of the Church in New France* (Toronto: McGraw-Hill Ryerson, 1976); J.H. Kennedy, *Jesuit and Savage in New France* (New Haven: Yale University Press, 1950).

10 Chauchetière, *JR*, 63 (1686): 141–245; *JR*, 61 (1679): 239–41; Henri Béchard, *The Original Caughnawaga Indians* (Montreal: International Publishers, 1976); E.J. Devine, *Historic Caughnawaga* (Montreal: Messenger Press, 1922); Gretchen Lynn Green, 'A New People in an Age of War: The Kahnawake Iroquois, 1667–1760' (Ph.D. diss., College of William and Mary, 1991).

11 The historical documents on Tekakwitha are conveniently available in *The Positio*, the compendium of materials used by the Vatican to determine whether she was worthy of Veneration. Cholenec, who headed the mission at Caughnawaga during Tekakwitha's stay there, wrote at least four versions of her life, which are usually but not entirely consistent. The 1696 'Life' (Document X in *The Positio*) is the most elaborate in describing Tekakwitha's virtues, trials, and posthumous miracles. Document XII, which also appears in Kip, is Cholenec's 1715 letter to Augustin Le Blanc and is a more straightforward account. Chauchetière's 'The Life of the Good Katharine Tegakoüita, Now Known as the Holy Savage,' probably first drafted in 1685 and revised or amended in 1695, is Document VIII in *The Positio*. Cholenec, Chauchetière, and Frémin (who apparently chose not to write a life of Tekakwitha) were the Jesuits stationed at Kahnawake during the time Tekakwitha lived there.

12 Chauchetière, *The Positio*, 121.

13 Cholenec, in Kip, *Early Jesuit Missions*, 83.

14 Chauchetière, *The Positio*, 125.

15 Catharine, Katharine, Katherine, Catherine, Kateri ('gadeli,' as it is pronounced among the Mohawks), and Katerei all appear in the records; Kateri seems to be the more accepted contemporary term.

16 Cholenec, in Kip, *Early Jesuit Missions*, 95.

17 Ibid., 105.

18 Ibid., 108.

19 Chauchetière, *The Positio*, 175.

20 Cholonec, in Kip, *Early Jesuit Missions*, 111; Cholenec, *The Positio*, 295.

21 K.I. Koppedrayer, 'The Making of the First Iroquois Virgin: Early Jesuit Biographies of the Blessed Kateri Tekakwitha,' *Ethnohistory* 40 (1993): 277–306.

22 Rudolph M. Bell, *Holy Anorexia* (Chicago: University of Chicago Press, 1985); Caroline Walker Bynum, *Holy Feast and Holy Fast: The Religious Significance of Food to Medieval Women* (Berkeley: University of California Press, 1987); Donald Weinstein and Rudolph M. Bell, *Saints and Society: The Two Worlds of Western Christendom, 1000–1700* (Chicago: University of Chicago Press, 1982).

23 Chauchetière, *The Positio*, 161, 165.

24 Peter Brown, *The Cult of the Saints: Its Rise and Function in Latin Christianity* (Chicago: University of Chicago Press, 1981).
25 Chauchetière, *JR*, 62 (1682): 175.
26 Cholonec, in Kip, *Early Jesuit Missions*, 98–9.
27 Chauchetière, *JR*, 63 (1686): 215–19; see also Cholonec, in Kip, *Early Jesuit Missions*, 106–8.
28 Chauchetière, *JR*, 62 (1682): 187.
29 See Axtell, *Invasion Within*; Jaenen, *Friend and Foe*; David Blanchard, '... To the Other Side of the Sky: Catholicism at Kahnawake, 1667–1700,' *Anthropologica* 24 (1982): 77–102. See also Henry Warner Bowden's discussion of the Hurons and the Jesuits in *American Indians and Christian Missions: Studies in Cultural Conflict* (Chicago: University of Chicago Press, 1981), 59–95; James P. Ronda and James Axtell, *Indian Missions: A Critical Bibliography* (Bloomington: Indiana University Press, 1978).
30 Jacques Gernet, *China and the Christian Impact: A Conflict of Cultures* (New York: Cambridge University Press, 1985); Charles E. Ronan and Bonnie B.C. Oh, *East Meets West: The Jesuits in China, 1582–1773* (Chicago: Loyola University Press, 1988).
31 *JR*, 58 (1673–4): 181–3; *JR*, 62 (1683): 199.
32 *JR*, 60 (1675): 61–3.
33 Le Jeune's 1634 Relation of his mission among the Montagnais, in *JR*, 7, shows in great detail how Jesuits deliberately competed with shamans to prove their superior access to supernatural authority.
34 *JR*, 6 (1634): 139; *JR*, 58 (1673–4): 191, 219–21; *JR*, 61 (1679): 229.
35 Chauchetière, *The Positio*, 115–16. See also *JR*, 5 (1633): 257–9; François-Marc Gagnon, *La conversion par l'image: Un aspect de la mission des Jésuites auprès des Indiéns du Canada au XVIIe siècle* (Montreal: Les Éditions Bellarmin, 1975).
36 Hazel W. Hertzberg, *The Great Tree and the Longhouse: The Culture of the Iroquois* (New York: Macmillan, 1966); J.N.B. Hewitt, 'Iroquoian Cosmology,' Part Two, *Annual Report*, Bureau of American Ethnology, 1925–6 (Washington, DC: 1928), 465.
37 For example, see Pamela Sheingorn, 'The Holy Kinship: The Ascendency of Matriliny in Sacred Genealogy of the Fifteenth Century,' *Thought* 64 (1989): 268–86. Also, for a fascinating discussion of how the Jesuits responded to Iroquoian matrilineality and their own need for a patriarchal authority structure to justify their role as 'fathers,' see John Steckley, 'The Warrior and the Lineage: Jesuit Use of Iroquoian Images to Communicate Christianity,' *Ethnohistory* 39 (1992): 478–509.

38 *JR*, 58 (1673–4): 185–9; Blanchard's '... To the Other Side of the Sky' discusses the rosary-wampum syncretism at length.

39 Chauchetière, *The Positio*, 162.

40 *JR*, 58 (1672–3): 77.

41 Daniel K. Richter, 'Iroquois versus Iroquois: Jesuit Missions and Christianity in Village Politics, 1642–1686,' *Ethnohistory* 32 (1985): 1–16.

42 Richter, *The Ordeal of the Longhouse*, 124–8.

43 Cholonec, in Kip, *Early Jesuit Missions*, 87.

44 Chauchetière, *The Positio*, 123.

45 Joseph François Lafitau, *Customs of the American Indians Compared with the Customs of Primitive Times* (Toronto: The Champlain Society, 1977), 2:240, 1:xxxi; J.N.B. Hewitt, 'The Requickening Address of the Condolence Council,' ed. William N. Fenton, *Journal of the Washington Academy of Sciences* 34 (1944): 65–85.

46 Lafitau, *Customs*, 1:71; *JR*, 60 (1675): 37.

47 Chauchetière, *The Positio*, 169, 137.

48 *JR*, 58 (1672–3): 77; Cholonec, *JR*, 60 (1677): 281.

49 Chauchetière, *The Positio*, 176.

50 Chauchetière, *JR*, 62 (1681–3): 179. See also Chauchetière, *JR*, 63 (1686): 203–5.

51 Arthur C. Parker, 'Secret Medicine Societies of the Seneca,' *American Anthropologist*, n.s., 11 (1909): 161–85; Lafitau, 2:54–5.

52 William N. Fenton, *The False Faces of the Iroquois* (Norman: University of Oklahoma Press, 1987).

53 Joyce Marshall, ed., *Word from New France: The Selected Letters of Marie De L'Incarnation* (Toronto: Oxford University Press, 1967).

54 Lafitau, *Customs*, 2:230–1, 237–8; for a comparison of Huron (Iroquoian) and Christian conceptions of the soul, see *JR*, 7 (1635): 293; *JR*, 10 (1636): 287. See also John Steckley's linguistic analysis of these concepts in Huron in 'Brébeuf's Presentation of Catholicism in the Huron Language: A Descriptive Overview,' *Revue de l'Université d'Ottawa / University of Ottawa Quarterly* 48 (1978): 93–115. Much of my perspective on Christian beliefs about the soul and the body is based on Caroline Walker Bynum's work, especially the articles collected in *Fragmentation and Redemption: Essays on Gender and the Human Body in Medieval Religion* (New York: Zone Books, 1991). Although her discussion refers to medieval Europe, she could just as easily have been describing the beliefs of seventeenth-century Jesuits, as revealed by their self-reflexive remarks on Iroquois differences in the *Jesuit Relations*.

55 Lafitau, *Customs*, 1:231–4; *JR*, 54 (1669–70): 65–73; Anthony F.C. Wallace, 'Dreams and the Wishes of the Soul: A Type of Psychoanalytic Theory among the Seventeenth Century Iroquois,' *American Anthropologist* 60 (1958): 234–48.

56 Lafitau, *Customs*, 1:230.

57 Ibid., 1:236, 243; 'Narrative of a Journey into the Mohawk and Oneida Country, 1634–1635,' in *Narratives of the New Netherland, 1609–1664*, ed. J. Franklin Jameson (New York: Charles Scribner's Sons, 1909), 137–62.

58 J.N.B. Hewitt, 'Orenda and a Definition of Religion,' *American Anthropologist*, n.s., 4 (1902): 33–46; Hope l. Isaacs, 'Orenda and the Concept of Power among the Tonawanda Senecas,' in *the Anthropology of Power: Ethnographic Studies from Asia, Oceania, and the New World*, ed. Raymond D. Fogelson and Richard N. Adams (New York: Academic Press, 1977), 167–84.

59 Lafitau, *Customs*, 1:218. See also Marina Warner, *Alone of All Her Sex: The Myth and Cult of the Virgin Mary* (New York: Alfred A. Knopf, 1976), 48–9, for a discussion of how the Christian ideal of virginity has roots in classical beliefs about virginity as a magic source of power.

60 Lafitau, *Customs*, 1:129–30.

61 Ibid., 1:217.

62 Ibid., 1:230–40.

63 Chauchetière, *The Positio*, 208.

64 Lafitau, *Customs*, 2:148–72; *JR*, 54 (1669–70): 25–35; Daniel K. Richter, 'War and Culture: The Iroquois Experience,' *William and Mary Quarterly* 40 (1983): 528–59; Thomas S. Abler and Michael H. Logan, 'The Florescence and Demise of Iroquoian Cannibalism: Human Sacrifice and Malinowski's Hypothesis,' *Man in the Northeast* 35 (1988): 1–26.

65 See Jaenen, *Friend and Foe*, 145; Steckley, 'Brébeuf's Presentation of Catholicism in the Huron Language,' 113.

66 Chauchetière, *JR*, 64 (1695): 125.

67 Blanchard, '... To the Other Side,' 97.

68 Chauchetière, *JR*, 63 (1686): 205.

69 Phillip Ziegler, *The Black Death* (New York: John Day Company, 1969), 86–98; see also Andrew E. Barnes, 'Religious Anxiety and Devotional Change in the Sixteenth Century French Penitential Confraternities,' *Sixteenth Century Journal* 19 (1988), 389–406, which is about a resurgence of penance during the crisis of the Protestant Reformation and simultaneous with Catholic-Huguenot violence.

70 See Axtell's discussion of the Jesuits' conflating hell and torture as a way to attract converts, in *The Invasion Within*, 114–15; Steckley, in 'The Warrior and the Lineage,' shows how the Jesuits described hell as worse than the ritual torture practised by northeastern tribes.

5 'She Was the Means of Leading into the Light': Photographic Portraits of Tsimshian Methodist Converts

CAROL WILLIAMS

While our knowledge of Native-American women's response to contact is fragmentary, women were represented in written and photographic documents generated by explorers, traders, colonial travellers, government officials, and missionaries between 1830 and 1880.[1] The editorial concerns expressed by eighteenth-century explorers and early nineteenth-century traders and travellers about women's dress, behaviour, mobility, labour, and morality established a distinct pattern and a judgmental tone that gave way to a uniform call for the reform of Native-American women by the mid-nineteenth century.[2]

During the trading era, Native-American women performed valuable labour and assumed new roles, working as guides, packers, and interpreters, and these working relations led to increased intimacy with Euro-American men.[3] Nisga'a and Tsimshian women became wives of convenience for traders, as these women and their mixed-race offspring were vital to the maintenance and survival of northern maritime forts.[4] Some highly ranked Haida, Coast Tsimshian, and Nisga'a women willingly provisioned the demand for sexual services, as these women understood there was profit to be made from the gender imbalance among the Euro-American traders and, after 1858, miners.[5] As early as 1850 male kin, too, profited by 'selling women, their daughters, and other women of low rank into white operated prostitution.'[6] But Euro-American observers interpreted the act of selling or trading sexual services as morally depraved and were unable to fathom how economics and social ambition might have compelled women, and their kin, into such transactions. With the arrival of missionaries and later with the appointment of government agents charged as overseers of Indian behaviour, interracial relations were unfavourably viewed, and this change in opinion led to disparaging views toward any relations with Native-American women. When Methodist missionary Jonathan Green visited the Queen Charlotte Islands and southeastern Alaska in 1829, he claimed 'that all the young women of the [Haida Kaigani] tribe visit ships for the purpose of gain by prostitution, and in most cases destroy their children, the fruit of this infamous intercourse.'[7] In bemoaning the fact that the offspring produced by mixed-race intimacy were subject to self-induced abortion, infanticide, or abandonment, Green did so less to mourn the loss of a child's life than to demonize women who performed such acts. With the mid-century arrival of Euro-American women settlers and the idealization of bourgeois femininity, the behaviour and roles of Native-American women were subjected to extraordinary scrutiny. Thereafter, intimate relations between Euro-American men and Native-American women were heartily disapproved because white women were now available for procreative purposes.

After 1870, missionization was generally embraced as a viable, and expedient, vehicle for the reform and assimilation of coastal Native Americans of British North America. The social evangelical movement, conducted by Catholic, Anglican, and Methodist missionaries, reinforced the policies applied by the regional Indian agents. Self-sufficient model Christian communities such as Metlakatla, founded in 1862 among the Tsimshian by William Duncan and the Anglican Christian Missionary Society, worked toward protecting Indians from the negative moral climate stimulated by the presence of miners during the gold rush.[8]

Yet in some circumstances, conversion was a means by which individual Native-American women improved personal status during turbulent times of change. Anecdotal accounts of two Tshimshian converts, Victoria Young and Elizabeth Diex, exemplified the success of Methodist evangelicalism among northwestern tribal groups. Yet the story of why Native-American women gravitated toward Christian conversion is more complicated than the brief mentions in missionary memoirs allow.

Taking a biographical approach, this essay investigates two honorific portraits produced between 1863 and 1879 of Young and Diex (see figs. 5.1 and 5.2) in order to illuminate the complex reasons why women converted. These two very different portraits help to reconstruct the lives of two individual women involved with the spread of Methodism among the Tsimshian at the northern coastal village of Fort Simpson. Notably, honorific portraits celebrate Native-American women as re-

5.1 Shu-dalth/Victoria Young and Thomas Crosby, taken on 15 July 1879 and entitled 'The Reverend Thomas Crosby and first nation's "Queen Victoria."' Photograph by Richard Maynard.

5.2 Elizabeth Diex, c. 1869–70. Photograph by Stephen Spencer.

spectable and sophisticated.[9] As such they went a long way toward disassociating Native-American women with prostitution and the increasing spread of venereal disease.

In their daily work, missionaries encouraged and stimulated cultural change, which they believed could be represented photographically. To advertise their success, missionaries used the formula of the conversion anecdote, frequently illustrated by a pair of photographs, one taken before conversion and another after. For outsiders, the before-and-after conversion story signified the Native-American rejection of physical modifications and garments associated with traditional ways, and the incorporation of settler dress signalled the adoption of Euro-American values. Missionary applications of photography contrasted with those of anthropologists, who, arriving at late century, considered cultural change as loss. With the intention of documenting vanishing cultural practices and artifacts, anthropologists used photography as a tool of preservation.

Missionaries quickly apprehended the propagandistic power of photographs placed alongside personal testimony, which seemed to tangibly confirm that evangelical activity among the Indians had yielded widespread cultural and spiritual transformation. Anecdotes and photographs placed in field reports, memoirs, public lectures, and newspapers advertised successes to sceptical audiences at home and abroad. Personal letters illustrated by photographs were sent to Britain from the missionary field and were frequently reprinted in newsletters like the *Methodist Missionary Recorder, Missionary Notices of the Methodist Church,* the *Christian Missionary Society Gleaner, Missionary Outlook,* or the *Christian Mission Society Intelligencer.* In 1907 honorific photographs of David Sallosalton and three other converts, Amos Cushan, Sarah Shee-at-ston, and Captain John Su-A-Lis, were used by Reverend Thomas Crosby in his memoir, *Among the An-ko-me-num or Flathead Tribes of Indians of the Pacific Coast by Thomas Crosby! Missionary to the Indians of BC,* to reinforce his missionary success in the region.[10] This account, like others of a similar genre, venerated the advancements made by evangelicals in Indian day and residential schools. Well-known Methodist missionary Charles Tate also used photography in public lecture tours not only to aggrandize his personal achievements but also to advocate continuing external financial support of his fieldwork at various stations in Indian villages along coastal British Columbia (see fig. 5.3).[11] Methodists working in the American West uniformly adopted this practice of advertising successes through illustrative campaigns in order to raise funds.

5.3 The handwritten caption on the front of the photograph reads, 'Chief Jacob Popcum [*sic*] – BC.' The handwritten caption on the back of photograph reads, 'A convert when stationed at Chilliwack, grand-daughter and great grandchildren.' The photograph was taken between 1874 and 1880 during missionary Charles Tate's appointment in Chilliwack, mainland British Columbia. Photographer unknown (possibly Charles Tate).

Archivist Daile Kaplan has noted, for instance, that the success or failure of campaigns waged by Methodists in territory south of the national border 'depended on the ability of photographs to convey a sense of mission to the viewer who responded with increased prayer and increased giving.'[12] Using the argument that Indian commitment to the faith was never instantaneous or sudden but demanded a steady application of scrutiny and pressure, the illuminated public lectures given by Charles Tate and others called for sustained funding from potential supporters in order to keep the sinner, or newly converted, within an ongoing spiritual embrace. It was necessary to convince supporters that true commitment to the faith could not be hurried. Caroline Tate, the missionary wife of Charles Tate, commented on the gradual process of conversion for a Kelsmat couple: 'Alex and his wife are both more sensible than the generality of them, and although not Christians are steady attendants at Church, and we hope that the truth is taking root in their hearts.'[13] Such evidence made requests for continued financial support of isolated missions and field missionaries in Indian villages more convincing. Missionaries, in general, had to overcome the public belief that Native Americans converted solely for self-interest or under pressure from priests or ministers, as evident in the caption accompanying Frederick Dally's photograph of Indians at prayer (see fig. 5.4), a pose struck at the encouragement of a priest.

Unpublished papers and lectures of Charles and Caroline Tate offer insight into the various ways photography proved useful. Though the precise content of Charles Tate's promotional public lectures may never be recovered, the economic, personal, and ideological motives for them were clear. On a year-long furlough campaign across Canada and the United Kingdom in 1897, Tate used the photographs he had collected during his various northwestern assignments to secure ongoing funding for Methodist evangelicalism among the Tsimshian, Sta:lo, and Coast Salish. And in 1898, Tate assembled thematic slide exhibitions and toured across British Columbia with a magic lantern projector, putting twenty-five years of his experience as a missionary to promotional effect. These public exhibitions, shown to both Euro-American and Indian audiences, were similar to a written memoir, as they were the means by which Tate dignified his personal contributions to Methodism after retirement. The titles of his lectures configured the ideological thrust of his repertoire around a 'before-and-after' transformation. In 1899, he projected a 'magic lantern exhibition at the Indian Church (in Victoria) ... showing mission work in different parts of BC, and the difference between Christian and heathen people.'[14] Between 1904 and 1915, Tate conducted another exhaustive speaking circuit exploring the topics of 'Indians – savage and civilized' and 'Manners and Customs of Indians in BC.'[15] Tate's intention to illustrate the miracles wrought by evangelicalism most likely showed Indians improved by Western styles of dress, physical decorum, and hygiene, all of which appeared to signify Christian piety and virtue. Through conversion, sinners found guidance along the evolutionary path from savagery to civility. Undoubtedly Tate described the experience of conversion for one of his Native followers, Captain John of Kultus Lake, 'who there [at

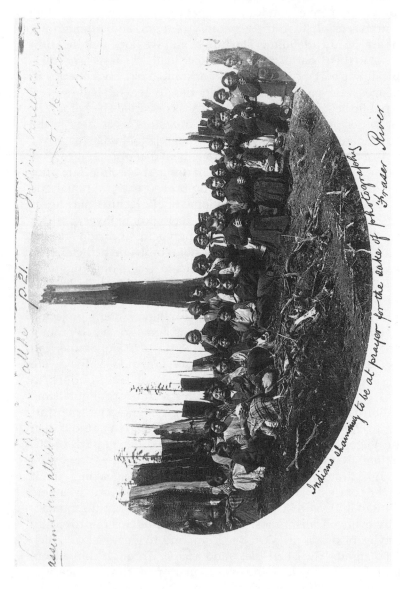

Indians shamming to be at prayer for the sake of photography's

5.4 Vignette photograph from Dally's Album no. 5, entitled 'Photographic Views of British Columbia, 1867–70.' The caption above the photograph reads, 'All the priests request all the Indians kneel down and assume an attitude of devotion. Amen.' The caption at the base of the photograph reads, 'Indians shamming to be at prayer for the sake of photography.' Photograph by Frederick Dally.

the Methodist's annual revival camp meeting], as he expressed it, buried his old heart in the ground, and left there his old ways.'[16]

Although much criticized as advancing assimilation, convert photographs and life histories found in missionary memoirs, notably, distinguished Native-Americans as accomplished individuals, an approach that contradicted the larger social inclination to homogenize. Photographs, although a fragmentary and incomplete record of an individual's multidimensional existence, confirm the cross-cultural encounters between individual Native Americans influenced by evangelicalism and various missionaries active in the region. For example, photographic portraits and descriptions of teen preacher David Sallosalton, who was stationed among the Nanaimo people beginning in April 1862, animated the public lectures, regional reports, and published memoirs of Thomas Crosby.[17] The photographs of Sallosalton, who died in October 1871 of tuberculosis at age nineteen, captured a brief interval in an eight-year process of acculturation and Christian conversion experienced by one young man. According to Crosby, 'Sallosalton was brought up in all the rites and customs of paganism.' About his initial encounter with Sallosalton, or Santana, his Indian name prior to conversion, Crosby observed 'a bright little fellow ... with no clothing on except a short print shirt, and painted up in the strangest fashion, with a tuft of his hair tied on the top of his head. Santana was a real flathead Indian, and had endured all the suffering belonging to such a barbarous custom.' And further, Crosby implied, Sallosalton's metamorphosis from savage to renowned Christian orator after his conversion at age eleven renovated the material, as well as spiritual, state of his existence. 'It was necessary,' declared Crosby, as if inscribing the ideological message of the photograph, 'to dress Sallosalton up a little more than he had been accustomed to if he was to live with a white man, and so a new suit of clothes was procured. He looked quite bright and neat in his new attire, and soon proved a useful and active assistant to the missionary in working inside and outside of the little home.'[18] Sallosalton's adoption of Euro-American dress, changed comportment, use of the English language, and dissemination of Christian beliefs among other Indians reflected a process of self-fashioning modelled by the dictates of his Methodist mentor.

Men and women who converted may have profited in several ways. First, conversion offered celebrated recognition and respect from the settler population. Second, as go-betweens on behalf of the Euro-American–headed missionary campaigns, converts commonly per-

DAVID SALLOSALTON,
An eloquent Indian Preacher of
British Columbia.
(1853-1871.)

5.5 David Sallosalton. Photographer unknown.

formed intermediary roles as educators and interpreters in villages of their kin, and in this way built bridges between the missionaries and the people. Finally, converts often received minor financial remuneration for services performed on behalf of the church. Thus convert photographs, like that of David Sallosalton, Victoria Young, and Elizabeth Diex speak not merely of the renovation of personal appearance but also to the acquisition of new forms of social status and new relations with Euro-American men and women of the ministry. Similar arguments have been asserted by Michael Aird about the photographic portraits of Australian Aborigine men and women, which provided insight into their response to overwhelming pressures to assimilate.[19] Photographs of this genre, Aird noted, reveal the ways in which individuals exercised an increment of control over their destinies in the face of oppressive government 'protection' policies. The acculturated convert who clearly demonstrated improvement by dressing in European garments was more likely to be accepted by settler society, as the proof of changed appearance seemed to be the expression of a willingness to incorporate the introduced economic, cultural, and spiritual system. Yet the convert photographs symbolized something else entirely for settlers and missionaries: the power of Christianity to move Indians from the degradation of pagan savagery. The photographs of upstanding church-going Indians confirmed missionary success.

Both Thomas Crosby and Charles Tate consistently emphasized the contributions of male indigenous converts on the coast and paid much less attention to the influence of women such as Diex and Young, who received abbreviated mentions in missionary memoirs. But a reconstruction of these written and visual fragments, set in profile with the Methodist's advocacy of missionary wives for the education and domestication of indigenous women and girls, enlarges our view of women's roles in assimilation and conversion. Exactly what means and measures were devised to lure and convert Native-American women? Determined to be the most effective routes for the reform of women and girls, residential schools, as well as mixed gender houses of worship, were quickly erected in tribal villages. As Thomas Crosby declared at the earliest stages of missionary activity among the Tsimshian at Fort Simpson, 'There is no part of our work here that is more trying and yet more important than that connected with the young women of the place; they are exposed to peculiar temptations and up to this time there has been no restraint to their course of sin ... they must be cared for , and in some cases the only way to save them is to take them to the mission house.'[20] Because of this, the pedagogical task of domesticating Native-American women and girls in the missionary's home and at gender-segregated schools, with the goal of insulating them from urban-based masculine corruption, fell to the wives and daughters of the clergy. Early on, Methodists and Anglicans adopted the policy of dispatching missionary husband-and-wife teams to the various coastal and interior villages, anticipating that the wives and daughters would assume an aggressive role in female reform work and that wives often replaced husbands when they were absent, as was the case when Caroline Knott Tate, who received her formal licence to preach in 1898, frequently stood in for her husband, Charles, during his absences.[21] Thomas Crosby honoured the contribution of his wife, Emma, as follows: 'The efficient state of the school is no doubt owing in a great measure, to the energy and wisdom of Mrs. Crosby, who, from the time of her arrival at the Fort [Simpson] has taken a deep interest in training the native mind, and having had such a thorough training herself, she was especially qualified to give it the best possible shape.'[22] The Department of Indian Affairs (DIA) also approved of the involvement of wives. For instance, the Indian agent's wife at the Cowichan Salish reserve 'began at once to help her husband with his work among the Indians ... and in his absence ... had many difficulties to settle and advice to give.'[23]

Caroline Knott Tate exemplifies how missionary wives were expected to guide Native-American women into the faith. After graduating from the Methodist school in Hamilton, Ontario, and before her marriage, Knott had accepted a position to teach at Thomas Crosby's day school for girls at Fort Simpson in October of 1876. In accord with Methodist policy, regarding missionary wives, she, like Emma Crosby, claimed duties within the female domain of the calling, including the 'training up' of women and children in domestic and household skills within the educational facilities built by the missionaries.[24] She and her husband later co-founded the Coqualeetza Industrial School for Indian students in British Columbia's Fraser Valley in 1887, and her ten-year reputation as a teacher of Indian women and girls was integral to the financial pledge granted to the school by the Toronto-based Methodist Women's Missionary Society.[25] Residential schools, she would claim, 'offered the only feasible plan of dealing with the children,' and, like others, she praised the inculcation of Indian girls with Christian ideals and European standards of domesticity and femininity. During special holiday events – which served as the Christian surrogate for traditional potlatch ceremonies – women and children were recruited by Knott Tate to collect and prepare the special foods distributed after the services, as 'the creation of native Christian mothers was a large element in the evangelistic effort.'[26] The annual celebrations, moreover, afforded a public stage for assessing whether individual women and girls had conformed to the codes of femininity expected of them.

Anglican reformers Mr and Mrs Henry Schutt similarly directed their attention to domesticating women when they established a women's mission house at Kincolith at the mouth of the Nass River, where a community of 150 Christianized and 60 unbaptized Nisga'a adults and children lived.[27] Their daughter Margaret Schutt, who was fluent in the local dialect and was often engaged as village interpreter, held her mother up as the feminine ideal to which the mission schoolgirls were expected to aspire. She recalled the daily regimen in 'home making and subjects of Christianity' whereby 'ten pretty Indian maidens were taken into the mission home, and became, under my mother's tutelage, efficient cooks and homemakers ... can still see them clad in neat, home-made dresses of brilliant hue, and large woolen shawls, walking off to church. The girls did the house work, taking turns, two each week, in the various phases of the home, run very smoothly and well, under my mother's immaculate housekeeping methods.'[28] As is evident, women's conversion under the auspices of the female-run mission house was not exclusively spiritual but required conforming with Euro-American habits of domesticity and housekeeping.

As the reconstruction of the life histories of Victoria Young and Elizabeth Diex demonstrates, it is unrealistic to assume that Native-American women and girls complacently submitted to missionary demands to convert and conform. While many coastal Native-American women did embrace Protestantism, this did not necessarily imply an absolute subordination to Euro-American ideologies. Rather, conversion was accepted, or resisted, for culturally specific individual motives. Victoria Young and Elizabeth Diex both originated from Tsimshian territory, yet their response to Protestantism and reasons for conversion significantly diverged. The photographs of Young and Diex, interpreted alongside statements by Thomas Crosby, Charles Tate, and others, expose the circumstances as women in search of stability in the face of social and cultural transformations wrought by contact.

Victoria Young, also sometimes identified by her Indian name of Shudalth, was a Gilutsau coastal Tsimshian noblewoman of the Kispaxatot clan.[29] In the sole photograph we have of her, Young stands next to

Thomas Crosby, who was stationed in Tsimshian territory at Fort Simpson beginning in 1874. His relationship with Young was first noted in a Methodist newsletter in February of 1876 when he mentions enclosing a 'picture of the chieftess Sudalth [sic], Victoria Young, as her name now is.'[30]

But why did the Methodists seek out converts in Tsimshian villages? Fort Simpson, built in 1831, and located at the mouth of the Nass River south of the Alaska panhandle, was one of many strategic trading posts founded by the Hudson's Bay Company on the Northwest Coast. Besides the prosperous fur trade conducted with 'King George's' men, indigenous residents earned their principal wealth from the seasonal run of small oily fish called oolachans, which they employed 'in every conceivable form, and for almost all purposes ... what they do not use they trade with the other tribes and with the white people.'[31] In 1856, British admiral James Prevost offered free passage to any missionary that the Christian Missionary Society could provide, proposing that Fort Simpson be the premier missionary station on the mainland northern coast because of its 'many advantages for prosecuting the objects of the mission' and claiming that missionaries working there would be protected by the company.[32] According to Prevost, Fort Simpson might also be advantageous as it gave missionaries access to approximately fifteen thousand members of coastal and interior tribes who converged there each spring to 'receive the commodities of the company in exchange for skins,' affording the opportunity for 'conversing with the natives, and giving them religious instruction. Here, too, a school might be opened for the native children, where they would receive an industrial as well as religious and secular education, and be secluded from the prejudicial influences of their adult relatives.'[33] Prevost's offer was accepted by an Anglican lay missionary of the Christian Missionary Society. William Duncan established the first mission at Fort Simpson but later relocated a number of Tsimshian coverts to greater isolation by creating a model village of Metlakatla in 1862.[34] The Methodists entered the community of Fort Simpson some ten years after Duncan's departure.

Taken on or around 15 July 1879 at Fort Simpson by Richard Maynard, the stereoscopic photograph commemorated a portentous political event in the Indian village attended by both Thomas Crosby and Victoria Young.[35] It was the occasion of a visit of the HMS *Rocket* carrying Israel Powell, the federal superintendent of Indian affairs. Powell's chief object was 'to visit the scene of the fishery disputes of [the nearby] Skeena [River].' On Powell's stopover at Fort Simpson, Young was one of six

Tsimshian representatives presenting a series of grievances to the government civil bureaucrat. In their formal address, 'presented and read by the Wesleyan missionary, Mr. Crosby,' the Fort Simpson Tsimshian demanded the Crown immediately resolve their conflict with the Hudson's Bay Company regarding 'the land question' and also that fishing grounds on the Nass and Skeena Rivers be preserved for the people. Powell reproduced a draft of the address in his report to the DIA the following month. The Tsimshian's grievances were signed by the six leaders 'on behalf of the Indian tribes residing at Fort Simpson.' One of these was 'Shu-dalth, or Victoria Young.' That Shu-dalth was the sole female signatory on this disposition made to the Crown attests to her elevated or noble status among the local people and in the eyes of Powell. In the address the Fort Simpson Tsimshian expressed alarm over the Hudson's Bay Company's claims to the land on which the village stood and questioned whether they might be subject to eviction. Phrased to appease the government's agenda of assimilation, they spoke of a fear of being displaced by the Hudson's Bay Company, which, they complained, 'kept many of our people from building and improving their houses,' and they hoped 'before too long to have all the old houses out of the way, and an entire new village.' At the time of Powell's visit, the total village population numbered approximately 900, and the Methodist Church, headed by Crosby, claimed a membership of 258, with 100 to 150 students attending the school. Undoubtedly scripted to a certain degree by Crosby, the Tsimshian's address transparently upheld the goals of the missionaries to eradicate the longhouses and support the mission school, which was determined to be of 'of great importance and benefit to our children and young people,' as was the Crosby Girls' Home tended by Mr and Mrs Crosby, described as 'a great blessing to our young women and to the whole community.'[36]

In his memoir, Crosby had insisted that Shu-dalth was crucial to the advocacy of Christianity among the northern Nishga'a and Tsimshian, and this appraisal matched descriptions of male converts celebrated by the Methodist leadership, such as David Sallosalton, Phillip MacKay, and William Pierce. Another Methodist minister described her as 'a woman who has great influence among her own people, and is much respected by the Nass people,' and on the occasion of her conversion, Crosby noted, 'she was generally very calm, dignified and deliberate, and was often a great help to the Missionary in counsel and advice among the people.'[37] According to Crosby, Shu-dalth meant 'New Woman,' and this title announced her status as a recent convert. After three months of spiritual instruction, Crosby had baptized the forty-eight-year-old Shu-dalth alongside her consumptive father, Eagle Chief Rapligidahl, in Fort Simpson on 2 January 1875.[38] In written records, her Christian forename, Victoria, and the surname of Young (and sometimes Yonge) were placed alongside 'Shu-dalth.' The consistent application of both names was meaningful as it emphasized her importance as cross-cultural intermediary but also suggested that she was not easily disabused of the Tsimshian convention of multiple names. Interestingly, although Crosby discussed the Indian convention of a double name in relation to David Sallosalton, he rarely employed Sallosalton's Indian name of Santana with the same degree of consistency.

Whatever his opinion on this matter, Crosby acknowledged Shu-dalth's ongoing influence and rank within the governance of the Fort Simpson Tsimshian when he stated, 'being a woman she did not always sit in council, although, on account of being a chief, she was often requested to do so. Whenever she knew that there was likely to be a tie vote on any important question, she would be there; and after nearly all the men had spoken, she would speak in her dignified way.'[39] Crosby's awe of her prestige and rank is visceral throughout his relatively brief commendations of her leadership. As head of a committee of home visitors, she also fulfilled what Crosby must have considered a more appropriately feminine role by attending to the sick and poor. As a councillor, Shu-dalth stood on the platform with other influential village elders of the village council to address villagers who assembled to discuss vital matters.[40] In their address to Powell, the people expressed an explicit request for self-governance through the village council, but phrased this request cautiously by firmly aligning themselves with the goals of the missionaries: 'The council is great benefit to the community, and does much with our missionary to keep peace and order in the village; they have a difficult and responsible duty to perform and we hope they may have a word of encouragement from you.'[41]

On another level, the photograph, like the carefully phrased Tsimshian address to Powell, served a self-promotional and propagandistic purpose for Thomas Crosby. Although government and Methodist aims for assimilation frequently coincided, there were occasions when the political aims of the government conflicted with those of the missionaries, who often lived closer to the people and exercised informed sympathy in ways government agents did not. As noted by Thomas Crosby in 1889, relations between the Indian Department in British Columbia and the Methodists had long been strained, with the government accusing the missionaries of causing trouble among the Tsimshian at Fort Simpson and the Haida at Skidegate.[42] The most common form of government control over missionary activity in remote villages was delivered through the granting or withdrawal of funds to village residential schools. In 1875, Powell established the basic criteria for support: 'Mission societies ... will take measures to increase the number of schools, and take advantage of the material assistance afforded by the government in granting a sum of money to every school which can show a certain average attendance of Indian pupils. On account of the migratory character of the Indians, great difficulty has been found in retaining an average attendance of thirty, the number required by a school to entitle it to the annual grant of $250.'[43] To prevent the loss of much-needed government financial support, the missionaries had to keep enrolment figures high. In addition, financial support was always tenuous. With Catholics, Anglicans, and Methodists competing for converts and the education of Indian children, the government also took care not to show any sectarian favouritism, as noted by one observer in 1870: 'Government although giving cordially to these missions every countenance and moral support in its power found it impractical to grant them any pecuniary aid from the consideration that by so doing it would be involved in the invidious position of appearing to give special state aid to particular religious bodies.'[44] As a result of this situation, the presiding missionary necessarily treated federal authorities' visits with care. It was in the mission's economic interest to represent its missionaries as obedient servants of the state and its policies. The function of the photograph taken on the occasion of Powell's visit in 1879 therefore had much to do with Crosby's aspiration to prove his qualifications to serve and educate the Tsimshian, especially following in the wake of the extremely popular Anglican ministry of William Duncan. With Shu-dalth at his side, Crosby's credibility was heightened and his acceptance among the Fort Simpson Tsimshian asserted.

Shu-dalth's participation in the formal process of negotiation with the federal government on the issue of territorial and fishing rights also motivated the taking of this photograph. That an older woman wielded political leverage through a position on the village council might have surprised Euro-American men like Powell. Shu-dalth's community status must have motivated Richard Maynard to document her for historical posterity. The photograph encodes a contrary powerful image of womanhood that not only challenged Euro-American patriarchal norms of femininity but also undermined the prevailing negative sentiment about Native-American women. Crosby's presence in the photograph affirms that he understood that Tsimshian women inherited power and position through age and matrilineality, a form of social organization fundamentally different from his own. That Shu-dalth exacted reverence and respect from Crosby to the extent that he thought it appropriate to be seen as her equal speaks not only of his ambition but also to her political and cultural prominence. Crosby, an intrusive but minority presence in a relatively remote community, could not afford to question Shu-dalth's rank, clan, or family ties. Undoubtedly, his wearing of Tsimshian garments and headdress for the photograph gestured toward reciprocity and respect for Shu-dalth and her kin.

In his written appraisals of Shu-dalth, Crosby avoided passing judgment on her behaviour and traditional dress. If it was customary of missionaries to view a Native-American woman's attachment to traditional ways and dress as incorrigible, Crosby's silence on this matter, reinforced by his wearing of ceremonial garments in the photograph, affirmed Shu-dalth's noble stature. Shu-dalth, despite Crosby's public declaration of her 'conversion,' demanded submission, and her role in the negotiations with the Crown protected her from the customary criticisms advanced by missionaries like Crosby. Crosby held precarious footing among Tsimshian constituents, and for this reason he necessarily had to sustain the trust of the people through strategic alliances. The photograph, then, is a visible testament of Crosby's respect for Shu-dalth driven by his aspiration to win approval. Thus the full-frontal defiant gaze of an influential woman named Shu-dalth proudly wearing Tsimshian ceremonial dress challenges the more commonplace impressions of hapless impoverished Indians represented in commercial portraits of indigenous street sellers, who were often shabbily dressed and rarely granted the respect of being identified by name or tribal affiliation. With the inclusion of ceremonially garbed Crosby, a 'civilized' Christian man of public repute, any moral shortcomings an uninformed viewer might project onto Shu-dalth were eliminated. For outsiders his civility and stature lent civility to her.

The head-and-shoulders studio *carte-de-visite* portrait of Methodist convert Elizabeth Diex, taken by Stephen Spencer around 1863, was less exceptional than Maynard's stereo card portrait of Shu-dalth and Thomas Crosby in Tsimshian garments. Although the photograph of Diex was taken prior to her conversion and possibly during the years when Diex laboured as a domestic in the household of Judge William Pemberton in Victoria, no photograph of Elizabeth Diex wearing traditional Tsimshian garments has been found.

As mother of hereditary Chief Skagwait (also known by the Christian name of Alfred Dudoward) of the Lower Skeena River Gitandau Tsimshian at Fort Simpson, Elizabeth Diex (also sometimes Deaks or Daix) was a woman of high status.[45] The story of Diex's remarkable transformation as recounted by Thomas Crosby, Caroline Tate, and Charles Tate was, in their view, demonstrated by her adoption of Euro-American dress and Christian habits and, most significantly, by her role in the conversion of her son Alfred in 1872 or 1873. Alfred had been educated at Metlakatla and in service to William Duncan, that mission's lay leader. Both Alfred and his wife, Kate, subsequently aided Thomas Crosby in his pedagogical and religious aspirations for Fort Simpson beginning in 1874. Educated at an Anglican school in Victoria, Kate Dudoward eventually taught at the Crosby Methodist School alongside Caroline Knott Tate and Emma Crosby. As Thomas Crosby asserted in 1875, 'Alfred and his wife still assist [in the schools], and I hope they will be favourably remembered by the [Methodist Central] committee. They are a great help to us indeed; we could not proceed without them.'[46] Alfred and Kate's daughter Alice would also teach in the Fort Simpson school. Conversion profited the family across three generations.

According to all missionary accounts, the Methodists' success at the formerly 'heathen' Fort Simpson originated with Elizabeth Diex, who had experienced a miraculous conversion at a revival meeting held at the Methodist Indian church in Victoria around 1872. This meeting stimulated a mass conversion of between forty and fifty Indians from various villages on the north coast.[47] Apparently Diex had been so enthralled with the words of indigenous convert Amos Shee-at-ston that a week later she sponsored a prayer meeting in her home that resulted in the subsequent conversions.[48] Soon afterward, she was baptized and accepted the Christian name of Elizabeth. Moreover, it was at this time that Diex introduced Alfred, who previously was 'a desperate and lawless character, living in riot and debauch,' to the 'peace and joy which she herself had found.'[49] She was, as Crosby recalled, 'a woman of commanding appearance and of great force of character, and exerted a powerful influence over her people,' so much so that she was 'the means of leading into the light quite a number of her own people who were wandering in sin on the streets of Victoria.'[50] These circumstances, metaphorically described as a 'rich harvest of precious souls,' quickly led to an invitation to Crosby to come to Fort Simpson for the purpose of establishing the mission and school. Arriving in February of 1874, 'he found hundreds of people hungering for the truth and eagerly waiting for a missionary.'[51] Crosby's description of Diex's spiritual transforma-

tion and the proof of her evangelical success across multiple generations of her family and tribe reinforced distinctions between those who
assimilated and those who did not. And Diex's contributions in preparing Fort Simpson for the spiritual work of the Crosbys and the Tates
matched Methodist beliefs that the spread of the faith among the Indians would take steady root only if aided by indigenous insiders. Caroline
Tate clarified this policy in her statement that 'a campaign is never won
by its officers alone. In the army itself lie the possibilities of victory or
defeat.'[52]

These two examples of Shu-dalth and Diex show that Methodists
clearly understood that the conversion and reform of women was
essential for the transformation of Indian culture and lifeways more
generally. In many ways their Methodist beliefs coincided with the
policies of the DIA and, in particular, with the DIA's legislative section
12 (1)(b) of the 1876 Indian Act. By defining who was and who was not
an Indian, the federal Indian Act not only increased social stratification
among Indian people but also caused women who married 'out' to non-
Native American men to lose their status. The children of these unions
also lost their status. Used for the alleged purpose of stimulating assimilation through behavioural change so that Indians would be 'culturally indistinguishable from other Canadians,' the act was effectively
segregationist.[53] For Indians, the act made matters of privacy – spiritual
activities, residential space, physical appearance, tribal and kin relations, child rearing, food-gathering activities, the consumption of alcohol, and other basic components of daily life – subject to state surveillance
and public regulation. It defined 'Indian' by three criteria supporting
patrilineality: any male person of Indian blood reputed to belong to a
particular Indian band, any child of this male person, and any woman
who is or was lawfully married to such a person. Those who were
excluded from holding status as Indians were illegitimate children,
individuals who had continuously resided in a foreign country for five
years, those classified as half-breeds who had benefited from treaties
elsewhere, and finally, as specified in section 12(1)(b) of the act, women
who married non-Native American men. These marriages 'out' were
supported by federal legislation, because women who married Caucasian men were no longer considered Indians. Missionaries stationed in
isolated villages were expected to support and enforce such policies.

For Native-American women, section 12(1)(b) of the Indian Act represented a decisive break with the preceding trade era when they had
leveraged economic and social opportunities from social affiliations

with foreign traders.[54] By 1876, the legislative proviso of section 12(1)(b) was an instrument by which Native-American women were encouraged to conform to Euro-American ideals of reproductive and marital behaviour. By declaring 'that any Indian woman marrying any other than an Indian shall cease to be an Indian within the meaning of this act, nor shall the children issue of such marriage be considered as Indians,' section 12(1)(b) disenfranchised women who married non-Natives from their cultural ancestry as Indians, divesting them of tribal privileges, property rights, reserve housing, and use of reserve burial grounds. Legally enveloped by the status of their husbands, women were ostracized from their own tribal and clan divisions and dispossessed of their ability, within matrilineal or bilateral structures, to transmit property and rights to their children. Moreover, the children of these marriages lost their status as Indians. As a result of these marriages, the British, patriarchal system of property and marriage law and the biologically related, nuclear, male-headed family gained increased footing.[55] Section 12(1)(b) acted to gradually reduce the number of Indians through the erosion of female ancestral lineage, a process that legislated assimilation. Given that mothers, grandmothers, and aunts were pivotal to the transmission of culture and language across the generations, the impact of section 12(1)(b) was grave. Although it is difficult to determine whether or how section 12(1)(b) was enforced within isolated villages like Fort Simpson, a formal marriage to a Euro-American man had concrete material and political implications for women. On the one hand, women were dispossessed of tribal privileges; yet, on the other hand, such marriages might afford an increment of respectability in the eyes of settlers and missionaries. After losing her Indian status by marrying a Caucasian man, conversion might have been an attractive choice for some women. A religious affiliation with the Methodists and their churchgoing membership may have permitted individual women to acquire an alternative form of status to replace that lost through a marriage.

Given the moral sentiment regarding the questionable respectability of Indian women and the changing legislative environment of the 1860s and 1870s, Elizabeth Diex's motivations for her Methodist conversion may have been directly associated with her relationships and, later, marriage to non-Native American men. Other circumstances, which occurred prior to her conversion in 1872, also may have influenced her decision to join the Methodists. Diex had borne her son Alfred with a French-Canadian man named Dudoward, but she subsequently resided 'in the habit of the country' with a Fort Simpson customs officer named Lawson. After initially declining his proposal of marriage because she 'feared he would desert her as other white men had done to their Indian wives,' she legally married Lawson.[56] Before her marriage to Lawson, Elizabeth Diex worked as a household servant to the prominent Judge Pemberton, but was dismissed from this position over an apparently wrongful charge of theft.[57] At this juncture, then, three notable actions were taken: Diex married Lawson, converted to Methodism, and, by 1872 or 1873, returned north to Fort Simpson. The humiliating event at the Pemberton household may have represented a turning point. Any respectability she might have earned among Victoria's urban élite from her formal marriage to Lawson or from her employee association with Judge Pemberton must have been lost. This episode, which occurred prior to her conversion, must have caused Diex considerable anguish and personal embarrassment, perhaps even shame, and may have been influential in her decision to return north and attempt to recapture her reputation with conversion. Therefore, by the time of her public commitment to Methodism, Diex had experienced intimate, but not wholly positive, encounters with Euro-American society in the southern economy of Victoria. Diex's exile from Victoria after her experience in the Pemberton household hints at the vulnerability, and in certain cases descent into destitution, experienced by northern women, many of whom necessarily went south in search of labour. Although northern coastal women ably adapted to the regional economic transformations by becoming day labourers, household domestics, door-to-door traders, and casual sex labourers, they placed themselves in settings not always safe or reputable. In contrast, men contracted out their expertise as interpreters, packers, canoeists, and trailblazers but were indisputably less susceptible to the injustices or abuses more likely to occur behind the closed doors of the private household. We may never recover the precise shape of the accusations leading to Diex's dismissal, but police charge books suggest that charges of theft were frequently brought against female domestic workers.[58]

As a woman who left the northern village of Fort Simpson in search of labour among the settler population of southern Vancouver Island, Diex's path to assimilation was more conventional than Shu-dalth's. Diex had possessed recognized status as a chieftainess among the Gitandau Tsimshian, but her intimate affiliations 'out,' first to Dudoward and later to Lawson, and her experience as a domestic in Victoria afforded her a familiarity with Euro-American culture and economy.

These experiences and associations must have tempered her status, or rank, among her own people at Fort Simpson. Her conversion to Methodism may have provided a means to re-enter the community at Fort Simpson, especially after the troubling episode in the Pemberton household. Although the reasons women like Diex aligned themselves with evangelical churches were varied and complex, the circumstances suggest that Diex's relationship to her own people at Fort Simpson may have changed, given her marriage to a white man and the legal scandal in Victoria. The authority she garnered with her new relationship with the Methodists, augmented by the conversions of her son and daughter-in-law, may have eased her return home.

Parallel to legislative reform, the missionization of women was yet another component of assimilation. For Native-American women, co-operation with missionaries promised benefits such as respectability, skills, wages, and status beyond the tribal hierarchies, during a complex time contoured by economic transitions and cultural change.[59] From what we know of the life of convert Elizabeth Diex, her renewed status as a public figure associated with Methodist conversion of the Tsimshian allowed her to regain some degree of the respect that may have been lost with her southerly migration, her marriage out of the tribe, and the accusations of theft. The existence of individual honorific photographic images of Diex and Shu-dalth, alongside public declarations made by prominent missionaries about these women, show that both had strategically adapted to a shifting political and social landscape during an era when the social actions of Native-American women were generally cast in an unfavourable light. They both made advantageous use of their associations with the missionaries and overcame the economic dependency and the accompanying despair that Native women would inevitably face after the turn of the century.

Between the eighteenth and late nineteenth century, Native-American women adapted to the new and ever changing economic and cultural demands of Euro-American exploration, trade, mining, missionization, and settlement. If, in an earlier economy, women from Haida, Tsimshian, and other northern tribes earned wealth and status through their sale of sexual services to explorers, traders, and miners, by the 1880s a growing dependency on social assistance from the federal DIA was recorded. The DIA attributed the rise of welfare dependency on the loss of nomadic, seasonally based hunting and gathering lifeways, the maladjustment to resource and industrial capitalism, and the decimation caused by imported diseases. As one agent reflected:

In 1880 the only visible means of livelihood of these people had disappeared. During the next twenty years they subsisted largely on the bounty
of the government. Tuberculosis spread among them, and after the manner of most newly introduced diseases, assumed the form of an acute
epidemic ... Early efforts at education almost failed owing to the high
mortality among the children in residential schools ... Housing and social
conditions were as bad as they could well be among a population which
had no experience whatever in living in settled locations.[60]

In retrospect, this agent's interpretation that Native Americans did not
fare well with trade and industrialization is not entirely convincing.
Women adapted by employing a multifarious range of economic strategies: by providing sexual and household services to bachelor traders
and miners, by the sale of goods and domestic services to private
households, and by marketing handmade goods to tourists. Some
individual women, like Diex and Young, and men, like Sallosalton and
others, sought new forms of social respectability and income by establishing what might be identified as professional relationships with missionaries and the agenda of reform.

Less apparent in official documents is the 'moral panic' of Euro-
Americans in response to Native-American women's involvement in
sexual commerce, hard labour, and community leadership. Exposing a
fundamental fear of women's economic and cultural agency, Euro-
American moral panic manifested itself in a widening call to reform,
what we now see as the imposition of repressive, culturally biased
models of femininity and domesticity. The misconceptions of Native-
American women held and promoted by Euro-Americans were tightly
bound with the long history of representing them as morally impoverished and fused to traditional ways and practices, but these views had
more to do with the construct of the Euro-American as modern saviour
and the countervailing claim that Indians were incompatible with modernity. The evidence retrieved from an interpretation of contemporary
photographs and missionary texts conveys a more progressive vision of
the Native-American woman's fight for survival.

By century's end, the pressure on indigenous men and women to
assimilate was intensified. By 1885, on the joint recommendation of
missionaries and regional Indian agents, a prohibition was passed for-
bidding the spiritual and cultural practices unique to Indian tribal
culture, including the potlatch, all winter ceremonies, secret societies,
dancing, and the use of tribal languages.[61] While the enforcement of the

prohibition remained in the hands of individual government field agents and was often unevenly prosecuted, it nevertheless made all Indians who engaged in rituals or ceremonies potentially criminals. In some agencies, field agents, like some missionaries and priests, openly tolerated the potlatch and local potlatch, and winter ceremonies persisted. Where they were suppressed, cultural traditions disappeared, were transformed, or went underground.[62] Under the dictates of these prohibitions, the garments proudly worn by Shu-dalth and Crosby in the Maynard photograph of 1879 would be unlawful.

NOTES

1 Robin Fisher, 'The Image of the Indian,' in *Out of the Background: Readings in Canadian Native History*, ed. Robin Fisher and Kenneth Coates (Toronto: Copp Clark Pitman, 1988), 169. See also Robin K. Wright, 'Depiction of Women in Nineteenth-Century Haida Argillite Carving,' *American Indian Art Magazine* 2.4 (1986): 36–45; Rayna Green, 'The Pocahontas Perplex: The Image of Indian Women in Popular Culture,' *Massachusetts Review* 16 (Autumn 1975): 678–714; Lilianne Ernestine Krosenbrink-Gelissen, *Sexual Equality as an Aboriginal Right: The Native Women's Association of Canada and the Constitutional Process on Aboriginal Matters, 1982–1987* (Saarbrucken: Verlag Breitenbach, 1991), 37; Carol Douglas Sparks, 'The Land Incarnate: Navajo Women and the Dialogue of Colonialism, 1821–1870,' in *Negotiators of Change: Historical Perspectives on Native American Women*, ed. Nancy Shoemaker (New York: Routledge, 1995), 142.
2 Marjorie Mitchell and Anna Franklin, 'When You Don't Know the Language, Listen to the Silence: An Historical Overview of Native Indian Women in BC,' in *Not Just Pin Money*, ed. Barbara K. Latham and Roberta J. Pazdro (Victoria: Camosun College, 1984), 17.
3 Lorraine Littlefield, 'Women Traders in the Maritime Fur Trade,' in *Native People Native Lands: Canadian Indians, Inuit and Metis* (Ottawa: Carleton University Press, 1987), 173–85; Sylvia Van Kirk, '"Women in Between": Indian Women in Fur Trade Society in Western Canada,' *Canadian Historical Association, Historical Papers* (1977): 31–46.
4 Carol Cooper, 'Native Women of the Northern Pacific Coast: A Historical Perspective,' *Journal of Canadian Studies* 27.4 (Winter 1992–3): 56; Margaret Blackman, *During My Time: Florence Edenshaw Davidson, a Haida Woman* (Seattle: University of Washington Press, 1992), 43–4.
5 Cooper, 'Native Women of the Northern Pacific Coast,' 58.

6 Ibid.

7 Jonathan Green, *Journal of a Tour on the Northwest Coast of America in the Year 1829* (New York: Charles Heartmen, 1915), cited in Blackman, *During My Time*. 43.

8 Jean Usher, *William Duncan of Metlakatla: A Victorian Missionary in British Columbia* (Ottawa: National Museums of Canada, 1974).

9 Alan Sekula, 'The Body and the Archive,' in *The Contest of Meaning: Critical Histories of Photography*, ed. Richard Bolton (Cambridge, MA: MIT Press, 1989), 343–90; John Tagg, *The Burden of Representation: Essays on Photographies and Histories* (London: Macmillan, 1988). In general, the honorific photograph celebrated the prestige and status of a sitter, whereas the repressive photograph was commonly used to identify and classify those persons who fell outside the norm.

10 Thomas Crosby, *Among the An-ko-me-num or Flathead Tribes of the Indians of the Pacific Coast* (Toronto: William Briggs, 1907), 208–23; see also Crosby, *Up and down the North Pacfic Coast by Canoe and Mission Ship* (Toronto: Methodist Mission Rooms, Missionary Society of the Methodist Church, Young People's Forward Movement Department, 1907). See also Crosby, 'Reminiscences' (1899), British Columbia Archives (BCA), H/D/R57/C88r.

11 Reverend Charles Montgomery Tate and Caroline Tate (née Knott), journals, letters, articles, and diaries, 1872–1932, BCA, add. mss. #303; Charles Tate, album, City of Vancouver Archives, add. mss. #225; Charles and Caroline Tate, clipping file, BC United Church Conference Archive.

12 Daile Kaplan, 'Enlightened Women in Darkened Lands – a Lantern Slide Lecture,' *Studies in Visual Communication* 10.1 (Winter 1984): 61.

13 Caroline Tate, 'Clayoquot Diary,' 24 February 1898, iii, BCA, add. mss. #303.

14 Charles Tate, 'Cowichan Diary,' 1 December 1899, BCA, add. mss. #303, box I, file 9.

15 Charles Tate, Diary, 30 March 1914, BCA, add. mss. #303, box 1, file 2. The first talk Tate refers to was given at Grandview Trinity Methodist Church in Vancouver, and the second took place in Sardis (Tate, Diary, 8 November 1914, BCA, add. mss. #303, box 1, file 2).

16 Charles Tate, letter from Chiliwack, 30 August 1876, *Missionary Notices of the Methodist Church*, 3rd ser., no. 11 (January 1877): 181.

17 Thomas Crosby, *Among the An-ko-me-num or Flathead Tribes of the Indians of the Pacific Coast*, 208–23. Sallosalton is also discussed in Charles Tate, Diary, volume dated 1876–7, 15, 16, and 17 November, BCA, add. mss. #303; see also John H. Wright, 'A Tribute to the Indian Evangelist' (1936), photocopied article, Nanaimo District Archives.

18 Thomas Crosby, *David Sallosalton: A Young Missionary Hero* (Toronto: Department of Missionary Literature of the Methodist Church, 1906), 8, 4–5, 11, 12.

19 Michael Aird, *Portraits of Our Elders* (South Brisbane: Queensland Museum Publication, 1993), 46.

20 Thomas Crosby, letter from Fort Simpson, 16 February 1876, *Missionary Notices of the Methodist Church*, 3rd ser., no. 8 (June 1876): 131.

21 Caroline Tate was licensed on 28 June 1898. See Robert Clyde Scott, 'Circuit Register of the Chilliwack Methodist Church,' unpublished manuscript, BCA, add. mss. #1299, box 2, file 3.

22 Thomas Crosby, letter, *Missionary Notices of the Methodist Church*, 3rd ser., no. 3 (June 1875): 55.

23 Mrs David Alexander, 'William Henry Lomas (Cowichan Indian Agent 1877–1881),' unpublished manuscripts, file #74A512, BCA, add. mss. #C2208; see also Margaret Elizabeth Schutt, 'Autobiographical Notes' (typed transcript), BCA, add. mss. #1213.

24 Jean Barman, 'Separate and Unequal: Indian and White Girls at All Hallows School, 1884–1920,' in *Indian Education in Canada*, vol. 1, ed. Jean Barman, Yvonne Hebert, and Don McCaskill (Vancouver: University of British Columbia Press, 1986), 110–31.

25 The Tates started Coqualeetza as a small day school at Squihala in 1879, and they reorganized in 1885 four miles upriver at Skowkale. In 1887 they received a grant of $400 from the Women's Missionary Society (Women's Missionary Society, untitled pamphlet [Toronto: Women's Missionary Society, 1925]; Caroline Tate, *Early Days at Coqualeetza* [Toronto: Women's Missionary Society, n.d.], BCA, add. mss. #303). See also Sadie Thompson, 'The Story of Coqualeetza,' BCA, add. mss. #N/A T37.

26 E. Palmer Patterson II, *Mission on the Nass* (Waterloo, ON: Eulachon, 1982), 144.

27 Henry Schutt, 'North Pacific Mission Report, Kincolith, February 1st, 1879,' *Church Missionary Intelligencer*, no. 4 (1879): 561.

28 Margaret Elizabeth Schutt, 'Autobiographical Notes' (typed transcript), BCA, add. mss. #1213, 1–2. See also Henry Schutt, 'Correspondence Out,' letter from Kincolith, Nass River, 3 May 1881, BCA, add. mss. #ECSch 4.

29 Victoria Young or Yonge was also identified in documents as Sudahl or Nishlkumik (Cooper. 'Native Women of the Northern Pacific Coast'). Crosby also refers to her 'official name as Neas-tle-meague' in Crosby, *Up and down the North Pacific Coast*, 383.

30 Thomas Crosby, letter from Fort Simpson, 16 February 1876, *Missionary Notices of the Methodist Church*, 3rd ser., no. 8 (June 1876): 131.

31 Reverend William Pollard, letter from Fort Simpson, April 1875, *Missionary Notices of the Methodist Church*, 3rd ser., no. 3 (June 1875): 55.

32 James Charles Prevost. 'Memorandum by a Naval Officer on the Eligibility of Vancouver's Island as a Missionary Station,' *Christian Missionary Society Intelligencer* (1856): 168.

33 Ibid.

34 Usher, *William Duncan of Metlakatla*; Robin Fisher, *Contact and Conflict: Indian-European Relations in British Columbia, 1774–1890* (Vancouver: University of British Columbia Press, 1992), 129–31.

35 In fact, O.C. Hastings, not Richard Maynard, was the official photographer on this expedition. Hastings was officially paid for ten weeks at five dollars per week, for a total of fifty dollars for photographs produced on the 1879 trip, as tabulated in a DIA annual report for 1880. However, Richard Maynard was aboard this tour of the HMS *Rocket*, and his embossed imprint appears on the stereocard depicting Shu-dalth and Crosby.

36 Israel Powell, *Report to the Department of Indian Affairs*, 25 August 1879 (Ottawa: DIA Annual Reports, 1868–1925), 112, 119–20 (BCA, NW 970.5 C212r).

37 Reverend Alfred E. Green, letter from the Nass River, 18 September 1977, *Missionary Notices of the Methodist Church*, 3rd ser., no. 16 (February 1878): 271; Crosby, *Up and down the North Pacific Coast*, 385.

38 Baptismal records indicated that Shu-dalth's father, identified by the Christian name of James, was dying of consumption (BCA, Methodist Church, Fort Simpson baptismal register).

39 Crosby, *Up and down the North Pacific Coast*, 385.

40 Powell, *Report to the Department of Indian Affairs*, 26 August 1879 (Ottawa: DIA Annual Reports, 1868–1925), 119–120.

41 Crosby, *David Sallosalton*, 8.

42 Thomas Crosby, 'Letter from the Methodist Missionary Society to the Superintendent General of Indian Affairs Respecting British Columbia Troubles, with Affidavits, Declarations, etc.' (1889), BCA, NWP 970.7 M592, ii

43 Canada, Sessional Papers, no. 8, *Report of the Deputy Superintendent General of Indian Affairs*, 4 February 1875 (Ottawa: DIA Annual Reports, 1868–1925).

44 Joseph Trutch, letter, 13 January 1870, in Israel Powell, 'Correspondence, Petitions, Accounts, Statements of Populations and Reports Relating to Indian Land 1861–1877,' BCA, add. mss. #GRO504.

45 Carol Cooper, 'Native Women of the Northern Pacific Coast: An Historical Perspective: 1830–1900,' *Journal of Canadian Studies* 27.4 (Winter 1992–3):

62; Jo-Anne Fiske, 'Colonization and the Decline of Women's Status: The Tsimshian Case,' *Feminist Studies* 17 (Fall 1993): 509–35.

46 Thomas Crosby, letter from Fort Simpson, 20 January 1875, *Missionary Notices of the Methodist Church*, 3rd ser., no. 2 (April 1875): 37.

47 Crosby, *Up and down the North Pacific Coast*, 19–22.

48 Ibid., 20.

49 Ibid., 21.

50 Ibid.

51 Thomas Crosby, letter from Fort Simpson, 20 January 1875, *Missionary Notices of the Methodist Church*, 3rd ser., no. 2 (April 1875): 37.

52 Caroline Tate, 'Family File, Notebook,' BCA, add. mss. #303, box 1, file 8.

53 Canada, Indian and Northern Affairs, *Indian Acts and Amendments, 1868–1950*, SC 1869, c. 6, sec. 6, p. 7. The section was amended by Bill C-31 in 1985. See Kathleen Jamieson, *Indian Women and the Law in Canada: Citizens Minus* (Ottawa: Canadian Advisory Council on the Status of Women and Indian Rights for Indian Women, 1978); Shirley Joseph, 'Assimilation Tools: Then and Now,' *BC Studies*, no. 89 (Spring 1991): 65–79.

54 Cooper, 'Native Women of the Northern Pacific Coast,' 63–4.

55 Terry Wotherspoon, *First Nations: Race, Class, and Gender Relations* (Scarborough, ON: Nelson Canada, 1993), 31; Jamieson, *Indian Women and the Law in Canada*, 1; Cooper, 'Native Women of the Northern Pacific Coast,' 47.

56 Vi Keenlyside, *They Also Came* (Duncan, BC: Yearbook Committee of the Duncan United Church, 1987), 7–12.

57 Bishop Edward Cridge, Memoranda Book, 7 September 1868, BCA, add. mss. #320 E B CV 87m.

58 Victoria Police Department, Charge Books (1873–1900); Gaol Charge Books (1874–82); Mug Shot Book #1 (8 July 1897–28 August 1904), Victoria Police Museum.

59 Margaret Whitehead, '"A Useful Christian Woman": First Nations' Women and Protestant Missionary Work in British Columbia,' *Atlantis* 18.1–2 (1993): 159; Clarence Bolt, *Thomas Crosby and the Tsimshian: Small Shoes for Feet Too Large* (Vancouver: UBC Press, 1992).

60 Canada, *Annual Report of Indian Affairs*, 31 March 1934 (Ottawa: Queens' Printer, 1934), 10.

61 Douglas Cole and Ira Chaikin, *An Iron Hand upon the People: The Law against the Potlatch on the Northwest Coast* (Vancouver: Douglas and McIntyre, 1990).

62 Ibid.

6 Categories and Terrains of Exclusion: Constructing the 'Indian Woman' in the Early Settlement Era in Western Canada

SARAH CARTER

In 1884 Mary E. Inderwick wrote to her Ontario family from the ranch near Pincher Creek, Alberta, where she had lived with her new husband for six months.[1] The letter provides a perspective on the stratifications of race, gender, and class that were forming as the Euro-Canadian enclave grew in the District of Alberta. Mary Inderwick lamented that it was a lonely life, as she was twenty-two miles from any other women, and she even offered to help some of the men near them to 'get their shacks done up if only they will go east and marry some really nice girls.' She did not consider the companionship of women such as 'the squaw who is the nominal wife of a white man near us,' and she had dismissed her maid, who had become discontented with her position as a servant. Inderwick had disapproved of a ball at the North-West Mounted Police (NWMP) barracks at Fort Macleod, despite the fact that it was 'the first Ball to which the squaws were not allowed to go, but there were several half breeds.' Commenting on the Aboriginal population that still greatly outnumbered the new arrivals, Inderwick wrote that they should have been 'isolated in the mountains,' rather than settled on nearby reserves, and that the sooner they became extinct the better for themselves and the country.

At the time of Mary Inderwick's arrival in the West, the consolidation of Canada's rule was not yet secure. The Métis resistance of 1885 fed fears of a larger uprising, and an uncertain economic climate threatened the promise of a prosperous West. There was a sharpening of racial boundaries and categories in the 1880s and an intensification of discrimination in the Canadian West. The arrival of women immigrants like Mary Inderwick after the Canadian Pacific Railway was completed through Alberta in 1883 coincided with other developments such as the railway itself, the treaties, and the development of ranching and farming that were to stabilize the new order and allow the re-creation of Euro-Canadian institutions and society. The women did not introduce notions of spatial and social segregation, but their presence helped to justify policies already in motion that segregated the new community from indigenous contacts.[2] The Canadian state adopted increasingly segregationist policies toward the Aboriginal people of the West, and central to these policies were images of Aboriginal women as dissolute, dangerous, and sinister.

From the earliest years that people were settled on reserves in western Canada, Canadian government administrators and statesmen, as well as the national press, promoted a cluster of negative images of Aboriginal women. Those in power used these images to explain conditions of poverty and ill-health on reserves. The failure of agriculture on reserves was attributed to the incapacity of Aboriginal men to become other than hunters, warriors, and nomads.[3] Responsibility for a host of other problems, including the deplorable state of housing on reserves, the lack of clothing and footwear, and the high mortality rate, was placed upon the supposed cultural traits and temperament of Aboriginal women. The depiction of these women as lewd and licentious, particularly after 1885, was used to deflect criticism from the behaviour of government officials and the NWMP and to legitimize the constraints placed on the activities and movements of Aboriginal women in the world off the reserve. These negative images became deeply embedded in the consciousness of the most powerful socio-economic groups on the Prairies and have resisted revision.

The images were neither new nor unique to the Canadian West. In 'The Pocahontas Perplex,' Rayna Green explored the complex, many-faceted dimensions of the image of the Indian woman in American folklore and literature. The beautiful 'Indian Princess' who saved or aided white men while remaining aloof and virtuous in a woodland paradise was the positive side of the image. Her opposite, the squalid and immoral 'Squaw,' lived in a shack at the edge of town, and her 'physical removal or destruction can be understood as necessary to the progress of civilization.'[4] The 'Squaw' was pressed into service and her image predominated in the Canadian West in the late nineteenth century, as boundaries were clarified and social and geographic space marked out. The either/or binary left newcomers little room to consider the diversity of the Aboriginal people of the West or the complex identities and roles of Aboriginal women. Not all Euro-Canadians shared in these sentiments and perceptions. Methodist missionary John McDougall, for example, in 1895 chastised a fellow missionary author for his use of the term 'squaw': 'In the name of decency and civilization and Christianity why call one person a woman and another a squaw?'[5] While it would be a mistake to assume a unified mentality among all Euro-Canadians, or, for example, among all members of the NWMP, it is nonetheless clear that the negative stereotype not only prevailed but was deliberately propagated by officials of the state.

Euro-Canadian Settlement of the West

Following the transfer of the Hudson's Bay Company territories to the Dominion of Canada in 1870, the policy of the federal government was to clear the land of the Aboriginal inhabitants and open the West to Euro-Canadian agricultural settlement. To regulate settlement the North-West Mounted Police (later Royal North-West and then Royal Canadian Mounted Police) was created and three hundred of them were dispatched west in 1874. A 'free' homestead system was modelled on the American example, and a transcontinental railway was completed in 1885. To open up the West to 'actual settlers,' seven treaties with the Aboriginal people were negotiated from 1871 to 1877, and through these the government of Canada acquired legal control of most of the land of the West. In exchange the people received land reserves, annuities, and, as a result of hard bargaining by Aboriginal spokesmen, commitments to assist them to take up agriculture as their buffalo-based economy collapsed. A Department of Indian Affairs with headquarters in Ottawa was established in 1880, and in the field an ever-expanding team of Indian agents, farm instructors, and inspectors were assigned to implement the reserve system and to enforce the Indian Act of 1876. The people who had entered into treaties were wards of the government who did not have the privileges of full citizenship and were subject to a wide variety of controls and regulations that governed many aspects of life.

Much to the disappointment of the federal government, the West did not begin rapid development until the later 1890s. There were small pockets of Euro-Canadian settlement, but in 1885 in the District of Alberta, for example, the Aboriginal and Métis population was more than 9,500 while the recent arrivals numbered only 4,900.[6] All seemed hopeless, especially by the mid-1880s when immigration was at a near standstill. Years of drought and frost and problems finding suitable techniques for farming the northern plains account in part for the reluctance of settlers, and the 1885 resistance of the Métis in present-day Saskatchewan did little to enhance the image the government wished to project of the West as a suitable and safe home.

Resistance to Settlement

The Métis were people of mixed Aboriginal and European ancestry who regarded the Red River settlement (Winnipeg) as the heartland of their nation. It was here in 1869–70, under the leadership of Louis Riel, that the Métis first resisted Canadian imperialism, effectively blocking Ottawa's takeover of the West until they had been guaranteed their land rights, their French language, and their Roman Catholic religion. But the victory negotiated into the Manitoba Act of 1870 soon proved hollow as the Canadian government adopted a variety of strategies to ensure that the Métis did not receive the lands promised them, and many moved further west.[7] In their new territories, the Métis again demanded land guarantees, but when the Canadian government largely ignored their requests, they asked Louis Riel to lead another protest in 1884. The Canadian government dispatched troops west and defeated the Métis at Batoche in May 1885. Riel was found guilty of treason and was hanged, as were eight Aboriginal men convicted of murder.

Despite desperate economic circumstances and deep resentment over government mistreatment, few of the treaty people of the West joined the Métis resistance, although at a settlement called Frog Lake, in present-day Alberta, some young Cree men killed an Indian agent, a farm instructor, and seven others, and in the Battleford district two farm instructors were killed. This limited participation became a rationale for the increasingly authoritarian regime that governed the lives of the treaty people. Anxious to see western development succeed in the face of all of the setbacks of the 1880s, the Canadian government restricted the Aboriginal population in order to protect and enrich recent and prospective immigrants.

Development of Stereotypes

Particularly irksome to many of the recently arrived 'actual settlers' was Aboriginal competition they faced in the hay, grain, and vegetable markets. Despite obstacles, many Aboriginal farmers had produced a surplus for sale. Settlers' particularly vocal and strident complaints led the government to curtail farming on reserves. To explain why underused reserves had become pockets of rural poverty, Indian Affairs officials claimed that Aboriginal culture and temperament rendered the men unwilling and unable to farm.

Plains women were also responsible: according to government pronouncements, they were idle and gossipy, preferring tents to proper housing because tents required less work to maintain and could be clustered in groups that allowed visiting and gossip. Reports of the superintendent general of Indian Affairs claimed that Indians raised dust with their dancing and the women's failure to clean it up spread diseases such as tuberculosis. Administrators blamed the high infant mortality rate upon the indifferent care of the mothers. The neglected children of these mothers grew up 'rebellious, sullen, disobedient and unthankful.'[8] While men were blamed for the failure of agriculture, women were portrayed as resisting, resenting, and preventing any progress toward modernization. As an inspector of Indian agencies lamented in 1908, 'The women, here, as on nearly every reserve, are a hindrance to the advancement of the men. No sooner do the men earn some money than the women want to go and visit their relations on some other reserve, or else give a feast or dance to their friends ... The majority of [the women] are discontented, dirty, lazy and slovenly.'[9]

The unofficial and unpublished reports of reserve life show that officials recognized that problems with reserve housing and health had little to do with the preferences, temperament, or poor housekeeping abilities of women. Because of their poverty, the people were confined in large numbers in winter to what were little better than one-room and one-storey huts or shacks that were poorly ventilated and impossible to keep clean, as they had dirt floors and were plastered with mud and hay. Tents and tipis might well have been more sanitary and more comfortable. One inspector of agencies noted in 1891 that women had neither soap, towels, wash basins, nor wash pails, and no means with which to acquire these.[10] Officials frequently noted that women were short of basic clothing but had no textiles or yarn to work with. Yet in official public statements, the tendency was to ascribe blame to the women rather than to draw attention to conditions that would injure the reputation of government administrators.

'Licentiousness' and Government Officials

Officials propagated an image of Aboriginal women as dissolute, as the bearers of sinister influences, to deflect criticism from government agents and policies. This image was evoked with particular strength in the wake of an 1886 controversy that focused upon the alleged 'brutal, heartless and ostentatious licentiousness' of government officials resident in western Canada.[11] The remarks of Samuel Trivett, a Church of England missionary on the Blood reserve in present-day southern Alberta, became the focus of the controversy. To a special correspondent for the *Mail* of Toronto, Trivett said that Indian women were being bought and sold by white men who lived with them without legally marrying them and then abandoned the offspring to life on the reserve.[12]

Trivett strongly hinted that some government agents were involved in licentious behaviour, an accusation seized upon by critics of the administration of Indian affairs in western Canada. In the aftermath of the Métis resistance of 1885, opponents of John A. Macdonald's Conservatives amassed evidence of neglect, injustice, and incompetence and were delighted to add immorality to this list. In the House of Commons in April of 1886, Malcolm Cameron, Liberal member of Parliament, delivered a lengthy indictment of Indian affairs in the West, focusing upon the unprincipled and unscrupulous behaviour of officials of the Indian department. Cameron quoted Trivett and further charged that agents of the government, sent to elevate and educate, had instead acted to 'humiliate, to lower, to degrade and debase the virgin daughters of the wards of the nation.' He knew of one young Indian agent from England, unfit to do anything there, who was living on a reserve in 'open adultery with two young squaws ... revelling in the sensual enjoyments of a western harem, plentifully supplied with select cullings from the western prairie flowers.'[13]

Cameron implicated members of the NWMP in this behaviour, wondering why it was that over 45 per cent of them were reported to have been under medical treatment for venereal disease. Cameron was not the first to raise the matter of police propriety in the House. Concern about possible improper relations between the police and Aboriginal women long predated the Trivett scandal and was one aspect of a larger debate in the press and in the House in the late 1870s over charges of inefficiency, lack of discipline, high desertion rates, and low morale in the force. Lieutenant-governor of the North-West Territories David Laird alerted NWMP commissioner James Macleod in 1878 that reports about immoral conduct were in circulation: 'I fear from what reports are brought me, that some of your officers at Fort Walsh are making rather free with the women around there. It is to be hoped that the good name of the Force will not be hurt through too open indulgence of that kind.

And I sincerely hope that Indian women will not be treated in a way that hereafter may give trouble.'[14]

Although Macleod and Assistant Commissioner A.G. Irvine denied that there was 'anything like "a regular brothel"' about the police posts, such reports persisted. In the House of Commons in 1880 Joseph Royal, a Manitoba member of Parliament, claimed that the NWMP was accused of 'disgraceful immorality' all over the West. Royal had evidence that at one of the police posts that winter there had been 'an open quarrel between an officer and one of the constables for the possession of a squaw ... and that one officer slapped another in the face on account of a squaw.' Royal had been informed that 'many members of the force were living in concubinage with Indian women, whom they had purchased from their parents and friends.'[15] In 1886 public attention was once again drawn to police behaviour. The *Mail* informed its readers that between 1874 and 1881 the police had 'lived openly with Indian girls purchased from their parents" and only the arrival of settlers had compelled them to abandon or at least be 'more discreet in the pursuit of their profligacy.'[16]

There is little doubt that Trivett and other critics based their accusations of both the police and government officials on some foundation, but remaining evidence is scanty and scattered. Missionaries depended to a large extent on the goodwill of the government and were rarely as outspoken as Trivett or John McLean, a Methodist missionary on the Blood reserve near Fort Macleod, who in 1885 characterized many reserve employees as utterly incompetent and urged the government to employ only married men 'of sterling Christian character.'[17] But missionaries were instructed in 1886 by Edgar Dewdney, lieutenant-governor of the North-West Territories, not to voice their accusations to the newspapers 'even if allegations against public officials were true,' as this would do more harm than good, would affect mission work, and could be used to stir up political strife.[18] Government officials generally investigated reports of government misconduct themselves, and this functioned to cover up or to mitigate such allegations. Similarly, members of the NWMP themselves looked into any complaints about the force's behaviour.

Marriages of Aboriginal Women and NWMP Members

There were members of the NWMP, especially among the earliest recruits of the 1870s and early 1880s, who formed relationships with

Aboriginal and Métis women, as did a great many other male immigrants of these years. Some of these were marriages of long standing, sanctioned by Christian ceremony or customary law. Lakota author/ historian John O'Kute-sica noted that six 'Red Coats' of the Wood Mountain Detachment in the early 1880s married Lakota women from Sitting Bull's band, and most of the couples, such as Mary Blackmoon and Thomas Aspdin, lived together to old age and death. One couple, Archie LeCaine and Emma Loves War, separated because she did not wish to move to eastern Canada.[19]

Other relationships were of a more temporary nature. Of course there were children. Cecil Denny, for example, while a sub-inspector at Fort Macleod, had a daughter with Victoria McKay, a part-Piegan woman who was the wife of another policeman, Constable Percy Robinson.[20] As a result of his involvement, Denny was forced to resign from the force in 1881 through a series of court cases that Robinson brought against him for 'having induced his wife to desert him and also having criminal connections with her.'[21] The child was raised by her mother on the American Blackfoot reservation. Assistant Surgeon Henry Dodd of the NWMP had a daughter who lived on one of the Crooked Lake reserves in the Qu'Appelle Valley. There is a record of this in the police files only because Dodd was granted leave to attend to her when she was very ill in 1889.[22]

D.J. Grier, who served three years with the NWMP beginning in 1877 at Fort Macleod, married Molly Tailfeathers, a Piegan woman, and together they had three children.[23] By 1887, however, Grier had remarried a white woman. For a short time the children from his first marriage lived with their mother on the Piegan reserve, but the two eldest were taken from her and placed in the care of Grier's parents, who had also settled in Fort Macleod. Grier was one of the most prominent men of the West. Renowned as the first commercial wheat grower in Alberta, he also served as mayor of Macleod for twelve years from 1901 to 1913.

Abuse of Aboriginal Women

John O'Kute-sica wrote at length about one unsuccessful Wood Mountain customary marriage, that of his aunt Iteskawin and Superintendent William D. Jarvis, an Englishman with the original contingent who was dismissed from the force in 1881. According to O'Kute-sica, his aunt consented to marry Jarvis because he promised that her brothers and sisters would have something to eat twice a day, and all of her people were in want and suffering. After only a few weeks of marriage, Jarvis, in a jealous rage, publicly assaulted Iteskawin at a Lakota 'Night Dance,' an incident that strained relations between the two communities, and she immediately left him.[24] On most of the few occasions that Aboriginal women laid charges against policemen for assault or rape, their claims were hastily dismissed as defamation or blackmail.[25]

Some government employees resident on reserves clearly abused their positions of authority. In 1882, for example, Blackfoot chief Crowfoot and his wife complained that the farm instructor on their reserve demanded sexual favours from a young girl in return for rations, and when an investigation proved this to be the case the man was dismissed.[26] Both the documentary and oral records suggest that several of the government employees that the Crees killed at Frog Lake and Battleford in the spring of 1885 were resented intensely because of their callous and at times brutal treatment of Aboriginal women. The farm instructor on the Musquoito reserve near Battleford, James Payne, was known for his violent temper – he once beat a young woman and threw her out of his house when he found her visiting his young Aboriginal wife. The terrified and shaken woman, who was found by her father, died soon after, and her grieving father blamed Payne, whom he killed in 1885.[27] Farm instructor John Delaney, who was killed at Frog Lake in 1885, laid charges against a man by the name of Sand Fly in 1881 so that he could cohabit with Sand Fly's wife. Delaney first claimed that Sand Fly had struck him with a whip, and when this charge did not result in the desired jail sentence, Delaney claimed that the man had beaten his wife. The farm instructor then lived with Sand Fly's wife, and the general feeling in the district, shared by the local NWMP, was that 'Mr. Delaney had the man arrested in order to accomplish his designs.'[28] As a Touchwood Hills farm instructor told a visiting newspaper correspondent in 1885, the charges of immorality among farm instructors on reserves were in many instances too true, as 'the greatest facilities are afforded the Indian instructor for the seduction of Indian girls. The instructor holds the grub. The agent gives him the supplies and he issues them to the Indians. Now you have a good idea of what semi-starvation is ...'[29]

Blaming Aboriginal Women

The most vocal response to the accusations of Trivett and other critics was not to deny that there had been 'immorality' in the West but to exonerate the men and blame the Aboriginal women, who were claimed to have behaved in an abandoned and wanton manner and were supposedly accustomed to being treated with contempt, to being bought and sold as commodities, within their own society. In defending the NWMP in 1880, the Toronto *Globe* emphasized that Aboriginal women had 'loose morals' that were 'notorious the world over' and that 'no man in the world was so good as to teach them better or to try and reform them in this respect.' These sentiments were echoed again and again in the wake of the 1886 controversy. The editor of the *Fort Macleod Gazette*, a former member of the NWMP, argued that whatever immorality there might have been came from the women themselves and from the customs of their society. They were prostitutes before they went to live with white men, who did not encourage this behaviour but were simply 'taking advantage of an Indian's offer.' The *Mail* told readers that Aboriginal males had sold their wives and children in the thousands to soldiers and settlers since the time of the French fur trade in exchange for alcohol, and that with the arrival of the police a great deal had been done to end this situation.[30]

The *Gazette* stressed, incorrectly, that there was no marriage in plains societies, simply a little lively bartering with the father and a woman could be purchased for a horse or two. The argument that Aboriginal women were virtual slaves, first to their fathers, and then to their husbands, was called upon by all who wished to deflect criticism from government officials and the NWMP. In the House of Commons in April 1886, Sir Hector Langevin defended the record of the government against Cameron's charges of immorality. Langevin claimed that to Indians marriage was simply a bargain and a sale and that immorality among them long predated the arrival of government agents in the North-West.[31]

The government published its official response to the criticisms of Indian affairs in the North-West in an 1886 pamphlet entitled *The Facts Respecting Indian Administration in the North-West*. A government official had again inquired into accusations about the misconduct of employees of the Indian department and, predictably, had found no evidence. The investigator, Hayter Reed, assistant commissioner of Indian affairs, was one of those unmarried officials who had been accused of' having Aboriginal 'mistresses' as well as a child from one of these relationships.[32] The pamphlet boldly asserted that Trivett was unable to come up with a shred of actual evidence, although the missionary vehemently denied this.[33] The pamphlet writer admitted that some men had acquired their wives by purchase, but claimed that this was the Indian custom, and that 'no father ever dreams of letting his daughter leave his wigwam till he has received a valuable consideration for her.' If the government stopped this custom, there would be loud protests, over and above the Indians' 'chronic habit of grumbling.' 'The Facts' insisted that it was not fair to criticize the behaviour of the dead, such as Delaney and Payne, who had 'passed from the bar of human judgment.'[34]

Endangered White Women

The real danger was not to Indian women but to white women, who might again be dragged into horrible captivity if critics encouraged Indians in their exaggerated, misled notions. Two white women, Theresa Delaney and Theresa Gowanlock, had been taken hostage by Big Bear's band following the events at Frog Lake. There were a great number of Métis and Aboriginal women (and men) hostages as well, but outrage and indignation did not focus upon them. Although Delaney and Gowanlock were fed and housed as well as their captors, and released unharmed, the government publication played up the perils, hazards, and threat to the safety of these women and others who might move west. The women's account of their two months of captivity stressed the 'savagery' of their captors, and the ever-present danger of 'the fate worse than death.'[35]

Following the period of heightened tensions within the Euro-Canadian community after the events of 1885 there was an increased emphasis upon the supposed vulnerability of white women in the West. Rumours circulated through the press that one of Big Bear's wives was a white woman being held against her will.[36] After a girl of about nine with fair hair and blue eyes was spotted on the Blackfoot reserve by an English artist accompanying Canada's governor general on a tour across the continent, in 1889, the story of a 'captive' white child attracted international attention and calls for a rescue mission. Indignant outrage was expressed, especially in the Fort Macleod newspaper, which called for prompt action to rescue the girl from 'the horrible fate that is surely in store for her.' The NWMP and Indian affairs officials assigned to look into the case knew all along that the child was not a captive at all but resided with her mother on the reserve. The captivity story functioned, however, to reaffirm the vulnerability of white women in the West and to provide a rationale for those who wished to secure greater control over the Aboriginal population.[37]

The Image of the 'Squaw Man'

The use of the term 'squaw man' to denote men of the lowest social class became increasingly frequent during the later 1880s. There was disdain for those within the community who did not conform to the new demands to clarify boundaries. Police reports blamed 'squaw men' for many crimes such as liquor offences or the killing of cattle. S.B. Steele of the NWMP wrote from the Fort Macleod district in 1890 that the wives of these men 'readily act as agents, and speaking the language, and being closely connected with the various tribes, their houses soon become a rendezvous for idle and dissolute Indians and half breeds, and being themselves in that debatable land between savagery and civilization possibly do not realize the heinousness and danger to the community ...'[38] The *Moosomin Courier* of March 1890 blamed the 'squaw-men' for stirring up trouble with the Indians in 1885 and prejudicing them against policies that were for their own good.[39]

Lives of Aboriginal Women

The overwhelming image that emerged from the 1886 'immorality' controversy was that of dissolute Aboriginal women. They, and the traditions of the society from which they came, were identified as the cause of vice and corruption in the new settlements of the prairie West. This was not an image shared or accepted by all Euro-Canadians in the West at all times, nor did the image bear resemblance to the lives of the vast majority of Aboriginal women. Women were not commodities that were bought, sold, or exchanged at will by men. Plains marriage practices entailed mutual obligations between the families of the couple and an ongoing exchange of marriage-validating gifts.

Aboriginal oral and documentary sources suggest that in the early reserve years, particularly in the aftermath of the events of 1885, women provided essential security and stability in communities that had experienced great upheaval. In these years of low resources and shattered morale, the work of women in their own new settlements was vital, materially as well as spiritually. Cree author Joe Dion wrote that when spirits and resources were low on his reserve in the late 1880s 'much of the inspiration for the Crees came from the old ladies, for they set to work with a will that impressed everybody.'[40] Aboriginal women also provided considerable assistance to new immigrants, particularly women. They were important as midwives to some early immigrants, and they helped instruct newcomers in the use of edible prairie plants and other native materials.[41] Aboriginal women formed what was described as a 'protective society' around the women and children hostages in Big Bear's camp in 1885, keeping them out of harm's way, but this aspect of the drama was absent from the headlines of the day.[42]

Constraints on Aboriginal Women

It was the image of Aboriginal women as immoral and corrupting influences that predominated in the non-Aboriginal society that was taking shape. Authorities used this characterization to define and treat Aboriginal women, increasingly narrowing their options and opportunities. Both informal and formal constraints served to keep Aboriginal people from the towns and settled areas of the Prairies, and their presence there became more and more marginal. While they may not have wished to live in the towns, their land-use patterns for a time intersected with the new order, and they might have taken advantage of markets and other economic opportunities, but townspeople believed that Aboriginal people did not belong within the new settlements that were replacing and expelling 'savagery.'[43] Their presence was seen as incongruous, corrupting, and demoralizing. Classified as prostitutes, Aboriginal women were seen as particular threats to morality and health. An 1886 pamphlet of advice for emigrants entitled *What Canadian Women Say of the Canadian North-West* was quick to reassure newcomers that Aboriginal people were seldom seen. The 320 women who responded to the question 'Do you experience any dread of the Indians?' overwhelmingly replied that they rarely saw any. Mrs S. Lumsden, for example, thought they were 'hundreds of miles away with sufficient force to keep them quiet.'[44]

Following the events of 1885, government officials as well as the NWMP made strenuous efforts to keep people on their reserves. A pass system required all who wished to leave to acquire a pass from the farm instructor or agent declaring the length of and reason for absence. A central rationale for the pass system was to keep away from the towns and villages Aboriginal women 'of abandoned character who were there for the worst purposes.'[45] There is evidence that some Aboriginal women did work as prostitutes.[46] Cree chiefs or the Edmonton district complained to the prime minister in 1883 that their young women were reduced by starvation to prostitution, something unheard of among their people before.[47] Officials attributed prostitution not to economic conditions but to what they insisted was the personal disposition or inherent immorality of Aboriginal women.[48] Classified as prostitutes, Aboriginal women could be restricted by a new disciplinary regime. Separate legislation under the Indian Act and, after 1892, under the Criminal Code governed Aboriginal prostitution, making it easier to convict Aboriginal women than other women. As legal historian Constance Backhouse has observed, this separate criminal legislation, 'with its attendant emphasis on the activities of Indians rather than whites, revealed that racial discrimination ran deep through the veins of nineteenth century Canadian society.'[49]

The pass system was also used to bar Aboriginal women from the towns for what were invariably seen as 'immoral purposes.' Women who were found by the NWMP to be without passes and without means of support were arrested and ordered back to their reserves.[50] In March of 1886 the Battleford police dealt with one woman who refused to leave the town by taking her to the barracks and cutting off locks of her hair. Two years later, the Battleford paper reported that 'during the early part of the week the Mounted Police ordered out of town a number of squaws who had come in from time to time and settled here. The promise to take them to the barracks and cut off their hair had a wonderful effect in hastening their movements.'[51]

Accustomed to a high degree of mobility about the landscape, Aboriginal women found that the pass system not only restricted their traditional subsistence strategies but also hampered their pursuit of new jobs and resources. Government officials further limited the women's employment and marketing opportunities by advice such as that given by one Indian agent, who urged the citizens of Calgary in 1885 not to purchase anything from or hire Aboriginal people, so as to keep them out of the town.[52] The periodic sale of produce, art, and craftwork in urban or tourist areas could have provided income to women and their families, as did such sales for Aboriginal women in eastern Canada. Studies of rural women in western Canada suggest that in the Prairie boom and bust cycle the numerous strategies of women, including the marketing of country provisions and farm products, provided the buffer against farm failure.[53] Aboriginal women were not allowed the same opportunities to market these resources.

The mechanisms and attitudes that excluded Aboriginal women from the new settlements also hampered their access to some of the services these offered. Jane Livingston, the Métis wife of one of the earliest farmers in the Calgary district, found that whenever there was a new policeman in Calgary, he would ask her and her children for passes and make trouble because of their appearance. On one occasion when a child was sick and she needed medicines from downtown Calgary, she rubbed flour into her face and 'hoped I looked like a white Calgary housewife' so that the new police constable would not bother her about a pass.[54]

Murders of Aboriginal Women

Community reactions to the poisoning of one Aboriginal woman and the brutal murder of another in the late 1880s in southern Alberta reflect the racial prejudices of many of the recent immigrants. In 1888 Constable Alfred Symonds of the NWMP detachment of Stand Off was accused of feloniously killing and slaying a Blood woman by the name of Mrs Only Kill by giving her a fatal dose of iodine. The woman had swallowed the contents of a bottle given to her by Symonds that apparently held iodine and had died the next morning. The same day, she had also eaten a quantity of beans that had turned sour in the heat. Although Only Kill died on Wednesday morning, the matter was not reported to the coroner until late on Friday night. The coroner claimed that by this time the body was too decomposed for post-mortem examination, and the coroner's jury decided that the deceased had come to her death either from eating sour beans or from drinking the fluid given to her by Symonds, who was committed to trial and charged with having administered the poison.[55] Constable Symonds was a popular and jocular cricketer and boxer, the son of a professor from Galt, Ontario.[56] In his report on the case, Superintendent P.R. Neale of the NWMP wrote to his superior, 'I do not think any Western jury will convict him.' Symonds appeared before Judge James E. Macleod, former commissioner of the NWMP, in August of 1888, but the crown prosecutor made application for 'Nolle Prosequi,' which was granted, and the prisoner was released.[57]

During the 1889 trials of the murderer of a Cree woman identified only as 'Rosalie,' who had been working as a prostitute, it became clear that there were many in Calgary who felt 'Rosalie was only a squaw and that her death did not matter much.'[58] Instead the murderer gained the sympathy and support of much of the town. The murder was a particularly brutal one, and the accused, William 'Jumbo' Fisk, had confessed and given himself up to authorities, yet there were problems finding any citizens willing to serve on a jury that might convict a white man for such a crime. The crown prosecutor stated that he regretted having to conduct the case, as he had known the accused for several years as a 'genial accommodating and upright young man.'[59] Fisk was a popular veteran of 1885, and he was from a well-established eastern Canadian family. At the end of the first of the Rosalie trials, the jury astoundingly found the accused 'Not Guilty.' Judge Charles Rouleau refused to accept this verdict, and he ordered a re-trial, at the end of which Rouleau told the jury to 'forget the woman's race and to consider only the evidence at hand,' that 'it made no difference whether Rosalie was white or black, an Indian or a negro. In the eyes of the law, every British subject is equal.'[60] It was only after the second trial that Fisk was convicted of manslaughter and sent to prison for fourteen years at hard labour. The judge intended to sentence him for life, but letters written by members of Parliament and other influential persons who had made representations to the court as to his good character, combined with a petition from the most respectable people of Calgary, persuaded him to impose the lesser sentence.

The people of Calgary tried to show that they were not callous and indifferent toward Rosalie by giving her 'as respectable a burial as if she had been a white woman,' although several months later the town council squabbled with the Indian Department over the costs incurred, as the department did not think it necessary to go beyond the costs of a pauper's funeral. As a final indignity, Rosalie was not allowed burial by the priests in the mission graveyard, although she had been baptized into the Roman Catholic Church, because they regarded her as a prostitute who had died in sin. The lesson to be learned from the tragedy, according to a Calgary newspaper, was 'keep the Indians out of town.'[61]

Aboriginal Women and Anglo-Saxon Moral Reformers

There was an intensification of racial discrimination and a stiffening of boundaries between Aboriginal and newcomer in the late 1880s in western Canada. In part this may have been because the immigrants exemplified the increasingly racist ideas and assumptions of the British toward 'primitive' peoples.[62] Like the Jamaica Revolt and the India Mutiny, the events of 1885 in western Canada sanctioned perceptions of Aboriginal people as dangerous and ungraceful and justified increased control and segregation.[63] Aboriginal women presented particular perils and hazards. The Métis of the Canadian West had fomented two 'rebellions' in western Canada, so that authorities wanted to discourage such miscegenation, which could potentially produce great numbers of 'malcontents' who might demand that their rights and interests be recognized.[64]

A fervour for moral reform in Protestant English Canada also began to take shape in the later 1880s. Sexual immorality was a main target and racial purity a goal of the reformers.[65] There were fears that Anglo-Saxons might well be overrun by more fertile, darker, and lower people who were believed not to be in control of their sexual desires. Attitudes of the moral reformers toward the inhabitants of the cities' slums were similar to categorizations of 'savages' as improvident, filthy, impure, and morally depraved. The 1886 accusations of Malcolm Cameron about the extent of venereal disease among the NWMP had led to an internal investigation of the matter, and although this proved that Cameron's claims were exaggerated, they were not entirely incorrect.[66] The concerns of the moral reformers, however, justified policies segregating Aboriginal and newcomer communities.

The Invalidation of Mixed Marriages

Also at issue in the West at this time was the question of who was to control property and capital, who was to have privilege and respectability, and who was not. The possibility that the progeny of interracial marriages might be recognized as legitimate heirs to the sometimes considerable wealth of their fathers posed problems and acted as a powerful incentive for the immigrants to view Aboriginal women as immoral and accustomed to a great number of partners. With the arrival of Euro-Canadian women, Aboriginal wives became fewer, and there is evidence, just as Trivett had suggested, that in the 1880s husbands and fathers were leaving their Aboriginal wives and children for non-Aboriginal wives. D.W. Davis, for example, began his career in Alberta as a whiskey trader at the infamous Fort Whoop-Up, but by 1887 was elected as the first member of Parliament for the Alberta District. He had a family of four children with a Blood woman by the name of Revenge Walker, but in 1887 he married an Ontario woman, Lillie Grier (sister of D.J. Grier), with whom he had a second family. Although Davis, like Grier, acknowledged the children of the earlier marriage and provided for their education, they were excluded from the economic and social élite in the non-Aboriginal community.[67]

While the validity of mixed marriages according to 'the custom of the country' had been upheld in Canadian courts earlier in the nineteenth century, this changed with the influential 1886 ruling in *Jones v. Fraser*. The judge ruled that the court would not accept that 'the cohabitation of a civilized man and a savage woman, even for a long period of time, gives rise to the presumption that they consented to be married in our sense of marriage.'[68] In 1899 the Supreme Court for the North-West Territories decided that the two sons of Mary Brown, a Piegan woman, and Nicholas Sheran, a founder of a lucrative coal mine near Lethbridge, were not entitled, as next of kin, to a share of their father's estate, as the judge found that Sheran could have but did not legally marry Brown while they lived together from 1878 until Sheran's death in 1882.[69]

Haunted by an Image

Negative images of Aboriginal women proved extraordinarily persistent. Their morality was questioned in a number of sections of the Indian Act. If a woman was not of 'good moral character,' for example, she lost her one-third interest in her husband's estate, and a male government official was the sole and final judge of moral character. As late as 1921 the House of Commons debated a Criminal Code amendment that would have made it an offence for any white man to have 'illicit connection' with an Indian woman. Part of the rationale advanced was that 'the Indian women are, perhaps, not as alive as women of other races in the country to the importance of maintaining their chastity.' The amendment was not passed, as it was argued that this could make unsuspecting white men the 'victims' of Indian women who would blackmail them.[70] By contrast, any critical reflections upon the behaviour of early government officials and the police in western Canada did not survive beyond the controversy of the 1880s. Ideological constraints, combined with more formal mechanisms of control such as the pass system, succeeded in marginalizing Aboriginal women and in limiting the alternatives and opportunities available to them.

Local histories of the Prairies suggest that by the turn of the century many of the settlements of the West had their 'local Indian' who was tolerated on the margins or fringes of society and whose behaviour and appearance were the subject of local anecdotes. 'Old Dewdney,' for example, an ancient, often flamboyantly dressed man, were a familiar sight in Fort Macleod. Local people exchanged stories about the exotic past of the old man and of their generosity and kindness toward him.[71] 'Nikamoos' or the Singer camped each summer by herself on the trail to the Onion Lake reserve agency in Saskatchewan. Among the white community, it was reputed that as a girl Nikamoos had run away with a policeman but that he had been compelled to leave her. The child she bore died and Nikamoos went insane.[72]

A solitary Indian woman known only as Liza camped on the outskirts of Virden, Manitoba, for many years until her disappearance sometime in the 1940s. By then Liza was thought to have been well over one hundred years old. She lived winter and summer in an unheated tent by the railroad tracks, although she spent the long winter days huddled in the livery stable and also at times crept into the Nu-Art Beauty Parlour, where she sat on the floor in front of the window, warming herself in the sun. Liza smoked a corncob pipe as she shuffled about the streets and lanes of Virden, rummaging in garbage tins. She bathed under the overflow pipe at the water tower, sometimes clothed and sometimes not, and dried off by standing over the huge heat register in Scales and Rothnie's General Store. To an extent she was tolerated and even assisted: town employees shovelled out a path for her when she was buried under snow, and it was thought that the town fathers supplied her with food from time to time. Children were half fascinated and half frightened by this ancient woman. Old-timers believed that Liza was there well before the first settlers, that she was among the Sioux who had escaped the pursuing American army in 1876, that she received regular cheques from the United States, and that she was capable of fine handwriting, where learned, no one knew.[73]

The presence of Liza, and the stories told about her, served to sharpen the boundaries of community membership and to articulate what was and what was not considered acceptable and respectable.[74] Liza was the object of both fascination and repugnance as she violated norms of conventional behaviour, dress, and cleanliness, representing the antithesis of 'civilized' Prairie society. Although economically and socially marginal, Liza was symbolically important. Her role attests to the recurrent pattern through which the new society of the West gained in strength and identity and sought to legitimate its own authority by defining itself against the people who were there before them. Liza was a real person, but what she represented was a Euro-Canadian artifact, created by the settlement. The narratives circulated about Liza were not those she might have told herself – of the disasters that had stripped her of family and community, or perhaps of her strategies in adopting the character role – and this folklore reflected less about Liza than about the community itself. Her solitary life was unique and in contrast to the lives of Aboriginal women; Liza was not representative of a Lakota woman within Lakota society. Yet her presence on the margins of the settlement was tolerated and encouraged in the way these women were not, as she appeared to fit into the well-established category of the 'squaw' that still served to confirm the Euro-Canadian newcomers in their belief that their cultural and moral superiority entitled them to the land that had become their home.

NOTES

The author thanks Hugh Dempsey for sharing his research with her and for his valuable suggestions as to other sources.

1 Mary E. Inderwick 'A Lady and Her Ranch,' in *The Best From Alberta History*, ed. Hugh Dempsey (Saskatoon: Western Producer Prairie Books, 1981), 65–77. In 1882 the North-West Territories were divided into four provisional districts named Assiniboia, Saskatchewan, Alberta, and Athabasca.
2 For an examination and critique of the argument that European women introduced segregation, see Margaret Strobel, *European Women and the Second British Empire* (Bloomington: Indiana University Press, 1991). See also Ann Laura Stoler, 'Carnal Knowledge and Imperial Power: Gender, Race and Morality in Colonial Asia,' in *Gender at the Crossroads of Knowledge: Feminist Anthropology in the Postmodern Era*, ed. Micaela di Leonardo (Berkeley: University of California Press, 1991), 51–101; and Stoler, 'Rethinking Colonial Categories: European Communities and the Boundaries of Rule,' in *Colonialism and Culture*, ed. Nicholas B. Dirks (Ann Arbor: University of Michigan Press, 1993), 319–52.
3 See Sarah Carter, *Lost Harvests: Prairie Indian Reserve Farmers and Government Policy* (Montreal: McGill-Queen's University Press, 1990).
4 Rayna Green, 'The Pocahontas Perplex: The Image of Indian Women in American Culture,' in *Unequal Sisters: A Multicultural Reader in U.S. Women's History*, ed. Ellen Carol DuBois and Vicki L. Ruiz (New York: Routledge, 1990), 15–21.
5 John McDougall, *A Criticism of 'Indian Wigwams and Northern Camp-Fires'* (Toronto: Printed for the author by W. Briggs, 1895), 12–13.
6 P.B. Waite, *Canada, 1874–1896: Arduous Destiny* (Toronto: McClelland and Stewart, 1971), 149.
7 D.N. Sprague, *Canada and the Métis, 1869–1885* (Waterloo, ON: Wilfrid Laurier Press, 1988).

8 Canada. *Sessional Papers*, annual report of the superintendent general of Indian affairs for the year ending 30 June 1898 (p. xix) and for the year ending 31 December 1899 (pp. xxiii, xxviii, 166); *Mail* [Toronto], 2 March 1889; Pamela Margaret White, 'Restructuring the Domestic Sphere – Prairie Indian Women on Reserves: Image, Ideology and State Policy, 1880–1930' (Ph.D. diss., McGill University, 1987); W.H. Withrow, *Native Races of North America* (Toronto: Methodist Mission Rooms, 1895), 114 (quoted).

9 Canada, *Sessional Papers*, annual report of the superintendent general of Indian affairs for the year ending March 1908 (p. 110).

10 Inspector Alex McGibbon's report on Onion Lake, October 1891, National Archives of Canada (NA), Record Group 10 (RG 10), records relating to Indian Affairs, Black Series, vol. 3860, file 82, 319–6.

11 *Globe* [Toronto], 1 February 1886.

12 *Mail*, 23 January 1886.

13 Canada, House of Commons, *Debates*, Malcolm Cameron, Session 1886, vol. 1, pp. 720–1.

14 E.C. Morgan. 'The North-West Mounted Police: Internal Problems and Public Criticism, 1874–1883,' *Saskatchewan History* 26.2 (Spring 1973): 56–9; Laird is quoted on p. 56.

15 Canada, House of Commons, *Debates*, 21 April 1880, Joseph Royal, Fourth Parliament, Second Session, p. 1638.

16 *Mail*, 2 February 1886.

17 John MacLean, 'The Half-Breed and Indian Insurrection,' *Canadian Methodist Magazine* 22.1 (July 1885): 173–4.

18 Edgar Dewdney to the Bishop of Saskatchewan, 31 May 1886, NA, RG 10, vol. 3753, file 30613.

19 Saskatchewan Archives Board (SAB), John O'Kute-sica Correspondence, collection no. R-834, File 17(b), p. 15.

20 *Blackfeet Heritage: 1907–08* (Browning: Blackfeet Heritage Program, n.d.), 171.

21 A.B. McCullough, *Papers Relating to the North West Mounted Police and Fort Walsh*, Manuscript Report Series, no. 213 (Ottawa: Parks Canada, Department of Indian and Northern Affairs, 1977), 132–3.

22 L. Herchmer to comptroller, 23 May 1889, NA, RG 18, vol. 35, file 499–1889.

23 Personal interview with Kirsten Grier, great-granddaughter of D.J. Grier, Calgary, 19 May 1993. See also *Fort Macleod – Our Colourful Past: A History of the Town of Fort Macleod from 1874 to 1924* (Fort Macleod: Fort Macleod History Committee, 1977), 268–9.

24 O'Kute-sica Correspondence (see note 19 above), p. 3.

25 See, for example, S.B. Steele to commissioner, Fort Macleod, 20 July 1895, NA, RG 18, vol. 2182, file RCMP 1895 pt. 2; and Gilbert E. Sanders Diaries, 20 October 1885, Edward Sanders Family Papers, M1093, File 38, Glenbow Archives.

26 F. Laurie Barron, 'Indian Agents and the North-West Rebellion,' in *1885 and After: Native Society in Transition,* ed. F. Laurie Barron and James B. Waldram (Regina: Canadian Plains Research Center, 1986), 36.

27 Norma Sluman and Jean Goodwill, *John Tootoosis: A Biography of a Cree Leader* (Ottawa: Golden Dog Press, 1982), 37.

28 Hugh A. Dempsey, *Big Bear: The End of Freedom* (Vancouver: Douglas and McIntyre, 1984), 117. See also *The Saskatchewan Herald* [Battleford], 14 and 28 February 1881.

29 Newspaper clipping, 'Through the Saskatchewan,' n.p., n.d, N.A. William Henry Cotton Collection.

30 *Globe,* 4 June 1880; *Macleod Gazette* [Fort Macleod], 23 March 1886; *Mail,* 2 February 1886.

31 Canada, House of Commons, *Debates,* Session 1886, vol. 1, p. 730.

32 William Donovan to L. Vankoughnet, 31 October 1886, NA, RG 10, vol. 3772, file 34983.

33 *Globe,* 4 June 1886.

34 *The Facts Respecting Indian Administration in the North-West* (Ottawa: 1886); quoted pp. 9, 12, 37.

35 Theresa Gowanlock and Theresa Delaney, *Two Months in the Camp of Big Bear* (Parkdale: Parkdale Times, 1885).

36 *Manitoba Sun* [Winnipeg], 7 December 1886.

37 Sarah Carter. '"A Fate Worse Than Death": Indian Captivity Stories Thrilled Victorian Readers: But Were They True?' *The Beaver* 68.2 (April/May 1988): 21–8; *Macleod Gazette,* n.d., quoted p. 22.

38 Canada, *Sessional Papers,* vol. 24, no. 19, annual report of the commissioner of the North West Mounted Police for 1890 (p. 62).

39 *Moosomin Courier,* 13 March 1890.

40 Joe Dion, *My Tribe the Crees* (Calgary: Glenbow-Alberta Institute, 1979), 114.

41 See Sarah Carter, 'Relations between Native and Non-Native Women in the Prairie West, 1870–1920,' paper presented to the Women and History Association of Manitoba, Winnipeg, February 1992.

42 Elizabeth M. McLean, 'Prisoners of the Indians,' *The Beaver* 278 (June 1947): 15–16.

43 David Hamer, *New Towns in the New World: Images and Perceptions of the*

Nineteenth Century Urban Frontier (New York: Columbia University Press, 1990), 17, 213.

44 *What Canadian Women Say of the Canadian North-West* (Montreal: Montreal Herald, 1886), 42–45; quoted p. 44.

45 L. Vankoughnet to John A. Macdonald, 15 November 1883, NA, RG 10, vol. 1009, file 628. no. 596–635.

46 S.W. Horrall, 'The (Royal) North-West Mounted Police and Prostitution on the Canadian Prairies,' *Prairie Forum* 10.1 (Spring 1985): 105–27.

47 Clipping from the *Bulletin* [Edmonton], 7 January 1883, NA, RG 10, vol. 3673, file 10,986.

48 Canada, *Sessional Papers*, annual report of the superintendent general of Indian affairs for the year ending 1906 (p. 82).

49 Constance B. Backhouse, 'Nineteenth-Century Canadian Prostitution Law: Reflection of a Discriminatory Society,' *Histoire sociale / Social History* 18 (November 1985): 420–2; quoted p. 422.

50 Canada, *Sessional Papers*, annual report of the commissioner of the North-West Mounted Police force for the year 1889, reprinted in *The New West* (Toronto: Coles Publishing Company, 1973), 101.

51 *Saskatchewan Herald*, 15 March 1886 and 13 March 1888 (quoted).

52 *Calgary Herald*, 5 March 1885.

53 See, for example, Carolina Antoinetta J.A. Van de Vorst, 'A History of Farm Women's Work in Manitoba' (M.A. thesis, University of Manitoba, 1988).

54 Lyn Hancock with Marion Dowler, *Tell Me Grandmother* (Toronto: McClelland and Steward, 1985), 139.

55 *Macleod Gazette*, 18 July 1888.

56 John D. Higinbotham, *When the West Was Young: Historical Reminiscences of the Early Canadian West* (Toronto: Ryerson Press, 1933), 260–1.

57 R.C. Macleod, *The North-West Mounted Police and Law Enforcement, 1873–1905* (Toronto: University of Toronto Press, 1976), 145. See also NA, RG 18, vol. 24, file 667–1888.

58 Donald Smith. 'Bloody Murder Almost Became Miscarriage of Justice,' *Herald Sunday Magazine*, 23 July 1989, p. 13. Thanks to Donald Smith, Department of History, University of Calgary, for allowing me to draw upon his sources on this case.

59 James Gray, *Talk to My Lawyer: Great Stories of Southern Alberta's Bar and Bench* (Edmonton: Hurtig, 1987), 7.

60 Rouleau quoted in Smith, 'Bloody Murder,' 15.

61 *Calgary Herald*, 24 July and 10 September (quoted) 1888; 27 February and 8 March (quoted) 1889.

62 See Christine Bolt, *Victorian Attitudes to Race* (Toronto: University of Toronto Press, 1971); Philip D. Curtin, *The Image of Africa: British Ideas and Action, 1780–1850* (Madison: University or Wisconsin Press, 1964); V.G. Kiernan, *The Lords of Human Kind: European Attitudes toward the Outside World in the Imperial Age* (Middlesex: Penguin Books, 1972); Douglas A. Lorimer, *Color, Class and the Victorians* (New York: Holmes and Meier Publishers, 1978); and Philip Mason, *Patterns of Dominance* (London: Oxford University Press, 1971).

63 Walter Hildebrandt, 'Official Images of 1885,' *Prairie Fire* 6.4 (1985): 31–40.

64 This is suggested by Backhouse, 'Nineteenth-Century Canadian Prostitution Law,' 422.

65 Mariana Valverde, *The Age of Light, Soap, and Water: Moral Reform in English Canada, 1885–1925* (Toronto: McClelland and Stewart, 1991).

66 NA, RG 18, vol. 1039, file 87–1886, pt. l.

67 Beverley A. Stacey, 'D.W. Davis: Whiskey Trader to Politician,' *Alberta History* 38.3 (Summer 1990): 1–11.

68 Sylvia Van Kirk, *Many Tender Ties: Women in Fur Trade Society, 1670–1870* (Winnipeg: Watson and Dwyer Publishing Ltd, 1980), 241; Constance Backhouse, *Petticoats and Prejudice: Women and the Law in Nineteenth-Century Canada* (Toronto: Osgoode Society, 1991), chapter 1; judge quoted in Van Kirk, 241.

69 Brian Slattery and Linda Charleton, ed., *Canadian Native Law Cases 3, 1891–1910* (Saskatoon: Native Law Centre, 1985), 636–44.

70 Canada, House of Commons, *Debates,* Session 1921, vol. 4, 26 May 1921, p. 3908.

71 *Fort Macleod – Our Colourful Past*, 217–18.

72 Ruth Matheson Buck, 'Wives and Daughters,' *Folklore* 9.4 (Autumn 1988): 14–15.

73 'Talk about Stories,' in *Anecdotes and Updates: Virden Centennial, 1982* (Virden: Empire Publishing Company, 1982), 57–9.

74 Diane Tye, 'Local Character Anecdotes: A Nova Scotia Case Study,' *Western Folklore* 48 (July 1989): 196.

7 Colonized Lives: The Native Wives and Daughters of Five Founding Families of Victoria

SYLVIA VAN KIRK

The fur trade history of the Pacific northwest is in many ways a trans-border story. Until the imposition of the border in 1846, most of the territory was known as the Columbia Department of the Hudson's Bay Company. The headquarters of this district was Fort Vancouver, but a network of posts stretched far up the coast into Alaska and was connected to posts in the interior by a system of river routes and pack trails (see fig. 7.1). The role that Native women played in the fur trade and the extensive family formation that resulted have been well-documented in previous studies.[1] What I shall look at here is the experiences of the Native women in five families who lived most of their lives at various posts in the Pacific northwest and then settled at Fort Victoria, capital of the Crown Colony of Vancouver Island, which had been created to forestall American expansion in 1849.

A look at a map of Victoria in 1858 (see fig. 7.2) illustrates the dominant position of the family properties of James Douglas, William H. McNeill, John Work, John Tod, and Charles Ross. These men had all been officers of the Hudson's Bay Company. All had indigenous wives, but of different tribal origins. Although all these officers had toyed with the idea of retiring to Britain or eastern Canada, there were several reasons why they chose to settle their families at Fort Victoria. Coming from the élite of the fur trade hierarchy, these men had both the desire and the wherewithal to purchase the expensive estates which the Company made available. In Victoria, in geographically familiar yet 'civilized' surroundings, they hoped to maintain their social and economic standing by becoming part of the landed gentry, which was envisioned as the élite class in an agrarian colonization scheme which was explicitly to replicate British social hierarchy.[2]

For the Native wives and children, however, adapting to life in colo-

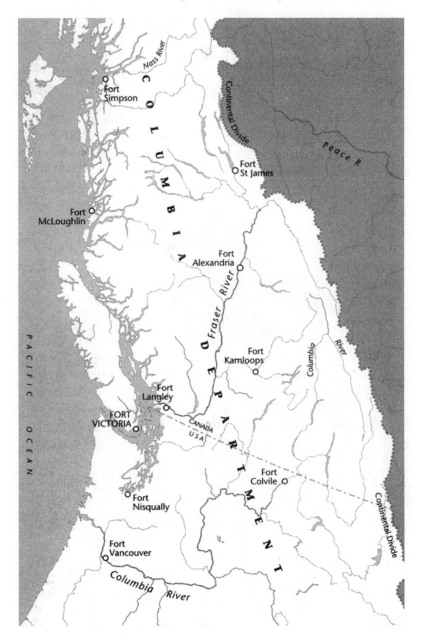

7.1 The Columbia Department of the Hudson's Bay Company. Map by Eric Leinberger.

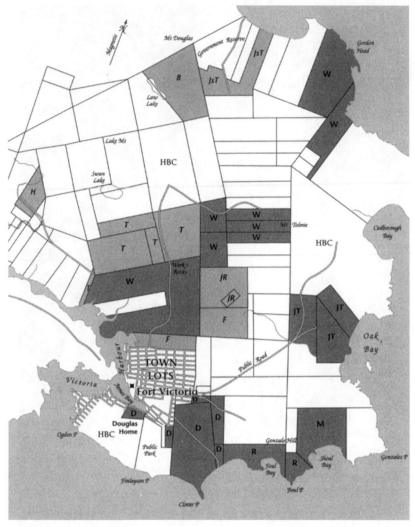

JT John Tod
   JsT James Tod (eldest son)
M William Henry McNeill
   B George Blenkinsop (son-in-law)
R Isabella Ross
   JR John Ross (eldest son)

D James Douglas
   H John S Helmcken (son-in-law)
W John Work
   F Roderick Finlayson (son-in-law)
   T William F Tolmie (son-in-law)

7.2 Victoria, 1858 (drawn from the Official District map). Map by Eric Leinberger.

nial settler society as opposed to that of a fur-trade post offered particular challenges. They were to be subject to an intensive program of colonization, designed to negate their indigenous heritage and to acculturate them to the norms and material culture of 'genteel' British society. As families with élite aspirations, there was little room for a middle ground, especially for the second generation: they could not build an identity which acknowledged the duality of their heritage. There were complexities in the intersection of the dynamics of gender, class, and race. As wives and mothers, the Native women in these five families were to find their social roles severely circumscribed. Daughters, however, succeeded much better than their brothers in adapting to the colonizing agenda of their fathers.[3] A fascinating window on the acculturation experience of these families is provided by the rich collection of portrait photographs which have survived in the British Columbia Archives and Record Service. Most of these photographs are from family albums, and the images preserved for family posterity (and public consumption) emphasize adaptation to British material culture.

In order to appreciate the social challenges faced by these families, it is necessary to sketch out their fur-trade background.[4] All of the Native women had married young, their unions initially being contracted according to the fur-trade marriage rite known as 'the custom of the country.' They produced large families, from seven to thirteen children, and the sex ratio was heavily weighted in a favour of daughters.

Significant to the social hierarchy of colonial Victoria was the fact that the governor in its formative years was Chief Factor James Douglas, whose wife Amelia, was part Cree. Her mother, Miyo Nipiy, had married her father, Chief Factor William Connolly, at Rat Portage (south of Hudson Bay) in 1803, and they had lived at various posts throughout Rupert's Land, before moving to Fort St James (in northern British Columbia) in the 1820s. There in 1828 the promising young clerk James Douglas took his superior's sixteen-year-old daughter, Amelia, for his 'country wife.' The Douglases soon moved to Fort Vancouver, where most of their thirteen children were born, but many did not survive to adulthood. When Douglas was given charge of Fort Victoria in 1849, his family consisted of his wife and five daughters. The only surviving son was born in 1851, followed by another daughter. Shortly after becoming governor, Douglas bought up large parcels of land and was one of the first to build a substantial home outside the fort. When Douglas was knighted in 1863 for his services to the colony, his wife gained the title of Lady Douglas.

Adjacent to the Douglas estate was that of the widow of Charles Ross. Ross only lived long enough to see Fort Victoria built in 1844. But he left his widow, Isabella, with the wherewithal to purchase her own estate, which made her the first woman to be an independent landowner in Victoria. The daughter of a French-Canadian *engagé*, Joseph Mainville, and his Ojibwa wife, Isabella had travelled far from her Aboriginal home and kin, after marrying Ross at Rainy Lake (now in western Ontario) in 1822. The Ross family numbered six boys and four girls, all of whom survived to adulthood.

The wife of Chief Factor John Work, who would become the largest landowner in the colony, was also the daughter of a French-Canadian *engagé* and a Native woman. Josette Legacé, whose mother was Spokane, grew up along the upper reaches of the Columbia River, where she and Work were married at Fort Colville in 1826. A redoubtable companion, she and her growing family moved with Work to various stations in the Columbia Department, including a fifteen-year stint at the northerly post of Fort Simpson at the mouth of the Nass River. The three boys and eight girls all lived to adulthood and settled in Victoria. The Work estate in the Hillside area encompassed over a thousand acres. Work died in 1861, his widow outliving him by thirty-five years.

Although often referred to as Indian, the wives of the above men were all of mixed descent. These marriages cut across class and ethnicity, however, they are still representative of fur-trade endogamy – the wives' fathers having been connected to the Company and the women themselves growing up within or near the fur-trade posts.

In the other two families, the McNeills and the Tods, the marriages harkened back to the old fur-trade alliances whereby officers married high-ranking Indian women whose connections were useful to advancing the husbands' commercial position. William H. McNeill was a Bostonian who first entered the Pacific coast trading in the 1820s for the firm of Bryant and Sturgis, in competition with the Hudson's Bay Company. His first wife was Kaigani Haida from northern British Columbia. Haida women were noted for their influential trading role, and this alliance undoubtedly helped to make McNeill such a successful trader that the company went to some lengths to lure him into its service in the early 1830s. There is no likeness of Mathilda, as she was known, but she was described as a large, handsome woman of dignified bearing. This long union produced twelve children, of whom seven girls and three boys survived to adulthood. The mother, however, did not long survive the birth of the last two, twin girls born in 1850. Thus it was a motherless family that McNeill settled in Victoria on a two-hundred-acre estate which encompassed much of south Oak Bay. Eventually McNeill took a second wife: this time, a high-ranking Nisga'a woman who was an active trader on the Nass River in her own right. Formally married in 1866, Neshaki (or Martha as she was baptized) retired with her husband to Victoria in the late 1860s. There were no children of the second union, this being the only one of the five families in which there was a stepmother who had to develop a relationship with a close-knit, already partially grown family.

Chief Trader John Tod's marital life, which had been considerably more irregular than many of his fur-trade contemporaries, had included an ill-fated marriage to an Englishwoman in the 1830s. This wife, having gone mad, was placed in an asylum in England, and Tod then returned to the far west where he took charge of Fort Kamloops. There in the early 1840s he took a new young 'country wife,' Sophia Lolo, eldest daughter of an influential local chief Jean-Baptiste Lolo *dit* St Paul and his Shuswap wife. In his retirement years on his estate in Oak Bay, Tod was thus surrounded by a young family, eventually numbering five boys and two girls.

In these families, the patriarchal role exercised by the British husbands and fathers was greater than usual because of their own cultural bias, which had increasing impact on the shaping of family life. This is not to deny that in fur-trade society, Native wives had brought their husbands valuable knowledge for the trade and even survival. There is ample testimony to the bonds of affection which developed, such as Work's writing: 'The little wife and I get on very well and she takes good care of myself and children.'[5] But there was also acknowledgment that Native wives, in spite of their fine qualities, were lacking in lady-like attributes. Work spoke of his wife as being 'simple and uninstructed'; Ross confessed that his wife was 'not exactly suited to shine at the head of a nobleman's table.'[6] That Indianness was not something to be celebrated is illustrated in Captain McNeill's poignant lament when his Haida wife died in 1850:

My poor Wife ... had been a good and faithful partner to me for twenty years and we had twelve children together ... the deceased was a most kind mother to her children, and *no* Woman could have done her duty better, although an Indian.[7]

The Native wives were subject to a program of anglicization along with their children, especially when the prospect of settlement loomed. Indeed, as early as the 1830s at Fort Vancouver several of these couples had had to deal with the racist implications which accompanied missionization. When the Reverend Herbert Beaver and his English wife arrived at the fort, Beaver castigated particularly the wives for living in sin and suggested that they be kept outside the fort gates. Douglas and other officers gallantly defended the honour of their wives and the morality of their domestic arrangements, but both Douglas and Ross sought to protect themselves from further insult by having their wives and children baptized and submitting to a Church of England marriage rite.[8]

As for the children, these fathers were active agents in the colonization of their families; they never seem to have questioned the desirability of acculturating them to British norms and customs. Though their private correspondence is filled with paternal concern for the welfare of their children, this was posited in terms of negating their Native background. It was never suggested that their First Nations heritage should be actively incorporated into their upbringing. At the fur-trade posts, the fathers took an active role in the education of their children, introducing them to the basics of English literacy and to Christian observances such as Bible reading and prayers. The critical role of mothers in socializing children, especially daughters, was severely truncated. Although there is certainly evidence of maternal devotion, mothers were tutored along with children in aspects of British material culture. But the fathers continually worried about their children growing up at isolated posts without 'proper education or example.' In 1834, for example, John Work wrote to a retired friend, Edward Ermatinger, 'I have now here four fine little girls, had I them a little brushed up with education, and a little knowledge of the world, they would scarcely be known to be Indians.'[9]

It had never been as common to send daughters as it was sons to eastern Canada or Great Britain for education, but for all it proved a risky and expensive business, even if they were entrusted to the care of relatives or friends. Thus fur-trade officers were eager to place their children at the first school established at Fort Vancouver in the 1830s. When this venture failed because of the mismanagement of the Reverend Beaver, Douglas and Work both placed their daughters with American missionaries in the Willamette Valley. Others did continue to cherish the hope of sending their children back home. Charles Ross, for example, felt that his promotion to Fort Victoria would enable him to support the education of his three teenaged children (two sons and a daughter) in England. Although the children were initially reported as 'much improved,' their progress was cut short by their father's untimely death. Relatives were soon expressing their dissatisfaction with the children, whom they found 'extremely indocile and addicted to habits incompatible with a residence in this country.' All three children were sent back to their mother at Fort Victoria in the fall of 1845.[10]

The transition from fur-trade post to colonial Victoria presented particular challenges for the Native wives of the fur-trade élite. While they have left us little direct record of how they felt, family correspondence and newspaper reports suggest something of the contours of their lives. Evidence indicates that the wives viewed settlement in Victoria as a more attractive alternative to being transported back to the alien environment of eastern North America or Great Britain.[11] Most of them had already proved their adaptability in moving with their husbands to various locations in the Columbia District, and had borne the loneliness which resulted from their separation from their own kin. As officers' wives, these women would have enjoyed a relatively privileged status within the forts; the move to colonial Victoria resulted in many changes. Materially, they now found themselves living on isolated estates in houses which attempted to replicate more completely a British lifestyle. Socially, in the colony, their status was threatened. However willingly they had responded to their husbands' tutelage, they were understandably at a disadvantage in providing social leadership, and invidious comparisons were quick to be made.

High class status could not protect these wives and even their daughters from racist jibes. It rankled some incoming settlers that Native families should stand so high in the social hierarchy. Numerous remarks were made by visitors and even working-class British immigrants that the society of the new colony was rather deficient because some of its leading officials were married to Native women. Shortly after her arrival from England in 1854, Annie Deans wrote home disparaging Douglas – a man who had spent his life among the North American Indians and got one for a wife could scarcely know anything about governing an English colony.[12]

An analysis of these wives suggests that they had varying degrees of success in adapting to the prescriptions laid out for them. This had to do with their own aptitude, the degree of familial support, and the role that they were expected to play. These social tensions were poignantly highlighted in the Douglas family, which because of its position was subject to particular scrutiny. Initially, Amelia Douglas kept in the background, partly because she didn't speak English very well. The social calendar was kept by her daughters and a Douglas niece who had come from Britain, but gradually Lady Douglas became comfortable in her role as the governor's wife. Douglas wrote proudly of his wife, after a New Year's levee in the early 1870s: 'Darling good Mamma was nicely got up and won all hearts with her kindness and geniality.'[13] When Lady Franklin visited Victoria in 1861, she was curious to meet the 'Indian' wife of the governor. She found Amelia to have 'a gentle, simple & kindly manner' and was fascinated that her Native features were less pronounced than in some of her daughters.[14] However shy she might have been in her public role, family correspondence indicates that Lady Douglas was a strong maternal presence in her own household. Described as 'a very active woman, energetic and industrious,' she supervised the domestic production of her household, which ranged from raising fine chickens to putting up fruits and preserves from the extensive orchard.[15]

By contrast, Josette Work seems always to have played an active role in the round of social entertainments, for which her home, Hillside House, became renowned in early Victoria. The following description of a New Year's celebration in 1861, by military officer Charles Wilson, was typical:

> There were about 30 at dinner – such a display of fish, flesh and fowl and pastry as is seldom seen. We danced until 12 & then all hands sat down to a sumptuous supper and then set to work dancing again until a very late hour ...[16]

'The Works,' he enthused, 'are about the kindest people I ever came across.' Indeed, Mrs Work earned the admiration of all who met her; even the American historian Hubert Bancroft acknowledged that 'in body and mind, the Indian wife was strong and elastic as steel.'[17]

Josette herself seems to have always been interested in adopting British fashion. A fine portrait of her, taken by S.A. Spencer, shows her every inch the Victorian matron – indeed, at a glance, she could be taken for Queen Victoria herself! During her long widowhood, she took an active role in the management of the family property. Very much the matriarch, she grieved over her sons' lack of success and premature deaths, but rejoiced in the widening family circle over which she presided, the result of her numerous daughters' successful marriages.

Josette Work and Amelia Douglas would have known one another from their earlier days at Fort Vancouver, and they remained fast friends, comforting one another in family trials and social rebuffs. As the youngest Douglas daughter wrote in her reminiscences: 'Mrs. Work was a most wonderful woman. She and my mother were the most loving friends and such rejoicing when Mrs. Work came to pay us a visit. She stood by my dear Mother on many sad occasions.'[18] These women were able to retain some of their Aboriginal ways and were noted for their kindness to incoming immigrant women, especially during childbirth and illness when their knowledge of Native medicine was particularly helpful. Dr J.S. Helmcken, who married the eldest Douglas daughter, remembered that his mother-in-law had rendered an Englishwoman, Mrs Yates, much assistance during a difficult confinement, notably by urging her to adopt the Native position of squatting down. Josette Work was well regarded as a midwife, Helmcken crediting her with saving the lives of babies of which he had despaired.[19] When this remarkable Métis woman of the Columbia Department died at an advanced age in 1896, she was eulogized for 'her usefulness in pioneer work and many good deeds.'[20]

Most of the wives experienced widowhood, although it affected their lives quite differently. The most difficult was that of the Widow Ross, who struggled gamely to build a respectable life for her family after her husband died prematurely in 1844. Buying her own estate was an unusual step for a woman in her position to take, but she relied on the support of her eldest son, John, who also purchased an estate in Victoria, and undoubtedly hoped the younger sons would help develop her farm. Documents from the 1850s reveal the Widow Ross actively involved in commercial transactions, selling farm produce and livestock, but by the late 1850s family troubles were brewing. Her younger sons were gaining a reputation around town for being wild, one running up such a debt that his mother publicly disowned him.[21]

Perhaps the offer of assistance with managing the estate made Isabella Ross succumb to the attentions of a young suitor from eastern Canada, one Lucius Simon O'Brien, whom she married in 1863. But the new stepfather was soon at odds with the family, as it quickly became apparent that he was intent on defrauding them. The conflict resulted in much unfavourable publicity. Isabella's distress resulted in her temporarily running away, an action which O'Brien used to try to tarnish

7.3 and 7.4 (above and opposite) Two portraits of Amelia, Lady Douglas, showing her acculturation to her role as the governor's wife.

her character. While he had been willing to overlook race while marrying the landed widow, once his plans went awry, he was certainly
prepared to play to racist stereotypes, publishing the following notice
in the Victoria *Daily Chronicle* in April 1864:

> Whereas My Wife, Isabella, has left my bed and board because I will not
> support her drunken sons, nor allow her to keep drunk herself, and have
> a lot of drunken squaws about her, this is to forbid all persons, harbouring
> her, or trusting her on my account, as I will pay no debts she may contract.

7.5 Josette Work as 'Queen Victoria.'

7.6 Isabella Ross in her widow's weeds.

A few days later, the youngest son, William, attempted to come to his mother's defence and charged that O'Brien was trying to swindle the family:

> His every act since his marriage has been to try to get everything from my mother, and turn us (the children) out of the house ... Will you do me and my mother the simple justice to publish this, as such a statement as O'Brien has made is calculated to injure both her and myself.[22]

When the family then began proceedings against O'Brien to prove that he was actually a bigamist, he apparently deserted up island, where he came to an untimely end a few years later. Isabella, assuming that his abandonment was as good as a divorce, resumed the title of the Widow Ross.

Through continuing family misfortune, Isabella found solace from other Native wives and also from the Anglican clergyman Edward Cridge, who had welcomed these families into his congregation. Cridge used to make regular visits to Mrs Ross to read and pray with her. The McNeills were her closest neighbours, but she also paid visits to old friends Amelia Douglas and Josette Work.[23] By the mid-1870s, when the last son remaining in Victoria died, the Ross estate could no longer be maintained and was sold off. In her last years, the Widow Ross was financially dependent upon Flora, her youngest daughter; Isabella ended her days in a little house on the grounds of the convent of the Sisters of St Ann, dying in 1885.[24]

The record is almost silent on the Victoria life of Sophia Tod. Tod himself, who carried on an extensive correspondence with former colleagues, does not mention her, although he comments extensively on his children. The most important document that remains is a striking portrait of her in European costume, which may have been taken at the time of her church marriage in Victoria in 1863 (see fig. 7.7). This photograph invites various readings, but it seems to indicate an ambivalence about the constraints of Victorian dress and customs. Tod's property was quite isolated from the rest of the community, and his wife seems to have been also; unlike some of the other Native wives, she had no previously established female social ties and she also had a young family to raise without the support of kin. Local legend implies that Sophia Lolo did not make a happy adjustment to life in Victoria; the Tod house, which is the only one of the original family dwellings surviving today, is reputed to be haunted by the ghost of an Indian woman.[25]

7.7 Sophia Lolo.

Martha (Neshaki), Captain McNeill's second wife, presents quite a contrast. As a high-ranking Nisga'a woman, she was used to an active commercial role, which she apparently continued in Victoria. In the 1860s, McNeill had constructed an imposing residence on McNeill Bay, to which Martha's Nisga'a kin were frequent visitors in addition to the McNeill siblings and their families. The Big House, which seems to have been a cross between a Scottish baronial hall and a Nisga'a longhouse, was home to the unmarried twins and their stepmother in the early 1870s.[26] A glimpse into their lives is provided by a unique little diary, chronicled by Rebecca, one of the twins, for several weeks in August and September 1875. This account underscores the importance of kin ties in the McNeill household; there were frequent comings and goings between the female members of the Big House and the homes of various McNeill children who had settled nearby. Again female ties had been formed earlier at Fort Simpson; in 1863, Martha had taken her stepdaughter Lucy on a trading expedition up the Nass River.[27] After McNeill died, however, it appears that Martha was closer to her own Nisga'a kin than to her stepchildren. Her will leaves the bulk of her portion of the McNeill estate to her own kin, but specifically requests that she be buried beside her husband in the Ross Bay Cemetery. It was left to a Nisga'a niece to see that wish carried out.[28]

A convert to Christianity, Martha was quite adept at travelling in both British and Nisga'a worlds. This would have been increasingly difficult for her highly acculturated stepdaughters. A stunning portrait of the five surviving sisters was taken by Victoria's famous woman photographer Hannah Maynard, likely around the time of their father's death in 1875 (see fig. 7.8). The as yet unmarried twins are standing at the back of picture. The three married sisters are seated: dominant on the right is Lucy, the eldest surviving sister. Mathilda, named for her mother, holds the family photograph album, while Fanny kneels by her side. With their elegant, if sombre, Victorian gowns and elaborate braided hairstyles, the picture exudes British gentility. At least the younger sisters would have directly benefited from the new agents of colonization, combined in the church and school, that the colony provided.

Schooling specifically for the children of the élite had been set up with the arrival of the first Anglican missionaries, Robert and Emma Staines, in 1849. The five families dominated the Fort Victoria school register in the first years; out of thirty pupils listed, there were four Douglases, five Works, three McNeills, three Rosses, and two Tods, mostly girls.[29] The girls were being groomed for marriage, with consid-

7.8 The five surviving daughters of Captain W.H. McNeill and his Haida wife, Mathilda, c. 1875.

erable emphasis on dress, deportment, and ladylike accomplishments. An English observer in 1860, in complimenting the schoolmistress, emphasized the class bias and the previous deficiencies in young ladies' education: 'Mrs. Woods has some 30 girls of the higher class here ... She is accomplished as well as highly educated we understand.

Even girls engaged to be married, placed themselves under her & were much improved.'[30]

For the daughters, success within the framework of the colonial élite was, of course, marriage to a British gentleman. The older daughters in these families had already an established pattern of marriage to aspiring young officers in the Hudson's Bay Company. It was not lost on incoming young clerks that their prospects could be enhanced by marrying 'a big-wig's daughter.' There were a number of notable weddings at Fort Victoria in the early 1850s; Work's daughters Sarah and Jane married Roderick Finlayson and William Fraser Tolmie respectively, and then the governor's eldest daughter, Cecilia, married the Company doctor, J.S. Helmcken. The social networking among the women in these families was underscored when Lucy McNeill married Hamilton Moffatt in1856, for her bridesmaids were Jane Douglas and Mary Work, who also soon married Company men.[31]

Advantageous as these marriages were, the social status of the younger sisters in the new world of the colony could not be taken for granted. A new element in the social scene was introduced with the arrival of the naval squadron in Esquimalt. The officers enthusiastically engaged in sponsoring balls and other entertainments, but could be quite scathing in ridiculing the young ladies' attempts to keep up with the latest English fashions. Charles Wilson's commentary in 1861 may have been kinder than most:

> Most of the young ladies are half breeds & have quite as many propensities of the savage as of the civilized being ... The ladies were nicely dressed & some of them danced very well, though they would look much better if they would only learn to wear their crinoline properly.[32]

Racism could indeed negate social aspiration. Although the younger Ross daughters featured at the balls given by the officers of the British Navy in the 1850s, they never attained the status they desired. According to Phillip Hankin, they were very fine looking girls, but 'they had a great deal of Indian blood in them and were supposed to be only on the edge of society.'[33] That race could trump class is seen in what is reported to have been an exchange between the governor's daughter Agnes and a young midshipman at one of these balls. Miss Douglas demurred at his invitation to dance as being beneath her station, saying, 'What would Papa say if I were to dance with a middy'; whereupon he haughtily replied, 'What would Mama say if I were to dance with a Squaw!'

7.9 James and Amelia Douglas's daughters (left to right) Agnes, Jane, and Alice, in one of the earliest photos taken at Fort Victoria, 1858.

In actuality, Agnes Douglas's station was such that she was to lead the way in a new trend of marriage patterns whereby the younger daughters began to marry British gentlemen attached to the colonial service. In 1862, she married a well-born recent arrival, Arthur Bushby, who was clerk to Judge Begbie.[34] The weddings of the Douglas girls became increasingly elaborate affairs, as did their education. These changes were epitomized in the experience of Martha, the governor's youngest daughter. Having been given the best education that the colony could afford, her father was gratified that 'she plays well, sings, has a taste for drawing, is well read, writes a good hand and a nice letter.' But he sent her off to England in 1872 to 'get rid of the cobwebs of colonial training and give her the proper finish.'[35] A portrait taken of Martha and her married sister Jane Dallas in London, inscribed 'For dearest, darling Mother,' illustrates how far the Douglas girls had come in both dress and deportment (see fig. 7.10).

Nothing in early colonial Victoria capped the wedding of Martha, who after her return to Victoria married another colonial official, Dennis Harris, in 1878. The bride and her numerous attendants wore elaborate gowns, imported from Paris, and most of Victoria's notables were among the guests. This pattern of marrying colonial officials or merchant settlers was followed in the Work, McNeill, and Tod families. In 1864, Fanny McNeill married bank clerk James Judson Young, who became provincial secretary, while in 1879 Rebecca married Thomas Elwyn, who had served as gold commissioner. In the Tod family, the eldest daughter, Mary, married an American settler, J.S. Bowker, from San Juan Island, while her younger sister married a successful merchant, J.S. Drummond.[36]

Certainly not all these marriages achieved the same class status. Of all the daughters in question, only the Ross girls were to marry Métis men. The eldest, Elizabeth, who had been sent to England for her education, married Charles Wren, a Métis who had immigrated from Red River to Oregon. After her death in 1859, he married a younger sister, Mary Amelia.[37] Flora, the youngest Ross daughter, is the only woman in this study for whom marriage was not a critical factor in maintaining her status. In 1859, she married Paul K. Hubbs, an American settler who was described as 'a white Indian,' but within a decade this marriage had dissolved.[38] Flora Ross went on to have her own career, becoming matron of the asylum at New Westminster. Like her mother, Flora Ross was a remarkable woman; the social respectability which is reflected in her portrait, taken in the 1890s, she had achieved in her own right (see fig. 7.11).

By the 1870s, it was current local opinion that while the sons in these founding families had amounted to very little and certainly did not do their fathers' names proud, the daughters had achieved notable success. As John Tod remarked on one occasion about the Work daughters: 'It is rather remarkable that so numerous a family of daughters should have all turned out so well, their exemplary good conduct having gained the universal respect of all their neighbours.'[39] Indeed, in the late nineteenth century, several of the Work daughters, notably Sarah Finlayson and Jane Tolmie, lived an opulent lifestyle, their husbands having become two of the most wealthy and influential men in the city. At their mansion-like homes, 'Rock Bay' and 'Cloverdale,' they were well known for their gracious hospitality.

7.10 Studio portrait taken in London of Jane Douglas (seated) and her younger sister, Martha.

7.11 Flora Ross, taken in the 1890s.

Yet social success in early Victoria did not come without a price. Although she had become Lady Douglas, Amelia had not forgotten her Cree heritage and pined for the old days. A visitor in 1881 observed that she 'often expresses a desire to see the Indian country before she dies,' and in spite of the fancy dishes presented at her table, 'she was more fond of bitter root, camas and buffalo tongue.'[40] Despite their marital and material success, the younger generation had the anxiety of living in an increasingly racist society – there was no guarantee that the stigma of Native blood could truly be transcended. These attitudes were painfully underscored by the American historian Hubert Bancroft, who denounced miscegenation as 'the Fur-traders' Curse' in his *History of the Northwest Coast*, published in 1886. Imagine what the genteel families, who had entertained him so hospitably upon his visit to Victoria some years earlier, must have felt upon reading his denigration of their maternal ancestors:

> I could never understand how such men as John McLoughlin, James *Douglas*, Ogden, *Finlayson*, *Work* and *Tolmie* and the rest could endure the thought of having their name and honors descend to a degenerate posterity. Surely they were possessed of sufficient intelligence to know that by giving their children Indian or half-breed mothers, their own old Scotch, Irish or English blood would in them be greatly debased, and hence they were doing all concerned a great wrong.[41]

For reasons that have nothing to do with miscegenation but resulted principally from a complicated intersection of racism and gender role expectations, the sons in the second generation were not successful in their fathers' terms; many, such as the Work and Tod sons, did not marry and died young. Leadership in the second generation in these families passed by and large to the white sons-in-law. Within the family circle, however, there was considerable loyalty and devotion shown to the widowed mothers, and kin ties were maintained by the daughters.

Evidence that bonds were strong between the sisters in the McNeill family is highlighted by a very interesting picture, taken in 1904, which features four out of the five sisters from the portrait taken thirty years early (see fig. 7.12). Again, Lucy Moffatt dominates the photo, obviously very much the matriarch of this part-Haida clan. Amelia Douglas and Josette Work remained the cherished centres of their families until their venerable deaths in 1890 and 1896 respectively.

But whatever the private family ties, as Christine Welsh so poignantly

7.12 The four surviving McNeill sisters in 1904; the woman in white is a daughter of Mathilda; she is holding her mother's cane.

testifies in her film *Women in the Shadows*,[42] the practice of hiding one's Native ancestry was an all too common response to the increasing racism of the late nineteenth and early twentieth centuries in the Pacific northwest and elsewhere. When they began to write family histories, male descendants made no mention of their distinguished maternal forebears, but rather played up the paternal Hudson's Bay Company

7.13 A page from Martha Douglas Harris's album, showing her mother and father and herself; Martha did the pen and ink drawing.

connections. Simon Fraser Tolmie, who became a premier of the province, fondly reminisced about growing up on the family estate 'Cloverdale,' but he hardly mentioned his mother and omitted all reference to his remarkable Work grandmother. In his family narrative of 1924, Donald H. McNeill was at pains to emphasize that his grandfather had been the first white settler of south Oak Bay; he did not acknowledge that he was descended from high-ranking Haida and Tongass women.[43]

It is significant that the only person to attempt to preserve an aspect of her Native heritage was the most acculturated Douglas daughter, Martha. When she was at school in England, her father had chided her for telling her mother's Cree stories – the world must not know that her mother was a Native. But in 1901, Martha Harris published a little book of Native history and folklore, which did include her mother's stories. In her preface, she lamented the destruction of First Nations heritage but only obliquely did she claim this as her own:

> As a little girl I used to listen to these legends with the greatest delight, and in order not to lose them, I have written down what I can remember of them. When written they lose their charm which was in the telling. They need the quaint songs and the sweet voice that told them, the winter gloaming and the bright fire as the only light. Then were these legends beautiful.[44]

NOTES

1 See Sylvia Van Kirk, *Many Tender Ties: Women in Fur-Trade Society in Western Canada, 1670–1870* (Winnipeg: Watson & Dwyer, 1980); and Jennifer Brown, *Strangers in Blood: Fur Trade Company Families in Indian Country* (Vancouver: University of British Columbia Press, 1980).
2 For an excellent discussion of the ideology behind the colonization scheme for Vancouver Island, see Richard Mackie, 'The Colonization of Vancouver Island, 1849–58,' *BC Studies* 96 (Winter 1992–3): 3–40.
3 For a further discussion of the differing experiences of the sons and daughters of these families in early Victoria, see Sylvia Van Kirk, 'Tracing the Fortunes of Five Founding Families of Victoria,' *BC Studies* 115–16 (Auturnn/Winter 1997–8): 149–79.
4 The following synopsis of the origins of these five families is derived mainly from Van Kirk, *Many Tender Ties*.

5 John Work to Edward Ermatinger, 15 February 1841, Edward Ermatinger Correspondence, British Columbia Archives and Records Service (BCARS).

6 Ibid.; 'Five Letters of Charles Ross, 1842–1844,' *British Columbia Historical Quarterly* 1 (April 1943): 107.

7 William McNeill to George Simpson, 5 March 1851, Simpson Correspondence Inward, D.5/30, Hudson's Bay Company Archives (HBCA).

8 For further discussion of the social controversy caused by the Beavers' arrival at Fort Vancouver, see Van Kirk, *Many Tender Ties*, 154–7.

9 John Work to Ermatinger, 13 December 1834, Ermatinger Correspondence, BCARS.

10 Walter P. Ross and Mary Tait to secretary, HBC, 13 June and 7 August 1845, A.1O/19 and 20, HBCA.

11 John Miles to Robert Clouston, 21 December 1858, E/B/C62A, BCARS.

12 Annie Deans Correspondence, 29 February 1854, E/B/D343, BCARS; see also Jane Fawcett to sister Emma, 24 June 1860, Edgar Fawcett Papers, Add. MS 1963, BCARS.

13 Marion B. Smith, 'The Lady Nobody Knows,' in *British Columbia: A Centennial Anthology*, ed. R.E. Walters (Toronto: McClelland and Stewart, 1958), 479.

14 Dorothy B. Smith, ed., *Lady Franklin Visits the Pacific Northwest* (Victoria, 1974), 12, 22–3.

15 Dorothy B. Smith, ed., *The Reminiscences of Doctor John Sebastian Helmcken* (Vancouver: University of British Columbia Press, 1975), 120.

16 George Stanley, ed., *Mapping the Frontier: Charles Wilson's Diary of the Survey of the 49th Parallel, 1858–1862* (Toronto: Macmillan, 1970), 135.

17 H.H. Bancroft, *Literary Industries* (San Francisco: History Co., 1890), 534.

18 Martha Douglas Harris, Unpublished reminiscences, BCARS.

19 Ibid.; Smith, ed., *Reminiscences of ... Helmcken*, 120.

20 Nellie de Bertrand Lugrin, *The Pioneer Women of Vancouver Island 1843–1866* (Victoria: Women's Canadian Club, 1928), 64.

21 Augustus Pemberton Diary, 1856–8, E/B/P37A, BCARS; *British Colonist*, 30 April 1859, p. 2; 20 and 21 May 1862, p. 3.

22 *Victoria Daily Chronicle*, 30 April 1864 and 4 May 1864. See also *British Colonist*, 26 August 1863, p. 3; 1 September 1863, p. 3; 27 September 1864, p. 3; and *Victoria Daily Chronicle*, 1 September 1863.

23 Bishop Edward Cridge Papers, vol. 7, 1868: pp. 68, 89, Add. MS. 320, BCARS.

24 *Victoria Daily Chronicle*, 24 April 1885; Carrie to Isabella, 17 August 1880, Wren Family Papers, BCARS.

25 John Tod Clipping File, BCARS.

26 Probate Records, Box 25, File 20 (1876), GR 1304, BCARS. The probate file of the McNeill estate contains a complete inventory of the contents of this house, which was auctioned off in 1876.

27 Captain McNeill's letterbook, A/B/20 Si22, BCARS; Helen Meilleur, *A Pour of Rain: Stories from a West Coast Fort* (Victoria: Sono Nis, 1980), 203.

28 Will of Martha McNeill, 18 September 1883, BCARS. Shortly before her death in 1883, Martha McNeill dictated her will in Chinook jargon to a mixed-blood interpreter, Margaret Hankin, who then translated it into English.

29 Fort Victoria, School Register, 1850–2, Add. MS 2774, BCARS.

30 Smith, ed., *Lady Franklin* Visits, 11, 15–16.

31 Christ Church Cathedral, Register of marriages at Fort Vancouver and Fort Victoria, BCARS; Smith, ed., *Reminiscences of ... Helmcken*, 297; Lucy Moffat Clipping File, BCARS.

32 Stanley, ed., *Mapping the Frontier*, 8, 45.

33 Philip Hankin Reminiscences, p. 166, BCARS.

34 Christ Church Cathedral, Register of marriages, BCARS.

35 W. Kaye Lamb, 'Letters to Martha,' *British Columbia Historical Quarterly* 1 (January 1937): 35.

36 Christ Church Cathedral, Register of marriages, BCARS; Robert Belyk, *John Tod: Rebel in the Ranks* (Victoria: Horsdal & Schubart, 1995), 187, 197.

37 Will of Charles Wren, 6 February 1864, Wren Family Papers, BCARS.

38 Christ Church Cathedral, Marriage register, BCARS; Gordon Keith, ed., *The James Francis Tullock Diary, 1875–1910* (Portland: Binford and Mort, 1978), 16; Cridge Papers, vol. 7, 1868, p. 32, BCARS.

39 John Tod to Ermatinger, 1 June 1864, Ermatinger Correspondence, BCARS.

40 Angus McDonald, 'A Few Items of the West,' *Washington Historical Quarterly* 8 (1917): 225.

41 H.H. Bancroft, *History of the Northwest Coast* (San Francisco: History Co., 1886), 2:650–1. I have indicated by italic all the officers who settled in Victoria. My attention was first drawn to this quote by reading Janet Campbell Hale's fascinating autobiography, *Bloodlines: Odyssey of a Native Daughter* (New York: Random House, 1993).

42 Christine Welsh's film *Women in the Shadows* was released by the National Film Board of Canada in 1991. She was able to trace her Native female roots back to Jane, a Cree woman who married George Taylor, a Hudson's Bay Company sloopmaster. One of their daughters, Margaret, was the 'country wife' of Hudson's Bay Company governor George Simpson in the 1820s.

43 See S.F. Tolmie, 'My Father: William Fraser Tolmie, 1812–1886,' *British Columbia Historical Quarterly* 1 (October 1937): 227–40; Donald McNeill, Personal record, 1924, BCARS.
44 Martha Douglas Harris, *History and Legends of the Cowichan Indians* (Victoria, 1901), 57.

8 Woman the Hunter: Ethnoarchaeological Lessons from Chipewyan Life-Cycle Dynamics

HETTY JO BRUMBACH AND ROBERT JARVENPA

Introduction

Faithful to its title, the 1968 *Man the Hunter* volume[1] rather dogmatically portrayed hunting as the exclusive role of males. In this vision of cultural evolution, men were characterized as 'cooperative hunters of big game, ranging freely and widely across the landscape.'[2] The exclusively male hunter model was constructed, in part, by a questionable manipulation of the original codings for subsistence variables in Murdock's 'Ethnographic Atlas'[3] and by ignoring contradictory evidence presented in the original symposium proceedings by several ethnographers. In essence, by narrowing and redefining the scope of 'hunting,' the symposium participants obscured women's very real participation in a behaviourally and culturally complex enterprise.

Dahlberg's edited volume, *Woman the Gatherer*,[4] served as something of a rejoinder, but it did this by highlighting the role of women as gatherers of plant foods, which often contributed more than half of some foraging people's subsistence. Thus, while one of its essays demonstrated the importance of female hunters among the Agta of the Philippines,[5] the volume at large has come to be best known for its discussion of women as plant gatherers 'par excellence.' Unfortunately, such extreme views, rendered as mutually exclusive 'man the hunter' versus 'woman the gatherer' models, have come to sum up the way many archaeologists interpret the economic roles of men and women.

Why women do not hunt or, more accurately, why some anthropologists have difficulty envisioning women as hunters is a complex issue best left for consideration in a separate essay. Despite a growing literature on the topic,[6] the ethnographic evidence for women as hunters has had negligible impact upon archaeologists interpreting artifacts, features, and other residues recovered at prehistoric sites. As Conkey and Spector have pointed out,[7] there is a deep-seated assumption that women in prehistory were 'immobilized' by pregnancy, lactation, and child care, and therefore needed to be left at a home base while the males ranged 'freely and widely across the landscape.'

If these rigid assumptions have merit, then what of the role of women in circumpolar arctic and subarctic societies where plant foods contribute very little to the diet in terms of calories? Do women play any role in the food quest in these environments?

Cultural Context and Research Methods

To address this problem and to shed light on the issue of women's contribution to subsistence, we turned to the methods of ethnoarchaeology, particularly the archaeological study of ongoing populations. Since the mid-1970s we have been engaged in carrying out ethnoarchaeological research among the Chipewyan, Cree, and Métis Cree populations of northwestern Saskatchewan. Much of this study has focused on the historical and ecological basis of ethnic-cultural adaptation and differentiation, including the roles of Native and European groups in the upper Churchill River fur trade.[8] This work involved survey and mapping of late eighteenth-, nineteenth-, and early to mid-twentieth-century sites, including extensive on-site collaboration with Native interpreters.

Additional research carried out in 1992 was directed at conducting a more systematic analysis of male and female interpretations of archaeological remains.[9] For analytical purposes, we adapted Spector's idea of 'task differentiation,'[10] a framework developed explicitly to break the bounds of androcentric bias in archaeology. Spector used the approach profitably in examining male and female activity patterns for the Hidatsa of the Great Plains. Ethnographic information on the historical Hidatsa was reanalysed to identify tasks performed by males and females, as defined on the basis of four dimensions: (1) social unit (age, gender, and kin relations of personnel cooperating in economic activity); (2) task setting (locations, locales, or geographic range of activity); (3) task time (frequency, seasonality, and other temporal contexts for activity); (4) task materials (implements, technology, and facilities employed in activity). The resultant patterning is suggestive of the ways that women's and men's lives differentially affect the formation of the archaeological record.

In our modification of Spector's approach, we interviewed both Chipewyan women and men, integrating questions concerning the social, spatial, temporal, and material dimensions of specific economic tasks. Additional data were derived from direct observation of such activities in living context. Maps were made of abandoned and still-occupied Chipewyan settlements and individual house sites, emphasizing locations and facilities used in performing relevant activities.

Because time constraints did not permit documentation of all tasks carried out by the Chipewyan, we concentrated on one set of activities: the acquisition and processing of food resources. Nine resources or resource clusters were identified to reflect the mammal, fish, and bird species emphasized by the women and men themselves and also those known to figure prominently in local diet and economy: moose, barren-ground caribou, snowshoe rabbit, beaver, muskrat, whitefish, lake trout, ducks, and various species of plants.[11]

While plant foods do not play a major role in terms of absolute caloric contribution, we included berries in the analysis as the most common plant food resource. Furthermore, to balance the Chipewyan's overwhelming emphasis on animal products, we added a general category of non-edible or non-food plant resources, including bark (for baskets and other containers), moss (baby diapering material), and medicinal plants, among other such resources.

For each animal or plant resource, we questioned informants about a comprehensive system of tracking, capturing or harvesting, and processing. For example, our informants' ultimate rendering of the 'moose system' included detailed knowledge on locating or tracking, killing, field butchering, transport to a residence or settlement, distribution or sharing of meat, final butchering and thin cutting, meat drying and storage, food preparation, hide smoking, and other usage of antlers, bones, fat, and body organs. Other resource 'systems' emerged with their own distinctive pathways and thereby provided extensive information on a range of activities through which animal and, to a lesser degree, plant products passed.

Formal questions concerning the four dimensions were posed to each consultant. These included information on the participants in specific tasks and their kin, marriage, or other ties. The seasonality or temporal scheduling of events was also recorded. Locations were determined either by having informants take us to the relevant places in the case of activities carried out at or near settlements, or by marking locations on maps for more distant areas. The material dimension was explored in much the same way. For some activities our informants were able to demonstrate with the actual tools and facilities employed, whereas other, more distant activities were explained verbally. Direct observation of ongoing hunts or other economic enterprise was possible in some instances. Maps were made of selected settlements and camps with their associated work areas and features. The emphasis on the material aspects of task performance was especially productive.

Each narrator recalled in some detail, and often with considerable emotion, his or her efforts in provisioning a family, whether it was snaring rabbits with a grandmother sixty years ago or butchering a moose with a husband that very week. In some instances, we were fortunate to be on the scene when hunting or food processing activities were occurring. These observationally enriched sessions lent an immediacy and clarity to some testimony.

By structuring interviews in this fashion and by posing the same range of questions to both women and men, we hoped to avoid or, at least, reduce biasing the results in the direction of our own gender stereotypes. We asked women about hunting and killing animals, and men about cooking meat and processing hides. For this we were rewarded. While some of our assumptions about gender were affirmed, we also learned that actual performance was far more flexible than we had thought.

Chipewyan Women Hunters

Perhaps the most interesting revelations were about women. We recorded, either through interviews or direct observation, considerable information on women's participation in the meat acquisition process (which includes all animal products hunted, trapped, or netted), their profound interest in tools and tool kits, and their investment in constructing features and facilities. We also added much to our previous knowledge regarding the complex technologies and procedures involved in women's processing and storage of dry meat, animal hides, and bone grease, and their usage of medicinal plants, among other matters.

One conclusion of this project is the simple but undeniable reality that women hunt. Although the women we studied do not dispatch large mammals as frequently as do men, they are inextricably involved in the broader system of provisioning through pursuit, harvesting, and processing of mammals, fish, and birds.

In recent years, hunting by both men and women has declined due to population increase, settlement nucleation, and mandatory schooling for youngsters, among other factors, but hunting still remains an important economic activity for most individuals. In June 1992, upon arriving at the small traditional Chipewyan settlement of Knee Lake, we found the community almost deserted. An elderly couple in their eighties and a middle-aged female resident were away moose hunting. A second elderly couple in their seventies and their forty-year-old daughter had recently returned from an extended moose-hunting trip. Drying and smoking facilities in the settlement contained evidence of recent success in the capture of moose and fish.

Ethnoarchaeological study of Knee Lake and several other communities provided us with a wealth of information on social units and task setting, time, and materials. One relevant observation is that while the tracking and dispatch phase of hunting usually takes place far from encampments and domestic settlements, the processing or the conversion of carcasses into meat, clothing, tools, and other useful items most often takes place at the residential settlements. Thus the materials produced by post-kill processing activities are spatially concentrated, unlike the archaeological residues created by kills, which are rarely recovered.

Another issue, however, will be highlighted here: the impact of life-cycle dynamics on women's hunting activities. While there is considerable individual variation in the intensity with which women participate in hunting, much of this variation is related to life-cycle dynamics. Adolescents and younger women are quite active, often as apprentices or partners to older relatives. It is within these mother-daughter or, more commonly, grandmother-granddaughter partnerships that many Chipewyan women learn necessary hunting and food-processing skills that aid them in adulthood and marriage. Many women in our interview sample remained active as hunters into their twenties, during the early years of marriage, either alone or with their husbands or other relatives. Most women reported a decline in long-distance travel for purposes of pursuing large mammals when in advanced pregnancy or faced with increased family responsibilities, although some women continued managing snarelines or fish nets closer to home. In their middle and later years, with a decline in child-rearing responsibilities, many of the women significantly increased their participation in a wide range of hunting activities.

Other Chipewyan women continued hunting sporadically throughout their lives. One woman, a middle-aged widow, regularly hunted moose and other game, and she also managed a trapline and fishing operations. Many of these activities she carried out independently, but she has teamed up with male and female partners. Another woman, widowed with three young children in the early 1920s, undertook the full range of hunting, fishing, and trapping tasks to feed her family.[12] In yet another instance, one of our informants noted that as a girl of fifteen she took on many adult responsibilities for her family when her father was permanently disabled. With some instructions from her father, she cut and transported logs and built her family's winter dwelling. With the help of even younger siblings, she tended the fish nets and rabbit snares that provided the bulk of her family's food supply for several years.

Samples of oral testimony underscore the close link between the intensity of women's hunting activities and their position in the family life cycle:

I always have hunted with my husband since early in our marriage. But I wouldn't go hunting after the third or fourth month of pregnancy ... I would help, together with my husband, pulling the moose out of the water and cutting it up in the bush. When I got back to camp, I would be the only one to do further butchering and making all the dry meat, as well as making the moosehide. Sometimes I would get help with hide making, like from my older daughter or another woman. In my early days of marriage, we would not haul the moose to Knee Lake village, but instead do all the butchering and hide making and all that in the bush, because it was hard to carry things a long way. (D.B., 70 years)

My grandparents, Bernard and Mary, would always hunt together in early marriage and also in their late marriage, but not in the middle years with children ... In the old days, when my grandmother was young, the women did all the men's jobs. They would shoot a moose, cut it up, bring it back with a dog team, and fish through the ice. And some women would be helpers or partners for making moosehide and fishing and call each other 'sitseni' ... If they bring in too many ducks, we would can duck meat in glass sealers. I did that for my grandma. Also with excess moose meat or any kind of meat we did that. Fall ducks [dul ingaii] we would also hunt. Before my first child I would go duck hunting with my husband. My husband did the shooting. We brought the whole ducks back home to clean. (A.M., 44 years)

I used to hunt rabbits with my mom. We had a little trail where we went. From our house we would cross a lake and go into the bush in winter [ca. 2.4 kms], and she would put rabbit snares. She would kill seven or eleven rabbits. I was seventeen years old. We would keep the skins for moccasin warmth. At the end of the trail my mom would kill a rabbit for a meal, make tea from snow, and have some bannock. We used snares. We would bring other rabbits back home whole. She would sometimes gut them and leave the hair on them and keep them frozen in a shed outside. We especially hunted rabbits in winter. But in summer my father and mother would snare rabbits in other places. (D.N., 64 years)

I have gone beaver hunting with my husband. But before marriage I used to paddle with my grandma ... for one day in a small canoe for beaver and muskrat hunting in the spring time. Sometimes we trapped and shot them. Sometimes my grandma made me shoot them, but often I missed. But I always caught them with traps ... Later, I always went with my husband. We would go on the same trail, yet we each individually set our own traps. (D.H., 40 years)

I learned from my mom and grandma how to trap muskrat and how to skin them. In older days both men and women trapped, because money was hard to get. ... Each woman had her own place for trapping so that it wouldn't overlap with brothers' or sisters' places. I would travel down the Churchill River in a canoe with Grandma to Dreger Lake, past Wagahonanci. I was seven or eight years old. We used an old-style wood-frame canvas canoe. They tear easily on rocks, and if we didn't have glue, we used 'bush gum' and applied it with hot steel to seal on the patch. The gum comes from a ... spruce. (J.D., 40 years)

When I was a young girl snaring rabbits at Dipper Lake, I did the work alone. I was nine years old when I started that. I used to be scared of wolves and things ... I would walk a distance away, like from here to the reserve [3.2 kms]. I'd bring back a load of rabbits sometimes, so that I'd leave some under the snow to get later. I'd snare rabbits all year round ... My father used to collect old string and soak them in rabbit blood, and we'd put them on a log to form stiff snare circles. (L.P., 73 years)

We used to trap fur, not only muskrats. I used to go with my grandparents to trap muskrats with metal traps, not snares. We would go trapping in Little Flatstone Creek and Mudjatik River ... When going out for muskrat we'd go out and camp for a couple days and then move the whole trapline, move it again, all the way down to the mouth of Little Flatstone and then working out way up to Patuanak. The skinning of muskrats, usually that's a man's job, but women would help if there were lots of animals. I am faster than my husband. My grandma used to make large birch-bark baskets, square but tall boxes, taller than wide. She would use these to store the dried muskrat meat ... We used to snare lots of rabbits at Little Flatstone, me and my grandmother. (L.N., 52 years)

As noted previously, most Chipewyan women reported a decline in hunting activities during the years when pregnancy and child-rearing responsibilities were greatest. A range of available government services, as well as Western technology, have triggered major changes in demography, with increased family size in recent history perhaps being the most relevant to this study. Although data are incomplete and somewhat difficult to compare, examination of three census lists revealed an increase in the number of reported sub-adult children over time. Shifts in family demography are central to our argument that changes in women's economic roles, particularly reduced involvement in hunting, occur quite late in history. Contemporary observations of family size and hunting, therefore, cannot be used uncritically to model prehistoric gender dynamics.

Three Chipewyan Censuses

1838 Census

In 1838 the Hudson's Bay Company (HBC) conducted a census of all its fur-trading posts, including the Ile à la Crosse post within the English River District, which served as the major point of trade for the southern Chipewyan or *Kesyehot'ine*, the people considered in this study.[13] Of the 489 Chipewyan enumerated for the English River District in that year, only 108 were identified by name. These 'Hunter's Names' were broad transcriptions of Chipewyan names (e.g., Chee na Gun, Jennay afsee, Houlcho Eazze) for adult male family heads and some of their male relatives and comrades.

The remaining 380 Chipewyan in the 1838 census were enumerated

Table 8.1. Chipewyan population data from censuses in the English River District, Canada

Census year	Men	Women	Boys	Girls	Followers and strangers	Total population
1838	108	119	107	103	52	489
1906	25	40	36	42	10*	153
1974	112	101	112	112		437

*'Other relatives' in this case included two males and eight females.

anonymously in columns following the roster of male family heads: 'Wives' (119 individuals), 'Sons' (107), 'Daughters' (103), and 'Followers and Strangers' (52) (see table 8.1). The listings provide a general picture of variation in family size and structure at that time. Since Catholic missionization did not penetrate the region until 1846, polygynous marriage was still common. Twenty-six of the named hunters, or nearly 24 per cent, had at least two wives, and some had three or four. Without information on age, however, one can only assume that 'Sons' and 'Daughters' represented sub-adult or dependent offspring who had not yet married or otherwise formed independent families. In the early twentieth century, Chipewyan grooms were on average about six years older than their brides, a pattern that may have held for the nineteenth century as well.[14] If so, young women may have been moving from the 'Daughters' to the 'Wives' category in their mid-teens, whereas a comparable transition for men may have been delayed until their early twenties.

More problematic for comparative purposes is the 'Followers and Strangers' category, suggesting a variety of dependants and hangers-on beyond the nuclear family. Only seventeen of the families, or about 16 per cent of all families, accommodated such individuals in 1838. The category was not used by the HBC in all its censuses, creating some ambiguity. Perhaps the most reasonable assumption is that 'Followers and Strangers' represented distant kin and/or friends, in some cases deriving from other regional bands, perhaps experiencing misfortune or hardship, and who formed temporary or short-term alliances with Chipewyan families in the English River District.

1906 Census

The year 1906 marked the beginning of Canadian federal involvement in local Indian affairs with the extinction of land title through Treaty

No. 10. The subsequent establishment of legally recognized bands and reserves affected the majority of the southern Chipewyan population, for whose attention the HBC and the French Roman Catholic Church had contended for decades. The annuity payment list for the English River Band of Chipewyan established in 1906 is simultaneously a census of the community. The seemingly low count of 153 individuals (table 8.1) does not reflect a massive population decline among Chipewyan since the early nineteenth century, however. The English River Band was one of several regional bands of southern Chipewyan in the old English River or Ile à la Crosse trading district. The 1906 population, therefore, is a regional subset of descendants of the 1838 population discussed previously.

The treaty roster listed 41 family units, most of them identified by named male heads (25), but many by named females (16). The latter apparently were widows, about a third of whom had dependent children. Catholic baptism had introduced French first names for most individuals, but older Chipewyan nomenclature was retained in surnames (e.g., Jean Baptiste Estralshenen, Marie Yahwatzare, Norbert Darazele). By this date, all marriages appear to be monogamous, another artifact of Catholic influence.

Although the 1906 census contains no information on age, it provides a tabular listing of 'Men' (25 individuals), 'Women' (40), 'Boys' (36), 'Girls' (42), and 'Other Relatives' (10) for each of the 41 named family units, paralleling the format used in the HBC's earlier census. In a similar vein, other than the named family heads, all remaining individuals are enumerated anonymously. If we assume that the ages and social positions of 'Sons' and 'Daughters' were parallel to that of 'Boys' and 'Girls,' and that 'Followers and Strangers' were roughly equivalent to 'Other Relatives,' then the two census documents are comparable.

1974 Census

A list of federally registered Indians in the English River Band for 1974, an annually updated document produced by the Canadian Department of Indian Affairs and Northern Development, represents the direct contemporary descendants of the Chipewyan community identified in the 1906 treaty census.[15] Barring radical rates of in-migration, therefore, the almost threefold rise in population (from 153 to 437) over seventy years (table 8.1) reflects the level of natural increase for this community. Occupying the settlements of Cree Lake, Dipper Lake, Knee Lake, Patuanak, and Primeau Lake, the English River Band has been the focus of our ethnographic and ethnoarchaeological work since the early 1970s.

Unlike the previous census documents, the 1974 registry identifies each individual by name, registration number, and family cluster, arranged in alphabetical order by surname. Some of these names retain the binary character of those in the 1906 treaty list (e.g., Joseph Dawatsare, Vitaline Deneyou), but many others have a more anglicized or Canadianized flavour (e.g., Gregoire Campbell, Mary Djonaire). In addition, a tabular format of codes indicates the marital status, religious affiliation, sex, and birth date of each individual, providing a level of specificity unavailable in the earlier censuses. There is nothing equivalent to the 'Followers and Strangers' or 'Other Relatives' categories, but for comparative purposes we can draw a distinction between adults and children in the 1974 census by using the age eighteen as a dividing line. The latter is a legal age of majority in the registry, at which time individuals are issued new registration numbers and separated into independent family clusters whether or not they have married.

Demographic Trends and Women's Burden

The general age- and sex-class data for the three time periods summarized in table 8.1 are used to generate sex ratios (SR) in table 8.2. These ratios generally indicate an excess of females over males in earlier history, with a remarkably unbalanced situation in 1906 (SR = 70). However, the ratio rebounds to a slight excess of males over females (SR = 105.16) by 1974. In such small populations, a combination of hunting accidents, disease, or other chance events could have easily reduced the male population at the turn of the century.

More relevant for the present discussion is the ratio of children to adults through history, expressed as a raw percentage in table 8.2. Chipewyan children account for 48.1 per cent of the total population in 1838. This increases to 51.0 per cent in 1906 and 51.3 per cent by 1974. The change is subtle, but it suggests an increasing burden for women who generally were, and are, responsible for the daily care and nurturance of young children and other dependent family members.

The final column in table 8.2 ('Children per woman') provides a more revealing means of interpreting women's child-care responsibilities over time. For example, the 1838 census material indicates an average of 2.8 children, with a range of 1–5, for each Chipewyan woman who was listed as having at least one child. The latter distinction is important. We

Table 8.2. Chipewyan sex ratios and sub-adult children per woman for three census periods

Census year	Adult sex ratio	Child sex ratio	Total sex ratio	Children as % of population	Children per woman
1838	90.76	103.88	96.84	48.1%	2.8 (R:1–5)
1906	62.50	85.71	70.00	51.0%	3.1 (R:1–8)
1974	110.89	100.00	105.16	51.3%	4.8 (R:1–12)

counted only those women with at least one child to generate this statistic. Because the census did not indicate the women's ages, we wanted some means of excluding elderly women with adult children, as well as very young women who had not yet started their own families.

By 1906, the comparable statistic had increased to 3.1 children, with a range of 1–8. More recently, in 1974, the figure had further increased to 4.8, with a range of 1–12. The averages tend to underestimate the total number of children a Chipewyan woman bore in her lifetime, since they represent family size at a single time. Thus, unborn children or adult children who had formed their own households were omitted. Nonetheless, these figures represent the average number of children a woman would have to care for at any time.

Conclusions

The ethnoarchaeology of hunting can be used to identity and reassess women and women's roles in the archaeological record. Several implications have emerged from our work.

1. Based on information concerning the spatial dimension of task performance, Chipewyan women that we studied tend to hunt closer to the home village or base than do men. In part, this range is due to women's greater concentration on smaller mammals, and men's on larger quarry, although the two patterns overlap considerably. When Chipewyan women report hunting activities carried out in the course of a day, they typically report several hours of travel, either by foot and/or canoe, from the home base. One archaeological implication of this is that catchment analysis of food resources located within 3 to 5 kms of a settlement site, or 5 to 10 kms, if water travel is likely, will encompass the food-animal resources of primary interest to *women*.

2. Spatial analysis of task performance *within* settlement sites reveals

that women's participation in hunting may be more easily identified in the archaeological record than that of men. The carcasses of small game animals are often returned whole to the village site for further processing. In contrast, kills involving one or only a few large animals are likely to take place far removed from the archaeologically more visible settlement sites[16] and hence may be more difficult to recover. Alternately, when large game animals were killed at some distance from the base camp, more common in earlier history, much of the community, including the women, would remove itself to the location of the kill. In such instances the processing of game animals, or the conversion of carcasses to meat, hide, and other usable products, was carried out at the newly established camp, primarily by women. In this case, the archaeological evidence in the form of faunal remains, hearths, and related features would evidence women's activities.

3. Moving from a general regional or inter-site analysis to more specific artifactual analysis, our study has demonstrated that women's activities are directly mirrored in the use of tools. Although the Chipewyan no longer use many stone tools, the women we studied maintained and curated all assemblage of implements used to process moose and caribou hides. Every older woman we interviewed owned a set of these tools, consisting of a selection of bone or metal scrapers, butchering knives, files, hide rougheners, and rope or cord to tie the hide to stretchers. These tools are carefully maintained; wrapped in a cloth or canvas and tied with string, cloth strips, or leather thong; and stored securely away in the house or tent.

These rather elaborate hide-processing kits are not what archaeologists would classify as 'casual' or 'pick up' tools to be used once and then discarded. If recovered archaeologically, they would no doubt be classified as 'high investment' or 'curated' tools. Far too often, such 'high investment' implements are uncritically perceived as indicators of male activity.[17] Yet it is apparent that women also made investments in the manufacture and curation of tools with which to carry out complex and multifaceted economic and domestic lives. Such behaviour was neither idiosyncratic nor casual. A more critical analysis of artifacts recovered archaeologically would undoubtedly reveal other evidence of women's contributions to the food quest in past times and places.

It should be noted that other tool kits or tool-kit-like assemblages are used by both Chipewyan women and men to carry out a variety of hunting, fishing, trapping, food-processing, and manufacturing tasks. As in the case of women's hide-making tool kits, and certain men's hunting and butchering kits, some of these other assemblages are spatially condensed both in use and in storage. However, other complexes of implements may have a more involved storage situation as items are frequently moved between various locations and activities. The composition and use of these other kits deserve a fuller discussion than is possible here.

4. Clearly women participated in a broad range of hunting activities. The level of participation varied from individual to individual, as well as from population to population, and according to life-cycle dynamics discussed previously, but it is apparent that it is not accurate to interpret all archaeological evidence of hunting and processing of animal products as indicators of an exclusively male enterprise.

A dramatic increase in the childbearing and child-rearing responsibilities of women, especially in the past seventy years, may go a long way toward explaining the decreased participation of some contemporary women.

NOTES

1 Richard B. Lee and Irven De Vore, eds, *Man the Hunter* (Chicago: Aldine, 1968).

2 Sherwood L. Washburn and C.S. Lancaster, 'The Evolution of Hunting,' in Lee and De Vore, eds, *Man the Hunter*, 293–303.

3 George P. Murdock, 'The Ethnographic Atlas: A Summary,' *Ethnology* 6.2 (1967).

4 Francis Dahlberg, ed., *Woman the Gatherer* (New Haven, CT: Yale University Press, 1981).

5 Agnes Estioko-Griffin and P. Bion Griffin, 'Woman the Hunter: The Agta,' in Dahlberg, ed., *Woman the Gatherer*, 121–51.

6 Richard K. Nelson, 'Athapaskan Subsistence Adaptations in Alaska,' in *Alaska Native Culture and History*, ed. Y. Kotani and W. Workman, Senri Ethnological Studies No. 4 (Osaka, Japan: National Museum of Ethnology, 1980), 205–32; Estioko-Griffin and Griffin; Hitoshi Watanabe, 'Subsistence and Ecology of Northern Food Gatherers with Special Reference to the Ainu,' in Lee and De Vore, eds, *Man the Hunter*, 68–77; Colin M. Turnbull, 'Mbuti Womanhod,' in Dahlberg, ed., *Woman the Gatherer*, 205–19; Eleanor Leacock, *Myths of Male Dominance* (New York: Monthly Review Press, 1981).

7 Margaret W. Conkey and Janet D. Spector, 'Archaeology and the Study

of Gender,' in *Advances in Archaeological Method and Theory*, vol. 7, ed. Michael Schiffer (New York: Academic Press, 1984), 1–38.

8 Hetty Jo Brumbach, 'The Recent Fur Trade in Northwestern Saskatchewan,' *Historical Archaeology* 19 (1985): 19–39; Hetty Jo Brumbach and Robert Jarvenpa, *Ethnoarchaeological and Cultural Frontiers: Athapaskan, Algonquian, and European Adaptations in the Central Subarctic* (New York: Peter Lang, 1989); Brumbach and Jarvenpa, 'Archaeologist-Ethnography-Informant Relations: The Dynamics of Ethnoarcheology in the Field,' in *Powers of Observation: Alternative Views in Archeology*, ed. Sarah Nelson and Alice Kehoe, Archeological Papers of the American Anthropological Association, No. 2 (Arlington: American Anthropological Association, 1990), 39–46; Brumbach, Jarvenpa, and Clifford Buell, 'An Ethnoarchaeological Approach to Chipewyan Adaptations in the Late Fur Trade Period,' *Arctic Anthropology* 19 (1982): 1–49; Robert Jarvenpa, 'The Hudson's Bay Company, the Roman Catholic Church, and the Chipewyan in the Late Fur Trade Period,' in *Le Castor Fait Tout: Selected Papers of the Fifth North American Fur Trade Conference, 1985*, ed. B. Trigger, T. Morantz, and L. Dechene (Montreal: St Louis Historical Society, 1987), 485–517; Jarvenpa and Brumbach, 'Ethnoarchaeological Perspectives on an Athapaskan Moose Kill,' *Arctic* 36 (1983): 174–84; 'The Microeconomics of Southern Chipewyan Fur Trade History,' in *The Subarctic Fur Trade: Native Social and Economic Adaptations*, ed. S. Krech (Vancouver: University of British Columbia Press, 1984), 147–83; 'Occupational Status, Ethnicity, and Ecology: Métis Cree Adaptation in a Canadian Trading Frontier,' *Human Ecology* 13 (1985): 309–29; 'Sociospatial Organization and Decision Making Processes: Observations from the Chipewyan,' *American Anthropologist* 90 (1988): 598–618.

9 Robert Jarvenpa and Hetty Jo Brumbach, 'Ethnoarchaeology and Gender: Chipewyan Women as Hunters,' paper presented at the ninety-second annual meeting of the American Anthropological Association, Washington, DC, 1993; 'Ethnoarchaeology and Gender: Chipewyan Women as Hunters,' in Research in Economic Anthropology, vol. 16, ed. Barry Isaac (Greenwich, CT: JAI Press, 1995), 39–82.

10 Janet Spector, 'Male/Female Task Differentiation among the Hidatsa: Toward a Development of an Archeological Approach to the Study of Gender,' in *The Hidden Half*, ed. P. Albers and B. Medicine (Washington, DC: University Press of America, 1983), 82–3

11 Robert Jarvenpa, 'Recent Ethnographic Research: Upper Churchill River Drainage, Saskatchewan, Canada,' Arctic 32 (1979): 355–65; *The Trappers of Patuanak: Toward a Spatial Economy of Modern Hunters*, Mercury Series,

Canadian Ethnology Service Paper, no. 67 (Ottawa: National Museum of Man, 1980).

12 Robert Longpre, *Ile à la Crosse* (Ile à la Crosse, SK: Ile à la Crosse Local Community Authority and Bi-Centennial Committee, 1977), 40.

13 Hudson's Bay Company, 'Ile à la Crosse District Indian Census, 1838,' B.239/a/10:fols.52a-57a, Hudson's Bay Company Archives, Winnipeg.

14 Brumbach and Jarvenpa, *Ethnoarchaeological and Cultural Frontiers*, 259.

15 Canada, Department of Indian Affairs and Northern Development, 'English River Band, Registered Indians as of June 30, 1974, Meadow Lake District' (1974).

16 Jarvenpa and Brumbach, 'Ethnoarchaeological Perspectives.'

17 Brian Hayden, 'Observing Prehistoric Women,' in *Exploring Gender through Archaeology*, ed. Cheryl Claassen (Madison, WI: Prehistory Press, 1992), 33–47.

9 Gender and Work in Lekwammen Families, 1843–1970

JOHN LUTZ

Recent studies of the interaction between gender, race, and colonialism in North America and the Pacific are forcing a reorientation of Canadian history. In the light of this new work, the settlement of Canada is exposed as a 'colonial project' that involved the displacement and marginalization of one people by another. Even more important, it is becoming clear that while the words 'colonial project' or even 'colonialism' are convenient shorthands, they do not describe a single process. What we call colonialism was a constellation of factors that had distinct, even contradictory, impacts on different indigenous people. It is increasingly apparent that colonization was a gendered process with differential impacts on Aboriginal women and men, impacts that depended, in turn, on age and social status.[1] This chapter develops an understanding of the gendered effect of colonization in Canada by examining the interplay of one of its elements – the economy – with gender, age, and social position in an Aboriginal community, over a 130-year time-span. It offers a microhistory focusing on the experience of one Aboriginal community, the Lekwammen (Songhees)[2] people, whose ancestral territory is now occupied by Victoria, the capital city of British Columbia.

A start has already been made in exploring the gendered impact of colonialism on Canadian Aboriginal people, but the conclusions so far have painted a one-sided picture. A dramatic illustration is Karen Anderson's examination of gender relations among the Huron and Montagnais. Anderson shows that, within the relatively short period of thirty years, the impact of colonial society (primarily through the church) in New France was to reduce dramatically the power of Aboriginal women vis-à-vis Aboriginal men. Eleanor Leacock, Jo-Anne Fiske, and

Ron Bourgeault, examining the impact of colonialism on other Aboriginal groups at other times, came to similar conclusions.[3]

Important and thought-provoking as these studies are, it would be a mistake to generalize that the gendered impact of the colonial interchange was always to weaken the social power of all Aboriginal women. Given the vast range of gender relations in pre-contact Aboriginal societies, it is not surprising that in some, women were relatively powerful, while in others they were relatively powerless.[4] As well, European colonists came from different countries, represented different churches and different economic systems, and had different agendas in their dealings with Aboriginal people. Thus, the gendered outcome of individual colonial interchanges depended on the nature of both the particular European and Aboriginal societies involved and the circumstances of their meeting. Moreover, west coast Aboriginal societies, like the European societies they encountered, were stratified according to age and status. Given these pre-existing social divisions, it seems possible that even within the gender-divided groups of men and women, costs and benefits of colonization would be unevenly distributed. There is some evidence that upper-class Aboriginal women, for example, may have seen their positions eroded, while their female slaves may have found their post-colonial position enhanced.[5]

This is not an attempt to argue that the Lekwammen case is more typical than the Huron or Montagnais experiences described by others, but it does underscore that the impact of colonization on gender roles was complex and varied. Using a microhistorical method, we can focus precisely on the variety of ways metahistorical processes, like colonization, manifest themselves in different contexts.[6] By taking a single community and piecing together lives, and the interconnections between lives, from fragments, painstakingly extracted from the many different hiding places of historical memory – local newspapers, reminiscences, parish records, census records, Indian agents' reports, letters, photos – it is possible to get to know something about practically everyone who lived in that community. Organizing these reminders of lives, births, deaths, descendants, and, most important, relationships, into scrapbooks covering six or seven generations allows a close, nuanced look at the effect of colonialism on gender.

The Lekwammen felt the impact of European society late, compared to many Canadian Aboriginal groups, but thereafter they experienced it with greater intensity. Their territory was selected as the site of Fort Victoria in 1843, and soon became the centre of European settlement in what is now British Columbia. When, in 1849, Vancouver Island became a British colony, Victoria became the capital and remained the most urban site in the colony, and later, in the province, until overtaken by Vancouver in the 1890s. With a city growing up in their midst, the Lekwammen felt all the administrative, religious, and social pressures of colonialism. But while Victoria's proximity had definite drawbacks, it also had possible benefits. Few Aboriginal groups were as well situated to take advantage of opportunities opened up by the new economy. Throughout the period covered here, economic relationships within Lekwammen society, and between the Lekwammen and immigrant society, reshaped gendered contributions to the household economy and gendered power more generally. By considering these changes over more than a century – beginning with contact, through the fur trade, establishment of the commercial fishery, global depression, world war, and post–Second World War welfare state economy – this chapter analyses the shifting nature of gender roles and power within Lekwammen society. This approach also reveals the multiple and contradictory interactions between gender and the colonial and post-colonial economies.

The Ethnographic Moment

The Lekwammen had only recently come together as a group when James Douglas arrived in their territory on the steamship *Beaver* in 1843 to establish a trading establishment. Previously, the ancestors of the people now called Lekwammen lived in villages occupied during the winter months on the islands and bays along the coast of southeast Vancouver Island (see map 9.1). In spring, summer, and fall they moved to seasonal campsites close to their fishing, hunting, or gathering grounds. Although they shared a common dialect, were neighbours with kin, and had ceremonial links to the others, these extended-family villages did not constitute a nation and did not act in concert in matters of peace or war.

Due to depopulation from European-introduced disease, which first swept the coast in the 1770s, and increased raiding by European-armed northern Aboriginal groups, most of these winter villages were deserted in the late eighteenth century. As protection against the northern raiders, the 1,000–1,500 remaining Lekwammen congregated into two fortified villages, one in Esquimalt harbour and a larger village, Sungaya, in what is now called Cadboro Bay.[7]

Most of the knowledge we have of Lekwammen social life comes

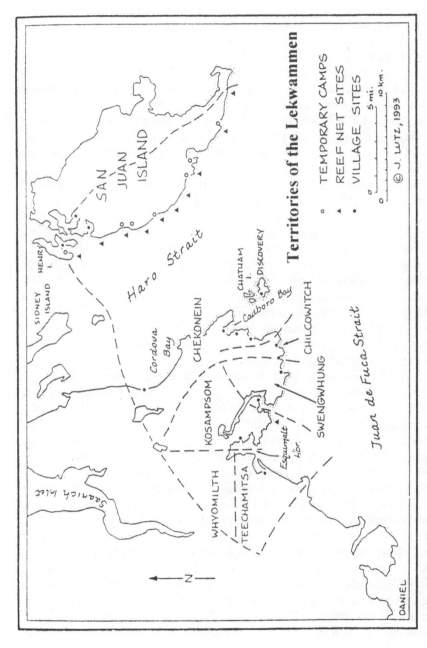

Map 9.1 Territories of the Lekwammen.

from the period that immediately brackets the arrival of Europeans in their territory. This is that 'ethnographic moment' that has come to be seen as 'since time immemorial.' Never mind that Aboriginal society, like all living societies, was continuously in flux, responding to new social and environmental pressures, including dramatic crises in the form of depopulation and concentration. This is the time when European observers found Aboriginal societies novel and recorded observations about them. When, beginning in the 1880s, ethnographers asked Aboriginal people to describe so-called 'traditional' lifestyles, they also heard a description of the time when most of the informants were raised, that is, the period surrounding the arrival of the fur traders.

Just as historic and ethnographic writing has privileged the contact era as 'time immemorial,' it has put a gendered spin on social relations. Virtually all the Europeans who left comments about Aboriginal people – explorers and ethnographers – were males. What they observed and where they interconnected with Aboriginal society were arenas of male society or of mixed society, but never the private realms of women's society.[8] At the very least, this means that we have a much more detailed rendering of men's society than women's. It also alerts us that the descriptions might tend to exaggerate the importance of men's society and diminish that of women. Much of what we can know of women's and children's activities must come from 'listening to the silence' in the existing accounts.[9]

The Lekwammen had a distinctly gendered political and production system, but the first European immigrants in Lekwammen territory made little mention of it. In north-coast Aboriginal societies like the Tsimshian studied by Fiske and Cooper and the Tlingit examined by Klein, descent was reckoned matrilineally. In these societies women were prominent, and Europeans frequently speculated about gender roles and the power of women. By contrast, the Lekwammen and other Coast Salish peoples, like Europeans, recognized descent bilaterally, from both paternal and maternal lines, with emphasis on the paternal. The Lekwammen's *siem*, heads of households that Europeans identified as 'chiefs,' were all male. This position, along with its prerogatives and obligations, generally passed from a *siem*, on his death, to his eldest son, and if there were no sons, then to a brother and his sons. Because he controlled access to major resource sites, a *siem* controlled the wealth of the household and managed the major items of property as well as ceremonial privileges.[10] Within each household, less important items were either the joint property of families or owned by individuals.

These included utensils of everyday use, wealth goods held in preparation for distribution, dogs, and spiritual knowledge derived from personal visions. Slaves were included among the private property of those who could afford them. Husbands and wives held their property separately; at death a husband's property would be transferred to his sons; a wife's property to her daughters.[11]

Although not so highly stratified as north-coast Aboriginal societies, the Lekwammen were divided into three classes: 'Good People' or nobles, from which the *siem* would be drawn; 'Worthless People' or commoners; and slaves.[12] By 1839 slaves apparently outnumbered commoners and nobles combined.[13] Villages consisted of a number of extended families each occupying a large winter house. Paul Kane, in 1847, described their 'lodges' as 'the largest buildings of any description that I have met with among the Indians. They are divided in the interior into compartments [using rush mats], so as to accommodate eight to ten families.' One Lekwammen house (at the abandoned village on Garrison Island) was later measured to be 400 feet by 40 feet.[14] Households usually consisted of a male *siem*, his brothers, sons, and all their wives and children. It was also common to have unmarried sisters, widows, orphans, and perhaps nephews included in the household, as well as slaves. Although blood relationship was theoretically as strong on the maternal side as the paternal, wives usually lived with their husband's family.

Except for the fact that a *siem* might have more than one wife, the newcomers could easily see him as an Aboriginal equivalent to an aristocratic patriarch – indeed they sometimes referred to important *siem* such as Chee-al-thuk of the Lekwammen as 'kings' and their wives as 'queens.'[15] Nonetheless, the *siem's* power lay strictly in his ability to persuade and reward. All decisions about collective action – when and whether to move to a seasonal camp, to hold a feast, to wage war – were made by the *siem* in consultation with family heads within households.[16]

In Lekwammen society men held the positions of economic and political power, but the practice of polygyny was, in part, a recognition of the importance of women as producers of goods and reproducers of labour. It was not uncommon for higher-ranking men to have more than one wife. Three seems to have been the maximum for all but the most prominent *siem*.[17] Since resources were generally abundant, the larger the family, the more labour available for accumulating surplus food and goods, and the higher the status a family could achieve. In

addition to enlarging the household, polygyny had other practical purposes. Marriages among high-status families were often diplomatic
unions, establishing a basis for friendly relationships between households, particularly households in different villages and different nations. This connection provided each set of in-laws with some access to
the resources controlled by the other and some measure of 'safe passage' through the others' territories. It also established a gift-exchange
cycle whereby one's in-laws would bring the rare and valuable commodities of their territory as gifts.

When it came to productive activities, men, women, children, and the
elderly had distinctive roles. Males and females worked in separate but
interdependent productive activities. The gendered division of labour
was maintained, at least partly, by the belief that women, during menstruation and following childbirth, had properties that drove away the
fish and animals depended on for food. If, at these times, a woman even
touched fishing or hunting equipment, it became unusable. If women,
at either of these times, had intercourse with males, male hunting/
fishing powers would be weakened or destroyed.

There is debate in the anthropological literature as to whether women
were considered 'polluted' at these times or endowed with a special,
uncontrollable power. Scholars who claim the latter argue that suggestions of women's 'pollution' come from male informants to male ethnologists. For the Lekwammen and their neighbours, it is clear that the
men, at least, saw women as polluted when menstruating and following childbirth. We have no surviving account from Lekwammen women,
but the autobiography of Mourning Dove, an interior Salish woman
culturally linked to the Lekwammen, accepts the term 'polluted' to
describe menstruating women.[18]

As a result of these prohibitions, only men fished and hunted; however, women made the baskets and other vessels in which the food
would be stored and preserved the catch so that food would be available throughout the year and for feasts. Men made the nets for catching
fish, deer, or ducks, but from twine made by women. Men secured most
of the protein in the Lekwammen diet; women produced the carbohy-
drates, starches, and other vegetables and fruits essential to their diet.
Men were not prohibited from doing 'women's work,' and for short
periods, where time was of the essence, some tasks, like harvesting
camas (a flowering plant with a starchy bulb that was a staple) or
shellfish, might involve whole households.[19]

Although tasks of production were specifically gendered, among the

Lekwammen gender was not necessarily determined by biological sex. Boas, in 1890, noted among the Lekwammen that 'sometimes men assume women's dress and occupations and vice versa.' He added that this custom was found all along the north Pacific coast.[20]

Food circulated in a 'subsistence economy' where individual gatherers and heads of families had some, but not total, control over its distribution. Other goods, including slaves owned by individuals and families, circulated in a 'wealth' or 'prestige economy.' The two economies functioned separately but were interconnected at various points.[21]

The most important reason for the production and accumulation of wealth goods in Salish society was the potlatch complex. 'Potlatch' is a Chinook jargon word for a variety of ceremonies among west-coast Aboriginal people that involve feasting, dancing, and, most importantly, the distribution of gifts. Although all the west-coast nations held potlatches, the occasions when they were held varied widely. For the Lekwammen and other Straits Salish, potlatches were held periodically to mark significant events, including marriage and the inheritance of rights such as those of the *siem*. Potlatches might also be held to clear away shame caused by oneself or one's family. Among the Lekwammen, a single potlatch was usually hosted by a number of families, each with its own event to memorialize. High-status recipients of potlatch gifts were expected to reciprocate with their own potlatches to maintain their relative social ranking.[22]

While subsistence production was shared relatively evenly between men and women, when it came to the production of prestige goods, women's contributions probably dominated. Men made a contribution through the acquisition of slaves in warfare and through manufacturing canoes, hunting implements, and regalia that might be given at a potlatch. Nonetheless, the most important items in the potlatch economy were blankets made by women. Woven from cedar bark, wool, and occasionally other fibres, blankets had a prestige value far exceeding their utility. Because of their value, portability, and divisibility, blankets also functioned as a medium of exchange. These were the first and most valuable items the Lekwammen offered to exchange with Europeans.[23]

Women and children gathered and prepared cedar-bark fibres for the warp. The main source for the wool was from the Lekwammen's only domesticated animal – a dog specially bred for its wool. Dog wool was supplemented by mountain goat wool received in trade from the Squamish and Nooksack on the mainland. Wool-bearing dogs were the property of women who kept them segregated, often on small islands, to prevent cross-breeding with other dogs. Myron Eells, speaking of the southern Lekwammen's neighbours, recorded that 'a woman's wealth was often estimated by the number of such dogs she owned.' Women sheared these special dogs, spun their wool, and wove the blankets on large looms.[24] In addition to the blankets, women also made baskets and mats as trade and potlatch items, harvested and stored the camas that was exchanged for the products of other nations, and tanned hides that were occasionally items of exchange.

When Europeans arrived in Lekwammen territory, they came to a society where political power was concentrated in the hands of elderly males, yet women had a measure of independence. Judith Brown has argued that women's power was commensurate with the value of and their control over the distribution of their own production.[25] Among the Lekwammen, women owned their own property and contributed the largest share of a household's wealth through the manufacture of important prestige items. They did not have much control over the distribution of these products.

The Colonial Moment

European colonization was less a matter of populating an empty land than of depopulating a full one. The missionary Bolduc estimated that he spoke to 1,200 people in the Lekwammen village of Sungaya in 1843. When James Douglas conducted his 1850 enumeration, he counted 700 Lekwammen. Their number had been reduced to 400 by 1859, to 285 by 1864, to 164 by 1891, and to a low of 117 in 1911.[26] The drastic population collapse is partly owing to the introduction of a dangerous form of home-brewed alcohol, but largely due to introduced diseases for which the Lekwammen had no immunity.

For those who survived, colonization brought a new economic system, based on wage labour, into their territory. The Lekwammen were surprisingly eager to participate – wages earned in a capitalist economy could be given away in the potlatch economy, thereby increasing workers' status in their own community. For their part, the immigrant Europeans were eager to employ the Lekwammen, but only in positions consistent with European ideas of racial hierarchy and appropriate gender roles. The Lekwammen – men, women, young and old – found that only certain jobs were open to 'Indians' according to racialized European beliefs that Aboriginal people were only suitable for menial work.[27]

The European arrival created some new opportunities and closed others, all of which affected Lekwammen gender relations. Lekwammen were hired primarily as labourers for construction, land-clearing, and ploughing and as paddlers for express-canoes. All these fell into the category of 'male work' in both the Lekwammen's and fur traders' worldview. The Lekwammen men who laboured for the fort were paid in factory-made blankets. Since blankets had been the main contribution of women to the Lekwammen economy, this new arrangement undermined women's economic importance. Moreover, the fur traders brought sheep to the island in 1849; after that, wool-bearing dogs, which had constituted the largest part of many women's personal wealth, lost their value and were left to interbreed with other dogs. By 1889 Franz Boas declared the special wool dogs 'extinct for some time.' Nonetheless, a small part of the women's blanket-making skill remained useful in the immigrant economy: shearing the dogs had been a woman's job among the Lekwammen; this may explain why sheep-shearing is the only labouring occupation at the fort for which women are named as workers.[28]

In addition to paid labour, and probably even more important as a source of new income, the Lekwammen supplied food to the fort. In this arena, as well, most of the provisions – fresh fish and game – were the products of male enterprise. Women contributed, to a lesser extent, through their control over potato crops (which the Lekwammen had been growing for several years by 1843) and in the harvest of clams and oysters for sale. In addition, women maintained their long-standing contributions to the subsistence economy.[29]

The immediate effect of the arrival of Euro-Canadians was to elevate the importance of Lekwammen men as producers of wealth relative to women. This might suggest that women's position ought to have been devalued as a result, but in fact this seems not to have been the case. Colonial society was almost entirely male. In looking for short-term or long-term relationships, the immigrant men courted Lekwammen women with some success. Charles Bayley, arriving in 1851, noted that outside the fort there were log shanties 'occupied by half breeds, Iroquois, French Canadian and Kanakas (Hawaiians) ... most of them living with native women.'[30] The declining productive role of women was offset by the increasing demand for Lekwammen women as marriage and sexual partners.

Although there is an absence of direct accounts, it seems likely these unions in the 1850s were similar to those described in the 1860s. In a fusion of indigenous and immigrant practices, the fur trader would offer the father of a Native woman or the owner of a female slave a 'bridal gift'; a variety of reciprocal obligations were probably initiated, but it seems that in general the new 'husband' felt less obligation and had less incentive to maintain the lifelong cycle of ritual exchanges that normally accompanied Lekwammen marriages. If the arrangement ceased to be satisfactory for either party, or if the man moved, his 'country wife' often returned to her family. From the comments of Bayley and the experience in other parts of the Pacific Northwest, it would seem that the overwhelming number of immigrant men, up to the 1858 gold rush at least, formed some kind of liaison with local Aboriginal women.[31] Given this extensive out-marriage on the part of the Lekwammen women, it is at first glance surprising that the gender balance of the local Aboriginal community continued to favour women by a small margin. Douglas's 1850 census of the Lekwammen showed 122 'men with beards,' 134 women, 221 boys, and 223 girls, totalling 700. Subsequent censuses show that the male-female ratio remained relatively constant.[32]

The out-marriage of Lekwammen women to immigrant men was apparently made up by women from neighbouring nations marrying into the Lekwammen. Aboriginal accounts of Lekwammen men marrying Swinomish, Twana, Cowichan, and Saanich women survive from this period. The presence of the fort made the Lekwammen wealthy compared to their neighbours, and therefore desirable as marriage mates. It was also valuable for distant nations to have relatives in Victoria, so that they could trade unmolested at the fort and have a place to stay when they came. Moreover, the Lekwammen had a reputation for being unusually clever and for having powerful spirit-allies.[33]

While many Aboriginal women formed long-term liaisons with the immigrants, others sold sexual services. Contemporary observers described this as 'prostitution,' but a closer look suggests the exchange of sex for payment, like other cross-cultural exchanges, had room for different interpretations on each side. Caroline Ralston argues in her study of Hawaiian women that 'the term "prostitution," with its undeniable sexist and moralistic connotations, is inapplicable as a description of the ... casual sexual encounters in which money or material favours are exchanged.'[34] At Victoria it seems certain that some of what the Europeans called prostitution was the coerced 'rental' of women slaves. From the first appearance of Europeans on the coast, the hiring out of women slaves to the fur traders and sailors had been a sideline venture for slaveholders. With the gold rush, opportunities for selling sex increased, but so did the avenues for slaves to escape their owners and seek protection from missionaries or kin. As slavery dwindled in importance in the 1860s, the transactions became more complex. There are a number of accounts, both in Aboriginal stories and in accounts by non-Aboriginal observers, that some women of other groups, the Haida, Tsimshian, and Tlingit as well as the Kwakwaka'wakw, used what the whites called prostitution to earn wealth independently of men in order to potlatch and enhance their personal status in their society.[35]

Overall, the first twenty years of the colonial encounter affected Lekwammen men and women differently depending on their location in Lekwammen society. Common women and men had, for the first time, the means to accumulate wealth and raise their status through their own potlatches. As a result, male and female members of the nobility found their relative status diminishing. With the decline of the patriarchal power system, common women probably experienced a relative increase in their political power. For slaves, the initial effect may have been to worsen their lot since male and females were rented out as manual labourers by their owners and female slaves were prostituted. But by the 1860s, the colonial encounter became a benefit to slaves. Missionaries and government officials offered refuge to runaways, and the Royal Navy worked to suppress the institution of slavery.

The Industrial Moment

Opportunities for the economic independence of women and the cash contribution of children and the aged, which had increased with the gold rush, increased even further in the late 1870s and early 1880s with the establishment of a salmon-canning industry. Whereas in other places colonial pressure was pushing Aboriginal women out of the public sphere of wage work,[36] on the west coast the new fish-canning factories appropriated the gendered division of work from Aboriginal societies: Native men fished and women mended nets and processed fish. The infirm looked after the infants, while even young children had work cleaning cans. In peak seasons, every available person would be brought in, and infants placed in a corner where they could be watched.[37] In addition to the Aboriginal gender division of labour, another element of the earlier economy, the separate personal property of husband and wife, continued into the industrial era. In the cash economy, the Lekwammen's Indian agent noted, 'among these Indians, the wife's purse is generally entirely separate from the husband's.' There was also continuity when it came to subsistence production. The Lekwammen people carried on their earlier gendered subsistence production and continued to pool their food resources. Food and wealth economies were kept separate.[38]

In the 1880s the canneries hired more Aboriginal men as fishers than they hired women as processors, but by the 1890s this ratio was reversed. Competition from European and Japanese fishermen eroded the demand for Aboriginal men, while a rapidly expanding canning industry and limits on Chinese immigration meant that demand for Aboriginal women workers continued to grow into the twentieth century.[39] This high demand for female cannery labour ensured that Native men with families were hired as fishermen. According to a prominent canner: 'The real reason that you want to have [cannery-owned boats] and get Indian fishermen is they bring their families around and you have Indian women and boys, and some of the men, not fishermen to work in the canneries.'[40]

Family-based production was also the norm for the Lekwammen's labour migration to the hop fields in the Fraser Valley and Puget Sound, which had begun demanding a large labour supply in the late 1870s. The hop-picking season closely followed the canning season, allowing families to participate in both. The Indian agent assigned to the Lekwammen noted that 'Indian women and children are always the most eager to go to the hop fields, where they always earn considerable sums of money.'[41] This new 'industrial' pattern was disrupted by the completion of the Canadian Pacific Railway in 1885, when some 6,000 laid-off Chinese labourers sought work in many of the industries where Aboriginal people dominated the labour force. At the canneries, Aboriginal women found that 'their places had been taken by Chinamen in cleaning and canning the fish.'[42] An Indian agent observed that even 'the poor Indian women and old men, their boys and girls, [who] used to make considerable money every summer picking berries,' had been 'ruined' by 'large numbers of Chinamen.'[43] The availability of impoverished Chinese workers reduced, but did not eliminate, the demand for the labour of Aboriginal women and children.

In the meantime, the new economy and disease were having a dramatic effect on household structure. In the early 1880s, the nuclear family extolled by the missionaries became economically possible in a way that it had not been before. Previously, a large household ensured the labour force necessary to harvest resources like camas and salmon, which were plentiful only for short periods. Now, with access to seasonal wage labour, a small household could earn enough to purchase a subsistence that was becoming less and less available from the land. Wage labour opportunities meant that even small families, with both parents and the elder children working, could accumulate sufficient wealth goods to hold their own potlatch, something that would have previously required the combined effort of a larger household. The Lekwammen responded to these economic and demographic forces by shrinking their household size. This is apparent in a comparison of Paul Kane's 1847 observation that households contained eight to ten families with Bishop Hills's 1860 comment that Chief Freezie's house contained only three small families. By 1910, the average Lekwammen household contained 2.3 people.[44]

The new economy and the shift to households built around nuclear families disadvantaged the elderly among the Lekwammen. Previously, the aged stood at the apex of Lekwammen society. The *siem* who controlled the most productive resources were often elderly men. The rituals and spiritual wealth of the community, on which the material wealth was thought to depend, were very much in the hands of the older members. As well, the practical experience of the elderly in everyday activities, ranging from gathering food to warfare, was of enormous importance to the household. The colonial encounter may have initially buttressed the importance of the elderly, so long as labour for the newcomers was organized by the *siem*, but the industrial order did not. According to the Indian agent assigned to the Lekwammen:

> The very old people who formerly lived entirely on fish, berries and roots, suffer a great deal through the settling up of the country ... With the younger men, the loss of these kinds of foods is more than compensated by the good wages that they earn, which supplement what they produce on their allotments; but this mode of life does away with their old customs of laying in a supply of dried meat, fish and berries for winter use, and thus the old people again suffer.[45]

Among the Lekwammen the disadvantaged elderly were most often widowed women.[46]

Changes in Lekwammen gender relations are also reflected in patterns of household formation. When the Europeans first arrived, marriages among the Lekwammen were arranged by parents with a view to making alliances. It was not uncommon for a *siem* to marry women much younger than himself. Although by 1891 no polygamous relationships show up in the census, males were, on average, four years older than their wives; several husbands were a decade older, and one was thirty-five years older than his wife. Two decades later, this situation had also reversed itself. In 1910 wives were, on average, a year older than their husbands, and it was not uncommon for a wife to be more than five years older than her husband. The older age of wives compared to their husbands may reflect women's increasing ability to choose their own partners, frequently marrying out into the large pool of non-Aboriginal bachelors.[47]

Shrinking household size put additional pressure on the remaining members to contribute to the household economy. The annual reports of the British Columbia Indian superintendent from 1902 to 1910 particularly focused on women's contribution:

> The Indian women, it may be remarked, are also money earners to no inconsiderable extent. During the canning season and at the hop fields they find profitable employment; they engage extensively in the manufacture of baskets, which they dispose of profitably to the tourists and others; they cure and dress deer and caribou skin, out of which they make gloves and moccasins, and they frequently find a market for dressed skins intact, they being useful for many purposes; mats from the inner bark of the cedar and rags are also made, some of which are of an attractive and superior quality; they make their own and their children's clothing, being much assisted in the latter by sewing and knitting machines; they also gather large quantities of berries, which in some cases they sell among the white people, a major portion is, however, dried for winter use; in doing chores and laundry work for white neighbours they also find considerable employment.[48]

The superintendent was reflecting on the provincial scene, but Lekwammen women could be found engaged in every activity he mentioned. True, the dressing of hides, gathering and selling of berries, and making of mats and baskets were less and less important as the Lekwammen's access to resources diminished. Instead, Lekwammen women expanded their sewing and knitting.[49] Sometime prior to 1872 Aboriginal women adapted their long-standing knowledge of spinning wool and weaving decorative blankets to the preparing of knitted woollen items, having learned knitting from the immigrants. Knitting what came to be called 'Cowichan sweaters' by the Cowichan people and other Coast Salish, including Lekwammen, later grew into a major source of income for women.[50]

As the Lekwammen gradually added kitchen gardens, a practice noted in the annual reports of the early 1890s, and as chickens became part of the domestic economy, women's and children's roles in household production expanded to include these responsibilities. By 1910 most Lekwammen homes had a chicken shed attached. There were probably others like Mrs Williams (Discovery Island band), who was responsible for sixty chickens and twenty-one geese; her daughter had her own flocks.[51]

After two decades of declining employment there was a considerable improvement in paid work for the Lekwammen in 1905 when J.H. Todd and Sons established the Empire Cannery on the nearby Esquimalt Indian reserve. Between 1907 and 1913, the new cannery and the labour shortages that accompanied a boom unprecedented since the gold rush guaranteed work for Lekwammen men and women.[52]

A detailed survey of the Lekwammen taken in November 1910 provides a clear picture of employment during the boom. The survey, done by the Indian agent, was part of an evaluation of the band's ability to manage the large sum of money that would result from the sale and relocation of their reserve. Even though it is unlikely that this survey captured all paid work, it offers a more complete picture than the earlier censuses since it indicates the main jobs held by the band members through the year, not just at the time of the survey.[53] Among the 31 men over 16 years old, stevedoring/longshoring was the biggest single source of work, employing 40 per cent (12) of the men full- or part-time. Other jobs included: general labourer (4), gardener (1), deckhand (1), logger or sawmill worker (2), laundry worker (1), construction worker (1), fish curer (1), and hunting/fishing guide (1). Of the 29 women over age 16, just over half were listed with occupations. Of these, four did domestic work, four cannery labour, four fishing/clamming (two on their own account and two with their husbands), two worked in a steam laundry, and one at fancy sewing work and hide tanning. Of those with no occupation listed, 11 were mentioned as housewives only and three were in school. The survey itself makes no mention of hop-picking, but the agent's correspondence makes it clear that 'nearly all' the Lekwammen migrated to Washington to pick hops for a few weeks each autumn leading up to 1910.

The industrial era had returned women to a place of importance and even dominance in producing wealth for Lekwammen households. While this had the potential to translate into a more significant political role for Lekwammen women, these changes occurred at the same time as the Canadian state intervened to restrict Aboriginal women's legal and political rights. The increasing economic independence of Lekwammen women in the 1880s was undermined by the application of the Indian Act of 1876, which dramatically weakened their legal and political position. According to the Act, women could not vote on matters concerning the band, nor could a woman serve as chief or councillor. In practice, this did not alter the political situation of Lekwammen women, who had not yet held political power, but it removed any flexibility for them to assume more power as productive relationships evolved.[54] More immediate in its impact was the Indian Act's stipulation that if an Aboriginal woman married a non-Indian or an Indian of a different band, she lost all rights to inherit her parents' house or land or to return to live with her birth family, even if her marriage ended in divorce or widowhood. Suddenly, Lekwammen women were much more dependent on their husbands.[55]

The state affected the Lekwammen economy in another way in 1885 when the Indian Act was revised to prohibit the potlatch. The intent of the anti-potlatch law was to hasten the assimilation of Aboriginal people by striking at the institution that tied their society together. Missionary Thomas Crosby had correctly concluded that 'the potlatch relates to all the life of the people, such as giving of names, the raising into social position, their marriages, births, deaths.' In prohibiting the potlatch, the government was banning the whole prestige economy, as well as the hereditary ownership of the subsistence economy's key resource sites, which could only be validated through potlatching.[56] Women, who had only begun to have independent means to participate in the potlatch economy, also found this route to social advancement cut off.

The state had another major impact on the Lekwammen economy and gender relations in 1911 when negotiations with the Lekwammen resulted in the sale of their downtown reserve and relocation to the suburbs (see map 9.2). The relocation suddenly placed the Lekwammen among the richest Aboriginal people in the province, though this wealth was not evenly distributed. As part of the settlement, the 41 heads of families received $10,000 in cash, plus the value of their 'improvements,' including houses, barns, stables, fences, and fruit trees. The Lekwammen insisted that the money be paid to them directly, not, as was required by the Indian Act, held in trust for them by the Depart-

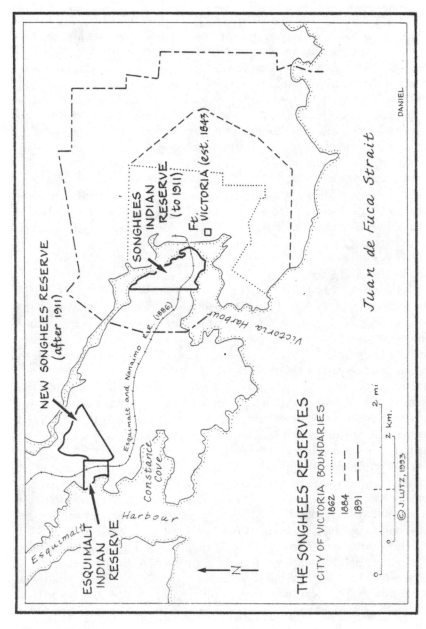

Map 9.2 Relocation of Songhees Reserve, Victoria Urban Area.

ment of Indian Affairs. This condition of sale was so extraordinary the federal Parliament had to pass special legislation to permit it.[57] Moreover, the decision to pay heads of families meant that most of the money went to the Lekwammen men. Of the forty-one groups considered families, thirty were headed by men, eleven by women. Two-thirds of the groups headed by men were married couples, some with children. Two instances where husbands gave their wives part of the settlement were explicitly mentioned in a report done by the Indian agent two years after the distribution. In one case, the wife received 30 per cent of settlement and in the other, 15 per cent.[58] But while wives did not benefit as much as husbands from the settlement, the elderly benefited disproportionately. Since they were considered heads of households, the seven Lekwammen widows each received the full cash payment of $10,000, as did the few widowers. For the first time since the breakdown of extended families, the Lekwammen elderly had some financial security.

Depression and War

The 1929 onset of the Great Depression, like the previous 1892 and 1914 depressions, seemed to hit the Lekwammen harder than their non-Aboriginal neighbours, and income statistics confirm this. Four years into the Depression, when the average Canadian income from wages and salaries was 61 per cent of its 1929 level, the average for registered Indians was down to 37 per cent of the 1929 level. In explaining this, the Department of Indian Affairs pointed to racism as the reason why Indians were in more need than others: 'The Indian was the first to be thrown out of work when the depression started and evidently will be the last to be again absorbed when the conditions improve.'[59]

When employment opportunities for Lekwammen men and women declined in the 1930s, they refocused on what remained of the subsistence economy as well as home manufactures, and then turned to relief payments for additional help. 'Relief' had first been given to the Lekwammen in 1888, when elderly members of the band received food that they were unable to gather from their declining subsistence base. Thereafter the state offered the destitute access to a new 'welfare economy.' By the 1930s, relief payments were paid 'in kind' to a value of $4 per month. This was less than one-quarter of the $16.50 non-Indians were getting in relief from the province and municipalities, as Mrs Dora Ross, a non-Aboriginal woman who became an 'Indian' through marriage, pointed out to the department. The agents, aware of the inadequate relief rates, encouraged Indians to return to subsistence activities or home manufactures as supplements. The importance of this non-wage income was highlighted by Mrs Ross: 'I can't possibly make out on the $4.00 [per month] grocery order ... The Indians here might make it do but they can do other jobs, also make sweaters etc. I have no means of adding anything to the allowance.'[60]

During the Depression, women's home production, particularly knitting, which had been a consistent supplement to employment income since the establishment of a cash economy, took on primary importance. Due to the home-based nature of the work, estimates of production are tenuous and hard to come by. One contemporary observer in the 1930s thought that Aboriginal women on southern Vancouver Island produced about five hundred sweaters a year. Sweaters were traded to storekeepers for food, until supply outstripped demand. Susan Cooper wrote the agent in March 1933: 'I owe a great deal to the store which I will pay by making sweaters [,] but the store keeper will not let me trade with sweaters for groceries any more after I pay him all because he has to[o] many sweaters on hand right now so that is why I am asking you for some groceries.' Later in the year, Elsie Kamia wrote the agent: 'I understand you are buying Indian sweaters[–]I have one made – the stores in town offer small money for them so I wondered if you could help us – many women in this reserve make them.' According to one knitter, a sweater in 1935 could bring in as much as $4.50; with wool costing only three cents a pound, the net payment to the knitter for each sweater would have been close to the $4.00 monthly grocery order available through relief.[61]

Knitting fit well with the other elements of the Aboriginal economy because it could be done in the evenings and seasons when there was little other work; it also allowed parents, particularly women, to work at home and provide their own child care, and it was an enterprise where most of the family could contribute. One knitter from southern Vancouver Island recalled about the early 1930s: 'I was eight years old when I started knitting with my mother. Our dad went fishing once in awhile but it was seasonal. My dad used to card the wool, my mom would spin and knit.' Another knitter, interviewed by Sylvia Olsen, recalled learning to knit from her mother before she was a teen: 'We were like contractors – we knit sleeves for mom – but we never got paid for it.'[62]

Another means of supplementing relief, pursue of supplementing relief, pursuer food and for sale, but this required transportation. 'Everybody is digging clams except me,' wrote Robbie Davis in 1934. 'I have no boat or canoe.' As a result, 'I wish you would give me relieve [*sic*] for it is about three weeks from the time I did went out of grocery ... please hurry.'[63] Hop-picking continued through the 1930s, but wages were so low that in 1932 many who went south did not even make enough to pay for their passage home, and so were stranded. Still, the inspector of Indian agencies, though he had previously tried to dissuade Indians from this annual migration, wished them well in 1933: 'Unfortunately there is nothing else for them in the way of employment in B.C., with the exception of those who may get work in the canneries.' Berry-picking, locally and in Washington state, took some off the relief roles for the summer, but they were back on again in the fall.[64]

The work situation started to change in 1939; by 1940 the relief list was down to twelve, and in 1943 it was down to four 'old widows and invalids,' according to Chief Percy Ross. Lekwammen men were all employed by 1942–3, many of them by the local shipyards trying to meet the wartime shipbuilding demand. Aboriginal women moved into new occupations, too, including wood processing and oil refining, as well as expanding their work in canneries, laundries, and garment manufacturing.[65]

Expanded wartime demand and the government's removal of Japanese Canadians from coastal areas combined to increase the need for Lekwammen labour in the fishing and canning industries. In 1944, the Empire Cannery added four herring canning lines to its three salmon lines, more than doubling its labour force. Herring canning also expanded the work season from the two summer months to include the four fall months. The annual payroll at the Empire Cannery jumped tenfold from its 1941–3 levels to $59,250 in 1944. The herring lines employed 40–80 Aboriginal women from September to December, in addition to the 15–20 who worked the summer on the salmon lines. The expanded demand drew Aboriginal women from all over southern Vancouver Island, as well as a few elderly Lekwammen men. The men who continued to fish made good incomes owing to high prices and absence of competition from ethnic Japanese.[66]

A couple of Lekwammen men enlisted in the military early in the war, and a few others were drafted later on, making a total of six who did military service. Compared to a $4 monthly relief cheque, the pay of an enlisted man looked pretty good. Mrs Frank and Mrs Dick received $85–$93 per month, which included a portion of their husbands' military pay plus a wife's and child's allowance.[67]

Whereas the Depression had pushed the Lekwammen back to the subsistence economy and to home production, the war drew Aboriginal men, women, children, and the elderly back into the workforce in a way that had not been seen since 1919. The agent's report for 1946 noted that 'women and elderly people, as well as the older children worked in the canneries and berry and hop-fields, both in British Columbia and the State of Washington ... Conditions were good and work plentiful for Indians of all ages.' Berry-pickers earned an unprecedented 85 cents an hour, and the hop companies paid pickers five cents a pound. 'Crops were good and the returns to the Indians were most satisfactory,' reported the agent.[68] Whereas in the 1930s there was virtually no paid labour to be found and families reverted to an economy based on subsistence and women's home production, in the early 1940s men and women, young and old, had as much work as they wanted.

Welfare Colonialism

Several factors came together in the immediate post-war period and reshaped the Lekwammen economy once again. First, the return of demobilized servicemen and ethnic Japanese from detention camps alleviated the wartime labour shortage. Second, and even more important in the long run, was an overall slackening in the demand for low-skill seasonal labour, which since the late 1880s had been the mainstay of the Lekwammen economy. In the meantime, tighter fishing restrictions further limited the subsistence economy. Finally, the state began a dramatic expansion of welfare payments to Indians.

The first evidence of the expanded welfare economy was the Family Allowance program instituted for all Canadians in 1945. Although payments were made for each child, cheques were payable to their mothers. Like knitting, Family Allowance provided year-round income and so was particularly valuable in the seasonal economy. The cash contribution of Lekwammen women to the household probably peaked in the late 1940s when Family Allowances could be added to June-to-December income from the Empire Cannery and sales of sweaters knitted from December to June.[69]

The closure of the Empire Cannery in 1951–2 was a major blow to Lekwammen participation in the post-war economy. Like so many other canneries on the coast, Empire fell victim to financial consolidation and technological change. Improved refrigeration techniques meant fish harvested at the firm's traps in Sooke could be transported to a cannery on the Fraser River and processed more cheaply there than by maintaining a separate cannery in Esquimalt. With its closing, Lekwammen women lost their most regular source of employment. Instead of six months' work next door to their home, what remained was one, or at most, two months' employment in the hop yards of Washington State. But even the demand for hop-pickers was declining. The hop fields that remained were experimenting with mechanical harvesters and Mexican labourers, so that by 1960 even this option was largely closed to the Lekwammen.

While the cannery jobs were shrinking, Aboriginal fishermen were also under increasing pressure. The Lekwammen's Indian agent (now called superintendent) remarked in 1954: 'With the return of numerous Japanese fishermen to the Pacific Coast, Indians are again finding it difficult to negotiate contracts with the fish canners who prefer to deal with the Japanese because of their dependability in paying accounts. Poor fishing conditions last year also resulted in the majority of Indian fishermen being financially "broke" during the winter months.'[70]

The same year that Empire closed, the federal and provincial governments extended Old Age Security allowances to Indians. Twenty-eight years after it was extended to other Canadians, Indians over seventy received the full old-age pension. Destitute Indians between sixty-five and seventy could also qualify for a pension. Four Lekwammen over age seventy were eligible for the $40/month payment.[71] For the first time in forty years, elderly Lekwammen could live independently, with a minimum level of comfort, or make a financial contribution if living with others.[72]

With the closure of work opportunities and the opening of social welfare programs to Aboriginal people, the importance of the wage economy fell. Families turned to an increasingly robust welfare economy, and Lekwammen women returned to their knitting. In his December quarterly report for 1955, the Lekwammen's Indian agent noted that 'requests for relief assistance have been unusually heavy ... Fortunately,' he added, 'the Indian women of this agency derive a very considerable income from knitting sweaters.'[73] By 1950 sweater production had increased so that there were three major sweater dealers on southern Vancouver Island. One of these, Norman Lougheed, was buying 1,500 sweaters a year. A decade later, he bought 5,000 sweaters in a single year. One indication of the value of the industry is the 1959 estimate, from one of the three main sweater dealers, that he paid $185,000 that year to Aboriginal knitters in the Cowichan Indian Agency, which included the Lekwammen.[74]

Barbara Lane noted that although Indian men had earlier helped with the knitting, this practice was dying out by the 1940s 'due to the modern prejudice that it is women's work.' The knitting industry, she concluded, 'has had far reaching effects on ... the status of women. The latter now have an independent year-round source of income, while the men are usually dependent on seasonal labour. The earning power of women has had repercussions in the marriage pattern and in family life generally,' giving women more independence.[75] For single mothers, knitting was even more important. Left with eight children when her husband died in the mid-1950s, Priscilla, a Saanich woman living on a reserve just north of the Lekwammen, recalled:

> I was knitting about seven sweaters a week at that time. I stayed up most of the night. I would first pack wood up from the beach for the fire. Then I would knit all night. I always liked knitting. All the kids would go to sleep and I would knit ... The kids had to eat and we had to work where ever we could.[76]

Although knitting sustained families in tough times in the 1950s and 1960s, as it had in the 1930s, by 1970 the money available from knitting was also in relative decline. Rising costs of wool and reduced prices from mechanical competition meant that knitters were making less than one dollar an hour in 1972 in exchange for 'both physically hard work in washing the wool and monotony.'[77] That year, Kathleen Mooney found that 'even the knitting of Cowichan sweaters, long an important source of supplementary [income], has become increasingly unprofitable. Although an Indian-owned and operated sweater store is located on the reserve, and people in ten of the 15 sample households used to knit regularly, only four continued to do so.'[78]

In 1954 the agent conducted a rough employment review and found the majority of Lekwammen men earned their living in unskilled intermittent jobs 'in neighbouring booming grounds and sawmills, and in various jobs in Victoria such as contracting, coalyards, etc.'[79] Aboriginal women's employment was evidently considered of such marginal importance that it was not counted. From the 1950s through to the 1970s, when non-Aboriginal women were increasingly attracted into retail, food and beverage, clerical, nursing, and teaching occupations, Aboriginal women were largely excluded from these jobs by a combination of inadequate academic preparation and racism.[80] Mooney's research shows that in stark contrast to earlier times, in these two decades

Aboriginal women were much less likely to be employed than non-Aboriginal women. Mitchell's 1972 study of Aboriginal women in a Victoria-area reserve confirms Mooney's research, finding that for those few who had employment, 'the median income for the year was an absurd $183.' By comparison, Indian men who lived on the reserve earned a median of $1,900, and non-Indian women in the Victoria area earned an average $2,600. Mitchell estimated the median income from all sources, including social assistance, for Indian women was $975 per year, compared to $3,400 for Indian men.[81]

Complete relief records survive for the Cowichan Indian Agency, which included the Lekwammen, for the year 1 April 1960 to 31 March 1961. During the peak summer employment season, a quarter of the Indians were receiving relief. Over the winter, when seasonal employment was scarce, just over 50 per cent were receiving relief.[82]

Comparing the late 1960s with the 1891 and 1910 censuses highlights the important transformations that had taken place in Lekwammen economic lives. The population of the Lekwammen band, 134 in 1890, was almost identical to the 131 in the band in 1967,[83] but the percentage of the population in the workforce had dropped dramatically. In 1891 the census showed 35 per cent of the Lekwammen with occupations, while a 1967 survey showed only 15 per cent had occupations.[84] Lekwammen men and, especially, Lekwammen women had become 'increasingly unemployed' in the twentieth century. Women were still able to participate to a small degree in the subsistence economy, but this had minuscule importance to the household economy compared to five and ten decades earlier. By 1970 women's main contribution to the household economy was through their claims on state welfare payments.[85]

Conclusion

The microhistorical method of asking wide-ranging historical questions in very localized contexts reveals the ebb and flow of economic and power relationships between men and women in a way that historical studies using blunter tools and coarser filters cannot. Focusing on gender and work, this study suggests that the gendered economic power depended on local factors like labour supply and demand, technological change, and pre-existing gender ratios in both indigenous and immigrant populations, as well as more general factors such as racial attitudes and government policies. At some moments in the colonial and post-colonial eras, Lekwammen women, taken as a whole, had a more important economic role in Lekwammen society than they did in the immediate pre-colonial period. At other historical junctures, they had less. And how women's economic contribution translated into other kinds of power in the household and community was also shaped by changes occurring in the broader political realm. When the Canadian state intervened in 1876 to exclude Aboriginal women from the official governing process on Indian reserves, it confirmed an earlier, pre-contact male control over this sphere. Given the complexity of changes, it is critical to realize that colonialism did not translate directly into a decline of the power of Aboriginal women vis-à-vis Aboriginal men.

Whereas Anderson and Leacock found that gender roles transformed rapidly and irrevocably after the arrival of Europeans in the Aboriginal societies they studied, the Lekwammen experienced a more drawn-out and fluid process.[86] Long-standing seasonal, gender, and family-based modes of organizing labour adapted and became integrated into colonial and industrial patterns and so persisted among the Lekwammen through to the 1950s. In these circumstances, gender roles inherited from the 'ethnographic moment' proved surprisingly resilient. To be sure, other facets of colonialism undermined the power of both Aboriginal women and men, as evidenced by the marginal economic position occupied by many Lekwammen in 1970 and by the decline in employment of both sexes compared to a century prior. Yet even this marginalization was relative to the original locations of individuals or their families in the pre-contact social structure. Nobles in Lekwammen society found themselves treated as anything but, as colonial society transformed into an industrial one. Yet, while colonial society also marginalized those who had been slaves in Aboriginal society, they were marginalized in common with all Aboriginal people and were no longer subject to the power of Aboriginal masters.

Microhistorical analysis reveals the gendered elements of the Canadian colonial project. Among the Lekwammen, men and women were affected by the arrival and persistence of Euro-Canadians in different and sometimes surprising ways – surprising because the complexity of the impact of colonialism over the long term has been missed in studies that have had broader spatial and shorter temporal scope. The history of the Lekwammen demonstrates the importance of long-term gendered analyses, while reminding us that gender only makes sense as an analytical category when linked to race, age, and social position.

NOTES

1 See especially Margaret Jolly and M. Macintyre, *Family and Gender in the Pacific: Domestic Contradictions and Colonial Impact* (Sydney, 1988).
2 Until recently the Lekwammen were known to Euro-Canadians as 'Songhees,' and this remains the legal name of the band and their reserve on the Department of Indian Affairs files. They have changed their name back to a term that identifies them by the dialect they speak.
3 Karen Anderson, *Chain Her by One Foot: The Subjugation of Native Women in Seventeenth Century New France* (New York, 1993); Jo-Anne Fiske, 'Colonization and the Decline of Women's Status: The Tsimshian Case,' *Feminist Studies* 17.3 (Fall 1991): 509–34; Eleanor Leacock, 'Montagnais Women and the Jesuit Program for Colonization,' in *Women and Colonization: Anthropological Perspectives*, ed. M. Etienne and E. Leacock (New York, 1980); Ron Bourgeault, 'The Indian, the Métis and the Fur Trade: Class, Sexism and Racism in the Transition from "Communism" to Capitalism,' *Studies in Political Economy* 12 (Fall 1983): 45–80.
4 Nancy Bonvillain, 'Gender Relations in Native North America,' *American Indian Culture and Research Journal* 13.2 (1989): 1–28.
5 Compare the different conclusions of Carol Cooper, 'Native Women on the Northern Pacific Coast: An Historical Perspective, 1830–1900,' *Journal of Canadian Studies* 27.4 (Winter 1992–3): 44–73, who looks at the upper- and mid-ranking Tsimshian women, with Fiske, 'Colonization and the Decline,' who focused only on the upper-ranked. Though there has been very little attention paid to slaves, I draw this conclusion for recent research by Susan Marsden, presented in 'The Life of Tahlama,' paper given to the BC Gender History Conference, Victoria, June 1995.
6 Microhistory is a method of historical analysis involving the detailed examination of individuals within a specific setting, such as a community, workplace, or household. See Giovanni Levi, 'On Microhistory,' in *New Perspectives on Historical Writing*, ed. Peter Burke (University Park, PA, 1991), 93–113. Although she does not use the term 'microhistory,' Dorothy Smith argues for this approach in *Texts, Facts and Femininity: Exploring the Relations of Ruling* (London, 1990).
7 Wilson Duff, 'Fort Victoria Treaties,' *BC Studies* 3 (Fall 1960): 3–57; Robert T. Boyd, 'Demographic History, 1774–1874,' in *Handbook of North American Indians*, vol. 7, ed. Wayne Suttles (Washington, 1990), 135–48.
8 The main ethnographers who have studied the Lekwammen, including such luminaries in the field as Franz Boas, Diamond Jenness, Charles Hill-Tout, Homer Barnett, and Wayne Suttles, have all been men using primarily male informants.

9 For a discussion of this problem as systemic in ethnographic literature, see Marjorie Mitchell and Anna Franklin, 'When You Don't Know the Language, Listen to the Silence: An Historical Overview of Native Indian Women in BC,' in *Not Just Pin Money*, ed. B.K. Latham and R.J. Pazdro (Victoria, BC, 1984), 17–36; Bonvillain, 'Gender Relations in Native North America.'

10 Laura Klein, '"She's One of Us, You Know": The Public Life of Tlingit Women, Traditional, Historical and Contemporary Perspectives,' *Western Canadian Journal of Anthropology* 6.3 (1976): 164–83; Homer Barnett, *Coast Salish of British Columbia* (Eugene, OR, 1955), 246–9.

11 Barnett, *Coast Salish*, 250–1

12 Hill-Tout believed the *siem* constituted a separate class and that there was an intermediary class who were not of the nobility but who had acquired considerable wealth. See Wayne Suttles, 'Private Knowledge, Morality and Social Classes among the Coast Salish,' in *Coast Salish Essays*, ed. Wayne Suttles (Seattle, 1987), 3–14; Charles Hill-Tout, *The Salish People* (Vancouver, 1977), 130.

13 J.M. Yale's 1839 census included one of the Lekwammen extended families. He records for them 12 families, which included 57 'people,' plus 70 male and female 'followers' or slaves. The large number of slaves may have been a recent adaptation (British Columbia Archives and Record Services [BCARS], B/20/1853, James Douglas, Private Papers, 2nd ser., 5–31).

14 Paul Kane, *Wanderings of an Artist* ... (1859; reprinted Edmonton, 1968), 152; Gary J. Morris, *Straits Salish Prehistory* (Lopez Island, BC, 1993), 11.

15 Chee-al-thuk was generally known to the whites as King Freezie. He was 'chief' of the Lekwammen until his death in 1864.

16 Barnett, *Coast Salish*, 241–4.

17 There are accounts from various sources, unfortunately none particularly reliable, that Chee-al-thuk had fifteen wives at one time. I believe this to be exaggerated. In the 1839 Yale census, cited above, there were 12 heads of families enumerated and only 14 mature women.

18 Thomas Buckley and Alma Gottlieb, *Blood Magic: The Anthropology of Menstruation* (Berkeley, 1982), 3–50. The most direct Salish male testimony comes from John Fornsby, 'John Fornsby: The Personal Document of a Coast Salish Indian,' compiled by June Collins, in *The Indians of the Urban Northwest*, ed. Marian Smith (New York, 1949), 287–341; Mourning Dove, *Mourning Dove: A Salishan Autobiography*, ed. Jay Miller (Lincoln, NE, 1986), 38, 42.

19 Wayne Suttles, *Economic Life of the Coast Salish of Haro and Rosario Straits* (New York, 1974), 57, 69, 235–40. Captain George Vancouver, visiting a Salish village in 1790, described how 'nearly the whole of the inhabi-

tants ... about 80 or 100 men, women and children, were busily engaged ... rooting up this beautiful verdant meadow in quest of a species of wild onion' (George Vancouver, *A Voyage of Discovery to the North Pacific Ocean and Round the World* [London, 1798; reprint, ed. W. Kay Lamb, 1984], 545).

20 Franz Boas, 'The Lku'ngen,' *Report of the British Association for the Advancement of Science* (1890), 571. Among some of the Lekwammen neighbours, we know of specific examples where women dressed as men and engaged in male occupations, including hunting. How this was reconciled with menstrual taboos is not known. See Wilson Duff, *The Upper Stalo Indians of the Fraser River of B.C.* (Victoria, BC, 1952), 79; Walter L. Williams, *The Spirit and the Flesh: Sexual Diversity in American Indian Culture* (Boston, 1986), 194–216.

21 Food was exchanged for other food and could only be converted into wealth indirectly; surplus food could be given as 'gifts' to one's in-laws, for which they were bound to return wealth goods. Otherwise, surpluses of food were only convertible through the freeing up of labour to be dedicated to the production of wealth goods. See Suttles, *Coast Salish Essays*, 15–25.

22 Ibid., 8, 17. There is an enormous ethnographic literature on the potlatch. A good bibliography can be found in D. Cole and I. Chaikin, *An Iron Hand upon the People* (Vancouver, 1990), 213–23.

23 Cecil Jane, *A Spanish Voyage to Vancouver and the North-West Coast of America* (London, 1930), 34–5; Vancouver, *Voyage of Discovery*, 524.

24 Myron Eells, *The Indians of Puget Sound: The Notebooks of Myron Eells* (Seattle, 1985), 122; F.W. Howay, 'The Dog's Hair Blankets of the Caost Salish,' *Washington Historical Quarterly* 9.2 (April 1918): 83–91. One of Paul Kane's paintings at the Royal Ontario Museum shows a Lekwammen woman weaving such a blanket and another spinning dog wool with a sheared dog in the foreground.

25 Judith Brown, 'Economic Organization and the Position of Women among the Iroquois,' *Ethnohistory* 17 (1990): 151–67.

26 Bolduc, in Father P.J. De Smet, *Oregon Missions and Travels over the Rocky Mountains in 1845 and 1846* (New York, 1847), 57–8; BCARS, James Douglas, Private Papers, 2nd ser., B20 1853; Captain Wilson, 'Report on the Indian Tribes Inhabiting the Country in the Vicinity of the 49th Parallel of North Lattitude,' *Transactions of the Ethnological Society of London*, n.s. 14 (1866): 275–332; National Archives (NA), RG 88, vol. 499, 1876–7; Canada Census, Manuscript 1891; Department of Indian Affairs, *Annual Report*, 1911; the Esquimalt band is counted with the Songhees.

27 For an elaboration of this point, see John Lutz, 'Work, Wages and Welfare

in Aboriginal–Non-Aboriginal Relations in British Columbia, 1843–1970'
(Ph.D. diss., University of Ottawa, 1994), ch. 2

28 Robert H. Ruby and John A. Brown, *A Guide to Indian Tribes of the Pacific Northwest* (Norman, OK, 1992), 225; Boas, 'Lku'ngen,' 566; W.F. Tolmie, 'Utilization of the Indians,' *Resources of British Columbia* 1.12 (1 Feb. 1884): 7.

29 Douglas to governor and committee, 27 Oct. 1849, in Hartwell Bowsfield, *Fort Victoria Letters, 1846–1851* (Winnipeg, 1979), 63; Sophia Cracroft, *Lady Franklin Visits the Pacific Northwest* (Victoria, BC, 1974), 79.

30 BCARS, E/B/B34.2., Charles A. Bayley, 'Early Life on Vancouver Island.' Sylvia Van Kirk, *Many Tender Ties: Women in Fur-Trade Society in Western Canada, 1670–1870* (Winnipeg, 1980), discusses the widespread phenomenon of fur traders marrying Aboriginal women and the benefits such liaisons brought to both parties.

31 Fornsby, 'John Fornsby,' discusses the prevalence in Puget Sound; see also Jean Barman, 'Imagining the "Halfbreed": British Columbia in the Late Nineteenth Century,' paper presented to the American Historical Association, 1992.

32 BCARS, James Douglas, Private Papers, 2nd ser., B20 1853; for more discussion of Lekwammen population changes, see Lutz, 'Work, Wages and Welfare,' ch. 6.

33 Fornsby is quite explicit about the relative wealth of the Lekwammen in his account of one such marriage between a Lekwammen *siem* and a Swinomish woman, in 'John Fornsby.' See also William W. Elmendorf, *Twana Narratives: Native Historical Accounts of a Coast Salish Culture* (Seattle, 1993), 41; BCARS, ms., Diamond Jenness, 'The Saanich Indians of the South-Eastern Tribes of Vancouver Island, BC' (1907), reprinted in Ralph Maud, ed., *The Salish People*, vol. 4 (Vancouver, 1978), 132–4.

34 Caroline Ralston, 'Ordinary Women in Early Post-Contact Hawaii,' in *Family and Gender in the Pacific: Domestic Contradictions and the Colonial Impact*, ed. Margaret Jolly and Martha Macintyre (Cambridge, 1989), 57.

35 Fiske makes this point in 'Colonization and Tshimshian Women,' 523. See also Cooper, 'Native Women of the Northern Pacific Coast,' 59; NA, Church Missionary Society (CMS), c.2/0 Appendix C, Reel A-105, William Duncan, First Report, Fort Simpson, Feb. 1858; Franz Boas, *Contributions to the Ethnography of the Kwakiutl* (New York, 1925), 93–4.

36 Ellice B. Gonzalez, *Changing Economic Roles for Micmac Men and Women: An Ethnohistorical Analysis* (Ottawa, 1981), 111.

37 When widowed, Lekwammen Sarah Albany worked in canneries, and her children, including future Lekwammen chief John Albany, earned ten cents an hour washing cans (Esquimalt Municipal Archives, 'Interview

with Joyce Albany'; BCARS, Add Mss, B/C21, Alfred Carmichael, 'Account of a Season's Work at a Salmon Cannery').

38 Canada, *Sessional Papers*, 1887, 5, 92; 1888, 13, 105. Studies of other coastal groups suggest that the separation of the earnings of husbands and wives was common elsewhere as well. See Cooper, 'Native Women of the Northern Pacific Coast,' 56; Klein, 'She's One of Us,' 67; Cairn Crockford, 'Changing Economic Activities of the Nuu-chah-nulth of Vancouver Island, 1840–1920' (Honours thesis, University of Victoria, 1991), 43.

39 Canada, *Sessional Papers*, 1883, 61, reports 1,300 Aboriginal men employed at fisheries and paid an average of $1.75 /day for a season of 90 days, while the canneries employed 400 Aboriginal women in the same season, who earned $1/day. See also Vowell in Canada, *Sessional Papers*, 1902, no. 27, 284–9; NA, RG 10, vol. 3988, file 154, 635, Lomas to Vowell, 30 March 1897; Canada, *Sessional Papers*, 1904, vol. 11, no. 27, 254–61.

40 NA, RG 10, vol. 1349, reel C-13917, item 412, Great West Packing Co., Ltd to W.R. Robertson, Cowichan Indian Agent, 20 Feb. 1913. See also British Columbia, *Sessional Papers*, 1893, 'BC Fishery Commission Report,' testimony of F.L. Lord, 117; NA, RG 10, vol. 3908, Black Series, file 106297-2, feel C-10160, 'Minutes of a Royal Commission at Victoria Involving the Fishing Privileges of Indians of British Columbia,' 1915.

41 Canada, *Sessional Papers*, 1887, 5, 92; 1888, 13, 105.

42 Ibid, 1885, 105.

43 Ibid; NA, RG 10, vol. 3772, file 35139, Loren P. Lewis to A.W. Vowell, 29 Jan. 1887

44 Canada, Census, Mss 1891, 1901; NA, RG 10, vol. 11, 050, file 33/3, part 7, 'Census of the Songhees Band of Indians,' 1910; Anglican Church of Canada, Ecclesiastical Province of British Columbia and the Yukon Archives (ACC), Bishop Hills' Diary, 17 Jan. 1860.

45 Lomas in Canada, *Sessional Papers*, 1888, 13, 105.

46 Mss. Census 1901; NA, RG 10, vol. 11, 050, 33/3, part 7. Among the Lekwammen there were seven widows in 1901 with an average age of 54 and three widowers with an average age of 67; in 1910 there were six widows with average age of 67 and two widowers, whose average age was 74. The special disadvantage that widows faced is discussed by Alice Bee Kasakoff, 'Who Cared for Those Who Couldn't Care for Themselves in Traditional Northwest Coast Societies?' *Canadian Journal of Native Studies* 12.2 (1992): 299–302; and Marjorie Mitchell, 'Social and Cultural Consequences for Native Indian Women on a British Columbia Reserve,' *Atlantis* 4.2 (Spring 1979): 179–88.

47 Of the eight single Lekwammen women under twenty-five in the 1901

census for which there was information on marriage, all married non-Indians. Only two of the nine single Lekwammen men under twenty-five listed in the 1910 census, and for whom marriage information is available, married non-Indians. Since Aborignal men less frequently married non-Aboriginal women, the pool of partners available to them declined. Four of the single Lekwammen men under twenty-five in 1901, who lived past forty, never married. This information is drawn from the Canada 1901 Mss. Census and compared to genealogy tables derived from estate files from 1903 to 1965, in NA, RG 10, Series B3g, reel 2739-40, file 37-3-23, and supplemented by the Cowichan agency correspondence files.

48 A.W. Vowell in annual report of the British Columbia Indian superintendent's office, 19 July 1906, in Canada, *Sessional Papers*, 1907, no. 27, 268; this passage is repeated nearly verbatim in all the reports through this decade.

49 As early as 1862, Bishop Hills found women sewing dresses on the Songhees reserve; in the 1880s when relief was issued to men, it included a shirt and trousers, but when issued to women, it included needles and nine yards of both flannel and cotton (NA, RG 10, vol. 3803, reel C-10, 141; Indian Affairs, Black Series, 53, 283, H. Moffat to superintendent general of Indian affairs, 21 Dec. 1888; ACC, Hills Diary, 1 Feb. 13 Mar. 1862).

50 Barbara Lane, 'The Cowichan Knitting Industry,' *Anthropology in British Columbia* 2 (1951): 18–10

51 NA, RG 10, vol. 11, 050, 33/3, part 7; BCARS, GR 1995, reel B-1454; transcripts, McKenna-McBride Commission, 10 June 1913, 198–9.

52 United Church Archives, Toronto, 78.092c, file 97, E.K. Nichols to A.B. Sutherland, 19 June 1909; *Colonist*, 13 June 1906, p. 9; 12 July 1907, p. 5; *Vancouver Province*, 18 September 1909, p. 1; Peter Baskerville, *Beyond the Island: An Illustrated History of Victoria* (Burlington, ON, 1986), 68.

53 The following information for 1910 is taken from NA, RG 10, vol. 11, 050, file 33/3, part 7, 'Census of the Songhees Band of Indians,' 21–5 Nov. 1910.

54 This has since changed with recent revisions to the Indian Act. See Bruce Miller, 'Women and Politics: Comparative Evidence from the Northwest Coast,' *Ethnology* 31. 4 (October 1992): 367–83.

55 Mitchell, 'Social and Cultural Consequences,' 183.

56 Thomas Crosby, *Among the an-ho-me-nums or Flathead Tribes of Indians of the Pacific Coast* (Toronto, 1907), 107.

57 The improvements were collectively valued at $20,172 (*Colonist*, 22 March 1916, p. 3; British Columbia, *Sessional Papers*, 1912, C270; Canada, *Statutes of Canada*, 1911, vols. 1–2, ch. 24, 225–7).

58 NA, RG 10, vol. 11, 050, file 33/3, part 7.

59 Department of Indian Affairs (DIA), 'Report of the Deputy Superinten-
    dent,' 1935, 10; J.L. Taylor, *Canadian Indian Policy during the Inter-War Years,
    1918–1939* (Ottawa, 1984), 93.
60 NA, RG 10, vol. 9, 170, file B-45, Mrs Percy Ross to H. Graham, 8 Jan. 1935;
    H. Graham to George Davidson, BC superintendent of welfare, 17 Jan.
    1935.
61 NA, RG 10, vol. 9, 170, file B-44, George Pragnell, inspector of Indian
    agencies, to secretary, DIA, 14 Dec. 1934; file B-48, Mrs Susan Cooper to
    H. Graham, Indian agent, 15 March 1933; Mrs Elsie Kamia to H. Graham,
    6 Dec. 1933; Ron Baird, 'World Famous Cowichan Sweaters,' in *BC Motor-
    ist* (Sept.–Oct. 1965): 10–11; and the 1935 price from a March 1994 inter-
    view with 'Priscilla' quoted in Sylvia Olsen, 'Cowichan Indian Sweaters,'
    unpublished paper, University of Victoria, 1994, 13. In his October 1930
    report, the inspector of Indian agencies wrote that in the Cowichan agency
    the sale of Indian sweaters was constantly increasing (NA, RG 10, vol. 9,
    170, file B-44, George S. Pragnell, inspector of Indian agencies, to the
    secretary of DIA, 26 October 1935).
62 'Cecelia' in Olsen, 'Cowichan Sweaters.'
63 NA, RG 10, vol. 9, 170, file B-45, Robbie Davis to H. Graham, 8 Dec. 1934;
    see also Mrs Percy Ross to H. Graham, 8 Jan. 1935.
64 NA, RG 10, vol. 9, 170, file B-44, George Pragnell to secretary, DIA, 15 June
    1933; Pragnell to secretary, DIA, 30 July 1932; file B-45, Frank George to H.
    Graham, 4 April 1933: 'Please continue my relief as the strawberries are
    getting in soon and then we won't be bothering you any more.'
65 NA, RG 10, vol. 9, 172, file B-57, Percy Ross to R.H. Moore, 21 May 1943;
    also file B-58. For women's occupations, see British Columbia, Department
    of Labour, *Annual Report*, in British Columbia, *Sessional Papers*, 1940–5.
66 Information on employment at Empire Cannery comes from University of
    British Columbia Special Collections (UBC-SC), J.H. Todd and Sons Busi-
    ness Records, boxes 2–6; DIA, *Annual Report*, 1944, 46.
67 NA, RG 10, vol. 9, 172, file B-58, Minutes of Songhees Band Council
    meeting, 25 June 1944; Percy Ross to R.H. Moore, 20 July 1944; Moore to
    W.A. Green, 19 Feb. 1945; file B-49, A.H. Brown, DND Dependents Allow-
    ance Board, to R.H. Moore, Indian agent, 14 April 1941.
68 DIA, *Annual Report*, 1946, 1947
69 In 1946 and 1947 the *Annual Report* of the Department of Indian Affairs
    noted that Cowichan sweaters were turned out 'in considerable quantity'
    at 'higher than prewar prices' (DIA, *Annual Report*, 1947, 206–7).
70 Ibid., 1954.

71 In 1948 the Department of Indian Affairs started paying Indians over seventy, $8 per month in lieu of Old Age Security. In 1950, this was raised to $25 per month (NA, RG 10, vol. 2375, file 275-3-4[1], 'Indians Transferred from Aged Assistance to Old Age Security,' 31 December 1951; NA, RG 29, Department of National Health and Welfare, vol. 1, 889, file R 170/110, J.I. Clark to Joy Peacock, 2 Nov. 1968).

72 NA, Vancouver Regional Repository (hereafter NA-VRR), RG 10, V1984–85/316, Box 21, file 988/29-5, part 1, Indian Affairs Branch to all Indian agents, 26 April 1948, 1 June 1950; NA, RG 29, vol. 1889, file R170/110, J.I. Clark, principal research officer, Department of Health and Welfare, to Joy Peacock, 2 Nov. 1968; *Thunderbird*, 1 June 1949, p. 8 and Nov. supplement, 1950, p. 4.

73 DIA, 974/21–1, vol. 1, J.V. Boys, 1 Feb. 1956.

74 DIA, Central Registry, Ottawa, file 9748/21-1, vol. 1, J.V. Boys, superintendent, Cowichan agency, 'Report for the Quarter Ending December 31, 1955'; E. Blanche Norcross, 'Cowichan Indian Sweaters,' *The Beaver* (Dec. 1945): 18–19; Norman Lougheed, quoted in Olsen, 'Cowichan Sweaters,' 16

75 Olsen, 'Cowichan Sweaters'; Lane, 'Cowichan Knitting Industry,' 14–17; NA, RG 10, vol. 9, 170, various letters; George S. Pragnell, inspector of Indian agencies, to secretary, DIA, 'Cowichan Indian Agency Report No. 6,' 26 October 1935.

76 Olsen, 'Cowichan Sweaters.'

77 Mitchell, 'Social and Cultural Consequences,' 183.

78 Kathleen A. Mooney, 'Urban and Reserve Indian Economies and Domestic Organization' (Ph.D. diss. University of Michigan, 1974), 89; the reserve she mentions is the Tsawout Reserve, thirty km north of the Lekwammen's.

79 NA, RG 10, vol. 6, 933, file 901/29-1, part 1, K.R. Brown to W.S. Arneil, 26 March 1954.

80 Joyce Albany's account of schooling provided by the Department of Indian Affairs shows that it was not up to the standard provided by the province in public schools. Moreover, high school was free for 'provincial tax-payers,' but Indians had to pay fees. Albany was hired as a secretary for a law firm and eventually the school board, but said that her sisters looked for work in Vancouver because they were known as 'Indians' in Victoria. See Esquimalt Municipal Archives, 'Joyce Albany Interview.'

81 Mooney, 'Urban and Reserve Indian Economics,' 399; Mitchell, 'Social and Cultural Consequences,' 183, 184.

82 In addition, 45 families received Family Allowance in the Cowichan

agency and 106 individual received old-age or disability pensions (NA-VRR, RG 10, V84–5, vol. 500351, file 41-12; DIA, Central Registry, Ottawa, file 208/29-1).

83 Canada, *Sessional Papers*, 1891; Capital Region Planning Board of BC, Indian Communities, appendix 1.

84 No Lekwammen women were listed as having an occupation in the 1967 survey.

85 In this respect, they fit into a national pattern evident in Linda Gerber, 'Multiple Jeopardy: A Socio-Economic Comparison of Women among the Indian, Metis and Inuit Peoples of Canada,' *Canadian Ethnic Studies* 22.3 (1990): 69–84.

86 A drawn-out process is also suggested by Cooper, 'Native Women of the Northern Pacific Coast,' and by Gonzalez, *Changing Economic Roles for Micmac Men and Women*.

10 The Woman's Lodge: Constructing Gender on the Nineteenth-Century Pacific Northwest Plateau

MARY C. WRIGHT

Gender and all manner of status and societal roles have come to be seen as constructed. People help define the categories of human groupings by their behaviour, their expectations, their ideas, their resistance, and by the way they treat each other. The understanding of woman as a biologically determined being is challenged (some would say over-turned) by cultural definitions resulting from human actions. And, of course, this defining of gender differs by group or culture and changes over time.

Female gender construction began at the woman's lodge among the Indigenous peoples inhabiting the Pacific Northwest Plateau at the beginning of the nineteenth century. A constellation of gender defini-tions, beliefs, and behaviours radiated from that place. In these women-built structures, all women passed their menstrual periods, girls' puberty rituals took place, children were birthed, baskets and other woman-produced articles were made, and teachings of what it meant to be a woman were passed from generation to generation.

The Plateau is an arid, often mountainous region drained by the Columbia, Fraser, and Snake rivers, or roughly occupying a region defined today by eastern British Columbia, Washington, and Oregon, all of Idaho, and parts of Alberta and Montana. A wide range of Indig-enous peoples made their home in the region, such as the Nez Perce in Idaho State, the Yakama of Washington State, and the Thompson, Lillooet, and the Okanagan in Canada. All included a woman's lodge among their buildings and their cultural practices. In a 1930s project defining the Plateau as a distinct cultural area, anthropologist Verne F. Ray found menstrual seclusion and girls' puberty rites, both sited in the woman's lodge, universal in the region. So much so, that he identified them as defining characteristics of Plateau culture.[1]

Investigating the woman's lodge as a *place* and as *space* proves to be a productive approach to understanding how gender was constructed for Plateau women. Cultural geographers have long studied human spatial patterning. Feminist geographers, expanding cultural geography's study of human spatial patterning, find women's use of space different from men's and women's places endowed with special meanings, protections, and practices. Applying some of the same inquiries and considerations of gender and space for non-European peoples, in this case the Indigenous peoples of the Plateau, shows the profound impact of gender on human construction of place and, vice versa, of spatial implications for the construction of gender.[2]

Control of the woman's lodge indicates the overall importance of women in the society at large, even as it serves as a marker for that power. The societal and cultural importance of Indigenous Plateau women can be traced to their economic contributions and control of distribution, the strength of the bilateral kinship system (where heredity and identity are calculated along both male and female lines), equal spiritual opportunities, and other cultural markers such as mobility and access to divorce.[3] Underneath these outward manifestations of women's power in the community at large were those behaviours and beliefs constructed internally, among women themselves, in the woman's lodge.[4]

American Indian women of the Plateau region built and controlled significant space within Native culture.[5] Shelter took two forms among the Plateau people. The winter lodge, built in sheltered valleys, was a pit house entered by ladders in the centre, with a dugout basement and overarching rafters covered with mats and earth. The summer or travelling lodge was smaller, more likely to be circular, without the deeply depressed flooring and with a different rafter structure. Women collected marshland tules and constructed mats needed for both structures. Buffalo robes later came to replace the mat covering for some groups. Women prepared the thirty to forty robes needed for the lodge and owned them.[6] The lodge's robes were valued at sixty to one hundred dollars total in mid-nineteenth-century currency.

Early-nineteenth-century fur traders and missionaries observed, often with surprise, the women's importance to the people's housing and the social practices that grew from that connection. Plateau women set up camp, including raising the mat lodges, then broke camp and dismantled the lodges when travelling and when returning to traditional villages. Their ownership of the lodge was recognized throughout the region. Upon divorce, a man's belongings were set outside the lodge door, while the woman retained the dwelling.[7]

A young woman built her own lodge for the puberty ritual. Later in her life, she would also build menstrual and birth lodges, as well as the dwellings needed for her family. These structures were built of materials the women gathered or produced, over the basement that women dug out themselves. The woman's lodges established the blueprint for the larger structures of the people, as well as providing the site for the important times and rituals of women's lives.

The Menstrual Lodge

The ritual practice of menstrual seclusion on the Plateau discloses the sited nature of girls' puberty rites. Passing on women's lore and wisdom occurred during puberty training. Women's training in the production of artifacts, such as basketry, leather goods, and quill (later beadwork) adornment, was also spatially defined in the menstrual lodge. Delivery of the next generation took place in the woman's lodge, where births occurred. For many girls, the menstrual lodge was where they insured a good future (that included health, prosperity, husband, and children) for themselves through ritual practices. The range of activities within the lodge and the weight of their importance for women mark the structure as culturally significant.

Given this cultural value, archaeologists have not assiduously searched for evidence of menstrual lodges within the Plateau or elsewhere. Remains of an excavated Yakima Valley village included small pits, eleven to thirteen feet in diameter, encircled with stones, located at the edge and downstream from the main housing site. These sites were not identified in the literature conclusively as menstrual lodges, yet they could be marks left by the woman's lodges.[8]

These findings are substantiated by testimony gathered in the 1970s from Native women who tell about the lodges former construction, physical structure, and setting, even though menstrual seclusion practices have declined. The nineteenth-century girl undergoing the puberty rite built the lodge herself, but women usually cooperated in the raising of other lodges. The lodge was usually a small circular pit house, with a dugout floor, pine poles, and mat covering. The menstrual lodge was secluded, or located downstream, at the edge of the winter village or summer encampment.

A Nez Perce elder reported in the 1990s, 'They had a place to go when they were menstruating – menstrual lodge ... There is one in Kamiah. You can see [it] on the other side of the second church, that little creek over there. You can tell because it is indented. It's down deep.' According to a Yakama woman interviewed in the 1970s, 'Long time, the women put up a hut, keep her outside [camp] for five days ... She stays in that mat tipi.'[9]

The terms of menstrual seclusion itself seem to have followed a geographic designation for some groups. 'The first menstrual period is called *tlo'gamug* ... [in] reference to the hole in the ground beneath the menstrual lodge ... all after periods [were] *alitska* (going outside),' reported Charles Hill-Tout for the Lower Lillooet Indians. Other Plateau villages used *zo'met* (abstaining from fresh meat) as their term.[10]

Whatever the term for the seclusion, selecting the place to build the lodge was all important. The away-from-camp location can be understood as insuring the health of the community. There was concern about the power of menstruating women negatively influencing the health of the community and men's power, tools, and hunting abilities. Menstruating women did not go to fishing sites or ceremonies. There were ritual and herbal remedies if by chance a woman contacted a man, the lodge, or others during her menses. It was not an all-or-nothing matter, but grandmothers and other elder women trained the younger generation to be careful in this regard.[11]

Rather than see menstrual restrictions in a negative light, until recently the standard Euro-American interpretation, we might see seclusion both as an acknowledgment of women's power and a mechanism to contain its potentially negative forces. Among the Cherokee, argues historian Theda Perdue, blood was believed to contain a being's life or spirit and demanded to be treated with ritual care, whether in menstruation, or childbirth, or, for men, in hunting and warfare. That many of the same rules – seclusion, purification, prayer – were followed by men during their blood-related war or hunting activities as by women during menstruation underscores that the blood was at issue, not the sex of the human interacting with it.[12]

There were also male-female similarities in Plateau culture. In fact, men were believed to have formerly menstruated. Coyote's decision to change the matter was influenced by both gender and spatial considerations. In *Memoirs of the American Museum of Natural History*, James Teit recounts a Shuswap menstruation myth:

> Coyote Makes Women Menstruate: Formerly the men menstruated, and not the women. When Coyote was working in the world, putting things to

right, he considered this matter, and said to himself, 'It is not right that men should menstruate. It is very inconvenient, for they do all the hunting and most of the traveling. Women stay more at home, and therefore it will be better if they menstruate, and not the men.' Whereupon he took some of the menstrual fluid from men, and threw it upon the women, saying, 'Henceforth, women shall menstruate, and not men. They shall menstruate once a month or with every moon.'

Perhaps it is not surprising, then, that in Plateau culture some practices transcended gender. Men also went into seclusion and purification before hunting or going to war. Both boys and girls underwent purification and were isolated when they sought a guardian spirit on the vision quest. Fathers followed restrictions, as did mothers, at birthing. Boys even let blood from cuts in their legs during a portion of their puberty training. It follows, then, as a wider cultural practice that women would go into isolation and undergo purification during this powerful time. Rather than see this as simply a pollution issue and a restriction of women, a broad societal pattern of spatial containment can be discerned.[13]

Just as shamans were honoured and feared among the Plateau peoples, menstruating women were revered and believed powerful. A modern contemporary Nez Perce woman reported in the 1980s:

[A] Woman is strong when she is pregnant, [a] woman is strong on her moon [menstruating] ... That's why she had to keep away from everybody. Women never went to medicine dances, war dances, stick games, or funerals. They were not supposed to be anywhere if they had their menstruation ... that's how they were separated ... Woman was very sacred when she had her menstruation or whenever she was pregnant.[14]

The lodge also may have been sited at a particular, secluded place due to its neutral or, alternately, supernatural qualities. A leading older woman who was respected in the community, one with appropriate powers and gifts, or the grandmother of the extended family chose the site and oversaw its construction. There might also have been spiritual reasons for building the menstrual lodge along a stream or by water. Two films give Native testimony on the spiritual power of Plateau water places. In *Places of the Falling Waters*, the Salish people define a waterfall as a spiritual, powerful place. In *Everything Change, Everything Change*, a girl's guardian spirit power included using water to replicate the lake location where she acquired it. Menstrual seclusion and especially the girls' puberty rite carried significant metaphysical content. The by-the-water site of the menstrual lodge, then, might have been potentially powerful space.[15]

Girls' puberty rite activities radiated from the menstrual lodge base. One spiritually significant activity among the Thompson people of Canada was for a girl near the end of her menstrual training to peck pictographs into the surface of a spiritually important rock or to use red paint to mark the stone. The powerful pubescent girl linked the two places by travelling from the menstrual lodge to the place of a rock appropriate for spiritually significant markers. The designs she made on the rock included lodges, pines, trails, and basketry connected to her training ritual. Not only was the menstrual lodge geographically significant in itself, but many of the spiritually powerful symbols representing it were geographic icons, such as trails and lodges. These same trail, lodge, and tree designs appeared in the headbands, hats, and baskets women made throughout their lives, connecting them back to the puberty lodge.[16]

The spot to build the menstrual lodge changed, of course, as the people migrated from place to place on their seasonal food-procuring rounds. In May they may have been digging roots, but by late summer they would pick berries at another mountain location. In early spring and autumn they would congregate at the fishing sites, or alternately they hunted elk and deer. Some travelled to the Plains to hunt buffalo. In each of these seasons, there would undoubtedly be preferred camps with special places where the menstrual lodge or lodges would be built year to year, appropriately away from community activity. One wonders whether these spots elicited the kind of stories and teachings (and, in this case, women's knowledge) that Keith Basso has noted in *Wisdom Sits in Places: Landscape and Language among the Western Apache*. The stories about menstruation, the puberty rite, and proper female behaviour sited in these different locales throughout the region surely were part of the lore passed on by the elders or stories shared by women who occupied the lodges together.[17]

Women living in close proximity have been shown to develop similar menstrual cycles over time. In *Blood Magic: The Anthropology of Menstruation*, Thomas Buckley argues that this synchrony of women's menstrual seclusion among California's Yurok people may have served as the timing for community rituals and male training. Menstrual synchrony among Plateau women of the community or family may have been difficult to establish because of these same seasonal rounds and a fluctuation in attendance. If menstrual synchrony developed on the

Plateau, it would seem logical that the winter village would be the time and place. The winter village was important in Plateau identity, and many of the tribal or band names by which the people are now known came from the rivers or valleys of their traditional winter village sites, or, alternately, the rivers were named for the people who resided nearby. If the women of the extended family who made up the winter village came, after several months, to menstruate at the same time, their joint seclusion would undoubtedly have been a powerful female ritual and community marker. Ethnographers have documented common menstrual lodges for the Tenino, Southern Okanagan, and the Nez Perce Plateau peoples.[18]

The girl or woman, then, built the menstrual lodge on an appropriate site using materials made by herself or by other women of the community. It was a place of seclusion and ritual, a place of spiritual potential, and a space for passing on women's knowledge and rituals. This woman's lodge space was the centre of Plateau women's gender identification.

Producing New Women

As a built environment on a selected site, the menstrual lodge was important women's space where new women were also constructed. Girls were taught, guided, and imprinted by the puberty rite passed on to them by female ancestors and monitored by the families' or community's elder women.[19]

Christine Quintasket, a Colville woman from the late nineteenth century known by her pen name of Mourning Dove, described from her own experiences the basic Plateau puberty rite. Traditional families of the Plateau, such as Quintasket's, still practised the rite in the late nineteenth century. James Teit found its use had declined from earlier in the century, according to the elders whose testimony he collected for Franz Boas. Quintasket reported:

> A girl started her fast at the first sign of menstruation, usually at an age between twelve and fifteen. She was ... not allowed to come in contact with her family for ten days. When she did return, she had to take several sweat baths and put on a complete change of clothes ... A girl prayed about motherhood at this time.[20]

The puberty rite was the culmination of an extensive training regimen for Quintasket:

When my mother and Teequalt [the elderly woman training her] began to anticipate my puberty, they became more serious in their instructions ... I was told to bathe and take on more responsibilities around the house. I was also made to run uphill without stopping until I reached the top ... From then on, I had to carry all the water in the house ... This was to give me energy for my lifework, my teacher explained. I carried all the firewood, worked beside my father in the fields, and went to round up the horses each day before my breakfast and daily cold water bath. While my sisters continued to play at will, I was obliged to do many duties about the tipi and cabin. It seemed I had to learn something new every day ... My eating was carefully watched and I was never allowed to fill up at meals as I had previously.[21]

In contrast to Quintasket's extensive prepuberty instruction, the girls of the Thompson people (Canadian Plateau) usually trained one year, and some longer, after the first menstrual cycle. To support her during this arduous training period, a girl's family moved away from the main village and stayed closer to her secluded lodge to assist her. The first four days of the puberty rite were the most intense, with fasting, physical exercise, ritual bathing, and instruction in women's traditional tasks. Imprinting or forecasting of health, ability, and good fortune of the girl's life seemed to be the goal of most of these practices. Intense physical activities such as running, digging trenches, going without sleep, washing with fir boughs, and continuous construction of basketry seem calculated to lure spiritual power, as well. Girls could attain such guardian spirits as basket, kettle, root digger, owl, porcupine, and huckleberry. With this training and the help of the spirits, a girl entered womanhood.[22]

Women from other Plateau groups also experienced intense training, according to recent informants. 'At puberty time for a girl, the Nez Perce had those menstrual lodges where women would go ... during her period ... they go there, and they stay there, her grandmother or mother would take her there and help them, explaining about it. She would stay there during that time,' recalled a Nez Perce woman in the 1980s.[23]

As appropriate to its important training function and spiritually powerful space, the puberty rite lodge contained implements designated solely for that place. Just as an altar, ciborium, and chalice help define the central ritual of the Christian church, so too does the drinking tube, the cup, and the scratching stick define the lodge rituals. Each had a defined purpose, as well as supernatural and gendered meaning. Not only was the menstruating woman powerful to others, but also to the environment and to herself. 'She couldn't touch her hair, and she had a certain cup to use, a special cup just for that,' recalled one Yakama woman. 'All the cups were made from cedar roots in those days.'[24]

Water, a source or location of spiritual power, was mediated in the puberty rite lodge by utensils that separated the power of the menstruating girl from drinking water. When in seclusion, the woman never drank from a stream or touched the water directly, but used a straw to separate herself from the water. The straw, a hollowed out bone tube among the Thompson, 'processed' the water for her use and helped circumvent negative impact from her to the water, or vice versa. Boys in puberty training among the Thompson also used a drinking tube. Shamans among some Plateau groups used straws in their healing ceremonies to 'suck' the disease or evil intention from their patient.

Within the lodge, girls in training, and later menstruating women, used a special cup for drinking. It 'contained' the water and its potential power, and separated the woman's power from it. The cup was made of cedar root among some groups and birchbark painted red among others, both highly regarded materials used in fiber or basket work by the women. While in menstrual seclusion within the woman's lodge, the care taken by the women for their own contact with water reinforced their caution necessary to protect men and community members from menstrual power.[25]

When using the lodge for puberty training, a girl was required to alter her diet. Among the Colville, 'a woman could not eat any freshly killed game without impairing the hunter's luck.' For the Yakama girl, 'her grandmother brings her food, just dry meat and fish and berries. She can't eat anything fresh ... She can eat anything [afterward]. But they used to say it's an Indian rule: can't eat anything fresh during that time ... that's to keep her stomach right.' The Nez Perce girl 'couldn't cook with or eat with anybody.' The food allowed in the woman's lodge, in other words, was 'cooked' by only having a woman process it and was never in its raw or male-tainted state.[26]

Careful disposal of the menstrual refuse usually took place within the lodge. Normally, the refuse was buried within the hole dug inside the menstrual lodge itself. It was never burned. This practice corresponds to others in the culture, such as the careful collection of hairs shed throughout life and the burial of these with the person at death. Afterbirth was also carefully disposed of, either hidden up a tree or buried, to protect the health of a newborn. Medicine people with evil intentions could use parts from a person to cast curses or steal power, so that in the powerful menstruation situation precautions were taken. Alternately, among the Thompson, in a ritual to increase a girl's power, a small amount of her first menses might be taken to a barren and rocky mountainside to be burned.[27]

Spiritual power or luck could be gained within the puberty lodge by the repetition of activities. For power the Thompson used the number four and the Yakama the number five. Some rituals were apparently performed in order to limit future menstrual flows to this prescribed number of days.

A scratching stick was another ritual tool used in the puberty rite. A girl was instructed never to touch herself, but instead to use the stick. Some of the same allusions listed above – mediating function, woman-made product – apply here as well. But in this case, the protection seems to be for a woman from her own power. How can that be?[28]

Other studies report that during the puberty rite the girls often collected wood or brought water for the entire camp. Obviously the supposed 'contamination' from the girl could be stymied if she channelled it in appropriate ways through work and providing needed services to the wider community. In some groups, the girl ran the ridges near the village in the early dawn hours, apparently not only to build stamina but also to chart the village's space or claim the trails somehow. These and the productive work done in the puberty lodge may have 'imprinted' the emerging woman with gender attributes and spatial command desirable to her life within the wider Plateau community.

Special attire and appearances within the woman's lodge were also important, perhaps carrying spiritual but certainly gendered significance. Although the patterning might vary, girls from all groups painted their faces red. All wore knee and ankle fringes decorated with deer-hoof rattles. Among the Thompson and some other groups, the girls wore their hair tied behind each ear and used a special headband or cap, had a special robe used for the first few days of the rite, and masked themselves when they emerged from their lodge at night.

These special implements, activities, rituals, and accomplishments helped transform the pubescent girl into a properly trained woman. She could now continue her training for matrimony. The Klamath of the Southern Plateau sponsored a community-wide dance to mark her new status, much as did the Luiseno of California and the Western Apache. Among the Yakama, she would now begin her string counting ball, marking important events by knotting the string and keeping it with her until death. For several Canadian Plateau groups, women's facial tattoos and ear or nose rings could now be worn. Her puberty training complete, the new woman would re-enact elements of the rite whenever she was secluded.[29]

Perhaps most important as she progressed through her life cycle, the Plateau woman would carry forward the training and teachings of gender roles that she received from her own grandmother, other female family members, and community elders. Some of the values imparted in the puberty training were to 'be pure, cleanly, honest, truthfull, brave, friendly, hospitable, energetic ... virtuous ... kindhearted to friends ... diligent ... modest ... charitable ... faithful ... industrious.' Important lessons of female-male relationships were disclosed, childbirth discussed, and family advice shared.[30]

The puberty rite's menstrual lodge was a spiritually powerful place where womanhood was constructed. Emergent women were trained there in the use and containment of power, imprinting the future with benefits by appropriately using special ritual implements and enacting proper gendered activities. Beyond the creation of new women, the menstrual lodge was the place for other productive activities that tied the secluded woman to other women and their shared Plateau culture. It was in the woman's lodge that they first made baskets, containers, mats, skin clothing, and other women's products.

Powerful Products

The siting of the menstrual lodge at the edge of the village, downstream or near water, can be thought of as a pathway, gateway, or boundary marker on the way to somewhere else. This connective function can be viewed in two ways. First, the things produced within the menstrual lodge were often intended for others within the wider extended family, for use at giveaways, or in ritual exchanges. Secondly, the thriving trade network among women on the Plateau for these same woman-made goods connected the activities in one community to the larger region. The scarce and valuable time needed to produce these utilitarian works of art could be found, a few days at a time, in the menstrual lodge.[31]

'She could work on anything though. That was for all women,' reports a Yakam woman in the 1970s. 'They were raised up and taken care of by grandmothers and aunts and taught to be good diggers, and how to make clothes and do things like that,' says a Nez Perce woman. 'The only time [a married woman] received a vacation was during her menstrual period, when she retired to a hut built away from the encampment. While in the hut she might tan skins,' explained Quintasket. The objects women produced were traded by women and sought by other women. These goods, it was believed, showed a woman's talents and spiritual gifts.[32]

Because of their particular home territory and its varying resources, tribal women 'specialized' in certain products. Klickitat baskets, Nez Perce sweetgrass sally bags, Salish parfleches, or Canadian Plateau birchbark baskets circulated in the region through the Indigenous trade fairs and at mutually used food resource sites. A talented tanner, quiller, or basket-maker became well known throughout the region, and her work was sought after. She passed her knowledge and her skill to young women in her family or band.[33]

Each menstrual seclusion after the all-important puberty ritual reinforced the special manifestation of a woman's power in the production and decoration of these products. Women could use their 'leisure' time in the menstrual lodge to make baskets, tanned-skin clothing, beaded objects, or the more mundane twine and tule mats. Perhaps the focus of much of the 'work' done during the puberty rite was to train the hands – as the articulators of a woman's creative power made manifest in menarche – in proper duties or habits or relationships with the object they produced.[34]

A Birthing Place

The importance of the woman's lodge in the construction of Plateau women's gender roles has been defined in three ways. First, the lodge was a woman-built structure using woman-made materials on a preferred site selected by women. Second, the lodge was the puberty ritual's site, where the elders trained up each generation in ways appropriate for women. Third, the lodge was a place of production, where skills were introduced to girls and where menstruating women made goods. Finally, the woman's lodge was also the site for another, equally significant, gender construction task. Birth is the fourth understanding of the lodge's importance.

It has been argued elsewhere that birthing and motherhood are powerful concepts for Indigenous women, central to the construction of their gender definition.[35] For women on the Plateau, the birthing experience replicated many practices of the puberty ritual itself. There was a very careful monitoring of foods consumed, behaviours were proscribed (no inappropriate looking, teasing the less fortunate, handling dead animals, or entering lodges backwards), and exercise and healthful living were required. In this case, however, the father as well as the mother followed strict rules. Among the Thompson, the birth mother did her hair up like a girl in puberty, was not to scratch herself, and for a first child both she and her husband 'had to go through certain ceremonies similar to the puberty ceremonies.' Among the Lillooet, after the birth, the entire family painted their faces red. The father and mother ritually bathed and sponsored a feast for family and friends.[36]

Perhaps most important, when a woman went into labour she used a woman's lodge for birthing. This lodge was constructed slightly larger than those used for menstrual seclusion. Otherwise, it followed the menstrual or puberty lodge schema. The woman might add a strap for gripping when contractions were intense. She might rely on an elder woman as a midwife. The afterbirth and any blood were handled in ways patterned by disposing of menstrual blood.[37]

Nez Perce testimony in the 1980s attests to enduring belief in the power of Plateau woman at the time of motherhood: 'Woman is strong when she is pregnant, woman is strong on her moon [menstruating]. She is creator at time of pregnancy.' Native women used the lodge in the nineteenth century not only to construct their definitions of gender and to produce new women, but also to bring forth new life and the people's future.[38]

Changes

It cannot be known precisely what challenged and changed the practices of nineteenth-century menstrual seclusion, Indigenous puberty rites, and the use of the birth lodge. Teit, whose ethnographic work has provided much of the detail for this analysis, noted the practices were already much reduced and some were lost by the end of the nineteenth century. He interviewed the Thompson people's eldest women for their memories and experiences, but was not as interested in outlining the then-current practices. He did not trace or consider how the new ways of the late nineteenth and early twentieth centuries might be old ideas or models wrapped in new ways. Instead, Teit writes, in 1906, 'Customs in connection with puberty have fallen into disuse. A very few families still make the girls pass through a ceremonial purification, but in a much modified form.'[39]

The forces of change can easily be conjectured, although to be certain a thorough investigation of these issues would be necessary. Apparently, contact with European and Euro-American culture and peoples challenged Indigenous women's practices. Epidemics, market economy, Christian missionaries, settlers to the Oregon Country, and, after the 1846 boundary decision, the United States government all had an impact on Plateau cultural practices. In the later nineteenth century, the mining rushes and the building of the railroads both north and south of the boundary line brought increased Euro-American populations and economic development to the interior. By taking girls away from their families and communities, boarding schools and Euro-American education contributed greatly to the dissolution of traditional practices.

Taking a spatial perspective, however, is also instructive. The challenge to Indigenous control of territories, especially with Euro-American population incursion, treaties with the United States that dissolved Indian title to the land, and the establishment of the reservations in the region, added to the pressure for change because some of the traditional places were no longer accessible, even with porous reservation boundaries and inventive Native circumvention of officialdom. The practice of seasonal food-gathering rounds was challenged in the nineteenth century by settler takeover of fertile root grounds and fishing sites, for instance.[40] Perhaps the woman's lodge, as another index of the Plateau-built environment, foundered as the people's geography became circumscribed.

Contemporary Women

Despite these changes, the enduring power of Indian women today may be due, in part, to its grounding in the birthing and menstrual lodges of the past.[41] The construction of gender and the foundation of women's power has shifted from the woman's lodge to new locations and situations. Awareness of the old ways and the woman's lodge tradition still circulates among the Plateau people, as much of the modern testimony cited in this study makes clear. Teaching young women the important values for women and appropriate gender roles continues despite the passing into disuse of the woman's lodge.

Today, young Indian women are singled out for important cultural roles. In first root ceremonies, they maintain traditional rapport with the land. As powwow and rodeo royalty, their beauty, traditional clothing, and honourable behaviour represent the best of their culture to their tribe and to others. In shawl and jingle-dress dancing, women's innovations in powerful ritual practices are celebrated. New practices that challenge and train young Native women bestow honour on them in their people's eyes. These new roles seem to serve much the same function in constructing young women as did the former puberty rites.[42]

Despite changes and modern challenges, Indigenous Plateau women continue in powerful gender roles. Their self-definitions, behaviour, and contributions show what it means to be an Indian woman today. The birth lodge, the puberty rite lodge, the menstrual seclusion lodge, as well as the family dwelling built and owned by the woman, show that previously the Plateau-built environment was almost exclusively under women's purview.[43] Women's gender construction came from this space, but also from the life-cycle connection established there between the newborn, the pubescent girl, the mature woman, and the elders. Their acquisition of spiritual power and their ritual practices were connected to their lodges' space and functions, as were societal honouring and male recognition of women's gender perogatives. Perhaps former female gender roles of responsibility for and honour from lodging has been transformed in today's world into responsibility for and honour from their work for the peoples' resistance, continuance, and power. As part of the larger Native-American cultural renaissance, the woman's lodge might yet return as a place to bolster American Indian women's self-definition and construction of gender roles.[44]

NOTES

1 For an overview of the Northwest Plateau cultural area, see *Handbook of North American Indians*, vol. 12, *Plateau*, ed. Deward E. Walker Jr (Washington, DC: Smithsonian Institution, 1998). For a shorter version, see Alice Kehoe's textbook, *North American Indians: A Comprehensive Account* (Upper Saddle River, NJ: Prentice-Hall, 1992), 382–98; Verne F. Ray, *Cultural Relations in the Plateau of Northwestern America* (Los Angeles: Southwest Museum, 1939), 52–61; and 'Cultural Elements Distribution, XXII: Plateau,' *Anthropological Records* 8.2 (1942): 202–6.

2 Good places to start in reviewing the literature in feminist geography are Gillian Rose, *Feminism and Geography: The Limits of Geographic Knowledge* (Minneapolis: University of Minnesota Press, 1993); and Linda McDowell, *Gender Identity and Place: Feminist Geographies* (Minneapolis: University of Minnesota Press, 1999).

3 Lillian Ackerman, 'Kinship, Family and Gender Roles,' in *Handbook of North American Indians*, 12: 515–24.

4 Mary C. Wright, 'Economic Development and American Indian Women in the Nineteenth Century Pacific Northwest,' *American Quarterly* 33.5 (1981): 525–35, and 'The Circle, Broken: Gender, Family and Difference in the Pacific Northwest, 1810–1850' (Ph.D. diss., Rutgers University 1996); Lillian Ackerman, 'Complementary but Equal: Gender Status in the Plateau,' in *Women and Power in Native North America*, ed. Laura A. Klein and Lillian A. Ackerman (Norman: University of Oklahoma Press, 1995), 77–100; and Lillian Ackerman, 'Sexual Equality in the Plateau Cultural Area' (Ph.D. diss., Washington State University, 1982).

5 I will use Indian, American Indian, Indigenous, and Native American interchangeably in this essay, although some of the peoples discussed herein are Canadian, where First Nation is the appropriate term.

6 Mary C. Wright, 'Places for the People: Indigenous Women as Builders in the Nineteenth-Century Pacific Northwest Plateau,' paper presented at the Western Association of Women Historians meeting, May 2001, Portland Oregon. For buffalo hide lodges, see Capt. E.F. Wilson, 'Report on the Indian Tribes Inhabiting the Vicinity of the 49th Parallel of North Latitude,' *Transactions, Ethnological Society of London* 4 (1866): 275–332; and Nicholas Point, *Wilderness Kingdom: Indian Life in the Rockies, 1840–47*, trans. Joseph P. Donnelly, S.J. (New York: Holt, Reinhart & Winston, 1967), 145, 174. The Yakama Cultural Heritage Center in Toppenish, Washington, has an excellent exhibit of traditional Plateau housing, including nearly life-size models of a pit house and a tule mat lodge. Visit their website at http://www.ohwy.com/wa/y/yakama.htm.

7 Peter Nabokov and Robert Eastman, *Native American Architecture* (New York: Oxford University Press, 1989), 174–87; Father Pierre de Smet, *Life, Letters and Travels of Father Pierre Jean De Smet, S.J., 1801–1873*, ed. Hiram Martin Chittenden and Alfred Talbot Richardson (New York: Kraus Reprint, 1969), 1012; Point, *Wilderness Kingdom*, 145; and Father Gregory Mengarini, S.J., *Recollections of the Flathead Missions Containing Brief Observations both Ancient and Contemporary Concerning this Particular Nation*, trans. and ed. Gloria Ricci Lothrop (Glendale, CA: Arthur H. Clark, 1977), 216–17, notes 19 and 20.

8 For a critique of archaeology's lack of interest in menstrual lodges, see Patricia Galloway, 'Where Have All the Menstrual Huts Gone?' in *Women in Prehistory: North and South America*, ed. Cheryl Claasen and Rosemary A. Joyce (Philadelphia: University of Pennsylvania Press, 1997), 47–62; Kenneth M. Ames et al., 'Prehistory of the Southern Plateau,' in *Handbook*

of North American Indians, vol. 12, 103–19; Dorothy Sammons-Lohse, 'Features,' in *Chief Joseph Dam Cultural Resources Project, Washington*, ed. Sarah K. Campbell (Seattle: University of Washington Press, 1985), 113; and Harlan L. Smith, 'The Archaeology of the Yakima Valley,' *Anthropological Papers of the American Museum of Natural History* 6.1 (1910): 51–7.

9 Caroline James, *Nez Perce Women in Transition: 1877–1990* (Moscow: University of Idaho Press, 1996), 80; and Helen Hersch Schuster, 'Yakima Indian Traditionalism: A Study in Continuity and Change' (Ph.D. diss, University of Washington, 1977), 120.

10 Charles Hill-Tout as quoted in James Teit, 'The Lillooet Indians,' in *Memoirs of the American Museum of Natural History*, ed. Franz Boas, 4.5 (1906): 296n8. In contrast, the euphemism for menstruation used among the Western Apache was 'grandmother's visit.' See Keith H. Basso, 'The Gift of Changing Woman,' *Bulletin 196* (Bureau of American Ethnology, Anthropological Papers) 76 (1966): 113–73.

11 Issues of pollution and seclusion are addressed in Thomas Buckley and Alma Gottlieb, 'A Critical Appraisal of Theories of Menstrual Symbolism,' in *Blood Magic: The Anthropology of Menstruation*, ed. Thomas Buckley and Alma Gottlieb (Berkeley: University of California Press, 1988), 3–50.

12 Theda Purdue, *Cherokee Women: Gender and Culture Change, 1700–1835* (Lincoln: University of Nebraska Press, 1998), 28–40.

13 James Teit, 'The Thompson Indians of British Columbia,' in *Memoirs of the American Museum of Natural History*, ed. Franz Boas, 2.4 (1900): 305; James Teit, 'The Shuswap,' *Memoirs of the American Museum of Natural History*, ed. Franz Boas, 4.7 (1909): 589–90; and Teit, 'Lillooet,' 261.

14 James, *Nez Perce Women*, 80–1. For a full discussion of this interpretation of menstruation as power, see Buckley and Gottlieb, eds, *Blood Magic*.

15 *Everything Change, Everything Change: Recollections of Ida Nason, an American Indian Elder*, prod. Patricia Branch Larson and Sandra Lewis Nisbet, dir. John Givens, 1986; Roy Begcrane and Thompson Smith, *Places of the Falling Waters*, prod. Dan Hart, Native Voices Public Television Workshop and Salish Kootenai College, 1991.

16 Teit, 'The Thompson Indians,' 218, 228, 264, 314, plate 19. Teit was married to a Thompson woman, spoke the language, and lived among the people for many years before doing his ethnographic work for Franz Boas. For these reasons, and because he was a sensitive man, we have very complete information about women's customs in the Canadian Plateau. See also Wendy Wickwire, 'Women in Ethnography: The Research of James A. Teit,' *Ethnohistory* 40.4 (1993): 539–62.

17 Keith H. Basso, *Wisdom Sits in Places: Landscape and Language among the*

Western Apache (Albuquerque: University of New Mexico Press, 1996). See also Steven Feld and Keith H. Basso, eds, *Senses of Place* (Santa Fe, NM: School of American Research Press, 1996).

18 Buckley, 'Menstruation and the Power of Yurok Women,' 187–209; and Ray, *Cultural Relations in the Plateau of Northwestern America*, 54.

19 For more about Plains women's puberty rites, see Marla Powers, 'Menstruation and Reproduction: An Oglala Case,' *Signs: Journal of Women in Culture and Society* 6.1 (1980): 54–65; Mark St Pierre and Tilda Long Soldier, *Walking in a Sacred Manner: Healers, Dreamers and Pipe Carriers – Medicine Women of the Plains Indians* (New York: Simon and Shuster, 1995): 67–76; and Marsha C. Bol and Nellie Z. Star Boy Menard, '"I Saw All That": A Lakota Girl's Puberty Ceremony,' *American Indian Culture and Research Journal* 24.1 (2000): 25–42

20 *Mourning Dove: A Salishan Autobiography*, ed. Jay Miller (Lincoln: University of Nebraska Press, 1990), 38–41, 67, 204, notes 7, 8, 9.

21 Miller, ed., *Mourning Dove*, 40–1.

22 Teit, 'The Thompson Indians,' 311–17

23 James, *Nez Perce Women*, 80

24 Schuster, 'Yakima Indian Traditionalism,' 120

25 Teit, 'Thompson Indians,' 313, 317; 'Shuswap,' 587–8, 612; 'Lillooet,' 264; and Schuster, 'Yakima Indian Traditionalism,' 120.

26 Miller, ed., *Mourning Dove*, 67; Schuster, 'Yakima Indian Traditionalism,' 120; and James, *Nez Perce Women*, 80.

27 For refuse burial, see Miller, ed., *Mourning Dove*, 204n7; Schuster, 'Yakima Indian Traditionalism,' 121, 165–79.

28 Teit, 'Thompson Indians,' 313, 314, 317; and Schuster, 'Yakima Indian Traditionalism,' 120. For a picture of a scratching stick, see Teit, 'Thompson Indians,' 312. The scratching stick was the ony material aspect of the girls' puberty complex found universally throughout the American West. See Harold E. Driver, 'Culture Element Distributions, XVII: Girls' Puberty Rites in Western North America,' *Anthropological Records* 6.2 (1941): 51.

29 Verne F. Ray, 'Cultural Elements Distribution, XXII: Plateau,' *Anthropological Records* 8.2 (1942): 203; Teit, 'Thompson Indians,' 311–17; Ray 'Cultural Elements,' 203–7; Joan Oxendine, 'The Lusieno Girls' Ceremony,' *Journal of California and Great Basin Anthropology* 2.1 (1980): 37–50; Basso, 'The Gift of Changing Woman,' 138–41; and Douglas Leechman, 'String Records of the Northwest,' *Indian Notes and Monographs* (New York: Museum of the American Indian, Heye Foundation, 1921), 16:5–47.

30 Teit, 'Thompson Indians,' 367; and Lillian A. Ackerman, *A Song of the*

Creator: Traditional Arts of Native American Women of the Plateau (Norman: University of Oklahoma Press, 1996), 22–3.

31 For examples of the creative work of Plateau women, as well as commentary on women's culture, see Ackerman, *A Song to the Creator*.

32 Schuster, 'Yakima Indian Traditionalism,' 120; James, *Nez Perce Women*, 80–1; and Miller, ed., *Mourning Dove*, 67.

33 Ackerman, *Song to the Creator*, explains this phenomenon well.

34 Ray, 'Cultural Elements,' 203.

35 Susan L. Rockwell, 'The Delivery of Power: Reading American Indian Childbirth Narratives,' *American Indian Culture and Research Journal* 19.3 (1995): 71–85. See also Margaret A. Kay, ed., *Anthropology of Human Birth* (Philadelphia: F.A. Davis, 1982) for essays by Veronica Evaneshko ('Tonawanda Seneca Childbearing Culture,' 395–411); Beverly Horn ('Northwest Coast Indians: The Muckleshoot,' 361–75); and Anne Wright ('Attitudes toward Childbirth and Menstruation,' 377–94). For another perspective on First Nations motherhood, see Jo-Anne Fiske, 'Child of the State, Mother of the Nation: Aboriginal Women and the Ideology of Motherhood,' *Culture* 13.1 (1993): 17–35.

36 Teit, 'Lillooet,' 260.

37 Teit, 'Lillooet,' 260–1, 'Shuswap,' 584, and 'Thompson Indians,' 305–10.

38 James, *Nez Perce Women*, 80–1.

39 Teit, 'Thompson Indians,' 228, 294, 312, and 'Shuswap,' 267, 269.

40 Janet H. Gritzner, 'Native American Camas Production and Trade in the Pacific Northwest and the Northern Rocky Mountains,' *Journal of Cultural Geography* 14.2 (1994): 47.

41 Teit, 'Thompson Indians,' 228, 294, 312, and 'Shuswap,' 267, 269.

42 See Tina Billedeaux, 'Young People Encouraged to Preserve Bitterroot Tradition,' *Char-Koosta News: The Official Publication of the Flathead Indian Nation*, 12 June 2000 (on-line at http://www.ronan.net/~ckn/fea.html).

43 Women also built the racks on which salmon and meats were dried. The sweat lodge, elementary hunting lodges, and fishing weirs were built by men.

44 For an encouraging report from another Native community, see Shirley Williams, 'Woman's Role in Ojibway Spirituality,' *Journal of Canadian Studies* 27:3 (1992): 100.

11 Taming Aboriginal Sexuality: Gender, Power, and Race in British Columbia, 1850–1900

JEAN BARMAN

In July 1996 I listened in a Vancouver courtroom as Catholic bishop Hubert O'Conner defended himself against charges of having raped or indecently assaulted four young Aboriginal women three decades earlier. His assertion of ignorance when asked what one of the complainants had been wearing on the grounds that, 'as you know, I'm a celibate man' encapsulated his certainty that he had done nothing wrong.[1] He admitted to sexual relations with two of the women, but the inference was clear: they had made him do it. They had dragged him down and led him astray. The temptation exercised by their sexuality was too great for any mere man, even a priest and residential school principal, to resist.

I returned home from that day, and subsequent days in the courtroom, deeply troubled. I might have been reading any of hundreds of similar accounts written over the past century and more about Aboriginal women in British Columbia. This essay represents my first attempt to come to terms with Bishop O'Conner and his predecessors, made more necessary on reading the National Parole Board's decision of March 1997. The Board denied Bishop O'Conner parole, subsequent to his conviction on two of the charges, because 'your recent psychological assessment indicates that you hold your victims in contempt,' and 'at your hearing today ... you maintain that ... you in fact were seduced.'[2] If I earlier considered that my response to my days in the courtroom might have been exaggerated, I no longer did so. My interest is not in Bishop O'Conner's guilt or innocence in a court of law, but, rather, in tracing the lineage of his attitudes in the history of British Columbia.

The more I have thought about Bishop O'Conner, the more I realize that those of us who dabble at the edges of Aboriginal history have ourselves been seduced. However much we pretend to read our sources 'against the grain,' to borrow from the cultural theorist Walter Benjamin, we have become entrapped in a partial world that represents itself as the whole world. Records almost wholly male in impetus have been used by mostly male scholars to write about Aboriginal men as if they make up the entirety of Aboriginal people.[3] The assumption that men and male perspectives equate with all persons and perspectives is so accepted that it does even not have to be declared.[4] Thus, an American researcher wanting to find out about her Aboriginal counterparts discovered that 'indigenous communities had been described and dissected by white men – explorers, traders, missionaries, and scholars – whose observations sometimes revealed more about their own cultural biases than about Native people. Misperceptions of Indian women were rampant because they were held up to the patriarchal model.'[5]

So what happens when we turn the past on its head and make our reference point Aboriginal women instead of Aboriginal men? We come face to face with Aboriginal sexuality or, more accurately, with male perceptions of Aboriginal sexuality. The term 'sexuality' is used here in its sociological sense as 'the personal and interpersonal expression of those socially constructed qualities, desires, roles and identities which have to do with sexual behaviour and activity,' the underlying contention being 'the social and cultural relativity of norms surrounding sexual behaviour and the sociohistorical construction of sexual identities and roles.'[6] In a useful summary of recent scholarship, English sociologist Gail Hawkes tells us that the word *sexuality* 'appeared first in the nineteenth century,' reflecting 'the focus of concerns about the social consequences of sexual desire in the context of modernity.' Christian dogma defined sexual desire 'as an unreasoned force differentially possessed by women, which threatened the reason of man' and the 'inherent moral supremacy of men.' According to Hawkes, 'the backbone of Victorian sexuality was the successful promotion of a version of women's sexuality, an ideal of purity and sexual innocence well fitted to the separation of spheres that underpinned the patriarchal power of the new ruling class.'[7] Sexuality, as Hawkes contextualizes the term, helps us better to understand the critical years in British Columbia, 1850–1900, when newcomers and Aboriginal peoples came into sustained contact.

Everywhere around the world Indigenous women presented an enormous dilemma to colonizers, at the heart of which lay their sexuality.[8] Initially solutions were simple and straightforward. During conquest local women were used for sexual gratification as a matter of course, just as had been (and still are) female victims of war across the centuries. If unspoken and for the most part unwritten, it was generally accepted that, so long as colonial women were absent, Indigenous women could be used to satisfy what were perceived to be natural needs.[9] No scruples existed over what the pioneering scholar on race Philip Mason has termed 'the casual use of a social inferior for sexual pleasure.'[10] The growth of settler colonies changed the 'rules of the game.' As anthropologist and historian Ann Laura Stoler astutely observes, drawing from her research on colonial Asia, 'while the colonies were marketed by colonial elites as a domain where colonizing men could indulge their sexual fantasies, these same elites were intent to mark the boundaries of a colonizing population, to prevent these men from "going native," to curb a proliferating mixed race population that compromised their claims to superiority and thus the legitimacy of white rule.'[11]

In British Columbia gender, power, and race came together in a manner that made it possible for men in power to condemn Aboriginal sexuality and at the same time, if they so chose, to use for their own gratification the very women they had turned into sexual objects. While much of what occurred mirrored events elsewhere, some aspects were distinctive.[12] Colonizers never viewed Aboriginal men as sexual threats,[13] whereas attitudes toward women acquired a particular self-righteousness and fervour. The assumptions newcomers brought with them shaped attitudes, which then informed actions. By the mid-nineteenth century Europeans perceived all female sexual autonomy to be illicit, especially if it occurred in the public sphere, considered exclusively male. Aboriginal women in British Columbia not only dared to exercise agency but often did so publicly, convincing men in power that their sexuality was out of control. To the extent that women persisted in managing their own sexual behaviour, they were wilded into the 'savages' that many newcomers, in any case, considered all Indigenous peoples to be.[14] That is, until Aboriginal women acceded to men in power by having their sexuality tamed according to their precepts, they were for the taking, an equation of agency with sexuality that encourages Aboriginal women's portrayal, even today, as the keepers of tradition. ...To avoid the image that men like Bishop O'Conner continue to project on them, Aboriginal women have had to be stripped of their agency past and present.

Prostitution

Indigenous sexuality struck at the very heart of the colonial project. British historian Catherine Hall has noted, in reference to Victorian England, that 'sex was a necessary obligation owed to men and not one which women were permitted to talk or think about as owed to themselves.'[15] Sexual independence, or circumstances where that possibility existed, was the ultimate threat to the patriarchal family. Children were considered to belong to their father, who had to have the assurance that they were indeed his biological heirs. As succinctly summed up by George Stocking in his history of Victorian anthropology, 'if the ideal wife and mother was "so pure-hearted as to be utterly ignorant of and averse to any sensual indulgence," the alternate cultural image of the "fallen woman" conveys a hint of an underlying preoccupation with the threat of uncontrolled female sexuality.' By the time Victoria came to the throne in 1837, 'the basic structure of taboos was already defined: the renunciation of all sexual activity save the procreative intercourse of Christian marriage; the education of both sexes in chastity and continence; the secrecy and cultivated ignorance surrounding sex; the bowdlerization of literature and euphemistic degradation of language; the general suppression of bodily functions and all the "coarser" aspects of life – in short, the whole repressive pattern of purity, prudery, and propriety that was to condition sexual behavior for decades to come.' Counterpoised to this stereotype were 'savages,' who were by definition 'unrestrained by any sense of delicacy from a copartnery in sexual enjoyments.'[16]

Any interpretation of events in British Columbia must adopt the language of colonialism as it was applied to Indigenous women's sexual independence. Around the colonized world the charge of prostitution, engaging in a sexual act for remuneration, was used by those who sought to meddle in Indigenous lives. Sexuality was not to be talked about openly, but prostitution and all that it implied could be publicly condemned. In other words, sexuality had to wilded into prostitution or possibly concubinage, cohabitation outside of marriage, in order for it to be tameable. Hawkes traces the fervour over prostitution back to Christianity, which both gave it prominence and held out promise for 'the redemption of the prostitute, the personification of polluting and uncontrolled women's sexuality.' Moving to the nineteenth century, 'Victorian sexual morality was focused on, and expressed through, the "social evil" of prostitution. Prostitution was discussed in such diverse venues as popular journalism, serious weekly reviews, medical tracts and publications from evangelical organizations devoted to the rescue of fallen women ... prostitution provided a forum within which to express, covertly, anxieties about, and fascination with, the characteristics of women's sexuality.'[17]

No question exists but that Aboriginal people in British Columbia viewed their sexuality differently than did colonizers. It is difficult, if not impossible, to reconstruct gender relations prior to newcomers' arrival, nor is it necessary to do so in order to appreciate the enormity of contact. The scholarship is virtually unanimous in concluding that, traditionally, marriages were arranged, with goods passing to the woman's family.[18] Intrusions of European disease, work patterns, and economic relations unbalanced Aboriginal societies and tended to atomize gender relations. Women possessed opportunities for adaptation not available to their male counterparts.[19] Many of the taboos normalized and universalized by Europeans simply did not exist in Aboriginal societies. If for Europeans sexuality had to be strictly controlled in the interests of assuring paternity, the link may have been less critical for Aboriginal people in that the group, rather than the immediate biological family, was the principal social unit.

To grasp the rapidity with which Aboriginal women became sexualized as prostitutes in colonial British Columbia, it is instructive to go back in time to another bishop, George Hills, first Anglican bishop of Vancouver Island. Arriving in Victoria in January 1860, he encountered a figurative tinder box, a fur-trade village which in just twenty months had been turned upside-down by the gold rush, bringing with it thousands of newcomers from around the world, almost all of them men. Bishop Hills was almost immediately condemning 'the profligate condition of the population.' 'The Road to Esquimalt on Sunday is lined with the poor Indian women offering to sell themselves to the white men passing by – & instances are to be seen of open bargaining.'[20] Bishop Hills's Methodist counterpart, Thomas Crosby, who arrived in the spring of 1862, was similarly struck by 'the awful condition of the Indian women in the streets and lanes of Victoria.'[21]

What newcomers constructed as prostitution did become widespread during the gold rush, just as it had existed to some extent during the fur trade. The evidence may be largely anecdotal, but it is consistent and, for some times and places, overwhelming.[22] Virtually all of the descriptions come from a colonial male perspective, but they are so graphic and diverse as to leave little doubt as to the circumstances. The most visible sites were seasonal dance halls where for a price miners could while away 'the long winter evenings' by interacting socially with Aboriginal women.[23] A New Westminster resident evoked its 'Squaw Dance-House' frequented by miners 'hastening to throw away their hardly earned gold.' Her description is graphic: 'As soon as eight or half-past struck, the music of a fiddle or two and the tramp of many feet began. Later on the shouts of drunken men and the screams of squaws in like condition made night hideous. Each man paid fifty cents for a dance, and had to "stand drinks" at the bar for himself and his dusky partner after each.'[24] Bishop Hills described 'houses where girls of no more than 12 are taken in at night & turned out in the morning – like cattle.'[25] Even while acknowledging dance halls' contribution to urban economies, the press repeatedly denounced the Aboriginal women whose presence made them possible, as in an 1861 editorial charging that 'prostitution and kindred vices, in all their hideous deformity, and disease in every form, lurk there.' In their San Francisco counterparts 'the females were at least civilized,' but 'here we have all the savagery of the ancient Ojibbeways [sic], with all the vice of a reckless civilization.'[26] If the decline of the gold rush from the mid-1860s put an end to dance halls' excesses and dampened down excitement over prostitution,[27] the wildness associated with Aboriginal sexuality had permeated settler consciousness.

Female Agency

Turned on their head, contemporary portrayals of Aboriginal women during the gold rush affirm their agency. Agency is by its very nature relational and interactive. Just as occurred during the fur trade[28] and in traditional societies,[29] Aboriginal women both initiated and responded to change. They scooted around, they dared, they were uppity in ways that were completely at odds with Victorian views of gender, power, and race. Some likely soon realized that, however much they tried to mimic newcomers ways, they would never be accepted and so might as well act as they pleased.[30] An Aboriginal woman 'dragged' the friend of a man who had assaulted her to a nearby police station 'to be locked up as a witness,' only to have him seek 'the protection of the police, which was granted' until she left.[31] The jury in a court case against a Victoria policeman accused of 'having attempted to ravish the person of an Indian squaw' was told that the verdict hinged on whether 'you believe the simple evidence of the three Indian women' and, 'after consulting together about one moment, [the jury] returned a verdict of "Not guilty."'[32] In some cases, Aboriginal women were encouraged or forced by the men in their lives. References abound to fathers selling their daughters 'for a few blankets or a little gold, into a slavery which was worse than death,'[33] exchanges likely viewed by some as only continuing traditional marital practices. Yet even missionary accounts hint at female agency, as with Bishop Hills's comment after unsuccessfully remonstrating with 'a woman making up a dress' for the dance house that night: 'Poor creatures they know these things are wrong – but the temptations are too strong.'[34]

Perhaps the most telling evidence of Aboriginal women's management of their sexual behaviour are the numbers who chose to live, at least for a time, with non-Aboriginal men. The nature of some decisions is suggested by Crosby's account of a twelve-year-old girl who, having 'refused at first to follow a life of sin,' 'was visited by a great rough fellow who, with his hand full of money and with promises of fine clothes and trinkets and sweets, coaxed her and finally prevailed upon her to come and live with him.'[35] ... Aboriginal women caught in the tumultuous world that was the gold rush sometimes had to make hard decisions, whether for material goods or personal safety. In such circumstances, a lonely miner's entreaties could be persuasive.

Non-Aboriginal men had their own reasons for entering into relationships. During the heady years of the gold rush, at least thirty thousand White men and several thousand Chinese and Blacks sought their fortunes in British Columbia. Most soon departed, for the difficulties of getting to the goldfields were horrendous, but however long they stayed, their utter loneliness in a sea of men cannot be discounted. The most fundamental characteristic of non-Aboriginal women in gold-rush British Columbia was their paucity[36] ... When a non-Aboriginal man saw an Aboriginal woman, what he may have perceived was not so much her Aboriginality as her gender and, certainly, her sexuality.

...

Although some of the relationships spawned by the gold rush extended through the couple's lifetime, many were fairly transient, two persons cohabiting for a time until one or the other decided to move on.[37] In most cases it was the man who did so, and, as one Aboriginal woman recalled,

Oh, it was hard on Indian wives, I guess,
But they always managed
To raise their children
Even if their husbands finished with them.[38]

Women might end relationships, as in the gold-rush town of Lytton in 1868 where a man 'lately left by his Indian wife who had had two children by him ... confesses having sown the seed he has reaped.'[39] Other women simply ensured that their husbands knew that they could leave if they wished to do so.

...

The various data from personal accounts, church records, and the manuscript censuses suggest that, in those areas of British Columbia opened up to Europeans during the gold-rush years, about one in ten Aboriginal women cohabited at some point in her life with a non-Aboriginal man.[40] The prevalence of such unions even caused the first session of the new provincial legislature, following entry into Confederation in 1871, to pass a bill, subsequently disallowed by the federal government, to legitimize children of unions between Aboriginal women and non-Aboriginal men whose parents wed subsequent to their birth.[41]

Taming Aboriginal Sexuality

By the time British Columbia became a Canadian province in 1871, Aboriginal women had been almost wholly sexualized.[42] The perception of widespread prostitution, and if not prostitution then concubinage, gave men in power the freedom to speak openly about matters that otherwise would have been only whispered.[43] Newcomers took for granted the fall as depicted in the Bible. Human nature was weak, and the biological man could easily be tempted to evil by his female counterpart, just as Bishop O'Conner considers himself to have been a century later. It was woman's place to be docile and subservient so as not to provoke man. For all those seeking to control Aboriginal peoples, women who exercised sexual autonomy had to be subdued. Conversion to Christianity held the key, for 'woman was always the slave or burden-bearer until the Gospel came and lifted her into her true social position,' which was essentially as man's handmaiden.[44] Whether missionaries, government officials, or Aboriginal men, the common perception was that the only good Aboriginal woman was the woman who stayed home within the bosom of her family. So an informal alliance developed between these three groups to refashion Aboriginal women.

This tripartite alliance, wherein men in power buttressed and comforted each other, was grounded in mutual expediency and, to some extent, in mutual male admiration. With entry into Confederation, responsibility for Aboriginal people shifted to the federal government under the terms of the British North America Act, and it did not take long for newly appointed officials to realize the enormous benefit to be had from establishing cordial relations with missionaries, who were already at work across much of the sprawling province. Officially, missionaries had no status, but unofficially they became the government's foot soldiers, and its eyes and ears. Aboriginal policy, as it developed in British Columbia, was to minimize official involvement in everyday affairs, which effectively meant letting missionaries have a free hand.[45] If disagreeing in many areas, including Aboriginal people's right to an adequate land base, government officials repeatedly commended missionaries for having 'taught, above all, the female portion of the community to behave themselves in a modest and virtuous manner.'[46] The other prong of the alliance crossed racial boundaries in the interests of gender solidarity and mutual self-interest. Members of the Indian Reserve Commission active across British Columbia in the mid-1870s left an extensive paper trail and repeatedly expressed approval of Aboriginal 'manliness' and of 'the industry of the men.'[47] Similarly, in missionary accounts it is almost wholly Aboriginal men who are given individuality and personality.[48] Men, particularly those who emulated colonial ways, needed to have suitable spouses, and for this reason too Aboriginal women had to have their sexuality tamed.

As for Aboriginal men, they were likely motivated by a shortage of women and also, some of them, by a desire to please their colonial mentors. Reports of a shortage are sufficiently widespread to be convincing. As early as 1866, Bishop Hills observed 'a scarcity of wives' among the northern Tsimshian, many of whose members camped in Victoria on a seasonal basis.[49] The Indian Reserve Commission's census of a decade later counted 1,919 Aboriginal persons in the area extending from Burrard Inlet north to Jervis Inlet, across to Comox, and down through the Saanich peninsula, including the Gulf Islands; of these, 979 were adult males compared with 919 adult females, and 94 male youth compared with 84 female youth.[50] The enumerator of the Southern Interior, extending from Lytton through the Nicola Valley, counted 884 adult males compared with 803 adult females and lamented 'the absence of females both adults and youths – those who should have been the future mothers of the tribe.'[51] Some Aboriginal men, in effect, made deals to behave in accord with missionary aspirations for them in exchange for getting wives.[52] Crosby described a visit to a Queen Charlottes village in about 1885, where local men promised him: 'Sir, if you will come and give us a teacher, we will stop going to Victoria. Victoria has been the place of death and destruction to our people, as you see we have no children left to us. All our young women are gone; some of our young men can't find wives any more; and we wish that you could help them to get wives among the Tsimpshean people.'[53]

The tripartite campaign to tame the wild represented by Aboriginal sexuality had two principal goals. The first was to return Aboriginal women home. The second was to desexualize Aboriginal everyday life, in effect to cleanse it so that the home to which women returned would emulate its colonial counterpart.

Returning Aboriginal Women Home

Marriage lay at the heart of newcomers' morality and, as anthropologist George Stocking concludes, 'it is perfectly clear that "marriage proper" meant proper Victorian marriage' whose 'purpose was to control human (and especially female) sexuality, so that there might be "certainty of male parentage."'[54] As summed up by historians Leonore Davidoff and Catherine Hall for England between the late eighteenth and mid-nineteenth centuries, 'marriage was the economic and social building block for the middle class.' 'Marriage became both symbol and institution of women's containment. It was marriage which would safely domesticate the burgeoning garden flower into an indoor pot plant; the beautiful object potentially open to all men's gaze became the possession of one man when kept within the house like a picture fixed to the wall.'[55]

In theory, two marital strategies could have tamed Aboriginal sexuality. One was to encourage non-Aboriginal men to wed their Aboriginal partners, the other to return Aboriginal women home to wed Aboriginal men. Either would have satisfied Victorian notions of marriage, but the alliance of interests that existed among men in power combined with growing racism to ensure that the second option would be favoured. As early as 1873 an agitated provincial official pointed to the federal government's responsibility for 'the care and protection of the native race in this Province, [and] so long as this shameful condition of things is suffered to continue unchecked, the character of that race in the social scale is practically a delusion.'[56] Reserve commissioners reported on conversations with chiefs at Nanaimo, where 'the evil of concubinage of their young women with the white men around were specially pointed out.'[57] By 1884 an Indian agent with an Aboriginal wife and grown daughters felt able to argue, perhaps with a touch of self-interest, that 'with the present state of civilization in the country and the abundance of white and educated half breed women – such a practice should be put a stop to in future.'[58] Aboriginal women were needed at home to service their menfolk.

For men in power, gender and race neatly dovetailed. Within the mix of pseudo-scientific ideas associated with Social Darwinism, newcomers accepted, as seemingly demonstrated by the triumph of colonialism and technological advances, that mankind had evolved into a hierarchy with Whites on the top and Aboriginal people near the bottom.[59] Persons of mixed race ranked even lower, for, to quote a colonial visitor, 'half-breeds, as a rule, inherit, I am afraid, the vices of both races.'[60] Concerns grew over 'a class of half-breed children ... who, under the bond of illegitimacy, and deprived of all incentives in every respect, will in course of time become dangerous members of the community.'[61] During the late 1870s such fears were exacerbated by a murderous rampage by the young sons of a Hudson's Bay trader and Aboriginal woman,[62] and given a sexual edge by female mixed-race students at a public boarding school becoming pregnant by their male counterparts.[63] While some encouragement was given to non-Aboriginal men to marry Aboriginal women with whom they were cohabiting, this was, for the most part, done somewhat grudgingly.[64] Petitions became a favoured means to compel Aboriginal women back home. The tripartite alliance developed a dynamic whereby Aboriginal men signed petitions orchestrated by missionaries, who then dispatched them to government officials to justify their taking action.[65] Both Catholic and Protestant missionaries participated, as did Aboriginal men across much of the province and numerous officials at various levels of government.

In 1885, Oblate missionaries stage-managed two identical petitions to the governor general that were affirmed with their marks by 962 Aboriginal men, including at least eighteen chiefs, from across the Cariboo and south through the Lower Fraser Valley. In the best English prose, the petitions 'beg[ed] to lay before your Excellency' that a 'great evil is springing up amongst our people' whereas 'on a dispute between a married couple, the wife leaves her husband and goes off the Reservation, and takes up with a bad white man, China man, or other Indian, and [they] live together in an unlawful state.' The men sought permission to 'bring back the erring ones by force if necessary.'[66] Caught up in the rhetoric to tame Aboriginal sexuality, the Ministry of Justice drafted an even broader regulation for consideration by the chiefs, one which made it possible to 'bring back to the reserve any Indian woman who has left the reserve and is living immorally with any person off the reserve.' The proposal was only derailed by the Ministry of Justice's suggestion, made almost in passing, that the Department of Indian Affairs should 'consider before it is passed whether or not the putting of it in force will lead to riots and difficulties between the Indians and the white people and others with whom the Indian women are said to be living immorally.'[67] Three of the four Indian agents consulted considered that this might well happen were chiefs given such authority. One of them acknowledged female agency in his observation that, 'while in some cases the Indian woman might be brought back without trouble, it would be impossible to keep her on a reserve against her will.'[68] The project was shelved, even though the Catholic bishop at New Westminster intervened directly at the federal ministerial level in an attempt to bypass the bureaucrats.[69]

The campaign to tame Aboriginal sexuality was not to be thwarted, and the Oblates were almost certainly behind a bolder petition dispatched in 1890 to the governor general. The chiefs of fifty-eight bands, again extending from the Cariboo through the Fraser Valley, indicated by their marks that they were 'much aggrieved and annoyed at the fact that our wives, sisters and daughters are frequently decoyed away from our Reserves by ill designing persons.' No means existed to return 'these erring women,' but, even were this possible, 'in most cases these women are induced to return again to their seducers.' Fearing that 'some of our young men who are sufferers will certainly take the law into their own hands and revenge themselves on the offending parties,' the petition sought 'a law authorising the infliction of corporal punishment by the lash.'[70] The advisability of 'legislation, making it an offence for a white man to have sexual intercourse with an Indian woman or girl without Christian marriage,' was referred to the Ministry of Justice,[71] which in this case pulled the plug. The ministry considered the legislation unnecessary, since 'the laws relating to the protection of females and for the punishment of persons who seduce or abduct them, apply to Indian women as well as to white women.'[72] Yet the campaign persisted, and later in 1890 the Indian agent at Lillooet urged, on behalf of 'the Chiefs of the numerous Bands around here,' that 'a severe penalty should be imposed upon any person, not an Indian, who, harbouring an Indian woman, does not deliver her up to the Chief of the Reserve.'[73]

At this point the enthusiasts may have stumbled. Acting largely independently of civil authority, the Oblates had allied themselves across much of the Interior with local Aboriginal men in order to effect control over everyday life.[74] As one Indian agent noted in the early 1890s, although the 'flogging habit has been abandoned for some years past' and fines are not so common as they once were, 'considerable sums of money are annually collected by the chiefs and their watchmen for the benefit of the churches whose functionaries attend to their spiritual welfare.'[75] In the spring of 1892 the Oblate missionary at Lillooet, the chief, and four other Aboriginal men were brought before the local magistrate, convicted, and given jail sentences for 'flogging a young girl ... on the report only of a fourth party' for some unspecified sexual activity. 'Without investigation *he* [priest] *ordered* 15 lashes. His plea was 1st ancient customs of the Indians & 2nd necessity for such punishment in order to suppress immorality.' The Indian agent who made the report considered both that the 'ancient customs' were not as portrayed by the missionary and that the local men should not have been punished so severely, since they 'believed the Priest to be their Commander in all Church matters – and that consequently they were obliged to obey him.'[76] The incident appears to have cooled the alliance between the Oblates and local men, who 'were astonished at the extent of the jurisdiction of the Courts of law, when even the dictates of a Priest should be upset and the Priest himself held accountable.'[77]

The Protestants could be just as enthusiastic as the Catholics in allying themselves with local men to keep women at home and then calling on federal officials to enforce what they could not effect by their own devices. In 1889 the Indian agent at Alert Bay, acting in concert with the local Anglican missionary, stopped a group of women from boarding a steamer to Victoria. His justification was that they 'went with the avowed purpose of prostituting themselves' and he 'had previously been requested by numbers of young men to prevent if possible their wives and sisters from going to Victoria.'[78] Reflecting the tripartite alliance's perspective, the Indian agent considered that 'nearly all the young women, whenever they leave their homes, whether ostensibly for working at the canneries or at the Hop Fields, do so with the ultimate idea of making more money by prostitution.'[79] The steamboat company vigorously protested, and the provincial Indian superintendent was luke-warm to the action, astutely observing that 'the Indian women and their friends come to Victoria, and other places in their canoes,' making their restriction practically impossible.[80] Nonetheless, the Indian agent and Anglican missionary did such a successful end run to federal officials as to persuade them to propose legislation to keep at home, by force if necessary, 'Indian women from the West Coast of British Columbia, who are in the habit of leaving their Villages and Reserves by steamers and by other mode of transport with the object of visiting the Cities and Towns of that Province for immoral purposes.'[81]

The proposed legislation hit a snag only after the federal minister of justice indicated 'that there is not at present sufficient material on hand to permit of the drawing up of a Bill fully dealing with the question.'[82] The minister requested the provincial superintendent to circularize Indian agents around the province. Even though the agents would likely have found it far easier to acquiesce to expectations than to dispute them, they were all, apart from those at Alert Bay and Babine in the Northern Interior, remarkably sanguine. On the west of Vancouver Island: 'I do not know of a single instance on this Coast where a young girl has been taken to Victoria or elsewhere for the purposes of prostitu-tion.'[83] His neighbour was 'not aware of any Indian women belonging to the Cowichan Agency who leave their Reservations for immoral purposes.'[84] In the Fraser Valley and Lower Mainland, 'there are very few immoral women.'[85] As for the Central Interior, 'the practice of Indian women leaving their Reserves for the purpose of leading im-moral lives is not common in this Agency.'[86] The Southern Interior agent offered a general observation: 'Indians are in their nature, in consequence of their training, habits and surroundings, far less virtu-ous than the average whites. Their morality should not therefore be judged by the standards of the white people. The Indian woman, al-though, as above stated, inclined to be worse in her morals, is naturally modest.'[87] The North Coast agent considered that the 'Indians have learned from sad experience the effects of immorality in the cities and are rapidly improving their conduct.'[88] Summarizing the responses, the provincial superintendent concluded that 'the few Indian women who may be found living an immoral life in our towns and Cities are less in number as a rule than of their white sisters.'[89]

Nonetheless, the depiction of Aboriginal sexuality as out of control was too attractive an explanation for missionary and government fail-ings to be abandoned. Just three years later, in 1895, a petition signed by thirty-four men from central Vancouver Island, all but one with their marks, demanded legislation to prevent 'our wives and daughters and sisters' from being 'carried to Victoria for illegitimate purposes.'[90] The British Columbia senator to whom the petition was addressed took its claims at face value and demanded that steps be taken to 'prevent the deportation of Indian women,' seeing that 'Indians are wards of the government under tutelage and not qualified to manage their own affairs wisely.' The senator, who simply assumed that Aboriginal women's sole role was to service their menfolk, emphasized that an 'increase, instead of a decrease, is much to be desired' in the Aboriginal population.[91] The federal response is interesting because, rather than quoting from the Indian agents' reports in their files, officials emphasized the difficulties of securing legislation. In doing so, they revealed, perhaps inadvertently, that women were de facto having their travel restricted by local Indian agents 'when requested by the husband or brother or anyone having proper authority, to stop a woman from going away, and so the men have the prevention of that of which they complain almost entirely in their own hands.'[92] The sexualization of Aboriginal women had far less to do with reality than with the needs, and desires, of men in power. So long as settler society perceived a need to tame Aboriginal sexuality, men in power could reorder Aboriginal society with impunity.

Reordering Aboriginal Society

Over time virtually every aspect of Aboriginal everyday life acquired a sexual dimension, thereby justifying its reordering. Aboriginal sexuality, or perhaps more accurately the fear of Aboriginal women's agency, became a lens through which traditional preferences in housing, social institutions, and child care were critiqued and found wanting.

The rhetoric condemning the 'big houses' inhabited by Coastal peoples made explicit Victorian fears of the body and of human sexuality. It also reflected Social Darwinian notions of the hierarchy of species, at the top of which lay Western societies premised on the monogamous conjugal family. The very existence of sites where more than a single family lived together was equated with immorality. No doubt existed but that, given the opportunity, men and women would act on their impulses. Davidoff and Hall have linked the subordination of women to the private home: 'Woman had been created for man, indeed for one man, and there was a necessary inference from this that home was "the proper scene of woman's action and influence ..." The idea of a privatized home, separated from the world, had a powerful moral force and if women, with their special aptitude for faith, could be contained within that home, then a space would be created for true family religion.'[93] So also in British Columbia, the single family home came to be seen as a necessary prelude to Christian conversion.

Men in power repeatedly lauded the single-family house, as in side notes on the Reserve Commission's census of Aboriginal people. At Burrard Inlet: 'The houses at this place have a pleasing appearance when viewed from the sea. They are mostly of the cottage style, white washed and kept cleaner in this than is usual with most Indians.' In contrast, along the Fraser River: 'Most of the houses of this tribe are of the primitive style. There are however several cottages kept and fitted up in a neat manner.' At Cowichan on Vancouver Island: 'There are a few tidy cottages – what they require is a desire and encouragement.'[94] Missionaries like Crosby were even more fervent and repeatedly linked housing to sexuality. 'The old heathen house, from its very character, was the hot-bed of vice. Fancy a great barn-like building, ... occupied by as many as a dozen families, only separated from each other by low partitions.' The interior seemed made for naughty deeds. 'Picture such a building, with no floor other than the ground, no entrance for light except the door, when open, and the cracks in the walls and the roof. Around the inside of such a building were ranged the beds, built up on rude platforms.' 'Is it any wonder that disease and vice flourished under such favorable surroundings?'[95] In sharp contrast stood 'the Christian home.' Crosby considered that 'the only way to win the savage from his lazy habits, sin and misery' was to 'be able and willing to show how to build a nice little home, from the foundation to the last shingle on the roof.'[96]

Fear of Aboriginal sexuality became frenzied in the rhetoric around the institution of the potlatch. Missionaries led the campaign against this social activity practised across most of the province, garnering support from government officials and over time from some converted Aboriginal men. Initially arguments focused on the event itself as being 'demoralizing,' leading to 'debauchery.'[97] Federal legislation banning the potlatch took effect at the beginning of 1885, but did not bring about wholesale conversion to Christianity. Missionaries soon sought both allies in Aboriginal men in search of wives and reasons, apart from themselves, to explain their failure to live up to their expectations for themselves.[98] The ethnographer Marius Barbeau concluded in 1921, after examining federal files on the potlatch, that, 'as the Church has not succeeded in making converts to any material extent ... there must be found a scapegoat, and as the potlatch already had a bad name, it was blamed.'[99]

The sexualization of the potlatch had a number of components, but centred on the supposed sale of Aboriginal women as wives or prostitutes to get the money to potlatch.[100] In 1893 a Toronto newspaper reported that a group of missionaries had witnessed 'blankets for potlatch procured at the expense of the virtue of women,' an event that the local Indian agent determined was sensationalized.[101] By the end of the century, the press was convinced that 'the potlatch is the inciting cause of three-fourths of the immorality that exists among Indian women.'[102] Writing shortly thereafter, the Indian agent at Alert Bay asserted that the younger generation of Aboriginal men supported his attempt to persuade his superiors in Ottawa to act against potlatching: 'It looks cruel to me to see a child 13 or 14 years of age put up & sold just like sheep or a nanny goat, to a bleary eyed siwash old enough to be her grand-father, for a pile of dirty blankets, which will in turn be Potlatched to the rest of the band, and all to make the proud Father, a big Injun,' rather than 'let her marry a young man whom I am sure she wanted.'[103] The Indian agent quoted a longtime missionary to make his point that 'the girls die off and the young men for the most part cannot get wives because as a rule they have no blankets or money unless they are sons of chiefs and the others cannot get wives until they are able to command a certain sum which is so difficult as they have to compete with the older men who hold the property.'[104]

The unwillingness to tolerate Aboriginal women's agency was a major factor in the determination to replace familial child care with residential schools operated by missionaries under loose government oversight. As attested by the scholarship, schools sought total control over pupils' sexuality, particularly that of girls.[105] The twinned concepts of Christian marriage and the Christian home depended on young women remaining sufficiently unblemished so that they could become good wives according to Victorian standards of behaviour. The attitudes and actions of Thomas Crosby and his wife, Emma, are instructive. Crosby considered that parents, 'though kind and indulgent to their children, are not capable of teaching and controlling them properly' and 'something must be done to save and protect the young girls ... from being sold into the vilest of slavery.'[106] 'On account of the prevalence of this traffic in Indian girls, many of the early missionaries were led to establish "Girls' Homes" for the rescue and further protection of these poor victims of this awful system.'[107] The taming that went on in the Crosbys' girls' home, as in residential schools across the province, left no doubt as to Aboriginal agency. As remembered by a Crosby school matron in the early 1880s, the girls required 'a great deal of Grace, Patience and determination, they were so obstinate and disobedient.'[108]

The wildness associated with Aboriginal sexuality explains attitudes toward a girl's transition from pupil to wife. Reflecting the assumptions of the day, the superintendent of the Children's Aid Society in Vancouver expressed relief that 'the savage was so thin and washed out' of two young women of mixed race, that they were able to find happiness with their White lovers. Yet this represented 'only a glimmer of light in the darkness.'[109] According to Crosby's biographer, 'girls stayed at the Home until they were married, at which time a new girl would be admitted.'[110] The full extent of missionaries' distrust of their charges is evident in the musings of another Crosby matron regarding the potential marriage of a fourteen-year-old student: 'It would seem sinful to allow such things to be mentioned if they were white girls, but here they are safer when married young.'[111]

Again, the informal alliance operated. Schools measured their success by numbers of girls who 'have married Christian Indians, have helped to build up Christian homes, to civilize the people generally and to aid in developing their own neighborhood.' 'Instead of a young man with his friends going with property and buying a wife, as was done formerly, many of our brightest young men tried to make the acquaintance of the girls in the Home.' Women might no longer be sold by their fathers, but they were no less commodities when it came to marriage. The Crosbys, like other missionaries, put a romantic spin around what was, in effect, a good being made available to a handful of men considered suitably Christian. 'There was no doubt in our minds that real, true love again and again developed between the young people who thus became acquainted. This acquaintance finally resulted in their marriage and the happy life that followed.'[112]

Consequences

By the end of the nineteenth century, settler society took for granted the interpretation that men in power put on Aboriginal women's agency. The ongoing frenzy over the potlatch is indicative. The press became ever more determined to expose its supposed basis in Aboriginal sexuality. 'Indian girl sold for 1,000 blankets' hit Vancouver streets in 1906.[113] The story makes clear that the supposed revelation about 'the awful Indian practice of potlatch' originated with an Anglican missionary who was disgruntled because a pupil had married someone other than the man she had selected for her. Later in the year, both Vancouver and Ottawa newspapers trumpeted 'Five Indian Girls Sold,'[114] a report that, on investigation, proved to be groundless.[115] A Vancouver paper headlined a year later, 'Squaw Sold for $400.00 at Alert Bay to a Grizzled Chief from Queen Charlottes.'[116] It turned out that, while two marriages had occurred, neither involved 'a grizzled chief,' and the local Indian agent considered the article to be 'very misleading.'[117] The press coverage prompted a host of women's voluntary associations across the country to demand legislation to 'put an end to this great blot on the Civilization and Christianity of Canada.'[118] Writing in 1921, a barrister who was the son of the former Indian agent at Alert Bay, and who represented Aboriginal people opposed to the potlatch ban, considered that 'the strongest reason for enforcing the law against the Potlatch is the question of Indian marriages ... It is also contended that women are bought and sold, [but] this is not true.'[119] Had the potlatch not been so successfully sexualized, it is doubtful that opponents could have maintained its illegality into the mid-twentieth century. The taming of Aboriginal sexuality had become a means to an end, as well as of course an end in itself, but the effects were no less detrimental to Aboriginal women.

For Aboriginal women, the consequences of the ceaseless rhetoric of scorn heaped on them in the interests of men in power were enormous. Some women acquiesced and returned or remained at home,[120] and the Crosbys delighted 'in visiting around among the villages, to pick out these Christian mothers who had the privilege of the "Home" life and training.'[121] In a broad sense, Aboriginal societies did come to mimic their colonial counterparts, which is not unexpected given federal policies and the material advantages to be got from doing so. An Aboriginal informant explained in 1950 how 'converts were sometimes termed "made white men," as they used different types of houses and they dressed in white men's clothes, while their heathen brothers ... indulged in all of the old rituals.'[122] Some women had the decision taken out of their hands. As more marriageable White women became available and attitudes hardened, numerous non-Aboriginal men shed their Aboriginal partners. The manuscript censuses for the late nineteenth century indicate that, while some of these women did return home and enter into new unions with Aboriginal men, others scraped along at the edges of settler society.

Other women continued to dare.[123] Many inter-racial unions survived the campaign to tame Aboriginal sexuality, in some cases by the partners legally marrying or retreating outward into the frontier, or by simply standing their ground.[124]

...

Most important, the campaign to tame Aboriginal sexuality so profoundly sexualized Aboriginal women that they were rarely permitted any other form of identity. Not just Aboriginal women but Aboriginal women's agency was sexualized. In the extreme case, their every act became perceived as a sexual act and, because of the unceasing portrayal of their sexuality as wild and out of control, as an act of provocation. By default, Aboriginal women were prostitutes or, at best, potential concubines. Their actions were imbued with the intent that men in power had so assiduously ascribed to them, thus vitiating any responsibility for their or other men's actions toward them. Sexualization of Aboriginal women's agency occurred within a context in which they were already doubly inferior by virtue of their gender and race, thus virtually ensuring that any Aboriginal woman who dared would become colonialism's plaything. Again, the stories are legion, be it the Okanagan Valley in the 1880s, Vancouver Island in the 1920s, the North Coast in the 1960s, or Bishop O'Conner. Sometimes the accounts embody a strong element of bravado, in other cases the wish fulfilment of lonely men, but in yet others a strong dose of action, as with O'Conner.

...

In a generally sympathetic account of a summer sojourn in 1966 at Telegraph Creek on the North Coast, a young American made clear that Aboriginal women's agency remained sexualized. 'More than they would have in the old days, I'm sure, they make fun of the Indians to me ... [for] their limber-limbed promiscuity.' A friend 'eats supper with me, chatting about the morals of Indian girls ("No morals at all if you scratch their stomachs a minute.").' Their every action became a sexual action; thus his vignette relating how 'earlier in the spring a girl appeared in the store, sent by her parents, and took up the broom and began to sweep, after the historical fashion of a squaw proposing to a white man.' For this young man, the wild which was Aboriginal sexuality remained mythic. Noting that 'in New York to dream of a woman is an unremarkable event' but 'here it invests the whole night with sexual urgency,' he repeatedly found himself tempted, as after 'I've had a day hearing stories of ... Indian women being mounted and screwed.' He resisted, but precisely because he did accept the equation of Aboriginal female agency with sexuality: 'Of course these Indian girls are too vulnerable to fool with, so I have only the past to keep me company in bed.'[125]

Hence we come full circle to Bishop O'Conner, who at virtually the same time that this young American was fantasizing acted on his impulses. Like so many men before him, he still considers himself to have been 'seduced' and, a full generation later, remains in his heart 'a celibate man.' I have no doubt that O'Conner feels himself to be sincere, just as I now have no doubt of the importance of newcomers' construction of Aboriginal women's sexuality for understanding events during that critical half century, 1850–1900, when your, my, and Bishop O'Conner's British Columbia came into being.

NOTES

Earlier versions of this essay were presented at the BC Studies Conference in May 1997 and, thanks to Elizabeth Jameson and Susan Armitage, at the Western Historical Association in October 1997. I am grateful to everyone who has commented on the essay, especially Robin Fisher at BCS, Elizabeth Jameson at WHA, and the two anonymous reviewers for *BC Studies*. The Social Sciences and Humanities Research Council generously funded the research from which the essay draws.

1 This statement by Bishop O'Conner was taken up forcefully in Reasons for Judgment, Vancouver Registry, no. CC9 206 17, 25 July 1996.
2 National Parole Board, Decision Registry, file 905044C, 21 March 1997.
3 The three best books for understanding Aboriginal people in British Columbia are, in my view, Robin Fisher, *Contact and Conflict: Indian-European Relations in British Columbia, 1774–1890* (Vancouver: UBC Press, 1970 and 1992); Paul Tennant, *Aboriginal Peoples and Politics: The Indian Land Question in British Columbia 1849–1989* (Vancouver: UBC Press, 1990); and Cole Harris, *The Resettlement of British Columbia: Essays on Colonialism and Geographical Change* (Vancouver: UBC Press, 1997), each of which is driven by a male perspective as to sources, authorship, subjects, and interpretation. Much the same observation might be made about the bulk of the ethnographic literature; a recent summary of the historiography (Wayne Suttles and Aldona Jonaitis, 'History of Research in Ethnology,' in

Handbook of North American Indians, ed. Wayne Suttles [Washington, DC: Smithsonian Institution, 1990], 84–6) does not even include private life or women, must less sexuality, as topics.

4 This general point is made by, among other authors, Sandra Harding in *The Science Question in Feminism* (Milton Keynes: Open University Press, 1986); Catherine Hall in *White, Male, and Middle-Class: Explorations in Feminism and History* (New York: Routledge, 1988); and Vron Ware in *Beyond the Pale: White Women, Racism and History* (London: Verso, 1992). A handful of exceptions by Canadian scholars are principally concerned with an earlier time period, as with Karen Anderson, *Chain Her by One Foot: The Subjugation of Native Women in Seventeenth-Century New France* (New York: Routledge, 1991); Sylvia Van Kirk, *Many Tender Ties: Women in Fur Trade Society, 1670–1870* (Norman: University of Oklahoma Press, 1980); and Ron Bourgeault, 'Race, Class and Gender: Colonial Domination of Indian Women,' *Socialist Studies* 5 (1989): 87–115. The two principal analyses of perceptions of Aboriginal people consider women, if at all, as extensions of their menfolk; see Robert F Berkofer, Jr, *The White Man's Indian: Images of the American Indian from Columbus to the Present* (New York: Vintage, 1979), and Daniel Francis, *The Imaginary Indian: The Image of the Indian in Canadian Culture* (Vancouver: Arsenal Pulp Press, 1992).

5 Jane Katz, ed., *Messengers of the Wind: Native American Women Tell Their Life Stories* (New York: Ballantine Books, 1995), 5.

6 David Jary and Julia Jary, *Collins Dictionary of Sociology,* 2nd ed. (Glasgow: HarperCollins, 1995), 590–1. It was 1914 before the *Oxford English Dictionary* got to the letters. All of its quotes were from the nineteenth century, and, while the first definition of sexuality was 'the quality of being sexual or having sex,' the second and third were the 'possession of sexual powers or capability of sexual feelings' and 'recognition of or preoccupation with what is sexual.' See Sir James A.H. Murray, ed., *A New English Dictionary on Historical Principles,* vol. 8 (Oxford: Clarendon Press, 1914), 582. Interest in the concept of sexuality, and more generally in regulation of the body, mushroomed with the publication of Michel Foucault's *History of Sexuality* in 1978 (Harmondsworth: Penguin, esp. vol. 1) and Peter Gay's *The Bourgeois Experience* in 1986 (Oxford: Oxford University Press, 2 vols). Particularly helpful for interpreting Foucault is Ann Laura Stoler's *Race and the Education of Desire: Foucault's History of Sexuality and the Colonial Order of Things* (Durham: Duke University Press, 1995).

7 Gail Hawkes, *A Sociology of Sex and Sexuality* (Buckingham and Philadelphia: Open University Press, 1996), 8, 14, 42.

8 This point underlies Ronald Hyam, *Empire and Sexuality: The British Experi-*

ence (Manchester: University of Manchester Press, 1990); and Margaret Strobel, *Gender, Sex, and Empire* (Washington: American Historical Association, 1993), which critiques Hyam's contention that empire enhanced men's sexual opportunities.

9 Among the more perceptive recent examinations of aspects of this topic are Margaret Jolly and Martha MacIntyre, eds, *Family and Gender in the Pacific: Domestic Contradictions and the Colonial Impact* (Cambridge: Cambridge University Press, 1989); Strobel, *Gender, Sex, and Empire*; Robert Young, *Colonial Desire: Hybridity in Theory, Culture and Race* (London: Routledge, 1995); Stoler, *Race and the Education of Desire*; and Frederick Cooper and Ann Laura Stoler, eds, *Tensions of Empire: Colonial Cultures in a Bourgeois World* (Berkeley: University of California Press, 1997).

10 Philip Mason, *Patterns of Dominance* (London: Oxford University Press for the Institute of Race Relations, 1970), 88.

11 Ann Laura Stoler and Frederick Cooper, 'Between Metropole and Colony: Rethinking a Research Agenda,' in Cooper and Stoler, eds, *Tensions of Empire*, 5. Although Stoler and Cooper co-wrote this introductory essay, the insight is clearly Stoler's, since it is her research on colonial Asia that is cited.

12 As diverse examples of a similar sequence, if not necessarily interpretation, of events, see Albert L. Hurtado, *Indian Survival on the California Frontier* (New Haven: Yale University Press, 1988), 160–92; and Caroline Ralston, 'Changes in the Lives of Ordinary Women in Early Post Contact Hawaii,' in Jolly and MacIntyre, eds, *Family and Gender*, 45–82. In *Capturing Women: The Manipulation of Cultural Imagery in Canada's Prairie West* (Montreal and Kingston: McGill-Queen's University Press, 1997), Sarah Carter links the sexualization of Aboriginal women on the Canadian prairies to their participation in the 1885 uprising (esp. 8–10, 161, 183, 187, 189).

13 In *Allegories of Empire: The Figure of the Woman in the Colonial Text* (Minneapolis: University of Minnesota Press, 1993), Jenny Sharpe argues that, after rebellions in India in the 1850s, raped colonial women provided the basis for racializing Indigenous peoples as inferior.

14 The concept of wildness is examined in Sharon Tiffany and Kathleen Adams, *The Myth of the Wild Woman* (Cambridge: Schenken, 1985).

15 Hall in *White, Male, and Middle-Class*, 61–2.

16 George W. Stocking, Jr, *Victorian Anthropology* (New York: Free Press, 1987), 199–200, 202.

17 Hawkes, *Sociology of Sex*, 14–15, 42.

18 Despite its male perspective, a good basic source, although limited to
    Coastal peoples, remains Suttles, ed., *Handbook of North American Indians*.
19 Especially useful is Carol Cooper, 'Native Women of the Northern Pacific
    Coast: An Historical Perspective, 1830–1900,' *Journal of Canadian Studies*
    27.4 (Winter 1992–3): 44–75, which points out that what newcomers la-
    belled prostitution sometimes simply continued traditional social struc-
    tures wherein some persons were deprived of their autonomy as 'slaves'
    (58) and traces the seasonal migrations of North Coast women to Victoria
    with their families.
20 24 September 1860 entry, Bishop George Hills, Diary, in Anglican Church,
    Ecclesiastical Province of British Columbia, Archives; also letter to the
    editor from C.T.W. in *Victoria Gazette*, 22 September 1860; and Matthew
    MacFie, *Vancouver Island and British Columbia* (London: Longman, Green,
    Longman, Roberts, & Green, 1865), 471.
21 Thomas Crosby, *Up and Down the North Pacific Coast by Canoe and Mission
    Ship* (Toronto: Missionary Society of the Methodist Church, 1904), 17. On
    the relevance of missionary accounts, see Jean and John Comaroff, *Of
    Revelation and Revolution: Christianity, Colonialism and Consciousness in South
    Africa* (Chicago: University of Chicago Press, 1991).
22 This contention is supported by Chris Hanna's extensive research on
    colonial Victoria, and I thank him for sharing his findings with me.
23 'Can Such Things Be?' *Victoria Daily Chronicle*, 16 November 1862.
24 Francis E. Herring, *In the Pathless West with Soldiers, Pioneers, Miners, and
    Savages* (London: T. Fisher Unwin, 1904), 173–5.
25 21 April 1860 entry, Hills, Diary; also entries of 12 August and 24 Septem-
    ber 1860, and 31 January 1862.
26 'The Dance Houses,' *British Colonist*, 20 December 1861. For events in
    California, see Alfred Hurtado, 'When Strangers Meet: Sex and Gender
    on Three Frontiers,' in *Writing the Range: Race, Class, and Culture in the
    Women's West*, ed. Elizabeth Jameson and Susan Armitage (Norman:
    University of Oklahoma Press, 1997), 134–7.
27 In *During My Time. Florence Edenshaw Davidson, a Haida Woman* (Vancouver
    and Seattle: Douglas & McIntyre and University of Washington Press,
    1982), 44–5, Margaret Blackman links the decline to the smallpox epidemic
    of 1862–3, but newspaper coverage suggests that the principal cause was
    fewer lone men.
28 On the maritime fur trade, see Lorraine Littlefield, 'Women Traders in the
    Maritime Fur Trade,' in *Native People, Native Lands: Canadian Indians, Inuit
    and Metis*, ed. Bruce Alden Cox (Ottawa: Carleton University Press, 1991),

173–85; and, on the land-based trade, Van Kirk, *Many Tender Ties*. Devens probes 'native women as autonomous, sexual active females' in seventeenth-century New France *in Countering Colonization: Native American Women and Great Lakes Missions, 1630–1900* (Berkeley: University of California Press, 1992), 25 and passim.

29 For a case study, see Jo-Anne Fiske, 'Fishing Is Women's Business: Changing Economic Roles of Carrier Women and Men,' in Cox, ed., *Native People, Native Lands*, 186–98.

30 On the concept of mimicry, see Homi Bhabha, 'Of Mimicry and Man: The Ambivalence of Colonial Discourse,' in Cooper and Stoler, eds, *Tensions of Empire*, 152–60.

31 'A Squaw Arrests a White Man,' *British Colonist*, 17 January 1862.

32 'Attempted Rape,' *British Colonist*, 17 August 1860.

33 Thomas Crosby, *Among the An-ho-me-nums, or Flathead Tribes of Indians of the Pacific Coast* (Toronto: William Briggs, 1907), 62.

34 1 February 1862 entry, Hills, Diary.

35 Crosby, *Among the An-ho-me-nums*, 63.

36 Adele Perry admirably tackles this and related topics in '"Oh I'm just sick of the faces of men": Gender Imbalance, Race, Sexuality, and Sociability in Nineteenth-Century British Columbia,' *BC Studies* 105–6 (Spring/Summer 1995): 27–43.

37 For a case study, see Jean Barman, 'Lost Okanagan: In Search of the First Settler Families,' *Okanagan History* 60 (1996): 8–20.

38 Mary Augusta Tappage, 'Changes,' in Jeanne E. Speare, *The Days of Augusta* (Vancouver: J.J. Douglas, 1973), 71.

39 27 May 1868 entry, Hills, Diary.

40 The base used is the greatly diminished Aboriginal population of about 25–30,000 following the devastating smallpox epidemic of the early 1860s. Another measure is the number of children resulting from the relationships, as indicated in the 'Supplementary Report' to British Columbia, Department of Education, *First Annual Report on the Public Schools in the Province of British Columbia* (1872), 38.

41 David R. Williams, *...The Man for a New Country: Sir Matthew Baillie Begbie* (Sidney: Gray's Publishing, 1977), 106–7.

42 The age-linked, equally essentializing counterpart was, of course, an absence of sexuality. Aboriginal woman as drudge is discussed in, among other sources, Elizabeth Vibert, *Traders' Tales: Narratives of Cultural Encounters in the Columbia Plateau, 1807–1846* (Norman: University of Oklahoma Press, 1997), 127–31, 136, and 233–9.

43 In referring to men in power, I do not mean to suggest that non-Aboriginal

women were completely absent from the discourse, but I do contend that, at least in British Columbia, their voices were muted compared to those of men; for a brief introduction to this literature, see Strobel, *Gender, Sex, and Empire*. Myra Rutherdale, in 'Revisiting Colonization to Gender: Anglican Missionary Women in the Pacific Northwest and Arctic, 1860–1945,' *BC Studies* 104 (Winter 1994–5): 3–23, discusses the priorities of female missionaries but without reference to sexuality.

44 Crosby, *Among the An-ko-me-nums*, 96.

45 See, for example, the private memorandum of Gilbert Malcolm Sproat, Indian reserve commissioner, Okanagan Lake, 27 October 1877, in Department of Indian Affairs (DIA), RG 10, vol. 3656, file 9063, C-10115.

46 Remarks enclosed with George Blenkinsop, secretary and census taker to Indian Reserve Commission, to Sproat, Douglas Lake, 20 September 1878, in DIA, RG 10, vol. 3667, file 10330.

47 Private memorandum of Sproat, 27 October 1877; and Alex C. Anderson and Archibald McKinlay, 'Report of the Proceedings of the Joint Commission for the Settlement of the Indian Reserves in the Province of British Columbia, Victoria, 21 March 1877,' in DIA, RG 10, vol. 3645, file 7936, C-10113.

48 Crosby, *Among the An-ko-me-nums*, esp. 206–32 and passim; and Crosby, *Up and Down*, passim.

49 24 May 1866 entry, Hills, Diary.

50 Census data included with Anderson and McKinlay, 'Report, 21 March 1877.'

51 Remarks enclosed with Blenkinsop to Sproat, 20 September 1878.

52 Such a contention is not inconsistent with Devens's view that Aboriginal men in the Great Lakes region more easily accommodated to missionaries' aspirations for them than did women; see her *Countering Colonization*.

53 Crosby, *Up and Down*, 270–1.

54 Stocking, *Victorian Anthropology*, 202.

55 Leonore Davidoff and Catherine Hall, *Family Fortunes: Men and Women of the English Middle Class*, 1780–1850 (London: Hutchinson, 1987), 322, 451.

56 Alex C. Anderson, J.F., to Sir Francis Hincks, MP for Vancouver District, Victoria, 26 August 1873, excerpted in undated memorandum of Anderson in DIA, RG 10, vol. 3658, file 9404, C-10115.

57 Anderson and McKinlay, 'Report, 21 March 1877.'

58 William Laing Meason, Indian agent of Williams Lake Agency, to L W. Powell, superintendent of Indian affairs, Lillooet, 25 March 1884, in DIA, RG 10, vol. 3658, file 9404, C-10115.

59 This topic is examined in Berkhofer, Jr, *White Man's Indian*, esp. 50–61;

Brian W. Dippie, *The Vanishing American: White Attitudes and U.S. Indian Policy* (Lawrence: University Press of Kansas, 1982), passim; Robert E. Bieder, 'Scientific Attitudes toward Indian Mixed Bloods in Early Nineteenth Century America,' *Journal of Ethnic Studies* 8 (1980): 17–30; and Robert Miles, *Racism* (London: Routledge, 1989).

60 R.C. Mayne, *Four Years in British Columbia and Vancouver Island* (London: John Murray, 1862), 277.

61 Anderson to John Ash, provincial secretary of British Columbia, 16 April 1873, excerpted in undated memorandum of Anderson, in DIA, RG 10, vol. 3658, file 9404, C-10115.

62 The fullest account of the events occurring in 1879 is by a descendant: Mel Rothenburger, *The Wild McLeans* (Victoria: Orca, 1993).

63 The sequence of events at Cache Creek School in 1877 was followed closely in the Victoria press.

64 Drawing on Stoler, Carter suggests that, on the Prairies, opposition grew out of fears of mixed-race children becoming heirs; see *Capturing Women*, xvi, 14–15, 191–2.

65 The constructed nature of all Aboriginal petitions is indicated by the alacrity with which missionaries and others warned federal officials about upcoming petitions 'purporting to come from the Indians,' but which were in fact being organized by an opposing religious group or others not to their liking, as with Alfred Hall, Anglican missionary, to superintendent of Indian affairs, Alert Bay, 5 October 1889, in RG 10, vol. 3816, file 57,045-1, C-10193.

66 Petitions of the Lillooet tribe of Indians and from Lower Fraser Indians, s.d. [summer and late fall 1885], and s.d. [summer 1885], in RG 10, vol. 3842, file 71,799, C-10148. On the Oblates' role, see memo from Bishop Louis d'Herbomez, OMI, to the governor general, s.d. [1887], in same.

67 George N. Burbidge, deputy minister of justice, to L. Vankoughnet, deputy superintendent general of Indian affairs, Ottawa, 3 February 1886, and enclosure, in RG 10, vol. 3842, file 71,799, C-10148.

68 W.H. Lomas, Indian agent of Cowichan Agency, to Powell, Quamichan, 20 May 1886; also draft of Vankoughnet to Powell, 13 February 1886; P. McTiernan, Indian agent at New Westminster, to Powell, New Westminster, 9 April 1886; Meason to Powell, Little Dog Creek, 25 March 1886; J.W. Mackay, Indian agent of Kamloops-Okanagan Agency, to Powell, Sooyoos [Osoyoos], 2 May 1886; and Powell to superintendent of Indian affairs, Victoria, 21 June 1886, in RG 10, vol. 3842, file 71,799, C-10148.

69 Memo-from d'Herbomez, [1887]; and Hector Langevin, minister of public

works, to John Macdonald, superintendent of Indian affairs, Ottawa, 25 April 1887, in RG 10, vol. 3842, file 71,799, C-10148.

70 Petition, New Westminster, 1 September 1890, in RG 10, vol. 3842, file 74799, C-10148.

71 Draft from Department of Indian Affairs to deputy minister of justice, 17 December 1890, in RG 10, vol. 3842, file 71,799, C-10148.

72 Draft of letter from Department of Indian Affairs to A.W. Vowell, Indian superintendent, Ottawa, 26 December 1890, in RG 10, vol. 3842, file 71,799, C-10148.

73 Meason to Vowell, Lillooet, 4 August 1890, in RG 10, vol. 3816, file 57,045-1 C-10193.

74 For the Cariboo, see Margaret Whitehead, *The Cariboo Mission: A History of the Oblates* (Victoria: Sono Nis, 1981).

75 Mackay to Vowell, Kamloops, 24 May 1892, in RG 10, vol. 3875, file 90,667-2, C-10193.

76 Meason to Vowell, Lillooet, 14 May 1892, in RG 10, vol. 3875, file 90,677-2, C-10193. The incident, its impetus in Oblate policy, and its aftermath are summarized in Whitehead, *Cariboo Mission*, 96–7. At the behest of Catholic authorities, the governor general remitted the sentences.

77 Mackay to Vowell, 24 May 1892.

78 R.H. Pidcock, Indian agent of Kwawkwelth Agency, to Power, Alert Bay, 3 April 1889, in DIA, RG 10, vol. 3816, file 57,045-1, C-10193.

79 Pidcock to Vowell, n.d., in RG 10, vol. 3816, file 57,045-1, C-10193.

80 Vowell to deputy superintendent of Indian affairs, Victoria, 25 March 1890, in RG 10, vol. 3816, file 57,045–1, C-10193.

81 Memorandum of superintendent general of Indian affairs to Privy Council of Canada, Ottawa, 20 February 1890, in DIA, RG 10, vol. 3816, file 57,045-1, C-10193.

82 John D. Thompson, minister of justice, to governor general in council, 1890, in RG 10, vol. 3816, file 57,045-1 C-10193.

83 Henry Guillod, Indian agent of West Coast Agency, to Vowell, Ucluelet, 22 August 1890, in RG 10, vol. 3816, file 57,045-1, C-10193.

84 Lomas to Vowell, Quamichan, 22 November 1890, in RG 10, vol. 3816, file 57,045-1, C-10193.

85 McTiernan to Vowell, New Westminister, 23 June 1890, in RG 10, vol. 3816, file 57,045-1, C-10193.

86 Meason to Vowell, Lillooet, 4 August 1890, in RG 10, vol. 3816, file 57,045-1, C-10193.

87 Mackay to Vowell, Kamloops, 4 July 1890, in RG 10, vol. 3816, file 57,045-1, C-10193.

88 C. Todd, acting Indian agent of North West Coast Agency, to Vowell, Metlakatla, 8 October 1890, in RG 10, vol. 3816, file 57,045-1, C-10193.

89 Vowell to Vankoughnet, Victoria, 25 February 1891, in RG 10, vol. 3816, file 57,045–1, C-10193.

90 Petition to Pidcock, Fort Rupert, 8 March 1895, in RG 10, vol. 3816, file 57,045-1, C-10193.

91 Senator W.J. Macdonald to minister of the interior, Ottawa, 6 May 1895, in RG 10, vol. 3816, file 57,045-1, C-10193.

92 Deputy superintendent general of Indian affairs to Vowell, Ottawa, 20 May 1895, in RG 10, vol. 3816, file 57,045-1, C10193.

93 Davidoff and Hall, *Family Fortunes*, 115.

94 Census date included with Anderson and McKinlay, 'Report, 21 March 1877.'

95 Crosby, *Among the An-ko-me-nums*, 49–50. On the related issue of domestic hygiene, see Michael Harkin, 'Engendering Discipline: Discourse and Counterdiscourse in the Methodist-Heiltsuk Dialogue,' *Ethnohistory* 43.4 (Fall 1996): 647–8.

96 Crosby, *Up and Down*, 74.

97 For example, Cornelius Bryant, Methodist missionary, to Lomas, Nanaimo, 30 January 1884; G. Donckel, Catholic missionary, to Lomas, Maple Bay, 2 February 1884; Lomas to Powell, Maple Bay, 5 February 1884; and Powell to superintendent general of Indian affairs, Victoria, 27 February 1884, in DIA, RG 10, vol. 3628, file 6244-1, C-10110.

98 This point is supported by DIA to Powell, 6 June 1884, in DIA, RG 10, vol. 1628, file 6244-1, C-10110; and stated explicitly in E.K. DeBeck, 'The Potlatch and Section 149 of the Indian Act,' Ottawa, 11 May 1921, in DIA, RG 10, vol. 3628, file 6244-X, C-10110; and in C.M. Barbeau, 'The Potlatch among the BC Indians and Section 149 of the Indian Act' (1921), in DIA, RG 10, vol. 3628, file 6244-X, C-10111.

99 Confidential memo to C.M.B., 17 February 1921, in Barbeau, 'The Potlatch.'

100 Douglas Cole and Ira Chaikin, in *An Iron Hand upon the People: The Law against the Potlatch on the Northwest Coast* (Vancouver and Seattle: Douglas & McIntyre and the University of Washington Press, 1990), 74–83, and Douglas Cole, in 'The History of the Kwakiutl Potlatch,' in *Chiefly Feasts: The Enduring Kwakiutl Potlatch*, ed. Aldona Jonaitis (Vancouver and New York: Douglas & McIntyre and American Museum of Natural History, 1991), 150–2, discuss sexual and marriage practices of the Kwakiutl as linked to the potlatch from a perspective which, while very informative and reliable, more or less accepts at face value the critiques of men

in power. In *Severing the Ties That Bind: Government Repression of Indigenous Religious Ceremonies in the Prairies* (Winnipeg: University of Manitoba Press, 1994), Katherine Pettipas essentially equates the perspective of males with the entirety of perspectives in reference both to the potlatch (90–6) and to the sundance. With a single exception noted only in passing (62), Joseph Masco does much the same in '"It Is a Strict Law That Bids Us Dance": Cosmologies, Colonialism, Death and Ritual Authority in the Kwakwa'wakw Potlatch, 1849–1922,' *Comparative Studies in Society and History* 37. 1 (Jan. 1995): 41–75.

101 *Empire* (Toronto), received 9 February 1893, and letter from Pidcock, 16 March 1893, in Barbeau, 'The Potlatch.'

102 Crosby, *Up and Down*, 316.

103 G.W. DeBeck, Indian agent of Kwawkwelth Agency, to Vowell, Alert Bay, 29 December 1902, and E.A. Bird, teacher at Gwayasdurus, to DeBeck, Alert Bay, 23 June 1902, in DIA, RG 10, vol. 6816, file 486-2-5, C-8538. The meaning of 'child marriage' is explored in Harkin, 'Engendering Discipline,' 646–7.

104 Bird to DeBeck, 23 June 1902.

105 Most recently, J.R. Miller, *Shingwauk's Vision: A History of Native Residential Schools* (Toronto: University of Toronto Press, 1996).

106 Letter from Thomas Crosby, *Missionary Outlook* 9 (1989): 100, cited in Clarence Bolt, *Thomas Crosby and the Tsimshian: Small Shoes for Feet Too Large* (Vancouver: UBC Press, 1992), 64; and Crosby, *Up and Down*, 85.

107 Crosby, *Among the An-ko-me-nums*, 63

108 Kate Hendry to sister Maggie, 26 December 1882, Kate Hendry Letterbook, British Columbia Archives, EC/H38.

109 C.J. South, superintendent, Children's Protection Act, to secretary, Department of Indian Affairs, Vancouver, 20 September 1905, in RG 10, vol. 3816, file 57,045-1, C-10193.

110 Bolt, *Thomas Crosby*, 64.

111 2 October 1886 entry of Agnes Knight, Journal, 1885–7, British Columbia Archives, F7/W 15.

112 Crosby, *Up and Down*, 89, 92–3.

113 'Indian Girl for 1,000 Blankets,' *Vancouver World*, 2 January 1906.

114 'Five Little Girls Sold at Alert Bay Potlatch,' *World*, 4 April 1906; and 'Five Indian Girls Sold, Vancouver B.C., April 6,' *Ottawa Journal*, 9 April 1906.

115 Letter to Vowell, 16 April 1906, in Barbeau, 'The Potlatch.'

116 'Squaw Sold for $400.00 at Alert Bay to a Grizzled Chief from Queen Charlottes,' *Vancouver Daily News Advertiser*, 6 April 1907.

117 Letter of William Halliday, 9 July 1907, in Barbeau, 'The Potlatch.'

118 The quotation is from Emily Cummings, corresponding secretary, National Council of Women, to minister of Indian affairs, Toronto, 19 February 1910, RG 10, vol. 3816, file 57,045, C-10193, which contains the many letters, often virtually identical in language, from the different associations.

119 DeBeck, 'The Potlatch and Section 149.'

120 Margaret Whitehead emphasizes this point in '"A Useful Christian Woman": First Nations' Women and Protestant Missionary Work in British Columbia,' *Atlantis* 18.102 (1992–3), 142–66.

121 Crosby, *Up and Down*, 92.

122 John Tate (Salaben), Gispaxloats, informant, recorded by William Benyon in 1950, in *Tshimshian Narratives,* collected by Marius Barbeau and William Benyon, ed. George F. MacDonald and John J. Cove, vol. 2, *Trade and Warfare* (Ottawa: Canadian Museum of Civilization, 1987), 207.

123 A fascinating question beyond the scope of this essay, which grows out of Foucault's work on power, concerns the extent to which some Aboriginal women internalized the assertions being made about them and considered that, yes, they must be prostitutes simply because they had been so informed so many times.

124 This topic is explored in Jean Barman, 'Invisible Women: Aboriginal Mothers and Mixed Race Daughters in Rural Pioneer British Columbia,' in *Negotiating Rural: Essays from British Columbia*, ed. R.W. Sandwell (Vancouver: UBC Press, 1998).

125 Entries for 16, 17, and 25 June, and 11 and 26 July 1966, in Edward Hoagland, *Notes from the Century Before: A Journal of British Columbia* (New York: Ballantine, 1969), 92, 96, 101, 141, 186, 250.

12 Native Women, Sexuality, and the Law

JOAN SANGSTER

In the early 1930s a young Ojibwa woman, Emma, living on a north-western Ontario reserve was sentenced to two years in the provincial reformatory for vagrancy. All the evidence against her centred on her supposed sexual promiscuity – including graphic evidence of her most recent sexual liaison – and the fact she had two illegitimate children. Although the Indian agent and RCMP appeared at the trial, the complaint appeared to have been made by her relatives and other community members. A petition was presented by the Indian agent, with the signatures of her cousins, aunts, uncles, grandfather, and others, asking that 'in the interests of the morality on the Reserve and the accused, she should be sent to a Reformatory.' Later, when parole was discussed, the agent claimed that opinion was not favourable among her family because of her 'reputation,' and he suggested that Emma be released into another community.[1]

In one sense, Emma's fate was not unusual: in mid-twentieth-century Canada, and especially after the Second World War, the numbers of First Nations women incarcerated in local and provincial correctional institutions increased steadily. While women like Emma were supposedly incarcerated for sexual offences, the most fundamental reasons for their conflicts with the law and subsequent imprisonment were material and social deprivation, cultural alienation, and systemic racism, combined with escalating social stresses on reserves and the increasing urbanization of Native peoples.[2] At first glance, Emma's apprehension at the insistence of her community also suggests that some First Nations were willing to use the powers of the Indian agent and Euro-Canadian law even to criminalize their own members, implying some 'acquiescence' to the process of colonization.[3] Although this is far too simplistic a characterization, this case does indicate the importance of probing the complex ways that Native women's sexuality was regulated, both through received Euro-Canadian law and also through its partial absorption into the social practices of First Nations peoples.

This article explores attempts to discipline the sexuality of Native women, examining the means and rationale for legal and moral governance, the interplay of customary Native law and Canadian law, and the resistance and responses of Native women, families, and communities to the imposition of new standards of conduct. The sexual regulation of Native and non-Native women alike was part of a broader project of nation-building: the creation of moral families, based on Western (largely Anglo) middle-class notions of sexual purity, marital monogamy, and distinct gender roles of the female homemaker and male breadwinner, was an important means of creating moral and responsible citizens, the 'bedrock of the nation,' as legal authorities never tired of saying.[4]

Yet, historically, the rights and representation of citizenship have also been linked to race, and nowhere is this more salient than in the operation of the law. As legal scholars have demonstrated, Canadian law played a significant role in constituting and reproducing racist ideology, and sanctioning discrimination, exclusion, and segregation in public policy, statute law, and judicial interpretation. In the early twentieth century, for instance, Asian women did not qualify as potential citizens, while Afro-Canadian women encountered second-class citizenship through the process of educational and social segregation.[5] Race was socially constructed through the law, with a racial hierarchy of white superiority clothed in rationales of necessity, progress, and even science sustained both by subtle ideological consent and by repressive coercion.[6] Race was also an integral ingredient of colonial relations articulated through the apartheid and paternalism of the Indian Act, which equated citizenship with disavowal of Aboriginal life and assimilation to the 'white' nation.

As we have seen, the sexual regulation of Native women sometimes intersected with that of poor and working-class non-Native women.[7] Both were drawn into the orbit of the Female Refuges Act, for instance, when they were presumed to overstep the boundaries of promiscuity, illegitimacy, or venereal disease. By the 1950s, more Native girls were also subject to the moral and sexual surveillance of the Juvenile Delinquents Act and Training School Act, though this, ironically, emerged from concerted attempts by bureaucrats and social workers to offer

Native girls equal social citizenship – that is, equal rehabilitation akin to poor and working-class girls.[8] The complex process of reforming the underclass and the colonized thus sometimes overlapped, claiming common goals – such as the inculcation of sexual purity and domesticity – and purporting a common familial model of citizenship.[9]

While recognizing intersection and overlap, we also have to acknowledge significant differences based on race and colonialism. Those differences are highlighted here, with particular emphasis on those women subject to the Indian Act. Attempts to remake First Nations sexual codes in a Euro-Canadian mould had long predated the twentieth century, but they assumed new legal and political dimensions over time. They were sometimes direct and coercive; they were also subtle, indirect, and ideological in nature, seeking to reshape the consciousness, conscience, and subjectivity of Native peoples. As the 'cutting edge of colonialism,'[10] the law was one crucial site of sexual regulation. While recognizing the many semi-autonomous spheres of formal and informal regulation-such as the overlapping assimilative projects of the missions and schools-the power associated with the Criminal Code and the Indian Act cannot be ignored.

Certainly, the 'normalizing power' of the law was never absolute, for the 'disciplinary project'[11] of colonialism was fraught with ambiguity, as indigenous peoples ignored, inverted, or attempted to manoeuvre within new, imposed forms of legal governance. Lingering systems of 'illegalities' – that is, non-observance, resistance, rejections of Canadian law, and alternative means of conflict resolution – existed in the cultures of Native peoples, but the power of new 'legalities'[12] imposed by the state and its apparatus was, by the twentieth century, more difficult to evade. After more than a century of physical encroachment and cultural belittling, Native peoples could be drawn into acceptance of some aspects of Euro-Canadian law. By erecting the boundaries of debate and shaping the definitions of crime and immorality, Euro-Canadian practices of justice gained some ground and were constructed upon existing social practices and forms of authority in Native cultures.

This complex process was experienced differently by Aboriginal women and men. For example, both Native women and men were subjects of an ongoing Euro-Canadian project to transform the Aboriginal family, an enterprise that implicitly challenged existing gender and sexual relations, portraying Native conventions as less civilized than white/Anglo ones. However, Native women were also perceived through a Euro-Canadian lens as 'wild women' symbolizing sexual excess, temptation, and conquest,[13] and thus they became the particular focus of white, masculine concerns about sexual control. Attempts to encourage conformity to a middle-class Euro-Canadian ideal, to re-structure the moral conscience of Aboriginal women, were thus shaped by the race and class relations of colonialism and simultaneously by related patriarchal images of sexual purity.

Colonialism, Customary Law, and Canadian Law

In twentieth-century Ontario, colonialism – that is, 'geographical incur-sion, external political control, social dislocation and the ideological denigration based on race'[14] – remained the defining characteristic of Native/non-Native relations. While colonialism has many faces, its dynamic often includes attempts to redefine the sexual codes and fam-ily relations of indigenous populations. Since the path-breaking writing of Franz Fanon, modern writers have wrestled with the oppressive yet contradictory sexual dynamics of colonial relations, exploring coloniz-ers' attempts to alter kin and productive relations through sexual con-trol, and also the more controversial cultural, psychological internalized anxieties and fantasies shaping sexual practices and desire in colonial encounters.[15]

...

In more recent, Foucauldian-inspired, explorations of colonialism, sex plays a ... prominent, if not dominating, role. Drawing on Foucault, though challenging his Eurocentrism, Ann Stoler argues that Foucault's European 'bourgeois sexual order' was constructed first in colonial contexts and that the racialization of sex central to colonial endeavours was imported back to Europe, redrawing European discourses on sexu-ality – a theme promoted also in Anne McClintock's culturalist inter-pretation of colonialism.[16] Stoler's exploration of Foucault, sex, and colonialism argues convincingly for new attention to the centrality of race to modern 'biopower,' including attempts to manage certain popu-lations deemed sexually 'deviant.'[17] Indeed, eugenic fears pinpointed by Foucault in his discussion of sexual regulation were inextricably connected to fears of intermixed, interracial colonial 'blood.' Stoler also highlights the way in which colonialism came to represent a contested cultural terrain of sexual order/disorder, which was reflected in the power struggles between the colonizers and the colonized and some-times within those groups as well.

Such reinterpretations of Foucault, in which race is integrated with his explorations of the discursive construction of sexuality and the creation of sexual subjectivities through power relations, have offered new angles of interpretation for sexual regulation and colonialism. Many, however, rest on historical evidence drawn from white minority colonial possessions (unlike the Canadian example), and we should be wary of the theoretical homogenization of all colonial societies over time. In addition, despite claims that sexual discourses and political economy are both addressed,[18] as is resistance, some of this scholarship remains ensnared within the cultural meanings of colonialism and the construction of the 'bourgeois' sexual self, 'ignoring the human agency [especially that of the colonized] within the structural processes' of colonialism.[19]

Related theoretical issues characterize debates concerning customary law.[20] The sexual regulation of Native women must be contextualized not only with attention to the broad picture of race and colonialism, but also with regard for the more precise, evolving relationship between Native custom, customary Native law, and Euro-Canadian law in Canadian history. Over the past two decades, Native peoples have embarked on the retrieval of customary practices of law and justice, sometimes encouraged by federal and provincial governments, that was prodded both by First Nations' demands for self-government and by an awareness that the criminal justice system has resolutely failed Aboriginal peoples, as victims and as defendants.[21] These efforts have encountered difficult questions: how does one historicize customary law, exploring its evolution over time, its relationship to power, domination, and resistance, its changing ideological purposes? How can one avoid 'freeze-framing' culture, extracting it from its material and historical moorings, and also avert its reinscription in new forms that disadvantage less powerful members of the Native community?

How can we discover, to begin with, how the sexual codes of conduct/misconduct in First Nations cultures changed over time, especially when Aboriginal cultures varied across Canada, and when many of the sources used to uncover past practices, including accounts by colonizers and anthropologists, are partial and invested with ideology, if not themselves entangled in colonialism? Oral tradition and testimony, often reflecting the fluid, social, pedagogical nature of Aboriginal law, may be used, but they are far more likely to be denigrated by Canadian courts, with their Eurocentric bias as to what is considered a valid historical source.[22]

Moreover, looking to Euro-Canadian courts to decide customary law has its own ironies and dangers, especially for women, as these courts have sometimes interpreted First Nations customs through the lens of patriarchal ideology and racial bias, for example, excusing violence against Native women as 'more natural' in Aboriginal cultures.[23] As Jo-Anne Fiske argues, having Canadian courts 'fix' a definition of Aboriginal customary law, especially if women are marginalized in this debate, may work against the interests of Native women.[24] Other national histories carry many warnings of the sexist and patriarchal misuse of customary law against indigenous women by European/white courts.[25] For Native peoples, in other words, customary law is currently an important 'political resource,'[26] an integral part of identity creation that has potential for decolonization, but also for divisiveness.

The dominant theme in many current accounts of Aboriginal customary law is the cultural dissonance between European and Aboriginal concepts of social order and dispute resolution.[27] Aboriginal law is described as process-oriented, rather than concentrating on rules and rights; the means of social control in Native cultures apparently included shaming or ostracism, at worst banishment, though mediation, reconciliation, and payment of compensation were also used to restore peace after a transgression of the social order. The important goal was community harmony, not punishment of the offender. Individual autonomy was protected, as well as community peace, with the established order a fine balance between the two. The teaching and control of elders were crucial to social order, and those lessons were gender-specific, as women's and men's roles were distinct, though a symmetry of equality is also implied. Indeed, some recent accounts, stressing the 'matriarchal' nature of some Native cultures, in which 'women were considered and treated as equal, respected, revered as lifegivers,'[28] suggest the ideological influence of a highly politicized 'maternalist' discourse within the contemporary Native women's movement.[29]

While the evidence showing some cultural divergence between Aboriginal and Euro-Canadian justice is indisputable, such accounts also risk reifying law in the realm of culture. Historical eras and changing social circumstances are conflated and tradition is presented as unmediated, creating a static, essentialized, and homogenized description of Aboriginal law. More historicized explorations of First Nations conflicts with Euro-Canadian law suggest that cultural dissonance was not the overriding theme in all periods or for all crimes.[30] Indeed, Native cultural survival went hand in hand with changing legal practices and political ideologies. Historians of colonial law in other countries have long argued that customary law is a process, in which custom is altered by indigenous/European colonial contact, by ongoing material and social crises, and by changing productive and kin relations. Most importantly, it is shaped by the relations of power and hegemony endemic to colonialism, including contests for power within indigenous groups.[31]

Establishing what constitutes 'tradition' is inherently ideological: this expert knowledge creates new hegemonic interpretations of society that can be used or abused by those exercising power. Any new 'inventions of tradition,' argue some committed to Aboriginal forms of justice, must be carefully scrutinized for their impact on existing gender or age power imbalances. The counsel of Patricia Monture-Angus, that Aboriginal justice is best seen as a 'process not a concept,' is well taken.[32] If we see customary law as historically constructed, framed by colonialism, shaped by material, social practices, a fluid cultural product embodying both domination and resistance, we can better understand Native women's encounters with Euro-Canadian laws governing sexual morality in the twentieth century and their attempts to accept, resist, or negotiate with them.

Managing Sex through Regulation of the Family

Attempts to regulate sexual and kin relations in order to assimilate, convert, or subjugate First Nations peoples have been noted in Canadian research on early contact and the fur trade, in discussions of Christianization and residential schools, and in explorations of state and mission attempts to reorder the domestic sphere of women on reserves.[33] As Karen Anderson has argued, this involved both direct coercion and the indirect 'colonization of the soul,' with the colonized literally coming to discipline themselves.[34] Feminist writers have often gravitated toward the early history of egalitarian Native societies, exploring the decline in women's status and the assault on women's sexual autonomy occasioned by colonialism, although recent research suggests the story is more varied and more complicated than a simple linear decline over time.[35] Nowhere is the example of reordering of kin relations more blatant than in the Indian Act, designed to create a patriarchal family unit in First Nations societies that already had a variety of kinship systems, including many matrilineal and matrilocal ones.[36]

...

The effect of Christianization was also a factor shaping Native culture. Despite the initial resistance of many communities to conversion, by the early twentieth century Christian imperialism had made deep inroads into Native societies.[37] Both Catholic and Protestant missionaries stressed the evils of premarital and extramarital sex and the damnation of those who abandoned monogamy and marriage, proclaiming this message from the pulpit and in the classroom. Residential schools also tried to inculcate sexual morals, stressing virginity before marriage, sexual purity, domesticity, and motherhood for girls.

Church and state efforts were directed by a deep-seated paternalism and a racist conviction that acculturation to Euro-Canadian values would benefit Native peoples. Similar premises shaped the Indian Act, though the precise contours of state assimilation changed over time, and as early as the 1920s assimilation was seen as almost infeasible by some bureaucrats. Admittedly, the Indian Act was contradictory, offering assimilation through segregation, advancing cultural denigration, but also creating a focus for Indian identity; it was also variously applied, ignored, or modified in different regions and by local Indian agents. As a study of two Ontario agencies also shows, Aboriginal peoples tried to subvert or manoeuvre around parts of the Act they found unacceptable.[38] However, its assimilative intent and its potential power to control Native peoples' lives cannot be denied. For example, Indian agents could act as justices of the peace or magistrates, prosecuting, trying, and convicting reserve inhabitants for infractions of the Act and the Criminal Code, a concentration of power quite unparalleled in Canadian law.

The agent's duty to monitor and record marriages and legitimate births was also mandated by the Indian Act (and was necessary to secure official Indian status). Federal Indian policy over the years also gave him a more general goal: to encourage Native families to assimilate to the image of the middle-class Anglo/white family. Marriage, adultery, sexual activity, and illegitimacy were all linked in the view of Indian Affairs; the surveillance of 'proper' marriages should theoretically police illegitimate births and also control the problem of adultery and sexual immorality. Both parsimonious motives and Christian moralism shaped the department's policies regulating the family. While the federal government clearly wished to limit those 'legitimate' status Indians eligible for treaty support, sexual control was also central to their overall policy of cultural assimilation, for monogamous, lifelong unions were seen as signs of sexual order / civilization, while deviations from this model were a sign that Native peoples remained attached to sexual disorder / primitive endurance.

The regulation of marriage was the first line of defence for the federal Department of Indian Affairs in its quest for sexual order. From the late nineteenth century on, Indian Affairs bureaucrats had to be continually reminded by the Department of Justice of the Connolly v. Woolwich case, which had accepted Native customary marriage as valid in 1867. While contemporary legal writers have cited this case as evidence of respect for customary law, the story is more complex. Customary unions were accepted because they were deemed similar to (the superior form of) Christian marriages, not out of respect for Native practice; the measuring stick of exclusive sexual coupling, monogamy, and a lifelong union led to court approval. As Department of Justice officials reminded Indian Affairs, customary unions were *only* legal 'where they were voluntary unions for life to the exclusion of all others, where there is cohabitation and normal marital duties.'[39] Euro-Canadian values remained dominant, setting out the boundaries of which sexual relations were 'normal' and 'legal.'

Also, there was an underlying ambivalence expressed by the Indian Affairs bureaucracy with this legal decision, and as a result there was debate over which forms of marriage should take precedence. Policy on Indian marriage was laid out in circulars by 1899 and was revisited regularly after the 1920s, particularly when the Second World War sparked debates about which Native soldiers' dependants were legitimate and could receive dependants' benefits.[40] However, the responses of agents to policy directives indicate that some viewed customary marriage suspiciously, as less genuine in commitment than Christian marriage. Agents, for example, worried that customary marriage would lead to 'barter in women' and 'desertion.'[41] Officials in Ottawa also thought more stringent legislation was needed, so that 'there could not be any loopholes for avoiding mutual marital obligations ... marriages must be mutual and exclusive unions.'[42] Jail and hard labour for six months was the solution proposed by one Indian agent for husbands who deserted. Such harsh treatment was presumably to correct people less socialized to Euro-Canadian ways. If they leave any marriage, said the Kenora agent in the 1920s, 'the parties should be punished, to teach the rest of the band they cannot act in this manner without being punished.'[43]

...

The suspicion expressed by the department and its agents that Natives treated marriage too cavalierly did not disappear easily. Indeed, waves of panic came and went over this entire period. 'Promiscuous and irregular cohabitation is increasing,' wrote one agent in 1944; marriage is seen as 'trivial,' just 'loose cohabitation.'[44] The basic reason for such attitudes, according to a western agent during the Second World War, was that 'Indians, [though they were] like the Irish in the way they make a living ... lacked moral fibre and religious conviction the white races had developed. Perhaps we expect too much of them,' he concluded, characterizing their customary marriages as 'not spiritual unions.'[45]

...

Punishment could be even more draconian than financial penalties: if unmarried partners lived together, charges of immorality were brought forward under the Indian Act and jail terms could result. This was especially true in the interwar period. In northern Ontario, 'Mary P, a treaty Lac Seul,' was brought before Agent Edwards and admitted to 'living as a wife, when she is not married.' Because she was ill, she did not serve her jail sentence, but her male partner did get one month in jail – a strong reminder that such discipline could be levied against men as well.[46] Another woman in the same agency also tried the route of pleading guilty 'to living with John S' to her RCMP inquisitors, but mercy was not the result. She was remanded and 'taken into Kenora' with her '2½ year old child, not yet weaned,' presumably to serve her sentence.[47]

Agents might also use their power to define who had the right to live on the reserve in order to break up illicit relationships. If one partner was not a status member of the band, he or she could be banished from the reserve. In one report of 1943, an agent who was 'asked to come and settle troubles' by the chief of one reserve mediated complicated charges of adultery and counter-adultery. When Nancy, an orphan from another reserve, finally admitted to her affair with a married man, the agent told her to 'stop the lies' or they would 'throw her off the reserve.'[48]

By the 1940s there is less evidence of jail terms for common-law relations – though some jail sentences were meted out for immorality. The department, noted Kenora agent Edwards, finally rescinded its earlier advice; regulations advocating the 'prosecuting of immorality,' he noted, 'had sent some to jail, then they were cancelled because we found we did not have the right to imprison treaty Indians for things [living common law] that others [whites] could legally do.'[49] As with other Indian Affairs policies, implementation of directives on marriage was uneven. Some agents decried and others defended customary marriage, though even those who defended the practice only did so if the relationships were lifelong. Edwards, a northern agent in the field for many years, eventually tried to tell Ottawa that 'immorality ... resulted from discouragement of customary marriage,' and he urged Ottawa to pass legislation giving 'Agents the power to marry people' (as in some Western provinces) because it was both financially and logistically impossible for Natives to go into urban centres, wait the three days required for licences, or find ministers to marry them.

Other agents were upset with the churches for complicating the issue by refusing to recognize customary marriage. One agent was furious with a Roman Catholic priest who married a man to a second wife, even though he had already been in a customary union for almost twenty years. The agent was concerned that the first wife and child would not receive financial support, but he was also irate that the Catholic Church was promoting the message that customary marriages could be easily dissolved. The wife was far more practical and less moralistic, indicating that the man should do as he wished, as long as she and their child were 'provided for.'[50]

Despite these variances, however, an underlying thread was apparent. Customary marriages were applauded if they looked exactly like Christian ones, if they were lifelong and monogamous, if husbands undertook their roles as providers, wives their roles as domestic caregivers. In the eyes of most agents, customary marriages might positively act as 'bulwarks against the raw passions and promiscuity'[51] of the Natives. Christian and 'legal' marriages were still better because they represented a more thorough internalization of prohibitions against extramarital sex and serial partners. Similar attitudes concerning common-law marriages characterized the moral regulation directed at non-Native poor and working-class women as well. Common-law unions were feared to be less binding and serious, and in the 1930s the Canadian Welfare Council (CWC) pressured the state to ensure legal mechanisms so that children could be removed from households tainted by adulterous 'immorality.' While the goal of encouraging sexually respectable families may have overlapped, the means of enforcement were distinct: the Indian Act offered the state and its agents more arbitrary, paternalist means of enforcing morality (whether they were successful or not), at least on reserves. On the other hand, the CWC never secured the prohibitions against adulterous and 'immoral' parents that it sought, in part because the judiciary was unsympathetic to such sweeping powers.[52]

Finally, it is revealing that only half of Native custom was embraced;

divorces, which had also been part of many Native cultures, were forbidden. This created enormous problems for those wanting to sever customary marriages, since they had no option of doing so as tradition had allowed, and if they did create a new union they could be charged with bigamy. Of the Native women sent to the Mercer Reformatory on bigamy charges during these years, one may well have been punished for such actions.[53] Ottawa was unequivocal when responding to one agent, who asked what to do when a woman left a 'husband who abused her,' escaped to a large city, and married another man. 'Use the provincial authorities and the Criminal Code,' the Department of Indian Affairs replied. 'Indian marriages are legal and binding and the guilty party should be punished.'[54]

Many Native women and men, especially in more remote areas, continued to practise and defend customary marriages, defining them as the courts originally did, as lifelong exclusive unions. They expressed regret and dismay if others abandoned the commitment made to these marriages. In one instance, a mother wanted the agent to intervene to help her daughter, who had been 'promised' in such a union, was pregnant, and had just found out that the father refused to marry her and was with another woman. 'Please help me with the law,' she pleaded.[55] In other situations, band councillors tried to impress on young people the importance of marriage, customary or Christian, and prohibitions against sex before marriage. One band sent a resolution to Ottawa, via their agent, asking for the power to enact the following rule on the reserve: 'young people are not to run after each other unless they want to marry.'[56]

In one long exchange over the marriage question, a slightly different view came from the Six Nations Reserve during the Second World War. Longhouse men, reported the agent, were 'incensed' when it was implied that their customary marriages were 'common-law' marriages. They took this as a great insult, presumably because the term 'common law' impugned their customary marriages as examples of immorality. The exchange would seem to suggest, at some level, internalization of the view that such common-law unions were immoral.[57]

The primary challenge from reserve inhabitants to the imposition of Euro-Canadian laws centred on the notion that marriage must be lifelong. Some used a variety of forms of marriage to move from one partner to the next, a practice facilitated by the hierarchy of marriages (some being perceived as more 'legal' than others) set out by the church and some agents. For example, they married in a church or civil ceremony the second time, claiming the first marriage was customary and did not count, using the Euro-Canadian denigration of customary unions as a rationale, almost as a form of informal divorce. They also reversed the strategy, going from church to customary marriage, in both cases, always infuriating the agent by subverting the law with its own murkiness. Their actions indicated the continuing non-observance of the Euro-Canadian ideal and ongoing 'illegalities' within Native cultures, as well as the desire within Native cultures to shape their own practices with regard to sexual and domestic relationships.

Sexual Immorality

If couples were able to support themselves and their children, leaving no one destitute, serial monogamy might be reluctantly accepted. The agents' disciplinary ire, however, was often focused on a more 'extreme' problem: promiscuity. Indeed, the fact that the Indian Affairs filing system designated a whole category for 'Immorality on the Reserves,' with almost all the complaints centring on sexual misbehaviour, indicates the importance of the agent's role as custodian of sexual morality. And the resulting persecutions and prosecutions reveal, most strikingly, the contradictory nature of sexual regulation on Native reserves.

Some of the cases of immorality that the agent pursued were classified as adultery; clearly, the policing of marriage and the prevention of promiscuity (or 'profligacy,' the word used in the Indian Act) were closely intertwined goals for the agent and for some prosecuting magistrates. The agent might act on his own accord or in concert with others on the reserve. Agents, of course, sometimes claimed to be paternal protectors of Indian women, especially young women, against 'lewd' white men or Indians ready to 'exploit' them.[58] In one such case in the 1950s, an agent wrote to a white railwayman in northern Ontario: 'It is [sic] been brought to my attention that you are spending a good deal of time with Mrs. X, before the death of her husband [and] after. Your time is obviously spent drinking and carrying on ... If brought to my attention again, I will ask the OPP to investigate with a view to arranging a charge against you and Mrs. X.'[59]

While the Indian agent might initiate legal proceedings against immorality, he might also be prodded to act by the band council or chief when they suspected crimes such as incest and sexual assault or, more often, when they objected to sexual immorality. The witnesses against one woman accused of 'profligacy' under section 101 of the Indian Act in 1933 were the chief and four councillors from her reserve. The RCMP and agent simply concurred that she 'had been carrying on in an immoral manner,' and she received one month in the Kenora jail.[60] The case of Emma, which opened this article, was also typical. Band councillors and reserve residents took up petitions, went to the agent or other authority figures such as the school principal with their complaints, and demanded action. As Robin Brownlie concludes succinctly about two Ojibwa Georgian Bay reserves in the interwar period, 'a woman charged with immorality had more to fear from neighbours and clerics than [from] the Indian Agent.'[61]

In another instance, a band councillor complained to a bureaucrat in Ottawa that the agent was ineffectual when it came to policing sexual immorality. He pointed out that the agent should have used treaty time (the once-a-year treaty payments) and other economic sanctions to punish these people. His letter is worth quoting at length as it sets out the complicated nature of these complaints, which reveal dissension within the community:

> I have just got back from X Reserve and found out that Joe A [and] widow Mary (Simon's wife) are going together although they have been told many times not to. Councillor Stephen found them sleeping together. Also that Will L has run away with Jane, wife of Pierre. Here, at M, Charly P, single, lives with the wife of WK. I have told the Indian Agent and nothing is done. If the first [couple] were punished we would not have the subsequent 3 couples living this way. I am a councillor and have all the Indians with me who revoke these misconducts ... Please keep order among the Indians for if this continues there will be murdering done by these husbands who are losing their legitimate wives. The Indians are disgusted with these 3 couples. The Indian Agent just tells them to be good and they only laugh and say they don't care. I tried to part Charly P and WK's wife but Charly took a big flashlight and threw it at my eye.[62]

The agent was called on the carpet by Ottawa and, indignant at the charge that he was ignoring immorality, suggested that the government make customary marriages easier and more binding.

...

Councils and chiefs, of course, were not autonomous from the agent's authority; they were often kept in a state of tutelage or were chosen for their acquiescent posture to the government. Their participation in sexual and marital regulation must be seen in this light. In some cases, it was also the result of their ties to Christian missions. But individuals often called on the agent to intervene as well, to bring home relatives who had abandoned marriages and gone astray, to correct immoral behaviour of daughters and wives. 'I need help from you,' wrote one grandmother to an agent, 'about my daughter, X, I don't like what I hear. My sister-in-law was in to visit me a while ago. It is awful what my daughter is doing. When a car goes through the reserve, she just jumps in and leaves her boys alone ... I don't want her to fool around and go to town ... please give her a good talking to.'[63] Another mother told the agent that she would accept her daughter's committal to a Toronto training school 'until she is of an age when she is able to work ... I'd like her to be there for her own good, and before she gets deeper into trouble.'[64]

Some band councils also took a dim view of women's illegitimate offspring, passing resolutions that 'no illegitimate children be adopted into the band.'[65] And the department periodically reminded agents never to register any illegitimate children, in part (like the bands) for financial reasons, but also because Indian Affairs claimed this would 'place a premium on immorality.'[66] Again, financial penalties were one way of chastising such mothers and warning others. After Mother's Allowances were made available to Ontario Native women, the monthly allotment was administered through the agent, who substituted as the province's moral investigator, cutting off the allowance if a woman had an illegitimate child.

Whatever band councils said, some families still welcomed and cared for illegitimate children and even tried to secure their status. Occasionally, too, chiefs and even agents 'intervened to plead for'[67] women with illegitimate children, asking that they be returned to the reserve and aided by the community. However, strains of negative moralism existed and, indeed, increased over time. Those families and communities who expressed reservations about taking in illegitimate children may have been influenced by the churches' moral lectures, but the reality of increasingly scarce resources on reserves was probably also crucial.[68] By the 1950s, Indian Affairs faced a new problem with illegitimacy: how to respond to Native women who now refused to have illegitimate children registered with the band because they were 'ashamed' of them. A social worker tried to get a stubborn Indian Affairs bureaucracy to change the policy, allowing women choice on this question. She noted that a Native woman she was advocating for 'was ashamed of her pregnancy ... and fears condemnation if her parents and community know [and] this is not an isolated case.'[69]

The Long Arm of Racism

Charges of immorality levelled against women on reserves might also lead to an appearance before a magistrate and a jail or reformatory sentence. In the early 1940s a young Native woman from southern Ontario was brought before the court by the Indian agent and local RCMP for drinking and 'dissolute' sexual behaviour and was subsequently sentenced under the Female Refuges Act to a term in the Mercer Reformatory. Though she listed her occupation as a 'domestic' who was looking after her father, the RCMP officer testified that 'she is transient, has no work,' and had been convicted on many alcohol charges, including 'brawling with white men.' While incarceration might be couched in paternalist rhetoric, the image of these women was undoubtedly racist. 'Have you been in the habit of getting drunk, have you? have you?' intoned the magistrate. 'I hope that by removing you, my girl, from unscrupulous white men and Indian soldiers you will start a new life. It is too bad that such a good looking Indian like you should throw yourself away,' he concluded condescendingly.[70]

...

The number of Native women incarcerated under the Female Refuges Act increased in the 1940s and 1950s, and Indian agents could play a central role in the sentencing process. One twenty-three-year-old woman living on a reserve was first incarcerated under the vagrancy statute, though the court was told she had also been charged with intoxication and 'was acting as a prostitute' near the reserve. The agent's report pronounced her a 'troublemaker on the Reserve' with a 'violent temper and [using] foul language,' though he added that a 'large portion of blame' for her situation was the fact she had 'no proper home to go to.' Three years later, she was incarcerated in the Mercer for the third time, now under the Female Refuges Act; although concerns with her 'dissolute' behaviour remained the same, her sentence was longer. The Indian agent now recommended parole to a sister in Toronto instead of returning her to the corrupting influence of her home on the reserve.[71]

...

While many of these convictions were for women who came from reserves, the long arm of the law also touched women far from the authority of the Indian agent. Linda, only seventeen, was convicted under the Female Refuges Act in the 1920s when she was 'living with a man not her husband.' She was found sleeping on a railway platform with him and was reported to have been travelling around the country, and was subsequently incarcerated.[72] To some extent, the sexual regulation of women like Linda resembled that imposed on non-Native women over this period. Many shared previous experiences of impoverishment, addiction, ill health, violence, and family dissolution. Some had also been in state care. Many were indicted by the 'immorality' or criminal records of their families. 'Her family history is a bad one,' noted a sentencing report for a Native woman that could easily have been written for countless inmates; 'her father is living with a woman not his wife and ... her mother is possibly worse than her, and certainly partly at fault for her behaviour.'[73]

However, the treatment of Native women differed in one important regard: the courts were influenced by racial stereotypes of Aboriginal women as weaker in moral outlook and more sexually promiscuous. Once incarcerated, they were often perceived to be less likely candidates for rehabilitation.[74] Also, Native women might become the disciplinary focus of fears concerning interracial sex. Even if anxieties concerning miscegenation were far less intense than in the nineteenth century, they could still be a factor in Native women's incarceration. As Jean Barman argues, the ideological outcome of a century of colonial efforts to 'tame' Native women's sexuality was the heightened 'sexualization' of all aspects of their lives, making them the inevitable target of legal and social regulation by the twentieth century.[75]

The issue of interracial sex was raised, for instance, in the case of an eighteen-year-old dishwasher, Anna, sent to the Mercer in 1942 from a northern city. Her trial also showed how, even when Native women moved to the city, the Indian agent from their 'home' reserve might be called in to testify against them. Anna's agent claimed she had appeared before him on the reserve three times for intoxication, and he had used the Indian Act to 'fine and warn' her. He further added that 'a doctor had informed him' Anna was now pregnant. The police chief also offered second-hand gossip: 'we hear she is in the family way ... Other stories that we hear around town are that she is drinking all the time ... [It is] not hard to believe [that] she is going into men's rooms.' The police constable who followed her, however, was very specific about whom she had sex with: '[I] noticed her a regular at the train station with white boys ... I've seen her in cafes with white boys, coming in and out.'[76] The magistrate was critical of the 'hearsay' evidence offered against Anna, but not critical enough: she was sent to the Mercer for eighteen months.

...

Tragically, incarceration for sexual immorality could simply become the first step in women's future conflicts with the law. One young woman, first convicted off the reserve for sexual immorality and sleeping with white men, later returned to the reformatory again and again, on charges of intoxication as well as sexual immorality and 'idleness,' a synonym in her case for increasing poverty, addiction, and destitution.[77] And tragically, women might also blame themselves, encouraged to admit their 'guilt' because of the potency of dominant definitions of morality. 'The surroundings' in the training school, wrote one young woman to her agent, 'will help me to better myself into the kind of girl my town would want me to be.'[78]

Indeed, the records of Native women who were imprisoned in the provincial reformatory, as well as of those sent to the training school, reveal families and communities themselves condemnatory of immoral sexual behaviour. Not only could Native relatives and communities play a role in turning a woman over to the police, but sometimes they also asked that a woman not get parole or at least not return to the reserve. 'She has been refused care by her own community,' it was noted of one imprisoned woman accused of immorality and prostitution. 'Her sister does not want anything to do with her, as she sends men over there and her sister says she does not want to live this kind of life.'[79]

Some families, however, were still less interested in debating or contradicting the designation 'immoral' for these women and more concerned with trying to secure sympathy or mercy for their relatives. Explaining her sister's downward spiral with alcohol and subsequent incarceration for immorality, a Native woman remarked to the authorities: 'her problems started after her first [illegitimate] child was born [because then] she had no self respect.'[80] Families thus tried to place the charge of immorality in the context of a woman's deprivation, alcoholism, or family dissolution. One sister, for example, wrote to the prison, pointing out that her sister was abused as a child, then was not allowed to marry the man she wished, as an explanation for her behaviour. However, it is revealing that direct denial of charges of sexual immorality came less frequently than rejection of the legitimacy of other convictions, such as those for alcohol infractions, indicating that, at some level, a colonialist project of 'colonizing' the sexual soul had been successful.

Colonizing the Soul

How then do we explain this process of sexual regulation, aimed at all Native peoples but more bluntly at women? First, the inordinate disciplinary power invested in the Indian Act and also the agent must be acknowledged. His job was to survey his subjects, to 'normalize' certain behaviours through a system of punishments and rewards, lectures, and advice.[81] Indian agents, as Robin Brownlie points out, were intermediaries with white society and the state, acting as both social workers and arbitrary, paternal rulers over people considered childlike. It was precisely the agent's combination of roles, encompassing necessity, aid, and repression, that solidified his power.[82] Though agents' aspirations to enforce sexual and marital morality varied from one community to another – as did their successes – knowledge of the agent's far-reaching potential to discipline, abetted by missions and schools, should not be ignored. Moreover, the Indian Act's patriarchal provisions concerning treaty rights, stipulating women's loss of status if they 'married out' (a provision finally removed from the Act in 1985), made women especially economically vulnerable to the agent's control.

Denied aid on reserves or simply searching out new lives, Aboriginal women might join the increasing numbers of First Nations people moving to urban centres. Even if they could escape the agent's purview – as Anna could not – they could not avoid the widespread racialized and gendered view of Aboriginal women. The long-standing European view of Aboriginal women in a 'dialectic of denigration and desire,'[83] as sexually licentious and in need of 'conquest,' meant they were the special mark of regulation by police and the courts.

The power of the law, of course, was tempered by women's attempts to elude or evade it, and on reserves by the outright rejection, at least by a minority, of the agent's moral authority. These people persisted in creating their own 'illegalities,' leaving marriages, changing sexual partners, ignoring pronouncements about illegitimate children. Others resisted the incursion of outside welfare and penal experts into community life. When a young woman who had been incarcerated in the Ontario Training School for Girls (OTSG) was released on parole, she returned to her reserve and became pregnant by the son of her neighbour. The placement officer sent out to retrieve her for reincarceration (as was the policy) was confronted by adamant relatives of the boy, who insisted that they would adopt the child, that the girl was not ready to settle down and marry yet, and that she should not be returned to the OTSG. We will 'settle things our own way,' they argued, 'in the long house tradition; we will do what is right.' In a rare recognition that they might be right, the officer left the families to work out a solution.

Significantly, though, this case was unusual. Moreover, it may be a mistake simply to equate Native communities' rejection of some Euro-Canadian laws with their embrace of Native custom; the story is more complex. Recognition of the changing nature of colonialism and its particular character in this later era of 'advanced colonialism' is important. Early contact accounts of some First Nations often stress women's sexual autonomy, the ability to divorce, and fewer prohibitions against non-marital sex. However, by the late nineteenth century, life histories and ethnographies emphasize lifelong marriages and premarital chastity as the ideal evidence of Christian missionary successes.[84] Even the Iroquois 'traditionalists,' notes one author, 'stressed marital fidelity' as a shared community value.[85] Descriptions of Ojibwa and Cree communities in the early twentieth century emphasized the importance of marriage as a cement to kin relations and community harmony, as a cooperative partnership in the battle for survival.[86] Few such accounts discuss sexual relations, though elders from a number of Native language groups referred to the existence of sexual taboos, prohibitions on extramarital sex, and the monitoring of such activity by the community, by elders, or (in some cultures) by shamans – a Foucauldian form of discipline, though certainly one distinct from that of the colonizers.[87]

By the mid-twentieth century, communities might be aware of the negative impact of Christian morals, but they were still deeply influenced by them. Edward Rogers, an anthropologist who worked for years with Ojibwa people in northern Ontario, noted in the 1950s that 'chastity and adultery, for *men* previously of little concern, now due to Christianity, are condemned. However, the Chief cannot command obedience to the "new ways" ... He wanted to intervene with a married woman having an affair, but the relatives said no.'[88] Traditional and Euro-Canadian/Christian morality overlapped as 'conflicting systems,' he argued, but the latter could be overwhelmed by the former. Previously, for example, 'there was little concern if a girl was pregnant. They simply asked the father to marry or support the child ... But the Christian taboo on premarital sex and the knowledge that pregnant girls will be hurt by European morality have led to recent concern with teen boys seducing girls.'[89]

In the interwar period some anthropologists went further, suggesting the internalization of patriarchal norms, claiming, for instance, there were signs of 'men feeling they have a sexual "right" to women.'[90] A controversial account of Ojibwa women in northern Ontario, Ruth Landes' *Ojibwa Woman*, described a culture in which women were valued less and subject to male violence and sexual control, a view that contradicted other anthropological accounts.[91] As a reinterpretation of Landes' work suggests, however, her own background and the intent of her female informant to relay stories of women's courage and hardship may have allowed Landes to 'hear' stories missed by other observers.[92] If sexual conflict and control existed, continues Sally Cole, this cannot be separated from the 'hard times'[93] increasingly affecting these communities, that is, declining resources, few opportunities for wage labour, and increasing government control.

In such circumstances, frictions were inevitable between older means of community control stressing mediation, reconciliation, and teaching of lessons and newer controls offered by Canadian law and the state. The increasing incursion of the state into Aboriginal communities also provided the possibility of some groups using the agent's power to exert or reassert theirs. As Tina Loo has argued in regard to British Columbia Aboriginals, 'some native peoples brokered the extension of the European state,'[94] drawing on legal powers outside of their traditional communities as possible levers of control within their communities. The hegemony of Canadian law offered the possibility of exerting moral governance over neighbours who were seen to be violating community sexual norms, with these norms an amalgam of Native and European tradition.

...

When the band councillors, as noted in the example opening this article, asked for the imprisonment of Emma to enforce morality, therefore, they were not simply enforcing custom but customary law as they saw it, with the latter already influenced by the lived experience and pressures of colonialism. Their attempt to regulate morality may have overlapped with the traditional power of elders teaching the young; they may have reflected the views of those who had absorbed Christian ideas; they may have represented one group establishing status over another; and they may have also represented the transfer and internalization of patriarchal values so strongly promoted by the colonizers – or all of the above.

Moreover, the community's exercise of moral regulation cannot be separated from the debilitating material effects of colonialism. On Ontario reserves, for example, the social consequences of so-called immorality were perceived to be worsening an already difficult situation: marriage desertion was linked to abandoned children and destitute wives, both real problems in the midst of increasing poverty. Moreover, as with the case of Emma, communities who urged that women be removed to the Mercer Reformatory may well have believed that the reformatory would actually *help* these women, even if we now know that the opposite was true.[95] Finally, it is revealing that a number of cases I have described involved elders monitoring the young. Similarly, one U.S. study of a tribal court argues that the majority of adultery charges were levelled at people under twenty-five: 'the enforcement of white man's morality was taking place in an old way; in effect, an elder was attempting to shape the conduct of his grandchildren.'[96] However, one crucial difference in the Ontario case was that such regulation was aided by outsiders from the Canadian state and that sexual behaviour was becoming more stringently disciplined, and in a more alienating manner. It might also be criminalized, with women removed from their communities to prisons and reformatories, where they were isolated, marginalized, and misunderstood.

Conclusion

The sexual regulation of First Nations women was thus fundamentally shaped by the social construction of 'race' through the law and by the politics of colonialism. Although Native and non-Native women alike were perceived to be pivotal to the broader nation-building project of creating 'moral' citizens and families, their encounters with the law also diverged, in part because Native women confronted a different legal regime and racialized surveillance, in part because Native communities drew on distinct cultural traditions as they grappled with the economic and social stresses of advanced colonialism.

As a 'cutting edge of colonialism,' the law was used as a central instrument of the state's attempts to assimilate Aboriginal peoples and reshape their cultures in a Euro-Canadian and middle-class mould. The Indian Act, government policy, and Indian agents were used to encourage nuclear, monogamous families that did not separate and in which men were protectors and earners, and women were sexually restrained, domestic, and a good moral influence. The Criminal Code, provincial courts, prisons, and reformatories might also be used, as a last resort, to refashion sexual morality and marital and family life. Both direct pressure – from financial penalty to imprisonment – and indirect proselytizing were part of this regulatory process. Indeed, ideological efforts to redefine public morality, to re-represent images of sexual order/disorder, to re-inscribe the sexual subjectivity of Native peoples – to colonize the soul – were critical to this project.[97]

As the cultural values of Native peoples were denigrated, the possibilities of articulating a distinct social-sexual code became more difficult, especially since schools, clerics, and missions often supported the agents. Indeed, the state was never the sole agent of regulation, as other powerful institutions, such as the Protestant and Catholic churches, prescribed influential discourses of sexual and familial moralism. Moreover, state officials, educators, and religious leaders employed existing internal family and community mechanisms of sexual and marital regulation in this process, and, conversely, some Native leaders and community members incorporated the Canadian law and the power of the agent into their attempts to secure community stability and order.

Regulation was never uncontested, complete, or uncomplicated. Clerics might oppose the policies of Indian agents on marriage; agents' own efforts to police morality varied widely; and Native communities and cultures responded with degrees of acceptance, negotiation, or resistance to these efforts. The latter is a critical point: the new legalities articulated by the state always overlapped with some lingering practices of non-observance or 'illegality.' Some Native women and their families rejected the imposed morality, though they could not always escape the consequences of this rejection, which, at worst, meant women's incarceration.

The context of colonialism and the hegemony of patriarchal Euro-Canadian laws thus frame the picture of sexual regulation, even if cultural persistence and individual resistance were part of the inner design. Within First Nations cultures, domination and resistance both existed, but not on equal terms. In colonial contexts, premised upon unequal social power and an ideology of racism, indigenous values were often more fragile, while the hegemony of those controlling legal knowledge was more authoritative.

Subversion of dominant ideologies always remains possible, and recently has become far more probable given the cultural renaissance and political organizing of the First Nations. However, in this ongoing debate over new forms of Aboriginal justice there is a troubling history to contend with: past colonial successes, the domination of Euro-Canadian law, and the overlap of Aboriginal and Euro-Canadian sexual regulation. Even if justice was process- rather than punishment-oriented at one time, by the mid-twentieth century colonialism had created new stresses, inequalities, and repressions within Aboriginal societies. The articulation of customary law and the reinvention of tradition on reserves, argues Carol La Prairie, is now complicated by the 'contemporary political economy of reserves,' faced not only with poverty but by new inequalities based on age and sex, and 'these may be in conflict with attempts to create new, ethically rooted participatory practices' of justice.[98] Attempts to construct new forms of 'popular justice' in post-colonial societies, though laudable, have in the past been jeopardized by the lingering, deeply entrenched legal ideologies of the previous colonial state.[99] Reinventing traditions will thus mean contending with and challenging a colonial past in which women's sexuality was prescribed and regulated, both by the colonizers and later within Native cultures, a process that created the power imbalances that Native women are now struggling to overcome.

NOTES

1 Archives of Ontario (AO), Record Group (RG) 20, Mercer Reformatory Records (hereafter Mercer), file 7057, 1930s.
2 For contemporary analyses of Native women's over-incarceration, see Ontario Advisory Council on Women's Issues, *Native Women and the Law* (Ottawa, 1989); Carol LaPrairie, 'Selected Criminal Justice and Socio-demographic Data on Native Women,' *Canadian Journal of Criminology* 24 (1982): 161–9. For a historical view, see Joan Sangster, 'Criminalizing the Colonized: Ontario Native Women Confront the Criminal Justice System, 1920–1960,' *Canadian Historical Review* 80.1 (March 1999): 32–60.
3 On political 'acculturation,' see Menno Boldt, *Surviving as Indians: The Challenge of Self-Government* (Toronto: University of Toronto Press, 1993), ch. 3.
4 The rhetoric of citizenship was often used by the Training School Advisory Board, as well as by some judges. See also Police Chief Draper, 'The Family Is the Fountain of All Morality for the Nation,' Toronto City Archives, Annual Report of the Chief of Police, 1944. On family, race, and nation, see E. Dua, 'Beyond Diversity: Exploring the Ways in Which the Discourse of Race Has Shaped the Institution of the Nuclear Family,' in *Scratching the Surface: Canadian Anti-Racist Thought*, ed. E. Dua and A. Robertson (Toronto: Women's Press, 1999), 237–60; Himani Bannerji, *The Dark Side of the Nation: Essays on Multiculturalism, Nationalism and Gender* (Toronto: Canadian Scholars Press, 2000), esp. ch. 3.
5 W.S. Tarnopolsky et al., *Discrimination and the Law in Canada*, 5th release (Toronto: Richard De Boo, 1997); J. St G. Walker, *Race, Rights and the Law in the Supreme Court of Canada: Historical Case Studies* (Waterloo, ON: Wilfrid Laurier University Press, 1997); Constance Backhouse, *Colour Coded: A*

Legal History of Racism in Canada, 1900–1950 (Toronto: University of Toronto Press, 1999).

6 This is drawn from Ian F. Haney Lopez, *White by Law: The Legal Construction of Race* (New York: New York University Press, 1996). On critical race theory and feminism, see also Sherene Razack, *Looking White People in the Eye* (Toronto: University of Toronto Press, 1998); Carol Aylward, *Canadian Critical Race Theory: Racism and Law* (Halifax: Fernwood Publishing, 1999); Kimberle Crenshaw, 'Race, Reform and Retrenchment: Transformation and Legitimization in Antidiscrimination Law,' *Harvard Law Review* 101.7 (May 1988): 1331–87.

7 I have been influenced by theories of 'intersectionality,' that is, the need to look at the intersection of class, race, and gender, rather than fixing on a single axis of oppression. See Kimberlé Crenshaw, 'Demarginalizing the Intersection of Race and Class,' *Chicago Legal Forum* (1989): 139–68; Crenshaw, 'Intersectionality, Identity Politics and Violence against Women of Colour,' *Stanford Law Review* 43 (1991): 1241–99; Rose Brewer, 'Theorizing Race, Class and Gender: The New Scholarship of Black Feminist Intellectuals and Black Women's Labour,' in *Theorizing Black Feminisms: The Visionary Pragmatism of Black Women*, ed. Stalie M. James and Abena P.A. Busia (London: Routledge, 1993); Patricia Williams, 'It's All in the Family: Intersections of Gender, Race and Nation,' *Hypatia* 13.3 (1998): 62–82.

8 Joan Sangster, 'She Is Hostile to Our Ways: First Nations Girls Sentenced to the Ontario Training School for Girls, 1933–1960,' in *Law and History Review* 20:1 (Spring 2002): 59–96.

9 The 'primitive and the pauper' were overlapping projects of colonialism and working-class reform, parallel projects for bourgeois reformers intent on reconstructing their home lives by inculcating the values of 'modern domesticity.' See John Comaroff and Jean Comaroff, *Ethnography and the Historical Imagination* (Boulder, CO: Westview Press, 1992), 289.

10 Martin Chanock, *Law, Custom and Social Order: The Colonial Experience in Malawi and Zambia* (Cambridge: Cambridge University Press, 1985), 4.

11 Peter Fitzpatrick, 'Custom as Imperialism,' in *Law, Society and National Identity in Africa*, ed. Jamil M. Abun-Nasr et al. (Hamburg: Helmet Buske Verlag, 1990), 22–3.

12 Michel Foucault, *Discipline and Punish: The Birth of the Prison* (New York: Vintage Books, 1995), 82.

13 Sharon Tiffany and Kathleen Adams, *The Wild Woman: An Inquiry into the Anthropology of an Idea* (Cambridge: Cambridge University Press, 1985).

14 James Frideres, *Native Peoples in Canada* (Scarborough, ON: Prentice Hall, 1983), 295–6.

15 For a review of this literature, see Ann Stoler, 'Making Empire Respectable: The Politics of Race and Sexual Morality in 20th Century Colonial Cultures,' *American Ethnologist* 16.4 (1989): 634–59.

16 Ann Laura Stoler, *Race and the Education of Desire: Foucault's History of Sexuality and the Colonial Order of Things* (Durham, NC: Duke University Press, 1995); Anne McClintock, *Imperial Leather: Race, Gender and Sexuality in the Colonial Contest* (New York: Routledge, 1995).

17 Stoler argues for the addition of 'race' and Europeans' obsession with interracial sex as the fifth of Foucault's 'strategic unities' (i.e., the Malthusian couple, the masturbating child, the perverse adult, and the hysterical woman).

18 Ann Laura Stoler and Frederick Cooper, 'Introduction,' in *Tensions of Empire: Colonial Cultures in a Bourgeois World*, ed. Stoler and Cooper (Berkeley: University of California Press, 1997), 19.

19 Laura Tabili, review of *Imperial Leather*, in *Victorian Studies* 40.3 (1997): 497. For another critical review of this book, see Tamara Jakubowska, *Race and Class* 38.2 (1996): 89–92.

20 Definitions of customary law vary. Martin Chanock's work makes a useful distinction between custom, a set of values and social practices maintaining order in pre-colonial times, and customary law, the product of interaction between missionaries, courts, administrators, and indigenous people in the post-contact period. A general definition is: a set of common practices, traditions, and norms accepted by the community, accompanied by moral pressure or other means of social control to maintain these practices. For definitions in Canada, see Scott Clark, 'Aboriginal Customary Law Literature Review,' paper for Manitoba's Public Inquiry into the Administration of Justice for Aboriginal Peoples, Winnipeg, 1990, 5–9.

21 The revelations of racism exposed by the Donald Marshall, Betty Osborne, and J.J. Harper cases, and subsequent inquiries, hastened this search. See Manitoba, *Report on the Aboriginal Justice Inquiry*, 1991; Nova Scotia, *Royal Commission on the Donald Marshall Prosecution, 1989*: *Equality, Respect (Ministers' Reference Report 34, Oct. 1991)*; Canada, Royal Commission on Aboriginal Peoples, *Aboriginal Peoples and the Justice System*, 1993; Law Reform Commission of Canada, *Report on Aboriginal Peoples and Criminal Justice*. See also Bryan A. Keon-Cohen, 'Native Justice in Australia, Canada and the USA: A Comparative Analysis,' in *Native People and Justice in Canada*, ed. Canadian Legal Aid Bulletin, Part 2 (1982), 187–258. Despite its proximity to the United States, Canada never imitated the establishment of Indian tribal courts. See Bradford Morse, *Indian Tribal Courts in the United States: A Model for Canada?* (Regina: University of Saskatchewan Law

Centre, 1980); Morse, 'Indigenous Law and State Legal Systems: Conflict and Compatibility,' in *Papers of the Symposia on Folk Law and Legal Pluralism*, 11th International Congress on Anthropological and Ethnological Sciences, vol. 1, ed. Harald Finkler (Ottawa, 1983).

22 On oral sources, see Julie Cruikshank, *Life Lived like a Story: Life Stories of Three Yukon Native Elders* (Vancouver: UBC Press, 1990). The classic case of oral traditions being denigrated is *Delgamuukw v. The Queen*. See Dara Culhane, *The Pleasure of the Crown: Anthropology, Law and First Nations* (Burnaby, BC: Talon Books,1998).

23 'There is a white man's law, traditional law and bullshit law. The latter is a distortion of traditional law by the legal system to justify violence against women' (Sharon Payne, 'Aboriginal Women and the Law,' in *Aboriginal Perspectives in Criminial Justice*, ed. Chris Cunneen [Sydney: Sydney Institute of Criminology, 1992], 37). For Canada, see Teressa Nahanee, 'Dancing with a Gorilla: Aboriginal Women, Justice and the Charter,' in Royal Commission on Aboriginal Peoples, *Aboriginal Peoples and the Justice System* (Ottawa, 1993), 359–82; Nahanee, 'Sexual Assault of Inuit Females: A Comment on Cultural Bias,' in *Confronting Sexual Assault: A Decade of Legal and Social Change*, ed. Julian Roberts and Renate Mohr (Toronto: University of Toronto Press, 1994), 192–204; Margo Nightingale, 'Judicial Attitudes and Differential Treatment: Native Women in Sexual Assault Cases,' *Ottawa Law Review* 23.2 (1991): 71–98.

24 Jo-Anne Fiske, 'The Supreme Law and the Grand Law,' *BC Studies* 105–6 (1995): 193.

25 Deborah Posel, 'State Power and Gender Conflict over the Registration of Customary Marriages in South Africa, 1910–70,' *Journal of Historical Sociology* 8.3 (1995): 223–56; Robert Gordon, 'The White Man's Burden: Ersatz Customary Law and Internal Pacification in South Africa,' *Journal of Historical Sociology* 2.1 (1989): 41–65.

26 Jo-Anne Fiske, 'From Customary Law to Oral Traditions,' *BC Studies* 115–16 (1997–8): 208.

27 Some of these gloss over differences between Aboriginal cultures; others are more specific. Michael Coyle sees similarities between Iroquois and Ojibwa laws in 'Traditional Indian Justice in Ontario: A Role for the Present?' *Osgoode Hall Law Journal* 24.2 (1986): 607–29. See also Patricia Monture-Angus, *Thunder in My Soul: A Mohawk Woman Speaks* (Halifax: Fernwood, 1995); Rupert Ross, 'Leaving Our White Eyes Behind: The Sentencing of Native Accused,' *Canadian Native Law Reporter* 3 (1989): 1–15; Rupert Ross, *Dancing with a Ghost: Exploring Indian Reality* (Markham, ON: Octopus Publishing, 1992); Rupert Ross, *Returning to the Teachings: Explor-*

ing Aboriginal Justice (Toronto: Penguin Books, 1996); Kjikeptin Alex Denny, 'Beyond the Marshall Inquiry: An Alternative Mi'kmaq Worldview and Justice System,' in *Elusive Justice: Beyond the Marshall Inquiry*, ed. Joy Mannette (Halifax: Fernwood, 1992), 103–8; Russell Smandych and Gloria Lee, 'Women, Colonization and Resistance: Elements of Amerindian Autohistorical Approach to the Study of Law and Colonialism,' *Native Studies Review* 10.1 (1995): 21–46; Marianne Nielsen and Robert A. Silverman, eds, *Aboriginal Peoples and Canadian Criminal Justice* (Boulder, CO: Westview, 1996), 243–58; *Canadian Journal of Criminology*, special issue on Aboriginal crime and justice (July-October 1992).

28 In Native societies, 'all were equal ... irrespective of handicap, age, sex' (Eileen Couchene, 'Aboriginal Women's Perspective of the Justice System in Manitoba,' paper for Manitoba's Public Inquiry into the Administration of Justice for Aboriginal Peoples, Winnipeg, 1990, 18. Though many scholars stress the egalitarian nature of Iroquois and Algonquin societies, few designate these as 'matriarchal' or female-dominated. This also seems to ignore evidence of more 'male-centred' Plains societies. See Laura Peers, *The Ojibwa of Western Canada, 1780–1870* (Winnipeg: University of Manitoba Press, 1994); John Milloy, *The Plains Cree: Trade, Diplomacy and War, 1790–1870* (Winnipeg: University of Manitoba Press, 1988). A recent examination of Dogrib (Dene) customary law points to traditions that include some patterns of male dominance and physical punishment of women – how much these are true 'customs,' how much customary law, is unclear. See Joan Ryan, *Doing Things the Right Way: Dene Traditional Justice in Lac La Martre, NWT* (Calgary: University of Calgary Press, 1995). For a recent overview exploring status in relation to patrilineal, matrilineal, and bilateral societies, see Ramona Ford, 'Native American Women: Changing Statuses, Changing Interpretations,' in *Writing the Range: Race, Class and Culture in the Women's West*, ed. Elizabeth Jameson and Susan Armitage (Norman: University of Oklahoma Press, 1997), 42–69.

29 Jo-Anne Fiske, 'The Womb Is to the Nation as the Heart Is to the Body: Ethnopolitical Discourses of the Canadian Indigenous Women's Movement,' *Studies in Political Economy* 51 (1996): 65–95.

30 Vic Satzewich, '"Where's the Beef?": Cattle Killing, Rations Policy and First Nations "Criminality" in Southern Alberta, 1892–1895,' *Journal of Historical Sociology* 9.2 (1996): 188–212; R.C. Macleod and Heather Rollason, '"Restrain the Lawless Savage": Native Defendants in Criminal Courts of the North West Territories,' *Journal of Historical Sociology* 10.2 (1997): 157–83; Tina Loo, 'Tonto's Due: Law, Culture and Colonization in British Columbia,' in *Essays in the History of Canadian Law: British Columbia and the*

Yukon, ed. H. Foster and J. McLaren (Toronto: Osgoode Society, 1995), 128–70.

31 Chanock, in *Law, Custom and Social Order*, argues that once custom was codified by the colonizers as text, customary law became *less* flexible than custom. See also Gordon Woodman and A.O. Obilade, eds, *African Law and Legal Theory* (New York: Dartmouth, 1995); Emmet Mittlebeeler, *African Custom and Western Law: The Development of Rhodesian Criminal Law for Africans* (New York: Holmes & Meier, 1976); Sally Faulk Moore, *Social Facts and Fabrications: Customary Law on Kilimanjaro, 1880–1980* (Cambridge: Cambridge University Press, 1986); Sally Engle Merry, 'Law and Colonialism,' *Law and Society Review* 25 (1991): 889–922; Douglas Hay and Frances Snyder, eds, *Law, Labour and Crime in Historical Perspective* (London: Tavistock, 1987); Mindie Lazarus-Black, *Legitimate Acts and Illegal Encounters: Law and Society in Antigua and Barbuda* (Washington: Smithsonian Institution Press, 1994).

32 Customary law in Africa was 'the most far reaching invention of tradition' (Terence Ranger, 'The Invention of Tradition in Colonial Africa,' in *The Invention of Tradition*, ed. T. Ranger and E. Hobsbawm [Cambridge: Cambridge University Press, 1983], 250). The invention of tradition may be taken for granted, for the debate concerns its usefulness for the present community, argues E.J. Dickson-Gilmore, in 'Finding the Ways of the Ancestors: Cultural Change and the Invention of Tradition in the Development of Separate Legal Systems,' *Canadian Journal of Criminology* 34.3–4 (July–Oct. 1992): 479–502. See also Monture-Angus, *Thunder in My Soul*, 242.

33 See, for example, Karen Anderson, *Chain Her by One Foot: The Subjugation of Native Women in Seventeenth-Century New France* (New York: Routledge, 1991); Sylvia Van Kirk, *Many Tender Ties: Women in Fur Trade Society* (Winnipeg: Watson & Dwyer, 1979); Jennifer Brown, *Strangers in Blood: Fur Trade Company Families in Indian Country* (Vancouver: UBC Press, 1980); Carol Devens, *Countering Colonization: Native American Women and Great Lakes Missions, 1630–1900* (Berkeley: University of California Press, 1992); Diane Rothenberg, 'The Mothers of the Nation: Seneca Resistance to Quaker Intervention,' in *Women and Colonization: Anthropological Perspectives*, ed. E. Leacock and Mona Etienne (New York, 1980); Carol Cooper, 'Native Women of the Northern Pacific Coast: An Historical Perspective, 1830–1900,' *Journal of Canadian Studies* 27.4 (1992–3): 44–75; Jo-Anne Fiske, 'Colonization and the Decline of Women's Status: The Tsimshian Case,' *Feminist Studies* 17.3 (Fall 1991): 509–36; Sally Roesch Wagner, 'The Iroquois Confederacy: A Native American Model for Non-Sexist Men,' in *Iroquois Women: An Anthology*, ed. W. Spittal (Ohsweken: Iroqrafts, 1990),

217–22; Elizabeth Tooker, 'Women in Iroquois Society,' in Spittal, ed., *Iroquois Women*, 199–216; Patricia Buffalohead, 'Farmers, Warriors, Traders: A Fresh Look at Ojibwa Women,' *Minnesota History* 48 (1983): 236–44. On residential schools, see Assembly of First Nations, *Breaking the Silence: An Interpretive Study of Residential School Impact and Healing as Illustrated by the Stories of First Nations Individuals* (Ottawa, 1994); J.R. Miller, *Shingwauk's Vision: A History of Native Residential Schools* (Toronto: University of Toronto Press, 1996); Jo-Anne Fiske, 'Gender and the Paradox of Residential Education in Carrier Society,' in *Women and Education*, ed. Jane Gaskell and Arlene Tigar McLaren, 2nd ed. (Calgary: Detselig Enterprises, 1991), 131–46; On the home and family, see Pamela White, 'Restructuring the Domestic Sphere – Prairie Indian Women on Reserves: Image, Ideology and State Policy, 1880–1930' (Ph.D. diss., McGill University, 1987).

34 Anderson, *Chain Her by One Foot*.

35 Nancy Shoemaker, 'The Rise or Fall of Iroquoian Women,' *Journal of Women's History* 2 (1991): 39–57, and her introduction to Nancy Shoemaker, ed., *Negotiators of Change: Historical Perspectives on Native American Women* (New York: Routledge, 1995); Jo-Anne Fiske, 'Fishing Is a Woman's Business: Changing Economic Roles of Carrier Women and Men,' in *Native People / Native Lands: Canadian Indian, Inuit and Metis*, ed. Bruce Walden Cox (Ottawa: Carleton University Press, 1988), 186–98.

36 Kathleen Jamieson, *Indian Women and the Law in Canada: Citizens Minus* (Ottawa: Minister of Supply and Services, 1978); Janet Silman, ed., *Enough Is Enough: Aboriginal Women Speak Out* (Toronto: University of Toronto Press, 1987); Susan Hynds, 'In
a Circle Everybody Is Equal: Aboriginal Women and Self-Government in Canada' (M.A. thesis, Trent University, 1996); Katherine Beatty Christe, 'Aboriginal Women and Self-Government: Challenging Leviathan,' *American Indian Culture and Research Journal* 188.3 (1994): 19–43.

37 Peter Schmaltz, *The Ojibwa of Southern Ontario* (Toronto: University of Toronto Press, 1996), 10; Robin Brownlie, 'A Fatherly Eye: Two Indian Agents on Georgian Bay, 1918–1939' (Ph.D. diss., University of Toronto, 1996), ch. 2; Sally Weaver, 'The Iroquois: The Consolidation of the Grand River Reserve in the Mid-Nineteenth Century, 1847–1875,' in *Aboriginal Ontario: Historical Perspectives on the First Nations*, ed. Edward Rogers and Donald Smith (Toronto: Dundurn Press, 1994), 213–57. On the west coast as well, argues Jean Barman with reference to sexual codes, 'Aboriginal societies did come to mimic their colonial counterparts,' which is not surprising given the advantages of doing so. See Jean Barman, 'Taming Aboriginal Sexuality: Gender, Power and Race in British Columbia, 1850–1900,' *BC Studies* 115–16 (1997–8): 263.

38 Brownlie, 'A Fatherly Eye.' On the history of the Act, see J.R. Miller, *Sky-scrapers Hide the Heavens: A History of Indian-White Relations in Canada* (Toronto: University of Toronto Press, 1989); John Tobias, 'Protection, Civilization and Assimilation: An Outline History of Canada's Indian Policy,' *Western Canadian Journal of Anthropology* 6. 2 (1976): 13–30; Brian Titley, *A Narrow Vision: Duncan Campbell Scott and the Administration of Indian Affairs in Canada* (Vancouver: UBC Press, 1987); Noel Dyck, *What Is This 'Indian Problem'? Tutelage and Resistance in Canadian Indian Administra-tion* (St John's: Memorial University of Newfoundland Press, 1991). On its uneven application, see Ken Coates, *Best Left as Indians: Native-White Rela-tions in the Yukon Territory, 1840–1971* (Montreal: McGill-Queen's University Press, 1991); Sarah Carter, *Lost Harvests: Prairie Indian Reserve Farmers and Government Policy* (Montreal: McGill-Queen's University Press, 1980).
39 NAC, Dept. of Indian Affairs, RG 10, vol. 7978, file 1-18-26, Dept. of Justice to Indian Affairs, quoted to Kenora agent, 8 July 1944, emphasis added.
40 NAC, RG 10, vol. 7278, file 1-18-26, 'Indian Marriage.' Letters between Dept. of National Defence and Indian Affairs discuss this issue during the war.
41 NAC, RG 10, vol. 3990, file 180/636, 'Policy re: Marriage,' 1908.
42 Ibid.
43 NAC, RG 10, vol. 8869, file 487, 'Immorality in Kenora,' Indian agent to Dept. of Indian Affairs, 19 Aug. 1919.
44 NAC, RG 10, vol. 7978, file 1-18-26, Manitoba inspector of agencies to Ottawa, 4 Dec. 1944.
45 NAC, RG 10, vol. 7978, file 11-18-26, Blackfoot agent Gooderham to Dept. of Indian Affairs, Feb. 1944. Although my sources and examples focus on Ontario, I have drawn on Indian Affairs files from other areas of Canada to indicate views that had some broad acceptance among Indian agents.
46 NAC, RG 10, vol. 8869, file 487, 18–6, 'RCMP Report,' 14 Aug. 1933.
47 Ibid., 30 June 1933.
48 NAC, RG 10, vol. 2991, file 216/447, 18 April 1943.
49 NAC, RG 10, vol. 8869, file 487, 18-6, Agent Edwards to Dept. of Indian Affairs, 25 Sept. 1941.
50 NAC, RG 10, vol. 9173, file B64, 19 Oct. 1927. This letter actually came from a western agent.
51 Deborah Posel, 'State Power and Gender: Conflict over the Registration of African Customary Marriage in South Africa c. 1910–1970,' *Journal of Historical Sociology* 8.3 (Sept. 1995): 241.
52 Joan Sangster, *Regulating Lives of Girls and Women: Sexuality, Family and the Law in Ontario, 1920–1960* (Toronto: Oxford University Press, 2001), ch. 5.

53 AO, Mercer case file 7644, 1930s. The case file is incomplete, but her father objected to her claims she could be paroled to 'an aunt in Parry Sound' as, he said, she didn't have an aunt in Parry Sound! 'She should serve her whole term. It is better for her to be in there,' he wrote. Although more than one Native woman was imprisoned for bigamy, it is not clear whether they were in customary marriages or not.

54 NAC, RG 10, vol. 8869, file 487, 18–6, letter from Ottawa to Ontario Indian agent, ca. 1920.

55 NAC, RG 10, vol. 11346, file 13, and 18-16, ca. 1956.

56 NAC, RG 10, vol. 9744, file 487, resolution of Whitefish Bay Council, sent to Dept. of Indian Affairs, Jan. 1939.

57 NAC, RG 10, vol. 7978, file 1-18-26, letter of Ontario agent to Dept. of Indian Affairs, 22 Feb. 1943.

58 The term was used by an agent from western Canada, but the paternalism was widely shared (NAC, RG 10, vol. 11415, file 984, 18-16, Agent Perry to Dept. of Indian Affairs, 31 May 1920). It was often articulated by magistrates in court cases as well. See AO, Mercer case file 93939: 'she [a young Native woman] is easy victim for unprincipled Indian and white men.'

59 NAC, RG 10, vol. 10721, file 484, 18-16, letter of Chapleau agent, 19 Nov. 1956.

60 NAC, RG 10, vol. 8869, file 487, 18-6, report of 16 June 1933.

61 Brownlie, 'A Fatherly Eye,' 67.

62 NAC, RG 10, vol. 8869, file 487, letter of councillor to Ottawa, 7 Feb. 1936.

63 NAC, RG 10, vol. 10721, file 484, 18-16, letter to Indian agent, May 1955.

64 NAC, RG 10, vol. 19680, file 48, 18-28, part 1, letter to agent, 13 Feb. 1958.

65 AO, Cape Croker Council, reel 1, minutes, 1 March 1920. There was also an account of parents refusing to take in their daughter and her illegitimate child. The priest tried to intervene in this case (AO, Cape Croker diary of mission priest, reel 3, 1933). See also R.W. Dunning, *Social and Economic Change among the Northern Ojibwa* (Toronto: University of Toronto Press, 1959), for discussion of an Ojibwa community's antipathy to illegitimacy, though not necessarily to premarital sex.

66 NAC, RG 10, vol. 2075, file 964, 'Immorality in West Bay Area,' circular from Indian Affairs.

67 AO, Mercer case file 11232, 1950s.

68 While many early accounts stress the ease with which all children were adopted into Native societies, constricted economic conditions probably made it more difficult to take in extended family members. Also the context in which the illegitimacy occurred related to acceptance of children. Children conceived when couples planned marriage were accepted

more than children whose parentage was unknown or whose mothers had numerous illegitimate children.

69 NAC, RG 10, vol. 8869, 1-18-16-2, part 1, 'Illegitimacy,' Nov. 1958. There was a long debate about this issue because Indian Affairs pointed out that the child's name had to be posted for the band to see if she/he was to have status.

70 AO, Mercer case file 9004, 1940s.

71 AO, Mercer case file, 12813 and 14305, 1950s.

72 AO, Mercer case file 8552, 1940s.

73 AO, Mercer case file 9434, 1940s. This description was for a woman living off the reserve. For discussion of the overlapping projects of sexual reform, see Joan Sangster, 'Defining Sexual "Promiscuity": "Race," Gender and Class in the Operation of Ontario's Female Refuges Act, 1930–60,' in *Crimes of Colour*, ed. Wendy Chan and Kiran Mirandanchi (Peterborough, ON: Broadview Press, 2002).

74 For images of Native women, see Daniel Francis, *Imaginary Indian: The Image of the Indian in Canadian Culture* (Vancouver: Pulp Press, 1992); Sarah Carter, 'Categories and Terrains of Exclusion: Constructing the "Indian Woman" in the Early Settlement Era in Western Canada,' in *Gender and History in Canada*, ed. Joy Parr and Mark Rosenfeld (Toronto: Copp Clark, 1996), 1–40. On the earlier period, see David Smits, '"The Squaw Drudge": A Prime Index of Savagism,' *Ethnohistory* 29.4 (1982): 281–306.

75 Barman, 'Taming Aboriginal Sexuality,' 237–67. On the United States, see Katharine Osburn, 'To Build Up the Morals of the Tribe: Southern Ute Women's Sexual Behaviour and the Office of Indian Affairs, 1895–1932,' *Journal of Women's History* 9.3 (1997): 10–27. It is important to distinguish, historically, between a colonial period when miscegenation was a primary anxiety of church and colonial officials, and the later twentieth century, when the 'segregation' of the reserve system made this a less potent anxiety for white officials and, indeed, for society.

76 AO, Mercer file 9332, 1940s.

77 AO, Mercer file 10279, 1940s.

78 NAC, RG 10, vol. 19680, file 43, 18-28, letter to Indian agent, ca. 1950.

79 AO, Mercer case file 9318, 1940s.

80 AO, Mercer case file 15182, 1950s.

81 Foucault, *Discipline and Punish*, 104–31.

82 Brownlie, 'A Fatherly Eye,' 152.

83 Sharon Tiffany and Kathleen Adams, *The Wild Woman: An Inquiry into the Anthropology of an Idea* (Cambridge, MA: Schenkman, 1985), 79.

84 It is also important to distinguish between persisting ideals and actual

practices. One American anthropological study claims that 'stable marriages' were first described as the normal practice, but on close question-
ing other practices, including 'husband stealing' and 'marital instability,'
were recounted. See Lillian Ackerman, 'Marital Instability and Juvenile
Delinquency among the Nez Perces,' *American Anthropologist* 73.3 (1971):
595–603.

85 Sally Weaver, 'The Iroquois: The Consolidation of the Grand River Reserve.'

86 Anastasia Shkilnyk, *A Poison Stronger than Love: The Destruction of an
Ojibwa Community* (New Haven: Yale University Press, 1985); Regina
Flannery, *Ellen Smallboy: Glimpses of a Cree Woman's Life* (Montreal: McGill-
Queen's University Press, 1995).

87 Irving Hallowell, *Culture and Experience* (Philadelphia: University of
Philadelphia Press, 1955); Irving Hallowell, 'Sin, Sex and Sickness in
Saulteaux Belief,' *British Journal of Medical Psychology* 18 (1939): 191–7;
Schmaltz, *The Ojibwa of Southern Ontario*; Edward Rogers, *The Round Lake
Ojibwa* (Toronto: Royal Ontario Museum, 1962).

88 Rogers, *The Round Lake Ojibwa*, B91.

89 Ibid. B47.

90 Hallowell, *Culture and Experience*, 304–5. Hallowell was looking at transplanted Ojibwa in Manitoba. See also Peers, *The Ojibwa of Western Canada*,
who argues that after migration, Ojibwa women might have seen a decline
in status due to absorption of values from the more male-oriented Plains
culture. Ojibwa elders in twentieth-century Ontario were also divided
over whether to oppose the 'marrying-out' clause (Schmaltz, *The Ojibwa of
Southern Ontario*, 199).

91 Ruth Landes, *Ojibwa Woman* (New York, 1938). As Carol Devens points
out, Landes describes a culture of separate and unequal spheres of men and
women that was a product of colonization. See Devens, *Countering Colonization*, 124–5.

92 Sally Cole, 'Women's Stories and Boasian Texts: The Ojibwa Ethnography
of Ruth Landes and Maggie Wilson,' *Anthropologica* 37 (1995): 3–25. Wilson
told her stories to convey images of resourceful women overcoming their
hardship and silencing, and Landes' background as a working-class
Jewish outsider in male academe may have attuned her ears to hearing an
'outsider's' story.

93 Ibid., 16.

94 Loo, 'Tonto's Due,' 129.

95 Sangster, 'Criminalizing the Colonized.'

96 Frederick Hoxie, 'Towards a "New" North American Indian Legal His-

tory,' in *Symposium on Contemporary and Historical Issues in Legal Pluralism: Prairie and Northern Canada* (Winnipeg: Faculty of Law, University of Manitoba, 1992), 7.

97 'The art of punishing, then, must rest on the technologies of representation' (Foucault, *Discipline and Punish*, 104).

98 Carol La Prairie, 'Community, Justice or Just Communities? Aboriginal Communities in Search of Justice,' *Canadian Journal of Criminology* 37.4 (1995): 521–45.

99 Sally Merry Engle, 'Popular Justice and the Ideology of Social Transformation,' *Social and Legal Studies* 1 (1992): 161–76, esp. 171: 'popular justice is often colonized by state law.'

13 Political Status of Native Indian Women: Contradictory Implications of Canadian State Policy

JO-ANNE FISKE

Introduction

For more than a century, anthropological interest in the status of Ab-original[1] women of North America has been shaped primarily by theoretical debates concerning the complex relationships between women's changing social position, social evolution, and economic transformation and, more recently, the penetration of colonizing state societies.[2] Since the 1970s, however, feminist scholars have redirected theoretical attention either to interpretations of how gender categories are conceptualized, symbolized, and privileged or to historical materialist analyses of women's status as measured by their relative autonomy and dependence, their control over human and economic resources, and their capacity to exercise public authority.[3] Historical materialists have concentrated on documentary research in their efforts to assess the impact of colonialism on women's socio-political status.[4] They have embarked on case studies to understand how the articulation between marginal community economies and capitalism establishes the material bases of women's empowerment.[5]

The latter body of literature reveals contradictions and ambiguities in women's lives that defy easy generalization. On the one hand, case studies suggest that contemporary Aboriginal women have relatively high political status vis-à-vis men within their own communities. That is to say, women are not disadvantaged in comparison to men in regard to access to elected office, appointment to administrative positions, employment, and economic advantages within domestic units.[6] On the other hand, these same studies also disclose the constraints women frequently confront: domestic violence, abuse related to alcohol dependency, the stress of parenting without male partners, and lack of intimate, stable relationships. It is evident, furthermore, that women within a community may experience a wide range of differences in their status, while individual women encounter considerable changes in their political position consequent to changing kinship statuses.[7] Discrepancies between actual functions women perform and the prevailing gender ideology create further paradoxes in women's status relative to men.[8] Moreover, in some instances women may have attained political advantage consequent to surmounting extraordinary hardships wrought by poverty.[9]

In the eyes of some, the excessive affliction of domestic violence, registered as the number one concern of women reporting to the Royal Commission on Aboriginal Peoples,[10] renders any analysis of the contradictions of women's status suspect. How, they ask, can factors indicating female empowerment be weighed fairly against the debilitation of domestic and sexual violence? Indeed, strong statements, supported by unequivocal evidence of the extent of violence, are made to this effect. Nahanee, for example, speaks of 'the almost total victimization of women and children in Aboriginal communities' and states, 'Violence against Aboriginal women has reached epidemic proportions according to most studies conducted over the past few years. This violence includes the victimization of women and their children, both of whom are seen as property of their men (husbands, lovers, fathers), or of the community in which they live.'[11] At the same discussion before the royal commission, Patricia Monture-Okanee and Mary Ellen Turpel reiterated their perceptions that violence leads the list of women's justice concerns. In Monture-OKanee's words, 'We must also accept that in some circumstances it is no longer the descendants of the European settlers that oppress us, but it is Aboriginal men in our communities who now fulfill this role.'[12] The truth of this oppression, viewed by these scholars as consequent to internalizing colonial oppression, which invariably foists a sexist/racist regime on the oppressed even while it privileges male power within the colonized community, cannot be questioned. Nonetheless, it is also seemingly apparent to many outside observers, and to some community members, that women do retain considerable influence and power even while they confront their male and colonial oppressors. Women's influence appears to derive from their education, which leads them to para-professional, administrative, and clerical positions in the First Nations' administration and social, health, and educational services. (Some Canadian data support this general view of positive influence: in 1986, 29 per cent of working Aboriginal women, as compared to 16.1 per cent of men, were in managerial or professional positions.)[13]

These contrary views beg the question, Is either view a misrepresentation or is the situation so complex that both may account truthfully for some aspect of women's shifting, complex experiences? This article explores the contradictory and ambiguous nature of women's political status vis-à-vis men within the internal political processes of Canadian Indian[14] reserve communities up to 1990. It examines the linkage between economy, domestic organization, and political processes, on the one hand, and the relationship between Indian women and the state, on the other.

Indian women have had their lives disrupted by state intervention to a greater degree than any other women of Canada and more extensively than their male Aboriginal peers. The very fact of this extensive intervention raises questions about the legacy of colonialism that has left Aboriginal women suffering a double jeopardy of sexist and racist discrimination, which are so intertwined that one can hardly be discussed without consideration of the implications of the other. Here a caveat is in order. It is true that many of the conditions described herein have not altered since 1990. However, 1991 marks a turning point in the degree to which provincial public policies have affected First Nations' political and economic practices.[15] To date, we have neither case studies nor comparative analyses on how these changes have affected gender relations in reserve communities. The most compelling situation, according to Nahanee, has been the transfer of judicial powers to communities, wherein a range of alternative sentencing practices and alternative justice systems has given rise to dubious treatment of male offenders at the expense of women's safety and well-being.[16] Moreover, as First Nations have gained greater administrative autonomy and have selected diverse strategies for decolonization, nationwide generalizations have been rendered more difficult.

The complex relationship between economic marginality, state intervention – which in itself is contrary, for the state can be the site of both oppression and protection – and the ambivalent status of Indian women calls for a feminist analysis of the ways in which the state organizes Indian women's daily lives and creates competing interests between women and men.[17] It also directs our attention to women's strategies and goals in political struggles engendered by state intervention, most significantly women's opposition to the state's enduring efforts to assimilate Indians and the more recent actions of some to reduce them to just another disadvantaged group within a multicultural society.

While it has been recognized that 'state policy towards the Indians, more than anything else, stands out as the most salient factor in explaining the relationship between Native and white Canadians'[18] and that Indian women, in particular, have been subjected to destructive racial and sexist policies, no systematic analysis has been offered of the impact of state policy on gender relationships. The paternalistic relationship between the state and Indian women is of particular salience in understanding their social position, for the Canadian Parliament has assigned Indian women fewer fundamental rights than their male peers and has subjected them to different definitions of their legal Indian status for more than a century. I suggest that assimilationist policies constitute elements of state patriarchy, in this case state organization of and control over reproductive relations that serve to define Indian identity.[19] Patriarchal policies and practices impinge upon marital and parental relations and constrain women's sexual and reproductive freedoms. Before analysing this coercive relationship, I will provide some useful definitions and a brief synopsis of relevant legislative history.

Definitions and a Brief History of Legislation

It has been more than a century since the first Indian Act (1876) consolidated colonial Indian policies and established the framework for Canada's administration of Indian people. This framework was premised on the paternalistic notion that, although Indian people were 'wards of the state' requiring 'protection,' they would eventually become 'civilized' and assimilate into broader society. The Indian Act (administered by the Department of Indian and Northern Affairs Canada [DINAC])[20] exercises exclusive power (allocated to the Canadian Parliament by the Constitution Act [1867])[21] to determine who shall be recognized as Indian, the criteria by which this status shall be accorded or lost, and the conditions under which said Indians must live in order to benefit from special treatment in federal law. From 1876 onwards, the terms *legal*, *registered*, and *status* have been used interchangeably to denote Indians recognized by the federal government and regulated by the Indian Act.

Status Indians are organized by the state into 'bands,' which were intended to function as the equivalent of municipalities (a curious notion, given that municipal governments are concerned with the administration and protection of private property and that some bands are an amalgamation of more than one community). Moreover, as government-designated administrative units, bands did not necessarily represent their members' perceptions of appropriate social boundaries. The term *First Nation* has gradually displaced *band*, although the two are not always congruent; some First Nations comprise a number of bands, while others do not. Bands (which are organized for administrative purposes by the state and which the minister of Indian affairs can create and destroy regardless of historical connections, cultural differences, or kinship affiliation) share corporate rights to lands and funds held in trust for them by the federal government. Federal Aboriginal-specific programs are largely confined to the status Indian population ordinarily residing on these reserves.[22] As resident reserve members, status women (and men) enjoy specific rights and privileges: membership in the band electorate, a share of the band's common resources, financial support for tertiary education, housing assistance, and financial aid from special Native economic development funds.

In contradictory efforts to assimilate Indians into mainstream society while allegedly protecting their lands from Euro-Canadian encroachment, the state has frequently revised the criteria it uses to assign legal status.[23] From its beginning, the Indian Act embraced the patriarchal terms of the Enfranchisement Act of 1869, which stipulated that Indian women who married non-Indian men would have their and their children's legal status revoked. At the same time, upon marriage to a status man, a non-Indian woman became a status Indian and consequently benefited from federal Indian programs. Children whose mothers were status Indians but who lived off the reserve were also deemed status Indians. In 1941, however, the father's status came to determine the fate of children living away from the reserve. The act was amended again in 1951 to further disadvantage women; now any woman losing status through marriage also lost her band membership and her rights to reside on the reserve, to inherit reserve property, and to share in the band's resources.[24]

Prior to amending the Indian Act in 1985, the state had imposed universal patrilineal criteria for band membership. Upon marriage, a woman was reassigned to her husband's band. Children born in wedlock were assigned to their parents' band; children born out of wedlock to status women became members of their mother's band (providing that no objections were raised and the ministry approved); sons born out of wedlock to non-Indian women and Indian men were registered in the father's band, but daughters of these unions were denied registration.[25]

Other early provisions of the act reinforced women's subjugation. Until 1951, women were excluded from the band electorate and barred from public meetings. Indian Affairs agents exercised considerable discretionary power over property inheritance. They allocated housing, agricultural land, and other valued resources to the benefit of men.

In 1985, following a long and bitter political struggle, efforts were made to redress the sexually discriminatory sections of the act and to make it conform to the equality provisions of the Charter of Rights and Freedoms (1982).[26] New legislation, popularly known as Bill C-31 (an Act to Amend the Indian Act), redefined who is and who is not a registered Indian. The sexually discriminatory passages of the old Indian Act were rescinded. Now marriage no longer affects legal status. Women who had lost status upon marriage became eligible for reinstatement to band membership and for re-registration as Indians under the act. Their children also qualified for registration and were granted contingent band membership, the latter to be ratified by the bands themselves. Bill C-31 also defined eligibility for various state benefits.

The new provisions created two official categories of Indians: (1) a charter group of reinstated women and all who had band membership prior to 17 April 1985 (when Bill C-31 took effect); and (2) a group of registered status Indians who are not guaranteed band membership and all its attendant rights and privileges, but who must apply to the band itself. The situation is further complicated by the act's provision that bands may now formulate and enact their own membership regulations. Consequently, a third category emerged: unregistered Indians with band membership.[27] In short, salient distinctions now exist between three socio-legal categories of Indians and band members – differences that generate unequal entitlement to valued resources and to special treatment under federal law.

At first blush, Bill C-31 appears to be an awkward compromise between guaranteeing individual equality rights and recognizing collective Aboriginal rights to self-determination. But it is much more than that. It empowers the Canadian state with new ways to intervene in reproductive relations; in fact, it expands the state's interest in where, when, and with whom women form intimate relations and rear their children. But these powers were not confined to the direct authority of the state. As elected band councils have assumed more authority over their members, their identity has altered and, with it, both their self-identifying discourse and their political strategies vis-à-vis their membership. To understand fully the impact of state interventions on gender relations, we must address the economic and political relations that have prevailed between reserve communities and the state, paying particular attention to the links between political processes and domestic organization. At this juncture, a second caveat is in order. Much of what follows, in particular the impoverishment of rural and small bands, remains the case for many First Nations. Lack of recent statistical data and comparative information on resource-rich and urban First Nations since 1991 precludes applying this study beyond 1990.

The Domestic Sector of Production and the Organization of Domestic Life

With rare exceptions, prior to 1990, the 596 Indian bands of Canada were wholly dependent on the federal government, which, in turn, limited economic and social benefits to status, reserve residents and (notwithstanding the actual number of reserve residents) calculated each band's fiscal entitlement according to this designated population base. Consequently, by devising new socio-legal categories with differing entitlement to benefits, the state aggravated community tensions. Even as populations grew[28] and resources dwindled, the state initiated the devolution of responsibilities, and First Nations assumed increasing responsibility for administering social and economic programs, putting further pressures on limited human and capital resources.

Analyses of the political processes in reserve communities suffering economic and social deprivation have led to the conclusion that internal political influence was gained by individuals acting as power brokers between the state and their community. Political influence is said to have rested on the ability to control scarce resources that circulated from the state.[29] These resources include funds for community administration, grants for community development projects and temporary job creation schemes, and subsidized housing for reserve residents. The degree of dependency generated is indicated by the high reliance on public sector jobs. In 1983, 63 per cent of on-reserve workers made their living from the public sector.[30]

Due to the paternalistic practices of 'welfare colonialism' or 'wardship,' a larger power base could not be created by the band council.[31] Compounding the restrictions of economic dependency was the fact that the state resisted relinquishing its bureaucratic control. The strict legal regime of the Indian Act limited local government authority to enacting minor bylaws and to routine administrative obligations. With very few exceptions, the First Nations lacked an independent fiscal base, such as the right to levy taxes or royalties on resources.

With the few exceptions of the Northwest Coast fishing villages, the large, semi-urban reserves, and those blessed by resource royalties, unemployment and underdevelopment have characterized reserve life. In rural and northern areas, in particular, wage labour opportunities were minimal, often sporadic, and consisted of relatively poorly paid or short-term jobs. Here the primary source of personal cash income came from programs administered by federal agencies. Community administration of social, educational, and cultural programs created the band's limited employment opportunities.[32] State assistance, either in the form of personal incomes or community development projects, rarely incorporated Native workers into the mainstream economy. Nor did it seem to alleviate substantial economic hardship. Reliance on state transfer payments meant that reserve communities primarily constituted a domestic sector of production, where the production of use-values was paramount. They operated at the periphery of capitalism. In areas where Native populations dominated, land-based productive activity was paramount.[33] Elsewhere, subsistence production combined with unearned income in the creation of use-values. As Peter Usher notes, 'The capitalist mode has been superimposed on the preexisting domestic mode, but the latter survives in modified form. The two coexist not as isolated, unconnected enclaves, but rather as interrelated parts of a larger social formation, that of industrial capitalism ...'[34]

Beginning in the 1960s but emerging more clearly in the 1970s and 1980s, the articulation of the domestic and capitalist modes of production generated complex ramifications for women. Within the domestic sector, reproduction and production overlapped and affected kin relations and household organization. In the First Nation reserve communities, individual households were rarely self-sufficient. Extended families, whether sharing a common household or otherwise, were the most stable economic unit. Kinship units were drawn together by a common need to share cash income, subsistence production, and labour. Exchanges of labour, goods, and services were reciprocal. An ethos of generosity and sharing prevailed across Native societies. Earned income and subsistence goods found their way into inter-household exchanges, thereby lessening the economic disparity of individual households and providing stability when household membership fluctuated and when access to resources was seasonally erratic.[35]

Cooperation and sharing enhanced women's social mobility. Collective responsibility for child care, for example, allowed women to pursue wage employment and education away from their communities. Similarly, pooling a range of subsistence goods and cash meant that women who were absent from seasonal subsistence production, whether they resided elsewhere permanently or only occasionally, could expect to share essential domestic provisions. Through collective labour and mutual support, women were relieved from performing domestic services for men and were protected from systematic economic dependence upon them. In fact, marriage did not necessarily improve women's economic well-being, since men often could not regularly or adequately support dependants. Indeed, marriage might be detrimental. A husband without either a cash income or the means to intensify use-value production became a drain on already limited resources. Faced with a difficult choice in circumstances over which they had little or no control, many women resigned themselves to forming autonomous households.[36] Wotherspoon and Satzewich, citing figures from the National Council on Welfare, report that, in 1986, 16 per cent of Aboriginal families were female headed. Because of the difficulty in obtaining accurate figures and the reluctance of some First Nations to participate in census enumerations, this figure may be low, as indicated by several case studies that report on the frequency of female-headed households.[37]

First Nation women's domestic choices were never entirely free of state intervention. State policies and practices directly and indirectly organized their daily lives in complex ways. State support for individuals has been organized around the provision of essential resources for women, children, and the elderly, which fostered development of uterine-based kin networks. Whether married or single, women favoured residing with or near their mothers, while single men, unable to be self-sufficient, relied on their own female kin.[38] Female-headed households were common; mothers raising children established their own homes or shared dwellings with female kin who distributed the burden of child care and economic resources.[39] Where women had relative wealth – for example, access to state transfer payments – and because they exercised control over essential provisions on which others depended, they played significant roles in inter-household relations.[40] The greater a woman's cash or subsistence contributions to the household economy, the larger the number of kin who depended, directly or indirectly, on her support.

Just as social assistance benefits bolstered women's inter-household influence, so, ironically, did coercive state policies. State interventions into family affairs were a case in point. Women lobbied the federal government for improved housing and essential community services, such as health care, recreation facilities, and education. Child apprehension practices, in particular, spurred women's kin networks and grassroots organizations into political action. Native families have been more likely than any others in Canada to have children removed to foster care or placed for adoption, primarily with Euro-Canadian homes.[41] In response, female-centred kin networks provided care when parents could not, while women's associations and band administrations formed child welfare committees and engaged in political lobbying.[42]

Confrontation with the criminal justice system also drew women into the political arena. According to the Canadian Human Rights Commission, the odds of Aboriginal women and men being imprisoned are higher than for any other Canadians.[43] With the extraordinary frequency of civil and criminal charges laid against their kin and the inordinately high rates of incarceration that disrupted their families, women and their associations politicized their distress and appealed to the state for alternative solutions.[44] Similarly, women challenged the state in order to protect Aboriginal resource rights, not infrequently arguing that, as nurturers and providers, women bear a particular obligation to oppose state encroachment.[45]

Nevertheless, the autonomy women gained from the relative security of their economic status, when compared to that of men, was not without paradox. In many ways, women paid dearly for their independence. Chronic poverty has been associated with health and social problems, not the least of which is alcoholism, an affliction that continues to generate considerable despair and interpersonal violence.[46] Conflict-ridden relationships have been common and brittle.[47] In the face of frequent domestic violence, women formed their own households or shared residences with female kin. (For one Aboriginal woman's viewpoint on violence, see Monture [1989].) As women established independent households, men were alienated from their children. Whether they desired it or not, women often had little choice in shouldering the primary, if not sole, responsibility for child care.[48] Not only were many women rearing their own children; they also gave economic and emotional support to their male kin's children. Nor did their maternal responsibilities end when children reached adulthood; rather, in a variety of ways, women continued to bear maternal responsibilities. Grandchildren had to be cared for when parents were unable to do so. Domestic conflicts had to be resolved. Domestic provisions and cash needed to be supplied in times of scarcity.

It is also true that within and between communities, women experienced their poverty and responsibilities differently. Due to internal, institutionalized divisions of rank, status, and prestige, some kin networks enjoyed greater benefits than others. Some women found themselves isolated from cooperative networks because of lack of kin. Elderly and middle-aged women without adult children and grandchildren, for example, suffered greater alienation and hardship than those with large extended families. Similarly, women's access to housing varied within communities. Here again, women of extended kin networks were more likely to secure a home as a consequence of their own and their kin's capacity to influence resource allocation.[49]

The pains of autonomy for women were rendered more problematic by the intrusive, patriarchal terms of the Indian Act, which further divided and harmed women. Most vulnerable were young women who had married into another band. Until they had adult children, or unless they had female kin within the band, they often endured considerable social isolation. They were perceived as outsiders, and their isolation was particularly pronounced if they were widowed, separated, or divorced.[50] Returning to their natal band was not easy. Prior to 1985, married women were automatically transferred to their husbands' bands; amendments to the Indian Act did not make returning to their natal band any easier. New membership provisions still empowered band councils with the right to decide if and under what terms former members might return. Isolated women experienced difficulty obtaining employment, securing educational assistance, acquiring a new home, or retaining a marital home following separation. Lack of access to education had long-term ramifications; as women's educational levels rise, the more likely they are to participate in community administration and politics. In contradistinction, women lacking these social resources were pushed to the community's margins.[51]

Gender conflicts were exacerbated by the return of reinstated women and their children to reserve communities. With reserve population increases of 32 per cent between 1985 and 1990, of which 60 per cent was due to Bill C-31, band administrations could not meet demands for post-secondary education.[52] In 1987, DINAC introduced a system of priorities for allocating funds that was meant 'to assure that students who would come from the regular stream for post-secondary education were not disadvantaged by taking funds and transferring them to Bill C-31 students.'[53] In consequence, when funds were exhausted, reinstated women suffered.[54] As women's associations report, in some regions reinstated women received lower rates of assistance than charter members of their bands. Furthermore, many women who were unable to return to a reserve were excluded altogether.[55]

Administrative staff, acting on behalf of elected councils, regulated home ownership and occupancy. However, house allocation was constrained by DINAC policy dictating the number of units and eligibility and by previous practices of DINAC agents. Historically, Indian agents favoured men when allocating home and land ownership. In most areas of Canada, ownership was registered with DINAC by 'certificates of possession.' Widows usually inherited their husbands' properties, but it was uncommon for single or divorced women to possess homes. Likewise sons, married or single, were favoured over daughters when inheriting parental property. In some communities, women remained unaware of their entitlement to certified possession.[56] Elsewhere, reinstated women face greater constraints. For example, at the Sawridge Reserve – a small band that is wealthy because of resource royalties – councils have specifically denied reinstated women the right to residency, thus denying them access to the social housing programs; on other reserves faced with housing shortages, elected councils have granted priority to original charter members at the expense of reinstated members and their families. Despite promises to the contrary, in the five years succeeding Bill C-31 the federal government failed to provide sufficient revenue to ensure homes for both reinstated women and charter members.

There is no federal legislation directly addressing the relationship between the Indian Act and provincial and federal family law, marital property laws, or marriage and divorce legislation (*Paul v. Paul* [1986] 1 SCR 306; *Derrickson v. Derrickson* [1986] 1 SCR 285).[57] Because provincial laws could not be enforced on Indian reserves (since reserve property falls under federal jurisdiction), women's access to stable housing varied from reserve to reserve. A First Nation government determined whether women were granted homes on the same basis as men and with the same security of possession. Such has been the case for the Stoney Creek Carrier, where mothers are granted housing priority.[58] In contrast, among the Maliseet of Tobique, New Brunswick, the quest for decent, secure housing and rights to marital property resulted in a political confrontation with the band council and the federal government. Unable to obtain homes, women resorted to an occupation of the council's offices and then, in July 1979, organized a protest march that drew nationwide attention and participation.[59] Women without home ownership were denied a source of power in domestic and economic arrangements, which had grave repercussions. Where women could not obtain certificates of possession to reserve land, for example, they could not establish businesses that required special premises. Consequently, they competed somewhat unequally with men for the financial and economic resources of the reserve.[60] And, of course, they were subjected to local politics as well as to formal state-level politics. They could not avoid the manoeuvres and manipulations of local politics.

Women's Political Status

Despite the contradictions women experienced and their uneven access to essential resources, women's domestic functions and status often facilitated rather than hindered their opportunities for political participation.[61] Because of the corporate interest in household provisions, the multiple demands on individuals' incomes, and an administrative priority to secure a living for community members, political considerations underlay virtually every decision concerning the allocation of common resources.

Political organization in reserve communities was by and large informal, characterized by face-to-face negotiations and subtle pressures radiating from kin-based social networks that perceived themselves to be in competition with each other.[62] Increasingly, however, through the 1970s and 1980s, these kin networks were female-centred. As female-headed households increased, so women's influence within the community rose. Similarly, as women's economic contributions grew relative to men's, women acquired greater control over the resources necessary to advance family status and political interests. Their influence over kin networks allowed women to shape and even to direct the course of public decision-making, whether it was through holding political or administrative offices or through promoting candidates for elected office.[63]

Women frequently achieved influence through their positions on advisory committees established by elected councils. Indeed, as the administrative responsibilities of reserve governments expanded, women were finding new opportunities to exert influence. Para-professional and managerial jobs created by the newly founded local bureaucracies not only generated employment for women; they fashioned new avenues for directing public affairs and public office.[64] From these administrative positions as well as from their voluntary associations, women sustained enduring influence over state officials.

In their struggle to improve the quality of family life, women faced many of the same pressing economic and social issues confronted by the elected band council: improving employment, housing, health, education, and recreational services and protecting resource rights from state and capitalist encroachment. This overlap of domestic and public concerns led women to present their political actions as an extension of their familial responsibilities, saying that their public behaviour carried the same meaning as their roles as women, mothers, and grandmothers.[65] In the eyes of the community, claims for houses, jobs, and development projects were closely tied to women's moral obligations to improve their own or their kin's immediate circumstances.

Women adopted diverse strategies to meet these objectives on a community-wide level. On their reserves, women's voluntary associations and service committees raised funds for community services, job creation programs, and community facilities. When the voluntary associations obtained funds for job creation, their leaders forged client/patron relationships with supra-parochial interests, further augmenting their political influence. Women's associations also created opportunities to inform women of tribal political issues, to generate female solidarity, and to deal directly and independently with intervening state agencies.[66] In consequence, acquired political and organizational skills and knowledge prepared women for public office and for political advocacy in a larger political arena.

Women also formed voluntary associations that embraced both status and non-status members in order to preserve social cohesion and to afford a sense of cultural continuity. Benefits from federal funds could be allocated by voluntary associations to status and non-status persons whether they were reserve residents or not. Among the Stoney Creek Carrier, for example, building projects sponsored by women's groups and funded by the Canada Employment and Immigration Commission and Canada Health and Welfare employed residents and non-residents regardless of their socio-legal status.[67]

Provincial and federal Aboriginal associations, such as the Homemakers of British Columbia and provincial and territorial member associations of the Native Women's Association of Canada (NWAC), established reserve-based chapters representing both status and non-status interests. These and like-minded associations confronted compelling issues like child apprehension and family violence, providing a unifying forum for status and non-status women. But their strength must not be exaggerated. State-imposed definitions of status and identity were never readily overcome; their effects on women have been divisive and enduring.[68] Although voluntary associations were effective in mitigating tensions within kin networks or small communities, they were less successful in bridging large-scale rifts between status and non-status groups. The scale of personal tensions and social strains created by state-imposed definitions of socio-legal status loomed too large for an easy solution. The crux of the contradictory base of women's empowerment lay in the patriarchal foundation of state definitions of Indian status.

Gender Implications of Socio-Legal Status and Self-Determination

Just as the consequences of domestic organization were contradictory and unevenly experienced within and between communities, so, too, were the social consequences of Bill C-31. Devised as a compromise between meeting the equality provisions of the Charter of Rights and Freedoms and granting limited recognition of Aboriginal demands for self-determination, Bill C-31, in fact, exacerbated gender tensions by imposing severe restrictions on women's personal lives and by bolstering state patriarchy. Once again, the issue was gender discrimination residing in state control over transmission of legal status. To start, as of 1985, Bill C-31 entitled children of persons holding status prior to 17 April 1985 to pass on status, while children of reinstated women could not do so unless they married registered status Indians. At the same time, Bill C-31 prevented reinstated females born out of wedlock to status fathers and non-Indian mothers from transferring status, while permitting their brothers born in the same manner to do so. Thus status has been effectively cut off after two generations of status/non-status unions.

Even more problematic for women has been the provision that children born out of wedlock are unable to transmit status to future generations unless their mothers could prove that the father was a status Indian. To do so, a woman was required to present a sworn affidavit of paternity to DINAC. Since, on average, 50–60 per cent of status women's children were born out of wedlock,[69] the ramifications of this intrusion were far-reaching. Overall, the policy undermined women's marital choices – for example, whether to adhere to customary marriage practices or to refrain from a legally sanctioned marital relationship. Because band administrations registered births and applications for status and because the federal state did not provide for unregistered children, increasingly women found themselves subjected to community surveillance. Band councils and administrators had a new interest in registering infants of unwed mothers and hence in having women divulge paternity. In consequence, women suffered further erosion of their domestic autonomy, and many faced conflicting pressures from their bands and the fathers of their children.[70]

Although state regulations disproportionately affected reinstated women, all status women faced new tensions as Indian peoples encountered contradictory demographic and economic pressures. The state was not the only interest group to benefit from regulating gender relations. Status Indian communities also had a vested, yet contradictory interest in regulating population growth and/or decline. In fact, the narrowly defined entitlements of Bill C-31, combined with high rates of intermarriage to non-status and non-Indian persons, may eventually result in a declining status Indian population.[71] More immediately, some families may find, within the next two generations, that they have no status members remaining.[72] With Bill C-31, reproduction of a status population established compelling household imperatives that, in turn, affect selection of marriage partners and women's choices concerning when and with whom to bear children.

Indeed, the legacy of Bill C-31 is a veritable Gordian knot that continues to confront Indian peoples. First Nations with few resources and little hope of economic development may, in the short term, suffer from population increases; ironically, in the long term, they may face a serious decline in a population for whom the government has a constitutional responsibility. This paradox is inextricably tied to First Nations' responses to women's demands for sexual equality and for state legislation compelling bands to devise membership rules and self-government structures consistent with the Charter of Rights and Freedoms.[73] Perpetuation of sexually discriminatory practices – whether perceived as customary laws or as internalized state practices – is likely to discourage women from remaining reserve residents and may carry the unintended consequence of further diminishing the status population.[74]

At the heart of this conundrum lies the conflict between Indian peoples and the Canadian state regarding self-determination. While the state continued to conceive of bands only as its designated administrative units, Indian peoples came to perceive themselves as First Nations whose Aboriginal rights included determination of citizenship, which has been seen as the necessary condition to prevent assimilation.

The struggle against assimilation lies at the core of gender tensions and the paradoxes confronting women. Women's organizations have consistently argued that total removal of sexual discrimination from the Indian Act should take precedence over self-determination. This position brought NWAC into conflict with the Assembly of First Nations (AFN), which had as its primary objective First Nation control over citizenship.[75] While NWAC and the women's associations it represented maintained that the various forms of differential treatment violated national and international human rights legislation, especially the Canadian Charter of Rights and Freedoms and the International Covenant on Civil and Political Rights, the AFN officially opposed (as did most status Indian groups) sexually discriminatory legislation. Nonetheless, its leaders argued that amendments to the Indian Act and appeals to state authority could not redress former wrongs or determine future conditions of citizenship. The AFN worried that the individualistic values of the charter would take priority over collective rights, the latter being, in the eyes of the AFN, consistent with Aboriginal tradition and essential to preservation of the special status of First Nations.

Aboriginal communities were slow to address tensions related to Bill C-31. The Canadian Human Rights Commission recorded growing numbers of complaints from women about violations of human rights, while, in January 1990, the Ontario Native Women's Association released media reports of increasing violence against women, in particular reinstated women seeking access to band resources. As of 1990, 232 of 596 bands controlled their own membership via band-designed membership codes. Codes varied in their restrictions, some calling for blood quantum, others adhering to patrilineal descent or other social criteria of eligibility. Some First Nations denied women educational assistance and residency rights, while others proposed membership codes that would exclude reinstated women from specific benefits.[76] The Sawridge band in Alberta, for example, not only proposed prohibiting Bill C-31 registrants from reserve residency; it turned to the courts in an effort to have Bill C-31 declared in violation of constitutional guarantees of Aboriginal rights.[77]

Community dispute settlement mechanisms were unable to resolve gender conflicts. Furthermore, the state retained power to override internal decisions. Gradually, women turned to the federal court system for redress of their wrongs.[78] Nonetheless, many reinstated women felt too vulnerable to contest gender discrimination, particularly recent residents on the reserve and women who experienced widespread opposition to their claims to corporate resources and state benefits.[79]

The ultimate irony was that women found themselves assimilating in order to resist state policies of assimilation; that is, they felt impelled to turn to the tools and rules of the state in order to secure their Indian status and its benefits. Appeals to external powers may well undermine Aboriginal autonomy and hence diminish the cultural and economic benefits of Indian identity. Turpel, for example, argues that internal challenges to Aboriginal government 'would be a dangerous opening for a Canadian court to rule on individual versus collective rights vis-à-vis Aboriginal peoples[;] it would also break down community methods of dispute resolution and restoration.' She further asserts that 'any case which presents a Canadian court with the opportunity to balance or weigh an individual right against a collective right ... will be an opportunity to delimit the recognition of Aboriginal Peoples as distinct cultures.'[80]

The struggle for self-determination, however, holds no guarantees of sexual equality. The state-imposed structure of elected band councils and the imposed definitions of *Indianness* have been internalized and institutionalized within the status Indian political structures. Inter-band unity of cultural groups has been effected primarily within political mini-bureaucracies variously known as tribal councils, confederacies, or unions, whose executive bodies comprise elected band chiefs or their delegates. This structure has been carried through to the provincial and national levels; AFN membership, for example, is composed of elected chiefs from most Canadian Indian bands. It remains male dominated and committed to status Indian interests.

The Assembly of First Nations has been legitimated by the government as a representative voice of the Indian peoples.[81] It has existed without any further conditions of identity imposed on its membership. Other political organizations, however, never proceeded as freely with respect to defining membership and goals. Organizations representing Indian women and non-status peoples as a whole have been subjected to state specifications as to their memberships. Moreover, government funding often determined the constituency of an organization as well as its mandate. In the 1970s, for example, funding regulations stipulated that Indian Rights for Indian Women represent both status and non-status women, a condition, according to Weaver, that brought about its demise.[82]

For a people who find themselves economically, politically, and culturally on the margins, the crucial issue is to develop forms of organization that express communal interests and neutralize the divisive effects of state policies. Aboriginal women faced the dilemma of identity and membership as defined by state socio-legal categories, while struggling to maintain and develop their collective sense of self as Aboriginal women. They have had to guard continually against the existential ambiguity and ambivalence heightened by Bill C-31.[83]

The struggle for self-determination and for clarification and protection of Aboriginal rights has carried further contradictions for women that are bound to open up social divisions and status conflicts. Federal responses to demands for self-determination resulted in greater decentralization of administrative control and increased fiscal responsibility of tribal councils. With DINAC money being targeted to tribal councils and their umbrella organizations, women's associations were denied direct funding, with the expectation that they would receive assistance from male-dominated political organizations.

What, then, are the implications of self-governing bands or tribal entities in light of the state's strategies of administrative decentralization and new definitions of Indian and Aboriginal identities? The first and most optimistic possibility is that self-determination will provide status female band members with greater political and social opportunities, as has been the case in the United States.[84] The second possibility is maintenance of the status quo. The already entrenched patriarchal strategies of the state authorities will continue. As noted, the disunity engendered by the Indian Act is now embedded in the Constitution. Recognition of Indian, Métis, and Inuit as distinct categories of Aboriginal peoples has exacerbated conflicts and cleavages between status and non-status groups. As status Indians and Métis fight for Aboriginal rights attached to a land base, they are moving to exclude non-status Indians, who apparently fail to qualify for a claim to a land base and fail to persuade the state of their own inherent Aboriginal rights. Nor do status Indians and Métis share common perceptions of their Aboriginal rights. Boldt and Long contend that 'inclusion and equation of Métis with Indian in the constitutional definition of Aboriginal peoples ... represents a dilution of special status for Indians ... [and] undermines the special rights of Indians and the exclusive jurisdiction of the federal government over Indians.'[85]

Deepening divisions between various Aboriginal groups are likely to escalate gender conflicts as well as to create rifts between networks of female reserve residents. Women's kin networks may fracture, and women's political status will be further jeopardized. In all likelihood, these strains will intensify as women seek to establish unifying associations of their own. Potentially, gender and intra-gender conflicts will deepen before they improve.

The third possibility is that divisive state policies will result in unbridgeable rifts among Aboriginal women and will weaken social links between female reserve residents and their migrant female kin. This may unfold as a consequence of state policies and/or from internal Native politics that unequivocally divide 'special rights groups' (status Indians and/or aggregations of status and non-status Indians with band membership) from 'special needs groups' (non-status and status women marginalized by lack of band membership, urban residence, and economic and social marginality). Special needs groups are not perceived as corporate bodies with moral rights and legal status accorded them as collectivities; rather, they are seen to be informal aggregates of individ-uals with individual needs and rights essentially coterminous with the rights and needs of any individual member of the democratic state. As a special needs group, Indian women can expect to be treated as any other body of minority women: individuals to be considered as beneficiaries of affirmative action programs and community programs aimed at ameliorating their cultural and social disadvantages. Should this be the case, their similarities to other minority women will become more marked, and a tendency to homogenize their problems will prevail. Clearly, special needs groups face unique structural barriers in their struggle to retain cultural identity and to further their social position within the dominant society. Associations of minority, economically disadvantaged women are often limited to a type of political activism based on strategies of public pressure and political embarrassment in their challenges to ethnic/racial/ gender discrimination. As members of marginalized ethnic groups, women derive strength from the informal influence of female-based kin networks and/or individual influence derived from material advantages. Theirs is not the strength of rights and duties devolving from state-recognized special status; furthermore, they lack access to and influence over local political structures of Indian band councils and First Nations associations.

In conclusion, the ambivalent position of women is, to a large measure, explained by contradictory outcomes of the welfare practices of the state, which unintentionally disempowered male kin by limiting their control over women's access to the means of livelihood, and by the explicitly patriarchal policies embedded in assimilationist strategies, which subjugated women to public authority exercised by the state and the political structures it supported. Not only do the assimilationist strategies constitute elements of state patriarchy; some First Nations argue that it is now in their communities' interests to regulate women's reproductive choices. Patriarchal policies embedded in the state's assimilationist strategies have created a paradoxical situation for women. Even as they struggle against state efforts to reduce them to just another disadvantaged group – threatened, as they are, with the possibility of being absorbed into mainstream society as an urban minority group – Indian women face the possibility that, in so doing, they will undermine the as yet fragile power of their reserve communities to recreate themselves as self-determining First Nations.

NOTES

The research for this paper was supported by Senate Research Grants of Saint Mary's University. An earlier version of the paper was delivered to the twelfth World Congress, International Sociological Association, Madrid, Spain, 9–12 July 1990.

1 In keeping with common usage, I use the terms *Aboriginal, Indigenous,* and *Native* interchangeably to refer to the descendants of the original peoples of North America. The term *Indian* is limited to the legal uses deriving from federal legislation that distinguishes registered Indians from all other Aboriginal peoples of Canada. For the most part, Aboriginal peoples have shed this usage, preferring *Aboriginal* and *First Nations* as identifying categories. *First Nations* more accurately reflects their social identity and historic relationship to one another and to the European colonizers with whom they first traded and signed treaties. The notion of First Nationhood also reflects their Aboriginal title to their traditional lands and resources and their struggles for self-determination. Throughout, I employ *Indian* and *First Nation* interchangeably where it is pertinent to restrict discussion to the legal category created by legislation and the ensuing self-identification of 'Indianness.'
2 Lucien Carr, 'On the Social and Political Position of Women among the Huron-Iroquois Tribes,' *Harvard University Peabody Museum of Archaeology*

and Ethnology Report 16 (1887): 105–24; William Beauchamp, 'Iroquois Women,' *Journal of American Folklore* 13 (1889): 81–90; Judith Brown, 'Economic Organization and the Position of Women among the Iroquois,' *Ethnohistory* 17.3–4 (1970): 151–67; Laura Klein, 'Tlingit Women and Town Politics' (Ph.D. diss., New York University, 1975); Louise Lamphere, *To Run after Them: Cultural and Social Bases of Cooperation in a Navajo Community* (Tucson: University of Arizona Press, 1977); Eleanor Leacock, 'Women's Status in Egalitarian Society,' *Current Anthropology* 19 (1978): 247–75, and 'Montagnais Women and the Jesuit Program for Colonization,' in *Women and Colonization: Anthropological Perspectives*, ed. Mona Etienne and Eleanor Leacock (New York: Praeger, 1980).

3 Peggy R. Sanday, 'Female Status in the Public Domain,' in *Women, Culture and Society*, ed. Michelle Z. Rosaldo and Louise Lamphere (Stanford, CA: Stanford University Press, 1974); Patricia Albers, 'From Illusion to Illumination: Anthropological Studies of American Indian Women,' in *American Anthropological Project on Gender and the Curriculum* (Washington, DC: American Anthropology Association, 1989).

4 Ron Bourgeault, 'The Development of Capitalism and the Subjugation of Native Women in Northern Canada,' *Alternate Routes* 6 (1983): 110–40, and 'Race, Class and Gender: Colonial Domination of Indian Women,' *Socialist Studies / Études socialistes* 5 (1989): 87–115; Leacock, 'Montagnais Women and the Jesuit Program for Colonization'; Alan Klein, 'The Political-Economy of Gender: A 19th Century Plains Indian Case Study,' in *The Hidden Half: Studies of Plains Indian Women*, ed. P. Albers and B. Medicine (Washington, DC: University Press of America, 1983).

5 Christine Conte, 'Ladies, Livestock, Land and Lucre: Women's Networks and Social Status on the Western Navajo Reservation,' *American Indian Quarterly* 6 (1982): 105–24; Albers, 'Autonomy and Dependency in the Lives of Dakota Women: A Study in Historical Change,' *Review of Radical Political Economics* 17.3 (1985): 109–34, and, 'From Illusion to Illumination'; Jo-Anne Fiske, 'Fishing Is Women's Business: Changing Economic Roles of Carrier Women and Men,' in *Native Peoples, Native Lands: Indian, Inuit and Métis in Canada*, ed. Bruce Aldan Cox (Ottawa: Carleton University Press, 1987); Martha C. Knack, 'Contemporary Southern Paiute Women and the Measurement of Women's Economic and Political Status,' *Ethnology* 28.3 (1988): 233–48.

6 Albers, 'Sioux Women in Transition: A Study of Their Changing Status in Domestic and Capitalist Sectors of Production,' in Albers and Medicine, eds, *The Hidden Half: Studies of Plains Indian Women*; Conte, 'Ladies, Livestock, Land and Lucre'; Knack, 'Contemporary Southern Paiute Women';

Robert N. Lynch, 'Women in Northern Paiute Politics,' *Signs* 11(1986): 352–66; Marla Powers, *Oglala Women: Myth, Ritual, and Reality* (Chicago: University of Chicago Press, 1986); Fiske, 'Native Women in Reserve Politics: Strategies and Struggles,' *Journal of Legal Pluralism and Unofficial Law* 30–1 (1990): 121–37.

7 Conte, 'Ladies, Livestock, Land and Lucre.'

8 Powers, *Oglala Women: Myth, Ritual, and Reality*.

9 Lynda Lange, 'Some Contradictory Effects of Internal Colonialism on the Situation of Dene Women of the Northwest Territories,' unpublished paper presented to the annual meeting of the Canadian Ethnology Society, May 1988, Saskatoon, Saskatchewan.

10 Teressa Nahanee, 'Dancing with a Gorilla: Aboriginal Women, Justice and the Charter,' in *Aboriginal Peoples and the Justice System: Report of the National Round Table on Aboriginal Justice Issues*, Royal Commission on Aboriginal Peoples (Ottawa: Minister of Supply and Services, 1993); in Patricia A. Monture-OKanee, 'Reclaiming Justice: Aboriginal Women and Justice Initiatives in the 1990s,' *Aboriginal Peoples and the Justice System*; Emma D. LaRocque, 'Violence in Aboriginal Communities,' in *The Path to Healing: Report of the Round Table on Aboriginal Health and Social Issues*, Royal Commission on Aboriginal Peoples (Ottawa: Minister of Supply and Services, 1993).

11 Nahanee, 'Dancing with a Gorilla,' 360–1.

12 Monture-OKanee, 'Reclaiming Justice,' 115.

13 Terry Wotherspoon and Vic Satzewich, *First Nations: Race, Class, and Gender Relations* (Scarborough, ON: Nelson, 1993), 14.

14 The Constitution Act (1982), recognized three categories of 'Aboriginal peoples': Indians, Métis, and Inuit. These categories do not accurately reflect the social identity and cultural boundaries of Aboriginal peoples; rather, they constitute a complex intertwining of ethnic and juridical meanings that have changed over time. Because the state has created statutory distinctions between these groups and because race-specific laws and policies have been applied differently to Indian women and men, this discussion is restricted to peoples recognized by the state as Indians.

15 Defeat of the Meech Lake Accord on constitutional reform and the Oka crisis in 1990 were dramatic signs of changing inter-government relations and, in themselves, signalled the urgency of the need for further changes. Responses varied from federal department to federal department, from province to province, and between Aboriginal associations. Although the struggle for constitutional change was defeated again in 1992, reform of inter-governmental relations quickened. One of the most controversial

moves was the establishment of the tripartite British Columbia Treaty Commission. Devolution of social, educational, health, and justice services by the federal government, already in motion, hastened and has been alternatively criticized for dumping complex responsibilities on under-resourced communities and praised as a step toward self-government. Local control of justice, moreover, has been criticized as an explicit transfer of state patriarchy to 'brown patriarchs,' and Aboriginal feminists fear that this particular surrender of power will further devastate women. The Inuit Women's Association's position was broadcast on *Sunday Morning*, CBC Radio, 25 March 1995, and reinforces the views expressed by Nahanee in 'Dancing with a Gorilla.' To date, however, we have no comparative studies of the impact of these changes on women as professional adminis-trators, employees, or clients of this new order of services. Fiscal restraint doubtless has had negative ramifications as well, and these also need analysis.

16 Nahanee, 'Dancing with a Gorilla.'

17 Aboriginal women are divided on the issue of feminist analyses and their contribution to understanding the unique history and social position of Aboriginal women. Aboriginal legal scholars (Teressa Nahanee and Sharon McIvor, for example) associated with the Native Women's Association of Canada have espoused the need for an Aboriginal feminist perspective that will analyse 'brown patriarchy' and identify solutions, while others have eschewed feminism altogether. Monture-OKanee adopts the position that feminist theories need careful scrutiny; what is useful in their analysis – but not necessarily ill-fitting solutions – must be taken up. She shares this position with Winona Stevenson, who states that she is not a feminist yet is not averse to looking for intersections with feminist analysis.

18 Peter Li, 'Introduction,' in *Race and Ethnic Relations* in *Canada*, ed. Peter Li (Toronto: Oxford University Press, 1990), 13; Kathleen Jamieson, *Indian Women and the Law in Canada: Citizens Minus* (Ottawa: Advisory Council on the Status of Women, reproduced by the minister of supply and services Canada, 1978); and 'Sex Discrimination and the Indian Act,' in *Arduous Journey: Canadian Indians and Decolonization*, ed. J. Rick Ponting (Toronto: McClelland and Stewart, 1986).

19 Use of the concepts *state* and *patriarchy* has been strongly contested in feminist scholarship. Both concepts have been perceived to obscure or distort the disparate, contradictory, and diffuse powers and practices of formal legitimate bureaucracies and of routine gender relations. While I acknowledge the constraints of these terms, I also recognize that no other terms adequately speak to the scope of power that legislated authority

wields over women's reproductive roles and gender subordination. Like Pateman, I hold that state patriarchy refers to the government of women by men and that, 'if we abandon the concept of patriarchy, the problem of the subjection of women and sexual domination will again vanish from view within individualist and class theories. The crucial question, therefore, is the sense in which it can be said that our own society is patriarchal.' Similarly, I maintain that to follow Allen's call to abandon feminist theories of the state is premature. Rather, what is needed is continuing, detailed study of the power relations that issue from legislated and bureaucratic intrusions into women's lives as authorized and implemented by various sites of state power. See Judith Allen, 'Does Feminism Need a Theory of the "The State"?' in *Playing the State: Australian Feminist Interventions*, ed. Sophie Watson (London: Verago, 1990), and Carole Pateman, *The Disorder of Women: Democracy, Feminism and Political Theory* (Cambridge: Polity Press, 1989), 35.

20 Reorganization and renaming of the federal department responsible for Indian affairs is not always reflected in popular usage of acronyms; most commonly, the department is still referred to as DIAND, Department of Indian Affairs and Northern Development.

21 Originally known as the British North America Act (1867), this legislation established the terms of Canadian confederation and designated the statutory jurisdictions of the federal and provincial governments.

22 Despite the state's efforts to impose universal regulations on all status Indians, considerable differences prevail. Indians of the Yukon and Northwest Territories, for example, do not reside on reserves; however, the same federal programs are available to them.

23 Sally M. Weaver, 'The Status of Indian Women,' in *Two Nations, Many Cultures: Ethnic Groups in Canada*, ed. Jean Leonard Elliot (Toronto: Prentice-Hall, 1983); 'Federal Policy-Making for Métis and Non-Status Indians in the Context of Native Policy,' *Canadian Ethnic Studies* 17.2 (1985): 80–102.

24 Not all the provisions for 'enfranchisement,' loss of legal Indian status, were directed against women. Provisions for voluntary enfranchisement, which promised full Canadian citizenship, attracted more men than women (although wives and minor children were involuntarily enfranchised with their husbands/fathers), and more men than women were involuntarily enfranchised upon receiving a professional education or residing away from the reserve in order to obtain employment. The effect of the enfranchisement policies has been to define Indian status more narrowly than was envisaged by the Constitution Act of 1982.

25 An extensive body of scholarship is available. For example, see Jamieson,

Indian Women and the Law; Lilianne Ernestine Krosenbrink-Gelissen, *Sexual Equality as an Aboriginal Right: The Native Women's Association of Canada and the Constitutional Process on Aboriginal Matters, 1982–1987* (Saarbrucken, Germany: Verlag breitenbach Publishers, 1991); Joyce Green, 'Sexual Equality and Indian Government: An Analysis of Bill C-31 Amendments to the Indian Act,' *Native Studies Review* 1.2 (1985): 81–95.

26 These changes did not come easily for disenfranchised women. As early as the 1950s, women were protesting against the gender discrimination inherent in the enforced enfranchisement that accompanied marriage to a non-Indian man. It was not until the 1970s, when Native women's organizations gained state funding and the support of non-Indian women's groups, that the issue went before the courts. Following a heated lobbying campaign and facing the hostility of male-dominated political associations that labelled them 'whitewashed women's libbers,' two women sought protection under the Canadian Bill of Rights. In 1973, the Supreme Court of Canada ruled that the act was exempt from the Canadian Bill of Rights, leaving women no recourse but to take their complaint to the United Nations Human Rights Committee. Embarrassed internationally in the face of the UN committee's ruling that the Indian Act breached the Covenant of Civil and Political Rights, the federal government finally amended the offending provisions.

27 Because of the high rates of miscegenation in some areas, a fourth category may emerge as non-Indian spouses are granted band membership and/or reserve residency rights.

28 Demographic data, generated by federal agencies, on the status Indian population are plagued with inconsistencies deriving from the problematic definition of *Indian* and from the absence of data regarding various bands that did not participate in census surveys. The most reliable estimates indicate that the 1986 population was 350,000, with 61–72 per cent ordinarily residing on reserves. Estimates of the number of individuals eligible for reinstatement range from 118,000 to 130,400. Data cited by DINAC in 1990 indicate that 15 per cent of the status population were registered under Bill C-31. See Canada, C-31, *Fifth Report of the Standing Committee on Aboriginal Affairs and Northern Development*, House of Commons, issue no. 46 (Ottawa, 1988); *Impacts of the 1985 Amendments to the Indian Act (Bill C-31)* (Ottawa: Minister of Supply and Services, 1990), module 4:ii.

29 Yngve Georg Lithman, *The Community Apart: A Case Study of a Canadian Indian Reserve Community* (Winnipeg: University of Manitoba Press, 1984), 785; Tod Larsen, 'Negotiating Identity: The Micmac of Nova Scotia,' in *The Politics of Indianness: Case Studies of Ethnopolitics in Canada*, ed. Adrian

Tanner, Social and Economic Papers no. 12 (St John's: Institute of Social and Economic Research, Memorial University of Newfoundland, 1983), 107.

30 Wotherspoon and Satzewich, *First Nations*, 62, citing Indian and Northern Affairs Canada, *Task Force on Indian Economic Development* (1986), 12.

31 Adrian Tanner, 'Introduction: Canadian Indians and the Politics of Dependency,' in Tanner, ed., *The Politics of Indianness*, 2.

32 DINAC reported in 1990 that 498 of the 596 bands administered social assistance funds (*Impacts of the 1985 Amendments of the Indian Act*, module 4:54).

33 The significance of male/female reciprocity in the domestic sector is made clear by Paul Drieben. He demonstrates the economic and social salience of women in traditional Ojibwa households by showing the losses felt by two husbands (and their children) on the sudden death of their wives in an airplane accident in 1983. Drieben notes, '[The women] were, in no exaggerated sense, the glue that bonded their families together, not only into a social unit but into an economic one as well, and when they were killed those bonds were destroyed' (Paul Drieben, 'A Death in the Family: The Strategic Importance of the Women in Contemporary Ojibwa Society,' *Native Studies Review* 6.1 [1990]: 83).

34 Peter Usher, 'The North: One Land, Two Ways of Life,' in *Heartland and Hinterland: A Geography of Canada*, ed. L.D. McCann (Scarborough, ON: Prentice Hall, 1982), 491.

35 Hugh Brody, *Maps and Dreams: Indians and the British Columbia Frontier* (Harmondsworth: Penguin Books, 1981); Fiske, 'Gender and Politics in a Carrier Indian Community' (Ph.D. diss. University of British Columbia, 1989); Kathleen Mooney, 'Suburban Coast Salish Inter-household Cooperation, Economics and Religious Movements,' *Culture* 7 (1988): 49–58.

36 Fiske, 'Carrier Women and the Politics of Mothering,' in *British Columbia Reconsidered: Essays on Women*, ed. Gillian Creese and Veronica Strong-Boag (Vancouver: Press Gang, 1992), 205; Julie Cruikshank, 'Matrilocal Families in the Canadian North,' in *The Canadian Family*, rev. ed., ed. K. Ishwaran (Toronto: Holt, Rinehart and Winston, 1976), 109; Lange, 'Some Contradictory Effects'; Janet Silman, *Enough Is Enough: Aboriginal Women Speak Out* (Toronto: Women's Press, 1987), passim.

37 Wotherspoon and Satzewich, *First Nations*, 101.

38 Fiske, 'Carrier Women and the Politics of Mothering,' 205; Silman, *Enough Is Enough*, passim; Cruikshank, 'Matrilocal Families in the Canadian North,' 115.

39 Statistics Canada reports that, in 1981, 20 per cent of families were headed by lone parents, while 18.8 per cent of family households were extended, that is, included adults other than marital partners. See Pamela White, *Native Women: A Statistical Overview* (Ottawa: Department of the Secretary of State, Canada, 1986), 21.

40 Women's and men's access to cash incomes varies greatly across Canada. Although Statistics Canada reports higher average earnings for men than for women, the relative stability of women's incomes is greater on reserves where unemployment is high and where men migrate for casual labour. In 1980, 51 per cent of status Indians either had no income or relied on government transfer payments. In 1986–7, 79 per cent of bands administered their own social assistance programs. See *Final Report: Task Force on Aboriginal Peoples in Federal Corrections* (Ottawa: Minister of Supply and Services for the Solicitor General, 1989), 72; White, *Native Women*, 22.

41 Patrick Johnston, *Native Children and the Child Welfare System* (Ottawa: The Canadian Council on Social Development, 1983); Patricia A. Monture, 'A Vicious Circle: Child Welfare and the First Nations,' *Canadian Journal of Women and the Law* 3.1(1989): 1–17.

42 Monture, 'A Vicious Circle.'

43 Canadian Human Rights Commission, *Annual Report* (Ottawa: Canadian Human Rights Commission, 1988).

44 *Creating Choices: The Report of the Task Force on Federally Sentenced Women* (Ottawa: Minister of Supply and Services for Correctional Services, Canada, 1990).

45 Fiske, 'Child of the State, Mother of the Nation: Aboriginal Women and the Ideology of Motherhood,' *Culture* 13.1 (1993): 17–36; Monture, 'The Violence We Women Do: A First Nations View,' unpublished ms., 1989; Marie Anne Battiste, 'Mikmaq Women: Their Special Dialogue,' *Canadian Woman Studies / Les cahiers de la femme* 10.2–3 (1989): 61–3; Osennontion and Skonaganleh:rá, 'Our World,' *Canadian Woman Studies / Les cahiers de la femme* 10.2–3 (1989): 7–19.

46 Ontario Native Women's Association, *Breaking the Silence: Report on Domestic Violence* (Thunder Bay: Ontario Native Women's Association, 1989); Nahanee, 'Dancing with a Gorilla'; Monture-OKanee, 'Reclaiming Justice'; Silman, *Enough Is Enough*, passim.

47 Ontario Native Women's Association, *Breaking the Silence.*

48 Lange, 'Some Contradictory Effects'; Ontario Native Women's Association, *Breaking the Silence*, passim.

49 Marjorie R. Mitchell, *Women, Poverty, and Housing: Some Consequences of*

Hinterland Status for a Coast Salish Reserve in Metropolitan Canada (Ph.D. diss., University of British Columbia, 1976); Silman, *Enough Is Enough*; Fiske, 'Native Women in Reserve Politics.'

50 Joan Holmes, *Bill C-31: Equality or Disparity?* (Ottawa: Advisory Council on the Status of Women, 1987), 26.

51 Jennifer Blythe, 'Career Choices by Women in Moosonee / Moose Factory,' unpublished paper presented to the First National Symposium on Aboriginal Women, Lethbridge, Alberta, October 1989; Fiske, 'Native Women in Reserve Politics.'

52 *Impacts of the 1985 Amendments to the Indian Act*, module 4:72.

53 C-31, *Fifth Report of the Standing Committee.*

54 George Erasmus, 'Introduction,' in *Drumbeat: Anger and Renewal in Indian Country* (Ottawa: Assembly of First Nations and Summerhill Press, 1989), 36.

55 C-31, *Fifth Report of the Standing Committee*, 56–7.

56 Personal communication, Native Women's Association, Nova Scotia (1988, 1990), and Indian Homemakers, British Columbia (1990); Holmes, *Bill C-31: Equality or Disparity*; Silman, *Enough Is Enough*; Ontario Native Women's Association, *Breaking the Silence.*

57 For a discussion of case law and the social and legal implications, see Ontario Native Women' Association, *Breaking the Silence*; Bradford W. Morse, 'Aboriginal Peoples and the Law,' in *Aboriginal Peoples and the Law: Indian, Métis and Inuit Rights in Canada*, ed. Bradford W. Morse (Ottawa: Carleton University Press, 1985), 8; Richard Bartlett, 'Indian Self Government, the Equality of the Sexes and Application of Provincial Matrimonial Property Laws,' *Canadian Journal of Family Law* 5 (1986): 188–95.

58 Fiske, 'Gender and Politics in a Carrier Indian Community,' 190, and 'Carrier Women and the Politics of Mothering.'

59 Silman, *Enough Is Enough*, 229.

60 Personal communication with Joan Holmes, October 1989; The Indian Homemakers Society, July 1990; The Native Women's Association, Nova Scotia, September 1989. Also see Krosenbrink-Gelissen, *Sexual Equality as an Aboriginal Right*, 65; Holmes, *Bill C-31: Equality or Disparity.*

61 See Albers, 'Autonomy and Dependency,' for comparable analysis of Native-American women in the United States.

62 See, for example, Lithman, *The Community Apart*, 149ff; Fiske, 'Native Women in Reserve Politics,' 125; Larsen, *Negotiating Identity*; Silman, *Enough Is Enough.*

63 Silman, *Enough Is Enough*; Blythe, 'Career Choices by Women in Moosonee / Moose Factory'; Fiske, 'Native Women in Reserve Politics.'

64 Fiske, 'Native Women in Reserve Politics'; Nora Bothwell, 'The Life of a Chief,' *Canadian Woman Studies / Les cahiers de la femme* 10.2–3 (1989): 33. Blythe, 'Career Choices by Women in Moosonee / Moose Factory,' 12.

65 Fiske, 'Carrier Women and the Politics of Mothering,' 205; Silman, *Enough Is Enough*, 234; Shirley O'Connor, Patricia Monture, and Norissa O'Connor, 'Grandmothers, Mothers, and Daughters,' *Canadian Woman Studies / Les cahiers de la femme* 10.2–3 (1989): 39; Marlene Brant Castellano, 'Women in Huron and Ojibwa Society,' *Canadian Woman Studies / Les cahiers de la femme* 10.2–3 (1989): 45.

66 Fiske, 'Native Women in Reserve Politics,' and 'B.C. Native Woman's Society,' *Canadian Woman Studies / Les cahiers de la femme* 10.2–3 (1989); Silman, *Enough Is Enough*, passim.

67 Fiske, 'Native Women in Reserve Politics,' and 'Carrier Women and the Politics of Mothering.'

68 Jamieson, *Indian Women and the Law in Canada*; Holmes, *Bill C-31: Equality or Disparity*; Krosenbrink-Gelissen, *Sexual Equality as an Aboriginal Right*, 55ff.

69 James Frideres, *Native People in Canada: Contemporary Conflicts* (Toronto: Prentice-Hall, 1988), 144; C-31, *Fifth Report of the Standing Committee*, 30.

70 I have spoken with women in ten communities representing four provinces. In each community, the women have divulged the stress imposed upon them either by men who do not wish to be identified as the fathers of their children or by councils whose interests are not consistent with those of the women. This stress is amplified when children are born of incestuous unions; women fear disclosure of this abuse, and councils desire to increase population through infant registration.

71 C-31, *Fifth Report of the Standing Committee*, 28–9.

72 Ibid.; Holmes, *Bill C-31: Equality or Disparity*, 25.

73 This position brings women into direct confrontation with First Nations' representatives, who argue that the Charter will disempower and constrain self-governance rather than protect Aboriginal rights. For a discussion of this viewpoint, see Menno Boldt and J. Anthony Long, 'Tribal Philosophies and the Canadian Charter of Rights and Freedoms,' *Ethnic and Racial Studies* 74.4 (1984): 478–93.

74 To my knowledge, no systematic research has been conducted on this issue. I rest my statements on personal conversations and general discussions arising in several conferences of First Nation women.

75 Fiske, 'Child of the State, Mother of the Nation'; Krosenbrink-Gelissen, *Sexual Equality as an Aboriginal Right*.

76 C-31, *Fifth Report of the Standing Committee*, 47, 57, 65.

77 Holmes, *Bill C-31: Equality or Disparity*, 20–1, 33.
78 At the time of this writing, women of the Hobbema band in Alberta are discussing court redress of their band's refusal to accept reinstated women and families as residents and to share band resources with them.
79 Holmes, *Bill C-31: Equality or Disparity*, 34.
80 Mary Ellen Turpel, 'Aboriginal Peoples and the Canadian Charter of Rights and Freedoms,' *Canadian Woman Studies / Les cahiers de la femme* 10.2–3 (1989): 153.
81 As an anonymous reviewer reminded me, legitimation by the state is no guarantee of credibility. The AFN was unable to persuade First Nations to adopt its stance on constitutional reform; it has lost members and continues to suffer internal discord.
82 Weaver, 'The Status of Indian Women,' 70.
83 The aftermath of Bill C-31 continues to be identified as the leading dilemma for First Nations. See Katherine Beaty Chiste, 'Aboriginal Women and Self-Government: Challenging Leviathan,' *American Indian Culture and Research Journal* 18.3 (1994), citing a 1993 survey by *Native Issues Monthly*, December 1993.
84 Albers, 'Autonomy and Dependency'; Powers, *Oglala Women;* Knack, 'Contemporary Southern Paiute Women'; Miller, 'Women and Politics.'
85 Boldt and Long, 'Native Indian Self-Government: Instrument of Autonomy or Assimilation,' in *Governments in Conflict? Provinces and Indian Nations in Canada* (Toronto: University of Toronto Press, 1984), 275.

14 'A Red Girl's Reasoning': E. Pauline Johnson Constructs the New Nation

VERONICA STRONG-BOAG

In the late nineteenth and early twentieth centuries, Canadians struggled to make sense of a colonial past, the Riel Rebellions, Native protest, feminist agitation, and the looming presence of a southern rival. The artists and writers who matured in these turbulent years offered some answers. Among this Confederation generation, E. Pauline Johnson is a unique example of a Euro–First Nation poet and non-fiction and short story writer. While well known in her own day, Johnson is largely remembered for producing Canada's best-selling book of poetry, *Flint and Feather*, and, in particular, for writing 'The Song My Paddle Sings,' which has been reproduced in a host of texts as a celebration of a northern nation.[1] More significantly, she developed a nationalist narrative in which Indians, Euro–First Nations, and women reject inferiority and claim an equal place. The daughter of a Mohawk-English union, Johnson publicly challenged the exclusionary nationalist narratives of her day.

Pauline Johnson articulates a racialized femininity that embodied and unsettled many of the middle-class conventions of late nineteenth-century Canada. Hers is one version of what Judith Butler has described as 'performative accomplishment' (1990: 271; 1993). Like today's performance artists,[2] Johnson 'wore' gender, race, and class in ways that could be both transgressive and reinscriptive. As she sought secure footing among the prejudices of her age, her messages seem sometimes ambiguous and ambivalent. In identifying her as a performer who highlighted issues of race and gender in her ongoing conversation with European Canada, I do not dismiss these conditions as in any way 'unreal' or as less significant because they are constructed in daily discourses. They remain critical sites of power and oppression in the real world. I wish rather to emphasize their construction, whether consciously or unconsciously, by Johnson and her audiences.[3]

In her efforts at communication, Pauline Johnson became one of those writers who, as postcolonial critics like Edward Said have suggested, endeavoured 'to rechart and then occupy the place in imperial culture forms reserved for subordination, to occupy it self-consciously, fighting for it on the very same territory once ruled by the consciousness that assumed the subordination of a designated inferior Other.'[4] To be sure, sometimes her arguments seem dispersed, fragmentary, and often undeveloped. As critics Bill Ashcroft, Gareth Griffiths, and Helen Tiffin point out in *The Empire Writes Back,* such limitations are typical of early postcolonial texts, which came 'into being within the constraints of a discourse and the institutional practice of a patronage system which limits and undercuts their assertion of a different perspective' (6). A reconsideration of Johnson as social critic and her work as a subversive narrative reveals a 'conscious effort to enter into the discourse of Europe and the West, to mix with it, transform it, to make it acknowledge marginalized or suppressed or forgotten histories' (Said, 216). Unlike some writers of Aboriginal ancestry who have chosen in the first instance to speak to a Native community, Pauline Johnson performed largely for European Canada (Silvera). So far as we can tell, few listeners and readers were Native. Through stage and published work, she tried to translate Aboriginal and Mixed Race experience into public images that settlers could value. In the process, she outlines a hybrid nationalist identity that denounces oppression and incorporates the inheritance of Native peoples and the recognition of women.

The Making of a Canadian Postcolonial Performer

Born in 1861 in southwestern Ontario to an activist Mohawk father, George Henry Martin Johnson, and an English-born woman from an abolitionist family, Susanna Howells, Pauline Johnson was reared in comfort on the Grand River's Six Nations territory. There, a respectable middle-class enthusiasm for canonical Romantic poets like Byron or Shelley mingled with a passionate commitment to protecting Indian people from the assaults of unprincipled Europeans.[5] Such views situated Johnson and her family within the mainstream of the liberal nationalism of her day.[6] Her élite family entertained leading individuals, from the governor general and Iroquois chiefs on down, exposing her to many of the burning questions of the day. Johnson's family, with its biculturalism, its liberal nationalism, and its middle-class privilege, provided a highly unusual vantage point from which to view the volatile mixture of influences that was to become modern Canada. It sharply distinguished her and, ultimately, her writing from the group of nationalist poets – Duncan Campbell Scott, Archibald Lampman, Isabella Valancy Crawford, Bliss Carman, Charles G.D. Roberts, and Wilfred Campbell – with whom she is commonly compared.

The Johnson household prepared its children to straddle the Aboriginal and European worlds, which, through trade and settlement, still remained closely connected for many nineteenth-century Canadians. As an interpreter and forest warden for the Department of Indian Affairs and a translator for the Anglican Church in the mid-decades of the century, Johnson's father[7] moved among different communities. His two sons and two daughters might have hoped to do the same. They were, as Pauline Johnson remembered in her short story 'My Mother,' 'reared on the strictest lines of both Indian and English principles. They were taught the legends, the traditions, the culture, and the etiquette of both races to which they belonged; but above all, their mother instilled into them from the very cradle that they were of their father's people, not of hers' (1987: 69). Despite such injunctions, status and nationality for the Iroquois are traced through the mother, not the father. Her identity as a Mohawk could not come in the traditional manner, but only from the federal Indian Act.

In the nineteenth century, the Grand River Mohawks remained a powerful and proud part of the Six Nations Confederacy, which had established Canada's most populous and prosperous Native community near Brantford in 1847 (Weaver 1994: 182; 1972). The territory itself was multinational, harbouring European-Canadians, blacks, the members of the Iroquois Confederacy, and a number of smaller allied tribes. During the nineteenth century a decisive split emerged between 'culturally conservative Longhouse people and the more acculturated Christians' (Weaver 1994: 183). The Longhouse faction championed traditional language, rituals, and governance (Shimony; Weaver 1972). Such views evoked little support among Anglican Mohawks like the Johnsons, who initially felt optimistic about their relations with the dominant society. The flourishing state of the Christian Grand River community in the last decades of the nineteenth century seemed full of promise to Iroquois Christians, who hoped to contribute to the emergence of a Native-European union (see Weaver 1994). Such optimism would later dissipate in rancour and despair. However, until the end of her life, Pauline

Johnson sought to express the positive vision of an inclusive nationality espoused by her family and others like them.

Johnson's access to the Mohawk community was limited by the fact that her English mother was never fully integrated into the Grand River territory. Close ties to her mother's relatives, schooling by a governess and in a city high school, and Pauline's residence throughout her twenties in Brantford's middle-class neighbourhoods, further undermined the influence of George Johnson and his father, John Smoke Johnson, both of whom were well-known Mohawk leaders, and that of her extensive Native family. Pauline Johnson stood on the periphery of even Grand River's Native community and 'its well-integrated system of values and morals' (Weaver 1994: 215).

Given her incomplete immersion, Johnson's performances as a Native woman, or 'Indian Princess,' always encountered problems of authenticity. One solution, as revealed in the deerskin dress she often wore, was to fabricate a synthetic pan-Indian stage presence that necessarily relied as much upon popular European fantasies of the Native as it did upon direct Aboriginal inspiration. Her reference to whites, such as William Lighthall and Charles Mair, for assistance in putting together a realistic stage presence (by whose standards?) captures her problems most poignantly.

Upon George Johnson's death in 1884, his widow and daughters, Pauline and Evelyn, permanently left the Six Nations territory and resettled in Brantford, a bustling industrial market centre.[8] Their shift from prominence in the Mohawk community to a socially inferior position in town mirrored the general decline in the situation of Mixed Race and Native peoples in Canada. The move also reinforced European cultural influences. Pauline attended and performed in theatrical amateur entertainments in Hamilton and Brantford and continued writing. Like many daughters of the middle class, she experimented with verse whose forms and themes often reflected the conventional sentiments of Victorian Canada.

Throughout Johnson's life, she claimed the literary traditions of Great Britain to be as much her own as were those of the Six Nations. The result is a cultural hybrid who juggles influences from both sides of her family as she seeks to bridge Canada's racial divide. In a world that typically thinks in terms of dualisms, Mixed Race individuals are troubling. As one contributor to the 1994 volume *Miscegenation Blues: Voices of Mixed Race Women* points out, those of plural ancestry 'embody some of the most unresolved contradictions in current human relations' (Green,

291). In their hands, 'nationality' can become 'unstable, mobile, and heterogeneous – a fluid process of negotiation rather than a rigid imposition of meaning' (Donaldson, 116). In the heyday of Euro-Canadian nation-building, Johnson faced an uphill struggle. Neither she nor her audiences could always be sure what she was expected to, or would, perform. Hers was a lifelong search for a credible and profitable means of enacting her own and Canada's hybridity.

The difficulty and loneliness of Johnson's position encouraged her to develop a style that made direct application to her listeners and readers. Much like other performance artists, she communicated in ways that are 'intensely intimate,' with an 'emphasis on personal experience and emotional material, not "acted" or distanced from artist or audience' (Forte, 255). Her efforts at emotionally direct communication, at the establishment of empathy, especially through the use of melodrama and comedy, encouraged a recognition of women's and men's, of Natives' and non-Natives,' shared humanity. Once she forged such bonds with her audience, Johnson could hope to create new space for First Nations and women in Canada's settler society.

As her long days at home from the age of eighteen until she gave a public recital in Toronto in 1892 at age thirty further reveal, a strong-minded Euro–First Nation spinster faced many handicaps in creating space for herself during the high age of British imperialism and paternalism.[9] While discrimination has always existed, the European-Canadian assessment of Indians had been deteriorating from an earlier emphasis on their 'fundamental humanity to one based on the theological and sociological theories which relegated them to the sub-human' (MacDonald, 103). Those of joint Native and European heritage also fared badly. The collapse of the Prairie resistances in 1870 and 1885 doomed the hopes of Louis Riel and others for recognition of the Euro–First Nations community. By the late 1880s, prospects for those claiming Native heritage looked bleak.

Native-Canadian writers emerged to address the ongoing crisis of their relationship with the dominant society. Penny Petrone charts evidence of resistance from an Indian and Euro–First Nations élite armed with a formal education and command of English. While protest came from many tribes, the Iroquois, with their long history of alliance with the British Empire, were especially prominent.[10] Not all Aboriginal participants in debates about the future of North America voiced opposition to European encroachment. One commentator has suggested that the handful of Native writers publishing in the United States at the turn of the century were basically assimilationist. 'Their characters accept white values and cultural traits, often rejecting the traditional way of life' (Larson, 36). There is also the question of resistance offered by the Aboriginal performers who peopled Wild West shows, burlesque halls, and popular entertainments of every kind in Europe, North America, and all around the world during these years. Their performances, constructed by themselves and the managers, negotiated complicated terrains of complicity and protest that are difficult to appreciate or evaluate.[11] In whatever fashion they confronted their common vulnerability, Native writers and performers contributed to the growth of pan-Indian sentiments in these years (Larson). In their preoccupation with relations with white society, they provide a critical backdrop for Pauline Johnson, the first Euro–First Nation or Native woman to assume a major public role in Canada.

The mid-nineteenth century also saw the birth of a generation of Canadians deeply influenced by the feminist movement. Johnson matured in a community debating women's roles, especially their right to higher education, paid work, and political power. Brantford and its surroundings produced, along with Native activists, Emily Stowe, Canada's first female school principal and, later, the founder of the country's first suffrage society (Bashevkin, ch. 1), and a crowd of pioneer female journalists. For a woman of ambition, Ontario in these years appeared full of promise. Johnson's uncertain position, an unmarried daughter in a widow's family, gave her particular reasons to rethink the situation of her sex and to join other women in asking questions of the new nation.

While the recurring racism of turn-of-the-century feminism has been described by scholars, the politics of gender and race are fluid and never uncomplicated (Bacchi; Valverde). A number of American suffragists had a special interest in the history of Native peoples. They were impressed by the presence of powerful women in the Iroquois Confederacy. For some feminists, Indian society appeared to supply 'an alternative to American patriarchy,' suggesting that male domination was neither inevitable nor omnipresent.[12] Pauline Johnson draws the same comparison in the *London Daily Express* in 1906:

> I have heard that the daughters of this vast city cry out for a voice in Parliament of this land. There is no need for an Iroquois woman to clamour for recognition in our councils; she has had it for upwards of four centuries ... From her cradle-board she is taught to judge men and their

intellectual qualities, their aptness for public life, and their integrity, so that when he who bears the title leaves his seat in council to join the league-makers in the happy hunting grounds she can use her wisdom and her learning in nominating his fittest successor ... The old and powerful chiefs-in-council never attempt to question her decision ... There are fifty matrons possessing this right in the Iroquois Confederacy. I have not heard of fifty white women even among those of noble birth who may speak and be listened to in the lodge of the law-makers here. (1987: 232)

Other Iroquois activists, desirous of outside, especially feminist, support, also emphasized the authority of their matrons.[13] As such arguments make clear, the politics of race and gender were not always at odds. In an age of multiple and overlapping protest movements, Johnson was well equipped to make critical connections between the politics of race and gender.

The decision to confront prevailing prejudice is far from easy. One Mohawk writer, Beth Brant, has recently reminded us:

To write or not to write is a painful struggle for us. For everything we write can be used against us. For everything we write will be used against us. And I'm not talking about bad reviews. I'm talking about the flak we receive from our own communities as well as the smug liberalism from the white 'literary' enclave. Writing is an act of courage for most. For us, it is an act that requires opening up our wounded communities, our families, to eyes and ears that do not love us. Is this madness? In a way it is – the madness of a Louis Riel, a Maria Campbell, a Pauline Johnson, a Crazy Horse – a revolutionary madness. A love that is greater than fear. A love that is as tender as it is fierce. (17)

It is just such a counter-discourse, essentially feminist and postcolonialist, that Johnson was to articulate on platforms in theatres, schools, and churches across the country after she entered the uncertain world of the paid recitalist in 1892. In these performances, she staged a femininity that was simultaneously and ambiguously raced. In a white ball gown, she offered herself as the epitome of upper-class Victorian womanhood. Minutes later, she would reappear as a passionate Aboriginal woman clad in leather and feathers.

Johnson's Indian ancestry enhanced her marketability, an appeal she capitalized on in her presentation as an archetypal 'Indian Princess' – someone, in other words, like Pocahontas in the American story, or

Molly Brant in the case of the northern colonies, who acts to redeem European men, saving them from the wilderness and the wilderness for them.[14] Here is both affirmation and repudiation of the middle-class conventions of gender and race. Johnson's ultimate dependence on the patronage of the dominant society required this ambiguity.

For the rest of her life, she orchestrated a public career that fed on melodrama, jingoism, and commercialism, together with a commitment to writing verse and stories that would both win the praise of literary critics and address the oppression of Native peoples and women. Her oral skills proved the key to earning a living, while her ability to publish poems and stories nourished her appeal to audiences and her claim to middle-class respectability.[15] While the results were uneven, as she herself painfully acknowledged,[16] Johnson persevered in struggling to translate her views into forms that would be simultaneously acceptable to both a cultural élite and popular audiences. In the process, she extended Native-American women's long-standing role – first exercised as mistresses, wives, and guides – as 'mediators of meaning between the cultures of the two worlds.'[17] Over the course of the twentieth century, Canadian audiences would find that Aboriginal performers, such as Grey Owl (in reality the transplanted Britisher, Archibald Belaney) and Buffy Sainte-Marie,[18] served in some measure as critical 'symbols in the Canadian-history enterprise' (Emberley, 18; Francis). In many ways, the reality faced by Aboriginal peoples is beside the point. Indian performers are often valued inasmuch as they can confirm Canada's particular relationship to the northern landscape and, ultimately, its difference from the United States. In the face of growing racism, however, Native roots jeopardized Johnson's efforts to parlay a talent for public expression and poetry into a living. As a public woman and as an Indian artist, she was to live on society's periphery, able finally neither to marry nor to guarantee her security.[19]

Marginality was further reinforced by Johnson's role as an interpreter and champion of a peripheral culture. Advocates and creators of Canadian literature had to fight hard to find a hearing. Only too often they found themselves on the defensive in the face of British and American aspirations to imperial domination and the colonialism of Canadians themselves. In her life and her work, Johnson had to negotiate many identities in the dominant culture's commercial and aesthetic markets. She had to sell to the very society she critiqued, her need for respectability and sympathy juxtaposed with a message that potentially unsettled conventions of race and gender.

Talking Race

Challenging a dominant narrative that held that 'to the majority of English speaking people, an Indian is an Indian, an inadequate sort of person possessing a red brown skin, nomadic habits, and an inability for public affairs'(Johnson 1900: 440) took courage. This boldness was recognized by her contemporaries. According to the nationalist poet Charles Mair, the effect of Johnson's 'racial poetry ... upon the reader was as that of something abnormal, something new and strange, and certainly unexampled in Canadian verse. For here was a girl whose blood and sympathies were largely drawn from the greatest tribe of the most advanced nation of Indians of the continent, who spoke out "loud and bold," not for it alone but for the whole red race, and sang of its glories and its wrongs in strains of poetic fire' (cited in Foster, 179). As one of a tiny group of North American Native women who challenged racism on stage and in writing, Johnson was a lonely figure.[20]

Her earliest contributions to public life – in 1884 at the reinternment of the Seneca orator Red Jacket, and, two years later, at Brantford's unveiling of a statue to the Mohawk chief Joseph Brant – identify heroic liberal figures who match any in the contemporary European national-ist lexicon.[21] Here are Natives of giant stature. Their merits and those of First Nations and Euro–First Nations peoples in general do not, as Johnson argues, meet with deserved respect. The history of Indian-white contact is the history of recurring ignorance and injustice. Pauline Johnson's inaugural recital in Toronto in 1892 electrified listeners with 'A Cry from an Indian Wife,' a passionate indictment of the crushing of the Prairie tribes in 1885, an encounter still fresh in memory and one that had sharply divided the country. Early 1890s articles, such as 'The Iroquois of the Grand River' and 'A Glimpse of the Grand River Indi-ans,' construct more realistic portraits to counter prejudices that fail to make critical distinctions among the tribes or to recognize their merits (cited in Keller, 111–12).

Johnson regularly pillories the prejudice that consigns all people of Aboriginal background to inferiority. In 1892, her powerful rejoinder to contemporary racism, 'A Strong Race Opinion on the Indian Girl in Modern Fiction,' catalogues and dismisses racist stereotypes that relegate Indian women to the losing side in war and in love (cited in Keller, 120–1). Poems like 'The Cattle Thief' and 'Wolverine' likewise reject the dehumanization that accompanies genocide. Audiences are asked to think of the Native characters as individuals with heroic qualities, more than a match for the erstwhile victors, who are, in turn, not in reality 'plucky Englishmen' but 'demons,' 'robbers,' and 'dogs' (Johnson 1972: 10–14, 226). In a nice reversal of conventions, the white intruders are reduced to non-humans. Johnson herself is not immune to racist constructions. In ways that are reminiscent of eugenic thinkers but also evoke older Native rivalries, she accords the Iroquois, the Cree, the Sioux, the Haida, and the Squamish superiority over other Aboriginal tribes. Faith in élite Natives armed her in struggles against those who sought to dismiss her and those she represented.

Throughout her life, Johnson wrote and performed works that starkly detail the ruin inflicted by newcomers and their governments. One short story, 'As It Was in the Beginning,' takes residential schools to task. Another, 'Her Majesty's Guest,' depicts the brutality of liquor-sellers, enemies who had, on three occasions, physically attacked her own father (Johnson 1989). Poems like 'Silhouette,' 'The Corn Husker,' and 'The Cattle Thief' dramatize the starvation that dogged the tribes in these years (Johnson 1972: 103, 7–9).[22] In face of injustice, cattle rustling is readily justified. As Johnson explains, in a revealing use of the first person, 'When *you* pay for the land you live in *we'll* pay for the meat we eat' (1972: 13 [author's emphasis]). In other passages, the hypocrisy of conquerors who 'had come with the Bible in one hand, the bottle in the other' is exposed.[23] Here are hard lessons about complicity and betrayal that audiences were not used to hearing.

In the early poems 'Ojistoh' and 'As Red Men Die,' Johnson attempts to create sympathy with dramatic portraits of idealized Native women and men who are every bit the equal of those found in the Scottish and English ballads with which listeners might be more familiar (1972). In deference to her audiences and no doubt to her need to earn a living, no poem portrays violence directed at newcomers. First Nations men and women are for the most part noble, long-suffering, generous, and open to reasonable overtures. In poems like 'Wolverine' and 'The Cattle Thief' (1972), and short stories like 'Catharine of the Crow's Nest,' they, rather than the European intruders, demonstrate humanity (1987). While Johnson sometimes despairs, as when she laments her 'dear dead race' in her story 'A Red Girl's Reasoning' (1987), she also insists on the 'innate refinement so universally possessed by the higher tribes of North American Indians' (1987: 103). She argues further that if you 'put a pure-blooded Indian in the drawing room ... he will shine with the best of you' (cited in Keller, 112). The Natives' 'adaptability to progress'

(1987: 104) makes them fully capable of entering the modern world. Her portrait of heroic and thoughtful Native figures stands in stark contrast to the 'disappearing race' chronicled in the poems of her more powerful contemporary, Duncan Campbell Scott of the federal Department of Indian Affairs.[24] Johnson's faith in the ultimate competitiveness of non-Europeans also helps explain her enthusiasm, in the poem 'The Man in Chrysanthemum Land,' for Japan's defeat of Russia in the 1904–5 war (1972: 158–9).[25] Like other liberal and anti-racist critics of her day, she interpreted that conflict as the belated triumph of non-Europeans over their would-be white masters (Martin).

In 1909, Johnson retired to British Columbia, a province that had by then become the centre of Indian protest.[26] Her assistance to Squamish chief Joe Capilano in 1906 when he and other representatives of BC tribes petitioned King Edward, like the long hours they spent together in Vancouver while he narrated the stories of his people and the assistance she gave to his son in public speaking, were in keeping with long-demonstrated sympathies. Johnson's relationships on the west coast also reflected the ties that increasingly connected Native peoples of different communities in the twentieth century.

The Legends of Vancouver (1911), published at the end of her life, reaffirms Johnson's persistent efforts to remap the Euro-Canadian imaginative landscape. As she reminds readers, the twin peaks that rise to the north of the city are not 'the lions,' so-named by a foreign-born settler with a mind for the exotic or the patriotic but 'without the love for them that is in the Indian heart' (1926: 3). The mountains have a far older indigenous history as 'the sisters' of Indian legend. Her retelling of Squamish stories unnames the land colonized by Europeans and evokes a powerful human landscape preceding their arrival.[27] The Native inheritance is located at the centre of human history in British Columbia and Canada. In such writing, Johnson suggests, as Edward Said has said of other resistance writers, that indigenous peoples have 'a history capable of development, as part of the process of work, growth, and maturity to which only Europeans had seemed entitled' (213).

Speaking of Women

While she tends to locate oppression primarily in racism, and she is most emphatic about its particular ill effects, Johnson remained sensitive to how women are damaged by the convergence of racial and sexual prejudice. She explains her double vision: 'I am a Redskin, but I am something else too – I am a woman' (1987: 13). Indeed, as A. LaVonne Ruoff has observed, Pauline Johnson's writing resembles that of many other female writers in the nineteenth century. In her stories 'the heroine encounters mistreatment, unfairness, disadvantage, and powerlessness which result from her status as female and child. The heroine accepts herself as a female while rejecting the evaluation of female with permanent children. In the course of the narrative women are rejected as sexual prey and a pragmatic feminism is embraced' (Johnson 1987: 19). The Mohawk writer Beth Brant has argued further that Pauline Johnson, in 'breaking out of the Victorian strictures of her day ... drew a map for all women to follow' (60–1). Unlike Euro-Canadian writers, Johnson identifies racism rather than patriarchy as the chief obstacle to the fair treatment of women.

Race could also be significant in empowering women. Johnson frequently roots her commitment to equality in Native traditions. In one story, 'The Lost Salmon Run,' a Squamish elder outlines this in describing her reception of a granddaughter: 'Very good luck to have a girl for first grandchild. Our tribe not like yours; we want girl-children first, we not always wish boy-child born just for fight. Your people, they care only for war-path; our tribe more peaceful ... I tell you why: girl-child may be some time mother herself; very grand thing to be mother' (1926: 37–8). Much the same argument about the value of women is made when Johnson points to the power of Iroquois matrons. These are influential figures who contest and, often, dominate the landscape.

Johnson's female characters, like her performances, are distinguished by passionate feeling. Polite conventions about heterosexual relations, with their common emphasis on female passivity and male initiative, are rare. A series of love poems, particularly those appearing after her own unhappy affairs, evoke female passion. The canoe figures significantly as an expression of, and vehicle for, women's desires for love and mastery. Her early work, 'The Song My Paddle Sings,' launches this preoccupation with lines like 'I wooed you long but my wooing's past; / My paddle will lull you into rest' and its reference to the river as a 'bed' and its waters as a 'breast.' Here, the heroine triumphs in the rapids that 'roar,' 'seethe and boil, and bound, and splash,' 'but never a fear my craft will feel' (1972: 29–31). In a later poem, 'The Idlers,' she again uses the first person to conjure up a memory of perfect passion. The male object of her erotic gaze is explicit:

Against the thwart, near by,
Inactively you lie,
And all too near my arm your temple bends
Your indolent rude
Abandoned attitude
And again
Your costume, loose and light,
Leaves unconcealed your might
Of muscle, half suspected, half defined;
And falling well aside
Your vesture opens wide,
Above your splendid sunburnt throat that pulses unconfined.

(1972: 59–61)

Disappointment eventually quells this optimism. Sleeplessness and despair dominate the poems 'Re-voyage,' 'Wave-Won,' and 'In the Shadows.' Days were now 'haunted' and 'dreary.' Even the speaker's 'arm as strong as steel' brings no salvation (1972: 65, 67).

By the time of Johnson's second volume of poetry, *Canadian Born* (1903), loss provides the major theme in 'Thistle-Down,' 'Through Time and Bitter Distance,' and 'Your Mirror Frame' (1972: 99, 105–6, 117–18). The author's lack of repentance about her feelings is perhaps, however, best captured in the poem 'In Grey Days':

Deep human love for others
Deep as the sea
God-sent unto my neighbour –
But not to me.
Sometime I'll wrest from others
More than all this
I shall demand from Heaven
Far sweeter bliss.   (1972: 131)

Such depiction of women's physical and emotional responses is unusual in the Canada of her day. In talking of passion and in embodying the very results of miscegenation, she was a controversial figure for her audiences. Were her presentations to be taken as proof that women sui generis had sexual desires? Or were they rather an expression of her Native heritage – in other words, a demonstration of inherent primitivism or even degeneracy? Just who was performing what? Such questions had to be negotiated afresh with each new set of listeners and readers.

Passion was not the only strong emotion requiring interpretation. Betrayal, violence, and death recur in Johnson's work. From her early narrative poem, 'Ojistoh,' in which a Mohawk woman murders a would-be rapist, to the later story 'As It Was in the Beginning,' again recounted in the first person, in which the Euro–First Nation heroine takes revenge on an unfaithful priest and a still more unfaithful lover (1987), she champions a stern code in which women are neither to be seized nor taken for granted. When Charles McDonald, in the short story, 'A Red Girl's Reasoning,' refuses to recognize the customary Native marriage between his wife Christie's parents, an issue which bitterly divided real-life Canadians in these years,[28] she responds, 'Why should I recognize the rites of your nation when you do not acknowledge the rites of mine?' (1987: 117).

If heterosexual relations spell trouble, Pauline Johnson joined other women writers in crediting her sex with strong maternal feelings. Remarkable mothers stand out in stories such as 'Catharine of the Crow's Nest,' 'The Next Builder,' 'Mother o' the Men,' and 'The Tenas Klootchman' (1987). In the first, an Indian woman, Maarda, shows newcomers the meaning of generosity when she rescues a white foundling. In the stories written for an American boys' magazine and published in 1913 as *The Shagganappi*, good women civilize sons, inspiring them to higher levels of honour and achievement. In her account of her own mother's life, Johnson lovingly portrays a woman who devotes herself to her children (1987). Ultimately it is women's maternalism that provides an important point of connection between the races. In 'A Cry from an Indian Wife,' the narrator describes her own agony at seeing her family and nation going to war. She nevertheless comments:

> Yet stay, my heart is not the only one
> That grieves the loss of husband and of son;
> Think of the mothers o'er the inland seas;
> Think of the pale-faced maiden on her knees.

These reflections, with their direct appeal to the enemy, cast doubt on 'the glories of war' and conjure up a common humanity (1972: 18).

Inspired by their capacity for nurture, women in general emerge, as did the Native women who make peace by marrying tribal enemies in poems such as 'Dawendine,' as the chief promise of a more just and peaceful world (1972: 118–21). In the story 'The Envoy Extraordinary,' the character 'old Billy' sums up these sentiments: 'these mother-wimmen don't never thrive where there's rough weather, somehow. They're all fer peace. They're worse than King Edward an' Teddy Roosevelt fer patchin' up rows, an' if they can't do it no other way, they jes' hike along with a baby, sort o' treaty of peace like' (1987: 138). This faith in women's special nature was a commonplace that Johnson, like a host of her feminist contemporaries, used to contest misogynist conventions.[29] Such shared assumptions added to her appeal for the U.S. *Mothers' Magazine*, in which she regularly published.

While Pauline Johnson self-consciously chose to speak as 'One of Them'[30] – as the Iroquois and, by extension, as all Native women of Canada – and their lives lay close to the centre of much of her writing, she maintained close friendships with non-Native women. Her first poem, appearing in the American magazine *Gems of Poetry* in 1884 is dedicated 'To Jean,' a white girlhood friend. During her itinerant career, she relied on women's work and emotional support. The suffragist Nellie McClung met the recitalist in the mid-1890s, and her response captures the response of many. In her autobiography she recollects that 'at her first word, we felt at home with her ... [this] charming, friendly woman' (1945: 35). That initial regard initiated a now lost correspondence of almost twenty years' duration.

The significance of female friendships is described in Johnson's short story 'Mother o' the Men.' Here Mrs Lysle (we never learn her first name) chooses to accompany her North-West Mounted Police husband to the Yukon. 'But there are times even in the life of a wife and mother when her soul rebels at cutting herself off from all womenkind, and all that environment of social life among women means, even if the act itself is voluntary on her part.' Later on, 'during days when the sight of a woman's face would have been a glimpse of paradise to her,' she 'almost wildly regretted her boy had not been a girl – just a little sweet-voiced girl, a thing of her own sex and kind' (1987: 182, 187). The author of these words had good reason to value her own sex. Her death from cancer in Vancouver in 1913 was made immeasurably easier by the life she had fostered among women. A host of correspondents encouraged her spirits. Efforts by the Women's Canadian Club, the Women's Press Club, and the Imperial Order Daughters of the Empire ensured no financial worries. A female world anchored her to the end.

What all this begs, of course, is the question of Johnson's own feminism. Certainly her maternalism is characteristic of the women's movement of her day. So, too, is her recognition of female strength and capacity (Prentice et al.). But as a recent reminder explains, 'Native women are feminist in a way that women of other culture groups, other religions, rarely understand ... Where differences arise between mainstream feminists and Native women they centre around causes of oppression and particularly racism. Whereas mainstream feminists see the primary cause of their oppression as patriarchal society, Native women are more inclined to see their oppression as arising from racism and colonialism' (Grant, 43). Johnson seems to fit this definition. Her poems and stories draw clear links between the treatment of women and the racism of the dominant society. Oppression rarely appears a simple relationship between sexes or races. Her female characters must first reject racialization to be recognized as fully human.

Creating a New Nation

While endeavouring to chart her course as a Native and as a woman, Pauline Johnson had to locate and define herself as a Canadian at a time when this identity was far from sure. This preoccupation, which is central to her writings, also revealed how far she had moved from the insistence of other Christian Iroquois on their status as allies of Great Britain rather than as citizens of Canada. Nationalisms in various forms competed for adherents and legitimacy (Berger). As the first post-Confederation collection of Canadian verse, *Songs of the Great Dominion* (1889), indicates, poets were among those who sought to capture the essence of what it meant to grow up in the northern half of the continent. A contributor to that influential volume, Pauline Johnson never gave up the effort to articulate a founding tradition of narrative and metaphor in the wider context of British cultural and political imperialism. Her championship of a cultural and racial 'hybridity' rooted in the northern landscape recalls her own family's efforts on the Grand River. Although Johnson has little to say about French Canada, she shifts the question of racial partnership away from the prevailing Eurocentrism to include Natives.

Membership in a family of Mohawk United Empire Loyalists (UELs) gave a special twist to Johnson's preoccupation with the nature of an identity separate from that of the United States and Great Britain. The patronage of British governor generals, literati, and salon hostesses, invaluable in establishing the credentials and the respectability of the Euro–First Nation poet, deepened her appreciation of and dependence on the centre of empire. Her early initiation in the English cultural canon kept her an enthralled captive. Lines in her poem 'My English Letter' provide eloquent testimony to this fascination. Referring to England as the 'Motherland,' and it is indeed the birthplace of her own mother, Johnson writes of exile:

> Although I never knew the blessed favour
> That surely lies in breathing English air.
> Imagination's brush before me fleeing.
> Paints English pictures, though my longing eyes
> Have never known the blessedness of seeing
> The blue that lines the arch of English skies. (1972: 76)

Such nostalgia seems typical of what Ashcroft, Griffiths, and Tiffin identify as the 'second stage of production within the evolving discourse of the post-colonial,' or 'the literature produced "under imperial license" by "natives" or "outcasts"'(5).

Like other élite Natives, Johnson has an ambiguous relationship with empire. As the descendant of British allies and the daughter of an English mother, she seeks to claim the culture of the imperial centre without accepting its denigration of the periphery. She rejects the racism while sharing some of the sentiments of imperialist contemporaries. Like the political economist and humorist Stephen Leacock, who thunders in his essay 'Greater Canada: An Appeal,' 'the Empire is ours too, ours in its history of the past, ours in its safe-guard of the present' (36), Johnson repudiates inferiority for Canada, Britain's legitimate heir. A unique blending of Old World and New World, it, not the 'old land,' is the 'beloved of God' (1972: 172, 79). Unlike Anglo-Canadian imperialists, however, she includes Native peoples as full participants in the imperial project. The hybrid empire she envisions is pluralistic and meritocratic.

Johnson's relationship with the rising power to the south is, in contrast, much less positive. Kinship with William D. Howells, the American man of letters, seems to have been disappointing. His dismissal of her work and apparent slighting of his Aboriginal cousins went hand in hand with the greater difficulty Johnson encountered with U.S. audiences, who tended, like some American literary critics at the end of the twentieth century, to appropriate her as a home-grown product.[31] Their relative rudeness, beginning with her 1896–7 tour south of the Great Lakes (it was claimed that they 'treated Pauline as if she too were a circus freak, though they were a bit awed by her obvious refinement and talent' [Keller, 234]), enraged her and helped confirm the benefits of the continuing British connection. Johnson also had a front seat on the American Indian wars of the late nineteenth century, and she shared with many Canadians the faith that matters were better north of the 49th.[32] When she envisions Canada's future, she insists that 'the Yankee to the south of us must south of us remain' (1972: 80).

For Pauline Johnson, like some contemporaries, British justice provides the critical imperial inheritance (Dean). The rule of law will allow Canada to escape American unrest and corruption. Revealingly, the United States is frequently 'othered' or, in a curious way, even orientalized in the accounts of Canadian imperialists like Johnson. A rebellious colony, the United States had repudiated its British inheritance and is thus susceptible to racial degeneration and despotism. In contrast, in Canada, the traditions of British law, with their promise of equality to all, supply an essential bulwark against the tyranny of the majority and allow minorities to survive. Johnson sums up her hope for a pluralistic future in a story entitled 'The Brotherhood': 'The Mohawks and the palefaces are brothers, under one law ... It is Canadian history' (1913: 220). Similar aspirations concerning the rule of law fuelled the continuing appeal by Native peoples to the courts, the Crown, and, eventually, the League of Nations and the United Nations, where they attempted to speak as the allies, not the conquered, of Great Britain (Drees).

Johnson identifies one institution as central to the maintenance of law and order and as symbolic of the significance of fair play among races. As Keith Walden has suggested, the North-West Mounted Police (NWMP) quickly emerged after their creation in 1873 as a major icon of the new nation (4). The NWMP, later the RCMP, provided an essential guarantee and evidence of Canada's regard for law and of its fundamental difference from the United States. Johnson's 'The Riders of the Plains' typically loomed as larger-than-life figures who, while few in number, were brave enough 'to keep the peace of our people and the honour of British law.' 'Felons,' 'rebels,' and the lawless, all of whom were only too likely to originate south of the border, have no place in the land of the Lion and the Union Jack (1972: 103). Although no disillusionment is found in Johnson's surviving work, Natives, in general, quickly learned, especially after 1885, that the Mounties were at least as much keepers as protectors.

For Johnson, fair dealing by national authorities not only upheld the principles of British justice, it also helped guarantee Canada itself. She insists that the Indian heritage is a key ingredient of national survival. At the dedication of Brant's memorial in 1886, she writes:

So Canada thy plumes were hardly won
Without allegiance from thy Indian son.

...

Then meet we as one common brotherhood
In peace and love, with purpose understood.

...

Today the Six Red Nations have their Canada. (Van Steen, 45–6)

Her tours across the country with their introduction to other First Nations offered her the opportunity to confirm their special relationship to the Dominion. In regard to the Sioux, her heroic hunters of the Plains, she explains: 'King Edward of England has no better subjects; and I guess it is all the same to His Majesty whether a good subject dresses in buckskin or broadcloth' (cited in Van Steen, 263). The appeal of Squamish chief Capilano to the same monarch in 1906 is the right of an ally and an equal.

While European newcomers may offer the advantage of British law, First Nations also bring important qualities to a biracial partnership. There is, of course, the courage and loyalty that stood at the core of Johnson's own family history, but there is also, contrary to the racist depictions of Natives as savage, a special proclivity for peacemaking. She employs a youngster in one story to speak for the newcomers in acknowledging 'brotherhood with all men ... We palefaces have no such times ... Some of us are always at war. If we are not fighting here, we are fighting beyond the great salt seas. I wish we had more of ... your Indian ways. I wish we could link a silver chain around the world; we think we are the ones to teach, but I believe you could teach us much' (1913: 213).

The peaceful inclinations credited to the original inhabitants of North America resemble the higher sentiments ascribed to women. Indeed, Indian women in her stories and poems are often the special champions and expressions of inter-group harmony. Whether nature or nurture creates this phenomenon is never clear. Today it seems best explained as part of the idealization of the oppressed that characterizes much resistance writing. The essential moderation of Johnson's appeal is reaffirmed by her associated message of the need for mutual forgiveness. She leaves it to a character to explain: 'Forgive the wrongs my children did to you. And we, the red-skins, will forgive you too' (cited in Van Steen, 263).

European settlers are also encouraged to reconsider their bloody history of contact with other peoples. Her poems 'Wolverine' and 'The Cattle Thief' testify eloquently to ignorance, irrationality, and violence, and their cost in Native lives. In one story, a formerly jingoistic hero reconsiders the Boer War and recants old allegiances. The death of a good friend makes him realize that 'the glory had paled and vanished. There was nothing left of this terrible war but the misery, the mourning, the heartbreak of it all' (1913: 211). Such reflections suggest Johnson's affinities with the liberal critics who questioned Britain's attack on the Boers (Schoeman; Koss; Page). The same critique of British morality informs her condemnation of the Christian churches' treatment of Natives. It also explains her contribution to the international condemnation of official France's anti-Semitism in the Alfred Dreyfus affair. In 'Give Us Barrabas,' she exposes supposedly civilized Europe as diseased, 'leprous,' without claim to moral authority (1972: 118–28).[33] In her writings, Native peoples supply Canada with ready sources of indigenous virtue.

The key to Johnson's understanding of the best course for the new nation is inclusiveness and partnership – between Native and British and between female and male. The highly visible women who crowd narratives are ultimately 'sisters under the skin.' In articulating key values, they are not passive bystanders in history but forces to be reckoned with. Their courage, loyalty, generosity, and persistence will anchor a young nation into the future. Pauline Johnson's Canada, like the 'land of the fair deal' proposed by Nellie McClung, charts an important place for women in the creation of civil society.

Superior qualities justify adoption into the Canadian 'tribe,' but Johnson also hopes that the fact of being 'Canadian-born' will itself create shared sympathies and qualities. The title poem of her second volume of verse suggests that offspring of aristocrats and common folk can grow up, like the members of the NWMP, in harmony and equality, the products of an essentially beneficent northern environment. The 'glory' of a 'clean colonial name,' of fresh beginnings, is enough to make 'millionaires' of all (cited in Van Steen, 271). In the new Dominion, Euro–First Nations individuals are well equipped to claim citizenship as their 'blood heritage' (ibid.). In one story, where a member of the British elite is typically required to draw the appropriate moral, a governor general repudiates the prejudices of lesser men in defending a Euro–First Nation boy: 'The blood of old France and the blood of a great aboriginal race [Cree] that is the offshoot of no other race in the world. The Indian blood is a thing of itself, unmixed for thousands of years, a blood that is distinct and exclusive. Few White people can claim such a lineage. Boy, try and remember that as you come of Indian blood, dashed with that of the first great soldiers, settlers and pioneers in this vast Dominion, that you have one of the proudest places and heritages in the world. You are a Canadian in the greatest sense of the great word ... you are the real Canadian' (cited in Van Steen, 272–3). As these remarks suggest, the issue of race was important – and dangerous.

Race could confer virtue and intermarriage, even among great 'races,' and it could compromise the purity increasingly valued by the racial theorists of the day. Hybridity might combine the best; it might also bring with it degeneration. In opting for hope, Johnson denies the prejudices of the age. The hybrid Canada she attempts to will into being is to repudiate the corrupt heritage of European racism.

Johnson's hopes appear especially rooted in the West, where she spent many of the later years of her life. 'Booster' poems, such as 'The Sleeping Giant' on Thunder Bay, 'Calgary of the Plains,' 'Brandon,' 'Golden of the Selkirks,' and, the most rambunctious of all, 'A Toast' (dedicated to Vancouver), celebrate the erasure of past differences (1972: 110, 158–9, 133, 96, 121–2). In the future, individuals and races are to be taken on their own merits. Such cities, like Canada itself, do not care who you have been, only what you may contribute to an emerging identity.

The nation described by Johnson struggles with racism and sexism. The future of Native and Euro–First Nations peoples absorb her, to the exclusion of any examination of how non-British Europeans and others might fit in. Confronted with the vulnerability of First Nations communities in her day, Johnson had no hope of taking back the country, of returning Europeans to their own homelands. However she might celebrate the virtues of Native peoples, she has to deal with the ongoing reality of injustice, of conquest and settlement, with no other explanation than, as one of her characters says, 'perhaps the white man's God has willed it so' (1972: 19). Her hopes rest with a renewal of the old partnership that had united the British and the Iroquois in the War of American Independence and with a recognition of women's value. In her attention to the injustices suffered by women and First Nations, Pauline Johnson voices something more than the 'sentimental nationalism' some critics have seen (Doyle, 50–8). In her hands, 'nationalism' becomes 'one of the most powerful weapons for resisting colonialism and for establishing the space of a postcolonial identity' (Donaldson, 8).

A Postcolonial Liberal Inheritance

We know little of how Pauline Johnson's audiences received her views and almost nothing of her reception by First Nations listeners. For the most part, only one part of a conversation has survived. To be sure, there are clues. A veteran of the 1885 Prairie campaign, in near tears upon hearing 'A Cry from an Indian Wife,' confessed, 'When I heard you recite that poem, I never felt so ashamed in my life of the part I took in it' (cited in Keller, 60). A host in a small Manitoba town was heard to say, by way of introduction, 'Now, friends, before Miss Johnson's exercises begin, I want you all to remember that Injuns, like us, is folks' (Keller, 121). The liberalism of the supposed 'colour blindness' embodied in these remarks suggests one influential source of support for Johnson. Her appeal to a tolerance and fair-mindedness based on a faith in a universal humanity convinced at least some receptive listeners. A few in her audiences understood some part of the message about First Nations, women, and Canada that she tried to deliver.

It is also clear that part of Johnson's appeal was her apparent lack of threat. Some listeners and readers, like one 1892 reviewer, enjoyed the fact that 'speaking through this cultured, gifted, soft-voiced descendant' was the 'voice of the nations who once possessed this country, who have wasted away before our civilization' (cited in Francis, 113). Representatives of dead or dying competitors for resources are easy to patronize, especially when they promise the illusion of a stronger national connection with the natural landscape. As Daniel Francis suggests in *The Imaginary Indian*, 'Having successfully subdued the Indians, Whites could afford to get sentimental about them' (123). Such scepticism is, however, only part of the story. It does not capture the common ambivalence and the outright opposition of some white Canadians to the abuses of European and male power. Johnson always had sympathizers. Her subversion of traditions that consign women and Natives to subordination and anonymity is significant, nourishing recurring liberal hopes for a more pluralist and egalitarian society. In her own way, like other resistance writers and performers at the turn of the century, Pauline Johnson prepared society to 'relinquish or modify' the idea of domination (Said, 200). Today she has literary heirs in Euro–

First Nations writers like Beatrice Culleton, Maria Campbell, Beth Brant, and Lee Maracle, who, too, name injustice and call for an equal partnership in a reformed nation (Lundgren; Brant).

NOTES

My thanks to the 'Race and Gender Group,' whose discussions have been supported by a SSHRCC Strategic Grant (1992–5). Thanks too for the comments of Gillian Creese, Julie Cruikshank, Margery Fee, Carole Gerson, Nitya Iyer, Jane M. Jacobs, Kathy Mezei, Dorothy Seaton, Donald Smith, Wendy Wickwire, Donald Wilson, and members of the audience at a talk based on this chapter that I gave to Native Studies and Women's Studies at the University of Toronto on 22 April 1996. I would also like to thank Lorraine Snowden for her research assistance.

1 This chapter employs the terms 'Indian,' 'Native,' 'Aboriginal,' and 'First Nation' to refer to the original human inhabitants of North America, excluding the Inuit peoples of the North. Turn-of-the-century Canada regularly referred to individuals and populations who are a product of Indian-French unions as Métis and to those who are a product of Indian-British unions as 'mixed bloods.' 'Half-breed' was used to refer to both groups. In order to avoid the racism embodied in such usage, I have used the term 'Euro–First Nation' to refer to such individuals and groups. 'European' is used in reference to individuals – Canadian and otherwise – whose families originate in the continent of Europe. So far as I have discovered, Pauline Johnson chose to refer to herself as Iroquois, Mohawk, Indian, and 'red' or 'redskin.'

2 For a fascinating discussion of contemporary women performing artists, see Forte. I would also like to thank Dr Merlinda Bobis (herself a performance artist) of the Faculty of Creative Arts, University of Wollongong, Australia, for her assistance in making this connection to Johnson.

3 For the limits and opportunities of 'performance,' see the essays in Diamond, especially the 'Introduction' by Diamond and Rebecca Schneider, 'After Us the Savage Goddess.'

4 Said (210). See also Turner, who provides a useful exploration of selected Canadian texts that attempt to create 'new discursive space' for a postcolonial nation. Turner focuses on Euro-Canadian writers, and Johnson is not a concern.

5 Her father, for example, was active, to the point of being assaulted by non-

Natives, in efforts to protect Indian timber and Indians from the liquor trade. See Keller and also Barron.

6 The classic feminist figure of this international liberalism was Lady Ishbel Gordon, Countess of Aberdeen, disciple of William Gladstone and founder of the National Council of Women of Canada in 1893. See Saywell, Strong-Boag.

7 On the role of children of Indian/European unions, see Brown (204–11). George M.H. Johnson was the son of Helen Martin (d. 1866), the daughter of the Mohawk George Martin and Catherine Rolleston (a woman of German background who was captured during a raid on Pennsylvania settlements), and John Johnson (1792–1886), hero of the War of 1812 and the speaker of the Council of the Six Nations. See also Smith (1987) for an important account of the efforts of one outstanding Euro–First Nation individual to find accommodation between the Native peoples and European settlers in early nineteenth-century Ontario.

8 On the development of Brantford's middle class, see Burley. Unfortunately, this study makes no mention of Native peoples and pays little attention to the role of women. See Johnston, especially chapter 10, for greater, although still limited, attention to the Iroquois Confederacy.

9 On British imperialism and patriarchy in these years, see Ramusack and Burton (469–81).

10 For instance, Dr Peter Martin or Oronhyatekha (1841–1907), Frederick Ogilvie Loft (1861–1934), Levi General or Deskeheh (1873–1925), and John Ojijatekha Brant-Sero (1867–1914) – all writers closely associated with the Grand River reserve – regularly challenged prejudices. Brant-Sero, for example, campaigned to win recognition of the Iroquois as the first United Empire Loyalists, founders of Canada itself. (See Petrone, chapters 2, 3, 4.)

11 See, for example, the case of the dancer described in McBride. My thanks to Trudy Nicks of the Royal Ontario Museum for drawing this volume and the issue in general to my attention. See also the related situation of the Australian Aborigines discussed in Poignant. My thanks to Kay Schaffer of the University of Adelaide for giving me a copy of this volume.

12 Landsman (274). See also Wagner. For a critical assessment of women's power in Iroquois society, see Tooker.

13 See Levi General or Deskeheh as cited in Petrone (104).

14 On this myth, see the now classic article by Green (1975: 698–714). See also Larson (chapter 2, 'The Children of Pocahontas').

15 Her efforts to combine European and Native traditions are also seen in the work of contemporary writers like Lee Maracle. See Lundgren (69).

16 See the comments in her letter to a friendly critic, cited in Petrone (82–3).

17 Kidwell (97). On the role of the wilderness and the function of Native guides, see Jasen (especially chapters 4 and 5).

18 See Smith (1990). Buffy Sainte-Marie is a folksinger and songwriter born at the Piapot Reserve in Saskatchewan in 1941.

19 See Keller on Johnson's failed romances and recurring financial problems.

20 Somewhat later, Iroquois women such as the American activists Minnie Kellogg (1880–1948) and Alice Lee Jemison (1901–64) would also assume major public roles as critics of European prejudice. Kellogg was born at the Oneida Indian Reservation in Wisconsin and educated at Stanford, Barnard, and Columbia's School of Philanthropy. She married a non-Indian lawyer and became an activist in the Society of American Indians and a powerful writer. She was the author of *Our Democracy and the American Indian* (1920). Alice Lee Jemison was born in New York State, graduated from high school, married a Seneca steelworker, and worked at various jobs while active as an outspoken critic of the American Indian Bureau. See Hauptman (1981: 12 and passim; 1986; 1985). At least one powerful speaker from another tribe also appeared somewhat earlier: Sarah Winnemucca (1844?–1891), an American Northern Paiute woman, who produced the autobiography *Life among the Paiutes: Their Wrongs and Claims* (1883). See Canfield. Unfortunately, we do not know whether Pauline Johnson knew of such women.

21 See, for example, her characterization of Red Jacket's thought as 'liberal, and strong, / He blessed the little good and passed the wrong / Embodied in the weak' (cited in Van Steen, 47).

22 See Carter; Andrews.

23 'My Mother' (1987: 64–5). See also her poem 'The Derelict' (1972).

24 See Titley. See also the more sympathetic view of Scott's treatment of Indians in Dragland.

25 Death and disappearance are also major themes for contributors to the section 'The Indian,' in Lighthall.

26 On British Columbia in these years, see the important studies by Barman and Tennant.

27 On 'unnaming,' see Ashcroft, Griffiths, and Tiffin (141). On similar efforts by other Native writers, see Petrone (chapters 2 and 3).

28 See Van Kirk (49–68).

29 See, for example, the arguments in McClung (1915).

30 Her nom de plume (1900: 440–2).

31 See, for example, the otherwise excellent 'Introduction' by A. LaVonne Ruoff (Johnson 1987).

32 See Prucha. On Canadian assumptions of superiority, see Owram.

33 On the significance of the Dreyfus affair as a touchstone for the liberalism of the day, see Wilson; Feldman.

WORKS CITED

Andrews, Isabel. 'Indian Protest against Starvation: The Yellow Calf Incident of 1884.' *Saskatchewan History* 28.2 (1975): 41–51.

Ashcroft, Bill, Gareth Griffiths, and Helen Tiffin. *The Empire Writes Back: Theory and Practice in Post-Colonial Literature.* London and New York: Routledge, 1993.

Bacchi, Carol Lee. *Liberation Deferred? The Ideas of the English-Canadian Suffragists, 1877–1918.* Toronto: University of Toronto Press, 1983.

Barman, Jean. *The West beyond the West: A History of British Columbia.* Toronto: University of Toronto Press, 1991.

Barron, F.L. 'Alcoholism, Indians and the Anti-Drink Cause in the Protestant Indian Missions of Upper Canada, 1822–1850.' In *As Long as the Star Shines and Water Flows: A Reader in Canadian Native Studies,* ed. I.A.L. Getty and A.S. Lussier, 191–202. Vancouver: UBC Press, 1983.

Bashevkin, Sylvia. *Toeing the Lines: Women and Party Politics in English Canada.* Toronto: University of Toronto Press, 1985.

Berger, Carl. *The Sense of Power: Studies in Ideas of Canadian Imperialism, 1867–1914.* Toronto: University of Toronto Press, 1971.

Brant, Beth. *Writing as Witness: Essay and Talk.* Toronto: Women's Press, 1994.

Brown, Jennifer. *Strangers in Blood: Fur Trade Company Families in Indian Country.* Vancouver: UBC Press, 1980.

Burley, David G. *A Particular Condition in Life: Self-Employment and Social Mobility, in Mid-Victorian Brantford, Ontario.* Toronto: University of Toronto Press, 1993.

Butler, Judith. 'Performative Acts and Gender Constitution: An Essay in Phenomenology and Feminist Theory.' In *Performing Feminism: Feminist Critical Theory and Theatre,* ed. Sue-Ellen Case, 270–82. Baltimore and London: Johns Hopkins University Press, 1990.

– *Bodies That Matter: On the Discursive Limits of 'Sex.'* London: Routledge, 1993.

Canfield, Gae Whitney. *Sara Winnemucca of the Northern Paiutes.* Norman: University of Oklahoma Press, 1983.

Carter, Sarah. *Lost Harvest: Prairie Indian Reserve Farmers and Government Policy.* Montreal and Kingston: McGill-Queen's University Press, 1990.

Dean, Misao. *A Different Point of View: Sara Jeannette Duncan*. Montreal and Kingston: McGill-Queen's University Press, 1991.

Diamond, Elin, ed. *Performance and Cultural Politics*. London and New York: Routledge, 1996.

Donaldson, Laura E. *Decolonizing Feminisms: 'Race,' Gender, and Empire Building*. Chapel Hill and London: University of North Carolina Press, 1992.

Doyle, James. 'Sui Sin Far and Onoto Watanna: Two Early Chinese-Canadian Authors.' *Canadian Literature* 140 (Spring 1994): 50–8.

Dragland, S.L. *Duncan Campbell Scott: A Book of Criticism*. Ottawa: Tecumseh, 1974.

Drees, Laurie Meijer. 'Introduction to Documents One through Five: Nationalism – the League of Nations and the Six Nations of Grand River.' *Native Studies Review* 10.1 (1995): 75–88.

Emberley, Julia V. *Thresholds of Difference: Feminist Critique, Native Women's Writings, Postcolonial Theory*. Toronto: University of Toronto Press, 1993.

Feldman, Egal. *The Dreyfus Affair and the American Conscience, 1895–1906*. Detroit: Wayne State University Press, 1981.

Forte, Jeanie. 'Women's Performance Art: Feminism and Postmodernism.' In *Performing Feminism: Feminist Critical Theory and Theatre*, ed. Sue-Ellen Case, 251–69. Baltimore and London: Johns Hopkins University Press, 1990.

Foster, W. Garland. *The Mohawk Princess: Being Some Account of the Life of Tekafhon-wake (E. Pauline Johnson)*. Vancouver: Lions' Gate, 1931.

Francis, Daniel. *The Imaginary Indian: The Image of the Indian in Canadian Culture*. Vancouver: Arsenal Pulp, 1993.

Grant, Agnes. 'Reclaiming the Lineage House: Canadian Native Women Writers.' *SAIL* 6.1 (1994): 43–62.

Green, Heather. 'This Piece Done, I Shall be Renamed. In *Miscegenation Blues*, ed. Carol Campber, 291–303. Toronto: Sister Vision, 1994.

Green, Rayna. 'The Pocahontas Perplex: The Image of Indian Women in American Culture.' *Massachusetts Review* 16.4 (1975): 698–714.

Hauptman, Lawrence M. *The Iroquois and the New Deal*. Syracuse, NY: Syracuse University Press, 1981.

– 'Designing Woman: Laura Minnie Cornelius Kellogg, Iroquois Leader.' In *Indian Lives*, Raymond Wilson and L.G. Moses, 159–86. Albuquerque: University of New Mexico Press, 1985.

– *The Iroquois Struggle for Survival: World War II to Red Power*. Syracuse, NY: Syracuse University Press, 1986.

Jasen, Patricia. *Wild Things: Nature, Culture, and Tourism in Ontario 1790–1914*. Toronto: University of Toronto Press, 1995.

Johnson, E. Pauline (Tekahionwake). 'One of Them (Pauline Johnson).' The

Iroquois Women of Canada.' In *Women of Canada. Their Life and Work*. Ottawa: National Council of Women of Canada, 1900.

– *The Shapgganappi*. Toronto: William Briggs, 1913.

– *Legends of Vancouver*. Toronto: McClelland & Stewart, 1926 [1911].

– *Flint and Feather: The Complete Poems of E. Pauline Johnson*. Toronto: Paperjacks, 1972 [1911].

– *The Moccasin Maker*. Introduction, Annotation, and Bibliography by A. LaVonne Brown Ruoff. Tucson: University of Arizona Press, 1987 [1913].

Johnston, Charles M. Brant. *Brant County: A History 1786–1945*. Toronto: Oxford University Press, 1967.

Keller, Betty. *Pauline. A Biography of Pauline Johnson*. Vancouver and Toronto: Douglas and McIntyre, 1981.

Kidwell, Clara Sue. 'Indian Women as Cultural Mediators.' *Ethnohistory* 39.2 (1992): 97–107.

Koss, Stephen. *The Pro-Boers: The Anatomy of an Anti-War Movement*. Chicago: University of Chicago Press, 1973.

Landsman, Gail. 'The "Other" as Political Symbol: Images of Indians in the Woman Suffrage Movement.' *Ethnohistory* 39.3 (1992): 247–84.

Larson, Charles R. *American Indian Fiction*. Albuquerque: University of New Mexico Press, 1978.

Leacock, Stephen. 'Greater Canada: An Appeal.' In *The Social Criticism of Stephen Leacock*, ed. A. Bowker, 3–11. Toronto: University of Toronto Press, 1973.

Lighthall, William D. *Canadian Songs and Poems: Voices from the Forests and Waters, the Settlements and Cities of Canada*. London: Walter Scott, 1892.

Lundgren, Jodi. 1995. '"Being a Half-Breed": Discourses on Race and Cultural Syncreticity in the Works of Three Métis Women Writers.' *Canadian Literature* 144 (Spring 1995): 62–79.

McBride, Bunny. *Molly Spotted Elk: A Penobscot in Paris*. Norman and London: University of Oklahoma Press, 1995.

McClung, Nellie L. *In Times like These*. Toronto: Thomas Allen, 1915.

– *The Stream Runs Fast*. Toronto: Thomas Allen, 1945.

MacDonald, Mary Lu. 'Red and White; Black, White and Grey Hats.' In *Native Writers and Canadian Writing*, ed. W.H. New, 92–111. Vancouver: UBC Press, 1990.

Martin, Christopher. *The Russo-Japanese War*. London and New York: Abelard-Schuman, 1967.

Owram, Douglas K. 'European Savagery: Some Canadian Reaction to American Indian Policy, 1867–1885.' M.A. thesis, Queen's University, Kingston, Ontario, 1972.

Page, Robert. *The Boer War and Canadian Imperialism*. Ottawa: Canadian Historical Association, 1987.

Petrone, Penny. *Native Literature: From the Oral Tradition to the Present*. Toronto: Oxford University Press, 1990.

Poignant, Roslyn. 'Captive Aboriginal Lives: Billy, Jenny, Little Toby and Their Companions.' In *Captured Lives: Australian Captivity Narratives*. Working Papers in Australian Studies, 85, 86, 87. The Sir Robert Menzies Centre for Australian Studies and the Institute for Commonwealth Studies. London: University of London, 1993.

Prentice, Alison, et al. *Canadian Women: A History*. 2nd ed. Toronto: Harcourt Brace, 1996.

Prucha, Francis P. *The Great Father: The United States Government and the American Indians*. Lincoln and London: University of Nebraska Press, 1986.

Ramusack, Barbara, and Antoinette Burton. 'Feminism, Imperialism and Race: A Dialogue between India and Britain.' *Women's History Review* 3.4 (1994): 469–81.

Said, Edward. *Culture and Imperialism*. New York: Vintage, 1994.

Saywell, John T., ed. *The Canadian Journal of Lady Aberdeen, 1893–1898*. Toronto: Champlain Society, 1960.

Shimony, Annemarie Anrod. *Conservatism among the Iroquois at the Six Nations Reserve*. Syracuse, NY: Syracuse University Press, 1994.

Shoeman, Karel. *Only an Anguish to Live Here: Olive Schreiner and the Anglo Boer War, 1899–1902*. Cape Town: Human and Rousseau, 1992.

Silvera, Makeda, ed. 'Maria Campbell Talks to Beth Cuthand: "It's the Job of the Storyteller to Create Chaos."' In *The Other Woman: Women of Colour in Contemporary Canadian Literature*, 264–70. Toronto: Sister Vision, 1995.

Smith, Donald. *Sacred Feathers: The Reverend Peter Jones (Kahkewaquonaby) and the Mississauga Indians*. Toronto: University of Toronto Press, 1987.

– *From the Land of Shadows: The Making of Grey Owl*. Saskatoon: Western Producer Prairie Books, 1990.

Strong-Boag, Veronica. *The Parliament of Women: The National Council of Women of Canada*. Ottawa: National Museums of Canada, 1976.

Tennant, Paul. *Aboriginal Peoples and Politics: The Indian Land Question in British Columbia, 1849–1989*. Vancouver: UBC Press, 1990.

Titley, E. Brian. *A Narrow Vision: Duncan Campbell Scott and the Administration of Indian Affairs in Canada*. Vancouver: UBC Press, 1986.

Tooker, Elisabeth. 'Women in Iroquois Society.' In *Canadian Women: A Reader*, ed. Wendy Mitchinson et al., 19–32. Toronto: Harcourt Brace, 1996.

Turner, Margaret E. *Imagining Culture: New World Narrative and the Writing of Canada*. Montreal and Kingston: McGill-Queen's University Press, 1995.

Valverde, Marianna. *The Age of Light, Soap, and Water: Moral Reform in English Canada, 1885–1925*. Toronto: McClelland & Stewart, 1991.

Van Kirk, Sylvia. '"The Custom of the Country": An Examination of Fur Trade Marriage Practices.' In *Essays on Western History*, ed. L.H. Thomas, 49–68. Edmonton: University of Alberta Press, 1976.

Van Steen, Marcus. *Pauline Johnson: Her Life and Work*. Toronto: Musson, 1965.

Wagner, Sally Roesch. '"The Root of Oppression Is the Loss of Memory": The Iroquois and the Earliest Feminist Vision.' In *Iroquois Women: An Anthology*, ed. W.G. Spittal, 223–8. Ohsweken, ON: Iroqcrafts, 1990.

Walden, Keith. *Visions of Order*. Toronto: Butterworths, 1982.

Weaver, Sally M. *Medicine and Politics among the Grand River Iroquois: A Study of the Non-Conservatives*. Publications in Ethnology, no. 4. Ottawa: National Museums of Canada, 1972.

– 'The Iroquois: The Grand River Reserve in the Late Nineteenth and Early Twentieth Centuries, 1875–1945.' In *Aboriginal Ontario: Historical Perspectives on the First Nations*, ed. E.S. Rogers and Donald B. Smith, 213–57. Toronto and Oxford: Dundurn, 1994.

Wilson, Stephen. *Ideology and Experience: Anti-Semitism in France at the Time of the Dreyfus Affair*. London: Associated University Presses, 1982.

15 The Colonization of a Native Woman Scholar

EMMA LAROCQUE

The history of Canada is a history of the colonization of Aboriginal peoples. Colonization is a pervasive structural and psychological relationship between the colonizer and the colonized and is ultimately reflected in the dominant institutions, policies, histories, and literatures of occupying powers. Yet, it is only recently that Canadian scholars from a variety of fields have begun to situate the Native/white relationship within this context of dominance-subjugation.[1] There is ample room in Canadian scholarship for macroscopic explorations of the dynamics of oppression. In other words, we must seek to understand what happens to a country that has existed under the forces of colonial history over such an extended period of time. We must seek to recognize the faces of both the colonizer and the colonized,[2] as they appear in society and in the academic community. We must become aware of the functions of power and racism, its effects on the Native population, and the significance of resistance.

Colonization has taken its toll on all Native peoples, but perhaps it has taken its greatest toll on women. While all Natives experience racism, Native women suffer from sexism as well. Racism and sexism[3] found in the colonial process have served to dramatically undermine the place and value of women in Aboriginal cultures, leaving us vulnerable both within and outside of our communities. Not only have Native women been subjected to violence in both white and Native societies, but we have also been subjected to patriarchal policies that have dispossessed us of our inherited rights, lands, identities, and families. Native women continue to experience discrimination through the Indian Act, inadequate representation in Native and mainstream organizations, lack of official representation in self-government discussions, under-

and/or unequal employment, and ghettoization of the educated Native woman, for example.[4] The tentacles of colonization are not only extant today, but may also be multiplying and encircling Native peoples in ever-tighter grips of landlessness and marginalization, hence, of anger, anomie, and violence, in which women are the more obvious victims.

The effects of colonization, then, have been far-reaching, and numerous issues remain to be examined, not the least of which is how colonization affects men and women differently.[5] As a long-standing scholar in Native studies, I especially wish to bring to this discussion some of my reflections about what confronts those of us who are not only Native and women but are also intellectuals and researchers caught within the confines of ideologically rooted, Western-based canons, standards, and notions of objectivity and research.[6] We are in extraordinary circumstances: not only do we study and teach colonial history, but we also walk in its shadow on a daily basis ourselves. What do we do with our knowledge as well as with the practices of power in our lives, even in places of higher learning?

I find it impossible to study colonial history, literature, and popular cultural productions featuring Native peoples, particularly women, without addressing the social and ethical ramifications of such study. To study any kind of human violation is, *ipso facto*, to be engaged in ethical matters. And we must respond – as scholars, as men and women, Native and white alike. These destructive attitudes, unabashed biases, policies, and violence that we footnote cannot be mere intellectual or scholarly exercises. They do affect Native peoples, real human lives. I believe there is a direct relationship between racist/sexist stereotypes and violence against Native women and girls.[7] The dehumanizing portrayal of the 'squaw' and the over-sexualization of Native females such as in Walt Disney's *Pocahontas* surely render all Native female persons vulnerable. Moreover, these stereotypes have had a profound impact on the self-images of Native men and women, respectively, and on their relationships with each other.[8]

In addition to the questions of the social purpose of our knowledge, we are confronted in scholarship with having to deal with Western-controlled education, language, cultural production, and history. For example, classically colonial archival and academic descriptions and data about Natives' tools, physical features, 'rituals,' or geography have been equated with objectivity,[9] while Native-based data has been subsumed under subjectivity. Native scholars, particularly those of us who are decolonized and/or feminist, have been accused of 'speaking in our own voices,' which is taken as 'being biased' or doing something less than 'substantive' or 'pure' research. Not only are such accusations glaringly ironic given the degree of bias, inflammatory language, and barely concealed racism evident in much of early Canadian historical and literary writing on Native peoples,[10] but they are also adversarial. Native scholars' contribution to contemporary scholarship is significant, for, in a sense, we bring 'the other half' of Canada into light. Not only do we offer new ways of seeing and saying things, but we also provide new directions and fresh methodologies to cross-cultural research; we broaden the empirical and theoretical bases of numerous disciplines, and we pose new questions to old and tired traditions. And often, we live with many anomalies. If we serve as 'informants' to our non-Native colleagues, for example, about growing up within a land-based culture (e.g., on a trap line), our colleagues would include such information as part of their scholarly presentations; it would authenticate their research. Yet, if we use the very same information with a direct reference to our cultural backgrounds, it would be met, at best, with scepticism, and, at worst, with charges of parochialism because we would have spoken in 'our own voices.'

Clearly, the tension in the colonizer/colonized dichotomy has not escaped the academic community, and much work needs to be done to acknowledge the dialectics of colonization in Canadian scholarship. And I, as a Native woman, am compelled to pursue and express my scholarship quite differently from the way my non-Native counterparts do. I do this by maintaining orality in writing, taking an interdisciplinary approach to genre, calling for ethical re/considerations (not to be confused with 'censorship') in the archiving of hate material, and openly (rather than covertly) referring to 'voice' within academic studies. My use of 'voice,' for example, is a textual resistance technique. It should not be assumed, as it so often is, that using 'voice' means 'making a personal statement,' which is then dichotomized from 'academic studies.' Native scholars and writers are demonstrating that 'voice' can be, must be, used within academic studies not only as an expression of cultural integrity but also as an attempt to begin to balance the legacy of dehumanization and bias entrenched in Canadian studies about Native peoples. Colleagues, publishers, editors, and readers of academic material need especially to acquaint themselves with the political nature of the English language, Western history, and other hegemonic canons of scholarly and editorial practices and criticism before they are in a position to appreciate what should most appropriately be understood as 'Native resistance scholarship.'[11] There is no basis for assuming that Native intellectuals are somehow more predisposed to bias than are white intellectuals.

The growing body of international literature on 'post-colonial voices' as expressed by non-Western scholars and writers should serve as an instructive reminder that Native scholars and writers in Canada are part of this non-Western international community. This is not to say that the colonial experience is 'in the past' for Canadian Native peoples; rather, it is to say that we are responding within the postcolonial intellectual context. As Ashcroft, Griffiths, and Tiffin put it, we are emerging 'in our present form out of the experience of colonization' and asserting ourselves 'by foregrounding the tension' with the colonial power by writing or talking back to 'the empire.'[12] We are challenging our non-Native colleagues to throw off 'the weight of' antiquity' with respect to hegemonic canonical assumptions, which continue 'to dominate cultural production in much of the postcolonial world.'[13] We are challenging them to re-evaluate their colonial frameworks of interpretation, their conclusions and portrayals, not to mention their tendencies of excluding from their footnotes scholars who are Native.[14]

There are many and varied layers of 'colonial' practices in current Canadian scholarship. Of interest is the less than judicious treatment of the Native women writers who contributed to *Writing the Circle*[15] by some critics who, among other things, exclude the theories, criticisms, creativity, and experience of these women.[16] A number of critical responses have based their theories about Native women writers on such small, repetitive, and highly selective samples[17] that it does raise troubling issues of exclusion, especially to those of us (both male and female) who are at once scholars, critics, and/or creative writers. We do present complexities in that we are crossing cultures, disciplines, and genres, and we obviously do not fit into conventional categories or ideological formulas. But we have been writing and footnoting at least as early as the 1970s, and our combined backgrounds of scholarship and marginalization as well as critical and/or creative works do model what is at the very heart of postcolonial discourse. It remains that as scholars we are all challenged to cross borders and to seek greater understanding. Western-based assumptions (including feminist, deconstructionist, and/or 'postcolonial' discourse) can no longer claim exclusive rights to the ways and means of academic methodology and insight.

The challenge is, finally, to ourselves as Native women caught within the burdens and contradictions of colonial history. We are being asked to confront some of our own traditions at a time when there seems to be a great need for a recall of traditions to help us retain our identities as Aboriginal people. But there is no choice – as women we must be circumspect in our recall of tradition. We must ask ourselves whether and to what extent tradition is liberating to us as women. We must ask ourselves wherein lies (lie) our source(s) of empowerment. We know enough about human history that we cannot assume that all Aboriginal traditions universally respected and honoured women. (And is 'respect' and 'honour' all that we can ask for?) It should not be assumed, even in those original societies that were structured along matriarchal lines, that matriarchies necessarily prevented men from oppressing women. There are indications of male violence and sexism in some Aboriginal societies prior to European contact[18] and certainly after contact. But, at the same time, culture is not immutable, and tradition cannot be expected to be always of value or relevant in our times. As Native women, we are faced with very difficult and painful choices, but, nonetheless, we are challenged to change, create, and embrace 'traditions' consistent with contemporary and international human rights standards.

Sadly, there are insidious notions within our own communities that we as Native women should be 'unobtrusive, soft-spoken and quiet,' and that we should not assume elected leadership, which is taken to mean 'acting like men.' The 'traditional Indian woman' is still often expected to act and dress like an ornamental Pocahontas / 'Indian Princess.' But who should our models be? How should we maintain the traditions we value without adhering to stereotype or compromising our full humanity? If one must look to the past for models and heroes, we might do well to take a second look at Pocahontas. The irony is that the real Pocahontas was neither unobtrusive nor quiet. Quite the contrary: she was in fact revolutionary – for the wrong cause, but revolutionary nonetheless!

If we wish to act on history rather than be acted on, we can ill afford to be silent or stay content in the shadows of our male contemporaries. Speaking directly to the exclusion of women's experience and the analysis of this exclusion, Joyce Green, a Native doctoral student in political science at the University of Alberta, writes: 'So much of women's experience has been classified as nondata. So much of women's analysis as women has been ignored by the academy and by the activists. The consequence is male-gendered theoretical and epistemological development that is presented as authentic reflection of the human condition ... But knowledge is dynamic, and there is nothing preventing the incorporation of new female and Aboriginal ways of knowing.'[19]

History demands of us to assume our dignity, our equality, and our humanity. We must not move toward the future with anything less. Nor can we pursue scholarship in any other way.

NOTES

1 There are fine works from various fields on the colonization of Canadian Native peoples. They include Patterson, *The Canadian Indian since 1500* (1972); Watkins, *Dene Nation* (1977); Berger, *Northern Frontier, Northern Homeland* (1977); McCullum and McCullum, *This Land Is Not for Sale* (1975); Shkilnyk, *A Poison Stronger than Love* (1985); Speck, *An Error in Judgement* (1987); A.D. Fisher, 'A Colonial Education System' (1981). Many more conventional studies have not placed the Native experience into any cohesive theoretical framework; instead, the emphasis has been on 'the impact of' the white man, his tools, his religion, and his diseases, and so forth. Fur-trade volumes, in particular, are replete with 'impact' notions and items.

2 I am suggesting, of course, that as Canadian peoples, both Native and non-Native, we may find ourselves, our respective experiences, mirrored in Memmi's *The Colonizer and the Colonized* (1967).

3 Racism and sexism together result in powerful personal and structural expressions in any society, but they are clearly exacerbated under colonial conditions. However, it should be noted that sexism, in particular, did not derive solely from European culture or colonization. As alluded to throughout this paper, there are indications of pre-existing patriarchy and sexism within Aboriginal cultures.

4 For a more detailed discussion on patriarchy, see my article 'Racism/ Sexism and Its Effects on Native Women' (1989). See also: Green, 'Constitutionalising the Patriarchy' (1993); Stacey-Moore, 'In Our Own Voice' (1993).

5 Further study is required on how colonization affects men and women differently. Diane Bell, a critical anthropologist, has pointed out that, while mainstream scholars have begun to 'develop more and more sophisticated models of colonial relations ... they have, for the most part, paid scant attention to the different impact of colonial practices on men and women,' which has led to creating 'a niche for the consolidation of male power;

... the most consistent outcome appears to be that while men assume the political spokesperson role, the women run the welfare structures' (1989: 6).

6 On the issue of non-Western intellectuals confronting Western hegemonic canonical assumptions in postcolonial writing, see Harlow, *Resistance Literature* (1987); Ashcroft, Griffiths, and Tiffin, *The Empire Writes Back* (1989); and Hitchcock, The *Dialogics of the Oppressed* (1992).

7 For a more detailed discussion on violence against Native women, see my article 'Violence in Aboriginal Communities' (1993). See also the Aboriginal Justice Inquiry of Manitoba, Government of Manitoba (1991); and the Ontario Native Women's Association's report, *Breaking Free: A Proposal for Change to Aboriginal Family Violence* (1989).

8 Native men and women have experienced and reacted to colonial influences quite differently. This is particularly evident with respect to gender roles and stereotypes. For further comment on this, see my articles 'Racism/Sexism and Its Effects on Native Women' (1989) and 'Violence in Aboriginal Communities' (1993).

9 There is an air of detachment to these descriptions, and it is this imperial aloofness that has been mistaken for objectivity. For a brilliant analysis of 'textual strategies of domination' through European descriptions of Native ethnography that give 'an appearance of impartiality,' see Duchemin, '"A Parcel of Whelps"' (1990).

10 For a discussion on inflammatory language that should qualify as hate literature, see my article 'On the Ethics of Publishing Historical Documents' (1988).

11 For a more detailed discussion, but in the context of literary treatment of Aboriginal themes and writers, see my 'Preface, or Here Are Our Voices– Who Will Hear?' (1990); see also my article 'When the Other Is Me: Native Writers Confronting Canadian Literature,' in *Human Ecology in the North*, vol. 4, to be published by the Circumpolar Institute, University of Alberta.

12 Ashcroft, Griffiths, and Tiffin, *The Empire Writes Back* (1989), 2.

13 Ibid., 7

14 Non-Native scholars are increasingly using Native sources that they, however, reformulate or discount as ethnographic or personal accounts; there has been a persistent tendency on the part of white intellectuals to disregard Native scholars and other intellectuals, apparently assuming that they cannot be 'of the people,' or cannot be 'objective.' Either way, Native-based scholarship is put in a no-win situation.

15 Perreault and Vance, eds, *An Anthology – Writing the Circle* (1990).

16 See, for example, Lutz, 'Confronting Cultural Imperialism' (1995). Lutz's article is wide-ranging but, in the context of discussing 'Stolen Stories'

(141–2), he lists *Writing the Circle* as one of the works criticized (led by two Native women) for 'cultural appropriation'; he then goes on to claim that 'most Native writers support' the debate without making clear whether by *debate*, he means the broad topic of cultural appropriation or the small controversy surrounding *Writing the Circle*. Lutz bases his conclusion on an extremely small representation, quite mysteriously (and uncharacteristically, as he usually treats Native literatures and writes with depth and scope) overlooking the theoretical ramifications of the fifty or so Native women writers involved in the production of *Writing the Circle*. For a similarly perplexing treatment of *Writing the Circle*, see also Emberley, *Thresholds of Difference* (1993).

17 Attention has been poured repeatedly and almost exclusively on three or four Native women writers in most 'Native issues' publication specials or literary conferences over the last five years. See, for example, articles by Agnes Giant, Noel Elizabeth Comic, Margery Fee, and Barbara Godard in W.H. New, ed., *Native Writers and Canadian Literature* (1990). I should emphasize that my comment is not intended to focus on the Native writers upon whom attention is lavished but on the literary and academic critics who persistently neglect to study the other several dozen or so Native writers in Canada.

18 Many early European observations as well as original Indian legends (e.g., Cree Wehsehkehcha stories I grew up with) point to pre-contact existence of male violence and sexism against women.

19 Joyce Green, 'Democracy, Gender and Aborginal Rights,' unpublished manuscript, November 1993, 15.

REFERENCES

Adams, Howard. 1975. *Prison of Grass: Canada from the Native Point of View*. Toronto: New Press.

Ashcroft, Bill, Gareth Griffiths, and Helen Tiffin. 1989. *The Empire Writes Back: Theory and Practice in Post-Colonial Literature*. London and New York: Routledge.

Bell, Diane. 1989. 'Considering Gender: Are Human Rights for Women Too?' Paper presented at the International Conference on Human Rights in Cross Cultural Perspectives, College of Law, University of Saskatchewan.

Berger, Thomas R. 1977. *Northern Frontier, Norther Homeland: The Report of the Mackenzie Valley Pipeline Inquiry*. Volume 1. Ottawa: Minister of Supply and Services Canada.

Brodribb, Somer. 1984. 'The Traditional Roles of Native Women in Canada and the Impact of Colonization.' *Canadian Journal of Native Studies* 4.1: 85–103.

Brownmiller, Susan. 1975. *Against Our Will: Men, Women, and Rape*. New York: Simon and Schuster.

Campbell, Maria. 1973. *Halfbreed*. Toronto: McClelland and Stewart.

Culhane Speck, Dara. 1987. *An Error in Judgment: The Politics of Medical Care in an Indian/White Community*. Vancouver: Talonbooks.

Duchemin, Parker. 1990. '"A Parcel of Whelps": Alexander Mackenzie among the Indians.' *Canadian Literature* 124–5 (Spring-Summer): 49–75.

Emberley, Julia. 1993. *Thresholds of Difference: Feminist Critique, Native Women's Writings, Postcolonial Theory*. Toronto: University of Toronto Press.

Fanon, Frantz. 1963. *The Wretched of the Earth*. New Yolk: Grove Press.

Fisher, A.D. 198I. 'A Colonial Education System: Historical Changes and Schooling in Fort Chipewyan.' *Canadian Journal of Anthropology* 2.1 (Spring): 37–44.

Fisher, Robin, and Kenneth Coates, eds. 1998. *Out of the Background: Readings on Canadian Native History.* Toronto: Copp Clark Pitman.

Green, Joyce. 1993. 'Constitutionalising the Patriarchy: Aboriginal Women and Aboriginal Government.' *Constitutional Forum* 4.4: 110–20.

Harlow, Barbara. 1987. *Resistance Literature*. New York: Methuen.

Hitchcock, Peter. 1992. *The Dialogics of the Oppressed*. Minneapolis: University of Minnesota Press.

LaRocque, Emma. 1975. *Defeathering the Indian*. Agincourt, ON: Book Society of Canada.

– 1988. 'On the Ethics of Publishing Historical Documents.' In *The Orders of the Dreamed: George Nelson on Cree and Ojibwa Religion and Myth, 1823*, ed. Jennifer S.H. Brown and Robert Brightman. Winnipeg: University of Manitoba Press.

– 1989. 'Racism/Sexism and Its Effects on Native Women.' In *Public Concerns on Human Rights*. Winnipeg: Human Rights Commission.

– 1990. 'Preface, or Here Are Our Voices – Who Will Hear?' In *An Anthology – Writing the Circle: Native Women of Western Canada*, ed. Jeanne Perreault and Sylvia Vance. Edmonton: NeWest Publishers.

– 1990. 'Tides, Towns and Trains.' In *Living the Changes*, ed. Joan Turner. Winnipeg: University of Manitoba Press.

– 1993. 'Violence in Aboriginal Communities.' In *The Path to Healing*, prepared by the Royal Commission on Aboriginal Peoples, 72–89.

Lutz, Hartmut. 1995. 'Confronting Cultural Imperialism: First Nations People Are Combating Continued Cultural Theft.' In *Multiculturalism in North*

America and Europe: Social Practices – Literary Visions, ed. Hans Braun and Wolfgang Klooss. Trier, Germany: Wissenschaftlicher Verlag Trier.

Manitoba, Government of. 1991. Aboriginal Justice Inquiry of Manitoba.

McCullum, Hugh, and Karmel McCullum. 1975. *This Land Is Not for Sale: Canada's Original Peoples and their Land – a Saga of Neglect, Exploitation, and Conflict*. Toronto: Anglican Book Centre.

Memmi, Albert. 1967. *The Colonizer and the Colonized*. Trans. Howard Greenfeld. Boston: Beacon Press.

New, W.H., ed. 1990. *Native Writers and Canadian Literature*. Vancouver: UBC Press.

Ontario Native Women's Association. 1989. *Breaking Free: A Proposal for Change to Aboriginal Family Violence*. Thunder Bay: Ontario Native Women's Association.

Patterson, E. Palmer. 1972. *The Canadian Indian since 1500*. Don Mills, ON: Collier-Macmillan.

Perreault, Jeanne, and Sylvia Vance, eds. 1990. *An Anthology – Writing the Circle: Native Women of Western Canada*. Edmonton: NeWest Publishers.

Shkilnyk, Anastasia M. 1985. *A Poison Stronger than Love: The Destruction of an Ojibwa Community*. New Haven: Yale University Press.

Stacey-Moore, Gail. 1993. 'In Our Own Voice: Aboriginal Women Demand Justice.' *Herizons* 6.4: 21–3.

Steiner, Stan. 1968. *The New Indians*. New York: Dell Publishing.

Van Kirk, Sylvia. 1980. *Many Tender Ties: Women in Fur-Trade Society in Western Canada, 1670–1870*. Winnipeg: Watson and Dwyer Publishing.

Watkins, Mel. 1977. *Dene Nation: Colony Within*. Toronto: University of Toronto Press.

Historiography of Aboriginal Women in Canada: A Select Bibliography

Interest in Aboriginal women has grown dramatically in recent years. We have included in this volume those readings that we consider the most provocative and the most accessible. To honour this burgeoning field and to suggest further reading, we also offer the following bibliography. While not comprehensive (what is?), it includes a range of methodological and theoretical works, as well as ethnographic and literary works, which highlight the increasingly diverse and interdisciplinary nature of this field.

Learning about Aboriginal Women: Issues and Methodologies

Cruikshank, Julie. 'Oral Tradition and Oral History: Reviewing Some Issues.' *Canadian Historical Review* 75 (Summer 1994): 403–18.

Cruikshank, Julie, in collaboration with Angela Sidney, Kitty Smith, and Annie Ned. *Life Lived Like a Story: Life Stories of Three Yukon Native Elders.* Vancouver: UBC Press, 1990.

Emberley, Julia. 'Aboriginal Women's Writing and the Cultural Politics of Representation.' In *Women of the First Nations: Power, Wisdom, and Strength,* ed. Christine Miller and Patricia Chuchryk, 97–112. Winnipeg: University of Manitoba Press, 1996.

– *Thresholds of Difference: Feminist Critique, Native Women's Writing and Postcolonial Theory.* Toronto: University of Toronto Press, 1993.

Fiske, Jo-Anne. 'By, For, or About? Shifting Directions in the Representations of Aboriginal Women.' *Atlantis* 25.1 (2000): 11–27.

– '"Ask My Wife": A Feminist Interpretation of Fieldwork Where the Women Are Strong but the Men Are Tough.' *Atlantis* 11.2 (Spring 1986): 59–69.

Foster, Martha Harroun. 'Lost Women of the Matriarchy: Iroquois Women in the Historical Literature.' *American Indian Culture and Research Journal* 19.3 (1995): 121–40.

Green, Rayna. 'The Pocahontas Perplex: The Image of Indian Women in American Culture.' In *Native American Voices: A Reader*, ed. Susan Lobo and Steve Talbot, 182–92. New York: Longman, 1998.

– 'Review Essay: Native American Women.' *Signs: Journal of Woman in Culture and Society* 7 (Winter 1980): 248–67.

Haig-Brown, Celia. 'Choosing Border Work.' *Canadian Journal of Education* 19:1 (1992): 96–116.

Jamieson, Kathleen. 'Sisters under the Skin: An Exploration of the Implications of Feminist-Materialist Perspective.' *Canadian Ethnic Studies* 13.1 (1981): 130–43.

Medicine, Beatrice. 'The Role of Women in Native American Societies: A Bibliography.' *Indian Historian* 8 (1975): 51–3.

Mitchell, Marjorie, and Anna Franklin. 'When You Don't Know the Language, Listen to the Silence: An Historical Overview of Native Indian Women in BC.' In *Not Just Pin Money*, ed. Barbara K. Latham and Roberta J. Pazdro, 17–34. Victoria: Camosun College, 1984.

Pierson, Ruth Roach. 'Experience, Difference, Dominance and Voice in the Writing of Canadian Women's History.' In *Writing Women's History: International Perspectives*, ed. Karen Offen and Ruth Roach Pierson, 79–107. Bloomington: University of Indiana Press, 1991.

Sunseri, Lina. 'Moving beyond the Feminism versus Nationalism Dichotomy: Anti-Colonial Feminist Perspective on Aboriginal Liberation Struggles.' *Canadian Woman Studies* 20.2 (Summer 2000): 143–8.

Turner Strong, Pauline. 'Feminist Theory and the "Invasion of the Heart" in North America.' *Ethnohistory* 43.4 (Fall 1996): 683–703.

Van Kirk, Sylvia. 'Towards a Feminist Perspective in Native History.' In *Papers of the 18th Algonquian Conference*, ed. William Cowan, 377–89. Ottawa: Carleton University Press, 1987.

Wickwire, Wendy. 'Women in Ethnography: The Research of James Teit.' *Ethnohistory* 14.4 (Fall 1993): 539–62.

The Fur Trade: Women's Involvement

Anderson, Karen. 'As Gentle as Little Lambs: Images of Huron and Montagnais-Naskapi Women in the Writings of the 17th Century Jesuits.' *The Canadian Review of Sociology and Anthropology* 25 (Nov. 1988): 560–76.

– 'Commodity Exchange and Subordination: Montagnais-Naskapi and Huron Women, 1600–1650.' *Signs* 11 (Autumn 1985): 48–62.

Brown, Jennifer S.H. 'Women as Centre and Symbol in the Emergence of Métis Communities.' *Canadian Journal of Native Studies* 3 (1983): 39–46.

– *Strangers in Blood: Fur Trade Company Families in Indian Country.* Vancouver: University of British Columbia Press, 1980.

Littlefield, Lorraine. 'Women Traders in the Maritime Fur Trade.' In *Native People, Native Lands: Canadian Indians, Inuit and Metis,* ed. Brian Cox, 173–85. Ottawa: Carleton University Press, 1987.

Perry, Richard. 'The Fur Trade and the Status of Women in the Western Subarctic.' *Ethnohistory* 26 (1979): 363–75.

Peterson, Jacqueline. 'Women Dreaming: The Religiopsychology of Indian-White Marriage and the Rise of Metis Culture.' In *Western Women: Their Land, Their Lives,* ed. Lillian Schissel, Vicki L. Ruiz, and Janice Monk, 49–69. Albuquerque: University of New Mexico Press, 1988.

Prezzano, Susan C. 'Warfare, Women and Households: The Development of Iroquois Culture.' In *Women in Prehistory: North America and Mesoamerica,* ed. Cheryl Claassen and Rosemary A. Joyce, 88–99. Philadelphia: University of Pennsylvania Press, 1997.

Sleeper-Smith, Susan. *Indian Women and French Men: Rethinking Cultural Encounter in the Western Great Lakes.* Amherst: University of Massachusetts Press, 2001.

– 'Furs and Female Kin Networks: The World of Marie Madeleine Reaume L'archeveque Chevalier.' In *New Faces of the Fur Trade: Selected Papers of the Seventh North American Fur Trade Conference, Halifax, Nova Scotia, 1995,* ed. Jo-Anne Fiske, Susan Sleeper-Smith, and William Wicken, 53–72. East Lansing: Michigan State University Press, 1998.

Van Kirk, Sylvia. 'The Custom of the Country: An Examination of Fur Trade Marriage Practices.' In *Canadian Family History: Selected Readings,* ed. Bettina Bradbury, 67–93. Toronto: Copp Clark Pitman, 1992.

– *Many Tender Ties: Women in Fur-Trade Society in Western Canada.* Winnipeg: Watson and Dwyer Publishing, 1980.

Missionaries and Education

Anderson, Karen. *Chain Her by One Foot: The Subjugation of Native Women in Seventeenth-Century New France.* London: Routledge, 1991.

Barman, Jean. 'Separate and Unequal: Indian and White Girls at All Hallows School, 1884–1920.' In *Indian Education in Canada,* Volume I. *The Legacy,* ed. Jean Barman, Yvonne Hebert, and Don McCaskill, 110–31. Vancouver: UBC Press, 1986.

Devens, Carol. *Countering Colonization: Native American Women and Great Lakes Missions, 1630–1900.* Berkeley: University of California Press, 1992.

– '"If We Get the Girls, We Get the Race": Missionary Education of Native American Girls.' *Journal of World History* 3 (Fall 1992): 219–38.
– 'Separate Confrontations: Gender as a Factor in Indian Adaptation to European Colonization in New France.' *American Quarterly* 38.3 (1986): 461–80.
Fiske, Jo-Anne. 'Pocahontas's Granddaughters: Spiritual Transition and Tradition of Carrier Women of British Columbia.' *Ethnohistory* 43.4 (Fall 1996): 663–81.
– 'Gender and the Paradox of Residential Education in Carrier Society.' In *Women and Education*, ed. Jane S. Gaskell and Arlene Tigar McLaren, 131–46. 2nd ed. Calgary: Detselig, 1991.
Haig-Brown, Celia. 'Warrior Mothers: Lessons and Possibilities.' *Journal for a Just and Caring Education* 4.1 (Jan. 1998): 96–109.
Leacock, Eleanor. 'Women's Status in Egalitarian Society: Implications for Social Evolution.' *Current Anthropology* 33 (Fall 1992): 225–36.
– 'Montagnais Women and the Jesuit Program for Colonization.' In *Women and Colonization: Anthropological Perspectives*, ed. Mona Etienne and Eleanor Leacock, 25–41. New York: Praeger Publishers, 1980.
Miller, J.R. '"The Misfortune of Being a Woman": Gender.' In *Shingwauk's Vision: A History of Native Residential Schools*, 217–50. Toronto: University of Toronto Press, 1996.
Neylan, Susan. *The Heavens Are Changing: Nineteenth-Century Protestant Missions and Tsimshian Christianity*. Montreal and Kingston: McGill-Queen's University Press, 2003.
Peers, Laura. '"The Guardian of All": Jesuit Missionary and Salish Perceptions of the Virgin Mary.' In *Reading beyond Words: Contexts for Native History*, ed. Jennifer S.H. Brown and Elizabeth Vibert. 284–303. Peterborough, ON: Broadview Press, 1996.
Raibmon, Paige. 'Living on Display: Colonial Visions of Aboriginal Domestic Spaces' *BC Studies*. 140 (Winter 2003): 69–89.
Whitehead, Margaret. '"A Useful Christian Woman": First Nations Women and Protestant Missionary Work in British Columbia.' *Atlantis* 18.1–2 (1992–3): 142–66.
Williams, Shirley. 'Women's Role in Ojibway Spirituality.' *Journal of Canadian Native Studies* 27.3 (1992): 100–4.

Contending with Colonization: Traditional Cultures, Changing Roles

Ackerman, Lillian. 'Gender Status in Yup'ik Society.' *Inuit Studies* 14.1–2 (1990): 209–22.

Alia, Valeria. 'Inuit Women and the Politics of Naming in Nunavut.' *Canadian Woman Studies* 11 (Fall 1994): 11–14.

Billson, Janet Mancini. 'Standing Tradition on Its Head: Role Reversal among Blood Indian Couples.' *Great Plains Quarterly* 11:1 (1991): 3–21.

Blackman, Margaret B. *During My Time: Florence Edenshaw Davidson, a Haida Woman*. Seattle: University of Washington Press, 1992.

– 'The Changing Status of Haida Women: An Ethnohistorical and Life History Approach.' In *The World Is as Sharp as a Knife: An Anthology in Honour of Wilson Duff*, ed. Donald. B. Abbott, 65–77. Victoria: British Columbia Municipal Museum, 1981.

Bodenhorn, Barbara. '"I'm Not the Great Hunter, My Wife Is": Inupiat and Anthropological Models of Gender.' *Inuit Studies* 14.1–2 (1990): 55–74.

Bourgeault, Ron. 'Race, Class and Gender: Colonial Domination of Indian Women.' *Socialist Studies* 5 (1989): 87–115.

– 'The Development of Capitalism and the Subjugation of Native Women in Northern Canada.' *Alternate Routes* 6 (1983): 110–40.

Brodribb, Somer. 'The Traditional Roles of Native Women in Canada and the Impact of Colonization.' *Canadian Journal of Native Studies* 4.1 (1984): 85–103.

Brown, Jennifer S.H. 'A Cree Nurse in the Cradle of Methodism: Little Mary and the Egerton R. Young Family in Norway House and Berens River.' In *First Days, Fighting Days: Women in Manitoba History*, ed. Mary Kinnear, 17–40. Regina: Canadian Plains Research Center, 1987.

Brown, Judith K. 'Economic Organization and the Position of Women among the Iroquois.' *Ethnohistory* 17 (1970): 151–67.

Carter, Sarah. 'First Nations Women of Prairie Canada in the Early Reserve Years, the 1870s to the 1920s: A Preliminary Inquiry.' In *Women of the First Nations: Power, Wisdom, and Strength*, ed. Christine Miller and Patricia Chuchryk, 51–76. Winnipeg: University of Manitoba Press, 1996.

Cooper, Carol. 'Native Women of the Northern Pacific Coast: An Historical Perspective, 1830–1900.' *Journal of Canadian Studies* 27.4 (Winter 1992–3): 44–75.

Danvers, Gail D. 'Gendered Encounters: Warriors, Women, and William Johnson.' *Journal of American Studies* 35.2 (2001): 187–202.

Drees, Laurie Meijer. 'Aboriginal Women in the Canadian West.' *Native Studies Review* 10 (1995): 61–73.

Emberley, Julia V. 'The Bourgeois Family, Aboriginal Women, and Colonial Governance in Canada: A Study in Feminist Historical and Cultural Materialism.' *Signs: Journal of Women in Culture and Society* 27.1 (2001): 59–85.

Fiske, Jo-Anne. 'Colonization and the Decline of Women's Status: The Tsimshian Case.' *Feminist Studies* 17 (1991): 509–35.

Green, Gretchen. 'Gender and the Longhouse: Iroquois Women in a Changing Culture.' In *Women and Freedom in Early America*, ed. Larry D. Eldridge, 7–25. New York: New York University Press, 1997.

– 'Molly Brant, Catherine Brant, and Their Daughters: A Study in Colonial Acculturation.' *Ontario History* 81.3 (1989): 235–50.

Klein, Laura F. 'Mother as Clanswoman: Rank and Gender in Tlingit Society.' In *Women and Power in Native North America*, ed. Laura F. Klein and Lillian A. Ackerman, 28–45. Norman: University of Oklahoma Press, 1995.

Leacock, Eleanor, ed. *Women and Colonization: Anthropological Perspectives*. New York: Praeger Publishers, 1980.

Medicine, Beatrice. 'Warrior Women': Sex Role Alternatives for Plains Indian Women.' In *The Hidden Half: Studies of Plains Indian Women*, ed. Patricia Albers and Beatrice Medicine, 267–80. Lanham, MD: University Press of America, 1983.

– 'The Role of Women in Native American Societies: A Bibliography.' *Indian Historian* 8 (1975): 51–3.

Monture-Angus, Patricia. 'Considering Colonialism and Oppression: Aboriginal Women, Justice and the "Theory" of Decolonization.' *Native Studies Review* 12.1 (1999): 63–94.

Phillips, Ruth B. 'Nuns, Ladies, and the "Queen of the Huron": Appropriating the Savage in Nineteenth-Century Huron Tourist Art.' In *Unpacking Culture: Art and Commodity in Colonial and Post-Colonial Worlds*, ed. Ruth B. Phillips and Christopher B. Steiner, 33–50. Berkeley: University of California Press, 1999.

Ridington, Robin. 'Stories of the Vision Quest among Dunne-za Women.' *Atlantis* 9.1 (Fall 1983): 68–78.

Schuurman, Nadine. 'Contesting Patriarchies: Nlha7pamux and Stl'stl'imx Women and Colonialism in Nineteenth-Century British Columbia.' *Gender, Place and Culture* 5.2 (1998): 141–58.

Shoemaker, Nancy. 'The Rise or Fall of Iroquois Women.' *Journal of Women's History* 2 (1991): 39–57.

– ed. *Negotiators of Change: Historical Perspectives on Native American Women*. New York: Routledge, 1995.

Smith, Erica. 'Gentlemen: This Is No Ordinary Trial: Sexual Narratives in the Trial of the Reverend Corbett, Red River, 1863.' In *Reading beyond Words: Contexts for Native History*, ed. Jennifer S.H. Brown and Elizabeth Vibert, 364–80. Peterborough, ON: Broadview Press, 1996.

Stahl, Dorinda M. 'Moving from Colonization to Decolonization: Reinterpreting Historical Images of Aboriginal Women.' *Native Studies Review* 12.1 (1999): 115–26.

Van Kirk, Sylvia. 'From "Marrying-In" to "Marrying-Out": Changing Patterns of Aboriginal/Non-Aboriginal Marriage in Colonial Canada.' *Frontiers* 23.3 (2002): 1–11.
– 'Colonised Lives: The Native Wives and Daughters of Five Founding Families of Victoria.' In *Pacific Empires: Essays in Honour of Glyndwr Williams*, 215–36. Vancouver: UBC Press, 1999.

Sexuality, Gender, and the Regulation of Women's Bodies

Barman, Jean. 'Invisible Women: Aboriginal Mothers and Mixed-Race Daughters in Rural Pioneer British Columbia.' In *Beyond the City Limits: Rural History in British Columbia*, ed. R.W. Sandwell, 159–79. Vancouver: UBC Press, 1999.
– 'What a Difference a Border Makes: Aboriginal Racial Intermixture in the Pacific Northwest.' *Journal of the West* 38.3 (July 1999): 14–21.
Benoit, Cecilia, and Dena Caroll. 'Aboriginal Midwifery in British Columbia: A Narrative Untold.' In *A Persistent Spirit: Towards Understanding Aboriginal Health in British Columbia*, ed. P.H. Stephenson, S.J. Elliott, L.T. Foster, and J. Harris, 223–47. Victoria: University of Victoria, Western Geographical Press, 1995.
Cannon, Martin. 'The Regulation of First Nations Sexuality.' *Canadian Journal of Native Studies* 18.1 (1998): 1–18.
Cruikshank, Julie. 'Becoming a Woman in Athapaskan Society: Changing Traditions on the Upper Yukon River.' *Western Canadian Journal of Anthropology* 5.2 (1975): 1–14.
Fiske, Jo-Anne. 'Carrier Women and the Politics of Mothering.' In *Rethinking Canada: The Promise of Women's History*, ed. Veronica Strong- Boag, Mona Gleason, and Adele Perry, 235–48. 4th ed. Don Mills, ON: Oxford University Press, 2002.
Gross, Julie. 'Molly Brant: Textual Representations of Cultural Midwifery.' *American Studies* 40.1 (Spring 1999): 23–40.
Jasen, Patricia. 'Race, Culture and the Colonization of Childbirth in Northern Canada.' *Social History of Medicine* 10.3 (Dec. 1997): 383–400.
LaRocque, Emma. 'Racism/Sexism and Its Effects on Native Women.' In *Public Concerns on Human Rights*. Winnipeg: University of Manitoba Press, 1988.
McGillivary, Anne, and Brenda Comaskey. *Black Eyes All of the Time: Intimate Violence, Aboriginal Women and the Justice System*. Toronto: University of Toronto Press, 1999.
Udel, Lisa J. 'Revision and Resistance: The Politics of Native Women's Motherwork.' *Frontiers* 22:2 (2001): 43–62.

Women and Work

Blythe, Jennifer, and Peggy Martin McGuire. 'The Changing Employment of Cree Women in Moosonee and Moose Factory.' In *Women of the First Nations: Power, Wisdom, and Strength*, ed. Christine Miller and Patricia Chuchryk, 131–50. Winnipeg: University of Manitoba Press, 1996.

Brown, Judith K. 'Economic Organization and the Position of Women among the Iroquois.' *Ethnohistory* 17 (1970): 151–67.

Brown, Rosemary. 'The Exploitation of the Oil and Gas Frontier: Its Impact on Lubicon Lake Cree Women.' In *Women of the First Nations: Power, Wisdom, and Strength*, ed. Christine Miller and Patricia Chuchryk, 151–66. Winnipeg: University of Manitoba Press, 1996.

Fiske, Jo-Anne. 'Fishing Is Women's Business: Changing Economic Roles of Carrier Women and Men.' In *Native People, Native Lands: Canadian Indians, Inuit and Métis*, ed. Bruce Alden Cox, 186–98. Ottawa: Carleton University Press, 1991.

Guard, Julie. 'Authenticity on the Line: Women Workers, Native "Scabs," and the Multi-Ethnic Politics of Identity in a Left-Led Strike in Cold War Canada.' *Journal of Women's History* 15.4 (Winter 2004): 117–40.

Leacock, Eleanor. 'History, Development and the Division of Labour by Sex: Implications for Organization.' *Signs: Journal of Women in Culture and Society.* Special issue on 'Development and the Sexual Division of Labour.' 7.2 (1981): 474–91.

Myszynski, Alicja. 'Race and Gender: Structural Determinants in the Formation of British Columbia's Salmon Cannery Labour Force.' In *Class, Gender and Region: Essays in Canadian Historical Sociology*, ed. Gregory S. Kealey, 103–20. St John's: Committee on Canadian Labour History, 1988.

Peers, Laura. 'Subsistence, Secondary Literature and Gender Bias.' In *Women of the First Nations: Power, Wisdom, and Strength*, ed. Christine Miller and Patricia Chuchryk, 39–50. Winnipeg: University of Manitoba Press, 1996.

The Law and the State

Backhouse, Constance. 'First Nations Laws and European Perspectives.' In *Petticoats and Prejudice: Women and Law in Nineteenth Century Canada*, 9–28. Toronto: Women's Press, 1991.

Bear, Shirley, and the Tobique Women's Group. 'You Can't Change the Indian Act?' In *Women and Social Change: Feminist Activism in Canada*, ed. Jeri Dawn White and Janice L. Ristock, 198–220. Toronto: James Lorimer and Co., 1991.

Chiste, Katherine Beaty. 'Aboriginal Women and Self-Government: Challenging Leviathan.' *American Indian Culture and Research Journal* 18.3 (1994): 19–43.

Fiske, Jo-Anne. 'The Supreme Law and the Grand Law: Changing Significance of Customary Law for Aboriginal Women of British Columbia.' *BC Studies* 105/106 (Spring/Summer 1995): 183–99.

– 'Native Women in Reserve Politics: Strategies and Struggles.' *Journal of Legal Pluralism and Unofficial Law* 30/31 (1990–1): 121–37.

Green, Joyce. 'Canaries in the Mines of Citizenship: Indian Women in Canada.' *Canadian Journal of Political Science* 34.4 (Dec. 2001): 715–38.

– 'Constitutionalising the Patriarchy: Aboriginal Women and Aboriginal Government.' *Constitutional Forum* 4.4 (1993): 110–20.

– 'Sexual Equality and Indian Government: An Analysis of Bill C-31 Amendments to the Indian Act.' *Native Studies Review* 1 (1985): 81–95.

Haig-Brown, Celia. 'Seeking Honest Justice in a Land of Strangers: Nahnebahwequa's Struggle for Land.' *Journal of Canadian Studies* 36.4 (Winter 2001): 143–71.

Jackson, Margaret A. 'Aboriginal Women and Self-Government.' In *Expressions in Canadian Native Studies*, ed. Ron F. Laliberte, Priscilla Settee, James B. Waldram, Rob Innes, Brenda Macdougall, Lesley McBain, and F. Laurie Barron, 355–73. Saskatoon: University Extension Press, 2000.

Jamieson, Kathleen. 'Sex Discrimination and the Indian Act.' In *Arduous Journey: Canadian Indians and Decolonization*, ed. J. Rick Ponting, 112–36. Toronto: McClelland and Stewart, 1986.

– *Indian Women and the Law in Canada: Citizens Minus*. Ottawa: Advisory Council on the Status of Women, 1978.

Kirkness, Verna. 'Emerging Native Women.' *Canadian Journal of Women and the Law* 2.2 (1987–8): 408–15.

Krosenbrink-Gelissen, Lilianne. 'The Native Women's Association of Canada.' In *Aboriginal Peoples in Canada: Contemporary Conflicts*, ed. James S. Frideres, 297–325. 5th ed. Scarborough, ON: Prentice Hall Allyn and Bacon Canada, 1998.

– 'Caring Is Indian Women's Business, but Who Takes Care of Them? Canada's Indian Women, the Renewed Indian Act, and Its Implications for Women's Family Responsibilities, Roles and Rights.' *Law and Anthropology* 7 (1994): 107–30.

– '"Traditional Motherhood" in Defense of Sexual Equality Rights of Canada's Aboriginal Women.' *European Review of Native American Studies* 7.2 (1993): 13–16.

Lawrence, Bonita. 'Gender, Race, and the Regulation of Native Identity in Canada and the United States: An Overview.' *Hypatia* 18.2 (Spring 2003): 3–31.

McGrath, Ann, and Winona Stevenson. 'Gender, Race, and Policy: Aboriginal Women and the State in Canada and Australia.' *Labour / Le Travail* 38 (Fall 1996): 37–53.

Monture, Martha. 'Iroquois Women's Rights with Respect to Matrimonial Property on Indian Reserves.' *Canadian Native Law Review* 4 (1987): 1– 10.

Nahanee, Teresa. 'Dancing with a Gorilla: Aboriginal Women, Justice and the Charter.' In *Aboriginal Peoples and the Justice System: Report of the National Round Table on Aboriginal Justice*, 359–82. Ottawa: Minister of Supply and Services, 1993.

Napoleon, Val. 'Extinction by Number: Colonialism Made Easy.' *Canadian Journal of Law and Society* 16.1 (2001): 113–45.

Pierre-Aggamaway, Marlene. 'Native Women and the State.' In *Perspectives on Women*, ed. Joan Turner and Lois Emery, 66–73. Winnipeg: University of Manitoba Press, 1983.

Robson, Robert. 'The Indian Act: A Northern Manitoba Perspective.' *Canadian Journal of Native Studies* 11.2 (1991): 295–331.

Sangster, Joan. 'Criminalizing the Colonized: Ontario Native Women Confront the Criminal Justice System, 1920–60.' *Canadian Historical Review* 80.1 (March 1999): 32–60.

Turpel, Mary Ellen. 'Patriarchy and Paternalism: The Legacy of the Canadian State for First Nations Women.' *Canadian Journal of Women and the Law* 6 (1993): 174–92.

Feminism, Writing, and Representation

Acoose, Janice. *Iskwewak. Kah'Ki Yaw Ni Wahkomakanak: Neither Indian Princesses nor Easy Squaws*. Toronto: Women's Press, 1995.

Anderson, Kim. *A Recognition of Being: Reconstructing Native Womanhood*. Toronto: Sumach Press, 2000.

Brant, Beth. 'The Good Red Road: Journeys of Homecoming in Native Women's Writing.' In *New Contexts of Canadian Criticism*, ed. Ajay Heble, Donna Palmateer Pennee, and J.R. (Tim) Struthers, 175–87. Peterborough, ON: Broadview Press, 1997.

– *Writing as Witness: Essay and Talk*. Toronto: Women's Press, 1994.

Chrystos. 'Askenet Meaning "Raw" in My Language.' In *Inversions: Writing by Dykes, Queers and Lesbians*, 237–47. Vancouver: Press Gang Publishers, 1991.

Cruikshank, Julie. 'Claiming Legitimacy: Prophecy Narratives from Northern Aboriginal Women.' *American Indian Quarterly* 18 (Spring 1994): 147–67.

Currie, Noel Elizabeth. 'Jeanette Armstrong and the Colonial Legacy.' *Canadian Literature* 124/125 (Spring/Summer 1990): 138–52.

Emberley, Julia. 'Aboriginal Women's Writing and the Cultural Politics of Representation.' In *Women of the First Nations: Power, Wisdom, and Strength*, ed. Christine Miller and Patricia Chuchryk, 97–112. Winnipeg: University of Manitoba Press, 1996.

– *Thresholds of Difference: Feminist Critique, Native Women's Writings, Postcolonial Theory*. Toronto: University of Toronto, 1993.

Gerson, Carole. 'Nobler Savages: Representations of Native Women in the Writings of Susanna Moodie and Catharine Parr Trail.' *Journal of Canadian Studies* 32 (Summer 1997): 5–21.

Godard, Barbara. 'Listening for the Silence: Some Native Canadian Women's Traditional Narratives.' In *The Native in Literature*, ed. Thomas King, Cheryl Calver, and Helen Hoy, 135–58. Oakville, ON: ECW, 1987.

– 'Voicing Difference: The Literary Production of Native Women.' In *Amazing Space: Writing Canadian Women Writing*, ed. Shirley Neuman and Smaro Kamboureli, 87–107. Edmonton: Longspoon/NeWest, 1986.

– *Talking about Ourselves: The Literary Productions of Native Women in Canada*. CRIAW paper, no. 11. Ottawa: CRIAW, 1985.

Grant, Agnes. 'Contemporary Native Women's Voices in Literature.' *Canadian Literature* 124/125 (Spring/Summer 1990): 124–32.

Haig-Brown, Celia, and Sophie Robert. '"Sophie Robert": Remembrances of Secwepemc Life: A Collaboration.' *Canadian Journal of Native Education* 19.2 (1992): 175–90.

Johnson, Rhonda, Winnona Stevenson, and Donna Greschner. 'Peekiskwetan.' *Canadian Journal of Women in the Law* 6 (1993): 153–73.

Monture-Angus, Patricia. *Thunder in My Soul: A Mohawk Woman Speaks*. Halifax: Fernwood Publishers, 1995.

Poelzer, Dolores T., and Irene A. Poelzer. *In Our Own Words: Northern Saskatchewan Métis Women Speak Out*. Saskatoon: Lindenblatt and Hamonic, 1986.

Rasporich, Beverly. 'Native Women Writing: Tracing the Patterns.' *Canadian Ethnic Studies* 28.1 (1996): 37–50.

Riddett, Lyn Anne. '"Finish I Can't Talk Now": Aboriginal and Settler Women Construct Each Other.' *Native Studies Review* 12.1 (1999): 49–61.

Ruffo, Armand Garnet. 'Out of Silence – the Legacy of E. Pauline Johnson: An Inquiry into the Lost and Found Work of Dawendine – Bernice Loft Winslow.' In *Literary Pluralities*, ed. Christl Verduyn, 211–23. Peterborough, ON: Broadview Press, 1998.

Silman, Janet. *Enough Is Enough: Aboriginal Women Speak Out*. Toronto: Women's Press, 1987.

Valaskakis, Gail Guthrie. 'Sacajawea and Her Sisters: Images and Native Women.' *Canadian Journal of Native Education* 23.1 (1999): 117–35.

Welsh, Christine. 'Women in the Shadows: Reclaiming a Métis Heritage.' In *New Contexts of Canadian Criticism*, ed. Ajay Heble, Donna Palmateer Pennee, and J.R. (Tim) Struthers, 56–66. Peterborough, ON: Broadview Press, 1997.

Special Issues Featuring Aboriginal Women

Hypatia 18.2 (Spring 2003).
Ethnohistory 43.4 (Fall 1996).
Canadian Literature 124/125 (Spring/Summer 1990).
Canadian Woman Studies 10.2–3 (Summer/Fall 1989).
Fireweed: A Feminist Quarterly 22 (Fall 1986).

Anthologies by and about First Nations Women

Albers, Patricia, and Beatrice Medicine, eds. *The Hidden Half: Studies of Plains Indian Women*. Lanham, MD: University Press of America, 1983.

Ahenakew, Freda, and H.C. Wolfart, eds. *Our Grandmothers' Lives as Told in Their Own Words*. Saskatoon: Fifth House Publishers, 1992.

Anderson, Kim, and Bonita Lawrence, eds. *Strong Women Stories: Native Vision and Community Survival*. Toronto: Sumach Press, 2003.

Bataille, Gretchen M., and Kathleen Mullen Sands, eds. *American Indian Women: Telling Their Lives*. Lincoln and London: University of Nebraska Press, 1984.

Etienne, Mona, and Eleanor Leacock, eds. *Women and Colonization: Anthropological Perspectives*. New York: Praeger, 1980.

Klein, Laura F., and Lillian A. Ackerman, eds. *Women and Power in Native North America*. Norman: University of Oklahoma Press, 1995.

Miller, Christine, and Patricia Chuchryk, eds. *Women of the First Nations: Power, Wisdom, and Strength*. Winnipeg: University of Manitoba Press, 1996.

Perreault, Jeanne, and Sylvia Vance, eds. *Writing the Circle: Native Women of Western Canada*. Edmonton: NeWest Publishers, 1990.

Shoemaker, Nancy, ed. *Negotiators of Change: Historical Perspectives on Native American Women*. New York and London: Routledge, 1995.

Spittal, W.G., ed. *Iroquois Women: An Anthology*. Ohsweken, ON: Oroqrafts, 1990.

Permissions

and Jane Samson. © 1999 University of British Columbia Press. Maps by Eric Leinberger. All rights reserved by the publisher.

Chapter 8: Hetty Jo Brumbach and Robert Jarvenpa, 'Woman the Hunter: Ethnoarchaeological Lessons from Chipewyan Life-Cycle Dynamics.' Reprinted by permission of the University of Pennsylvania Press. *Women in Prehistory: North America and Mesoamerica*, ed. Cheryl Claassen and Rosemary Joyce. © 1994 University of Pennsylvania Press. All rights reserved by the publisher.

Chapter 9: John Lutz, 'Gender and Work in Lekwammen Families, 1843–1970.' Reprinted with permission of the Publisher from *Gendered Pasts: Historical Essays on Femininity and Masculinity in Canada*, ed. Kathryn MacPherson, Cecilia Morgan, Nancy M. Forestell. © 1999 University of Toronto Press. All rights reserved by the publisher.

Chapter 10: Mary C. Wright, 'The Woman's Lodge: Constructing Gender on the Nineteenth-Century Pacific Northwest Plateau,' *Frontiers: A Journal of Women Studies* 2, No. 1: 1–18. By permission of the publisher.

Chapter 11: Jean Barman, 'Taming Aboriginal Sexuality: Gender, Power, and Race in British Columbia, 1850–1900,' *BC Studies: The British Columbian Quarterly* 115–16 (Fall-Winter 1997–98): 237–66. By permission of the publisher.

Chapter 12: Joan Sangster, 'Native Women, Sexuality, and the Law.' Reprinted with permission of the publisher from *Regulating Girls and Women: Sexuality, Family, and the Law in Ontario, 1920–1960* by Joan Sangster. © 2001 University of Toronto Press. All rights reserved by the publisher.

Chapter 13: Jo-Anne Fiske, 'Political Status of Native Indian Women: Contradictory Implications of Canadian State Policy,' *American Indian Culture and Research Journal* 19, No. 2: 1–30. By permission of the publisher.

Chapter 14: Veronica Strong-Boag, '"A Red Girl's Reasoning": E. Pauline Johnson Constructs the New Nation.' Reprinted with permission of the publisher from *Painting the Maple: Essays on Race, Gender, and the Construction of Canada*, ed. Veronica Strong-Boag, Sherrill E. Grace, Avigail Eisenberg, and Joan Anderson. © 1998 University of British Columbia Press. All rights reserved by the publisher.

Chapter 15: Emma LaRocque, 'The Colonization of a Native Woman Scholar.'

Illustration Credits

Index